GREGORY'S
SERMON
Synopses

GREGORY'S
SERMON
Synopses

200 EXPANDED SUMMARIES

HUPOMONE PRESS

FORT WORTH, TEXAS

© Copyright 2001 · Gregory Ministries

4220-05

ISBN: 1-4243-0923-9

Dewey Decimal Classification: 252

Subject Heading: SERMONS

Library of Congress Card Catalog Number: 91-24724

Publisher: Hupomone Press, 2006

Printed in the United States of America

Unless otherwise indicated, all quotations from the Scriptures are from the *Holy Bible New International Version,* © 1973, 1978, 1984 by International Bible Society. Used by permission. All Scriptures marked (KJV) are from the *King James Version* of the Bible; (NKJV) from the *New King James Version.* Copyright © 1979, 1980, 1982, Thomas Nelson, Inc., Publishers. Used by permission; (ASV) from the *American Standard Version;* (NASB) from the *New American Standard Bible.* © The Lockman Foundation, 1960, 1962, 1963, 1968, 1971, 1972, 1973, 1975, 1977. Used by permission.

Library of Congress Cataloging-in-Publication Data

Gregory, Joel C., 1948-
    Gregory's sermon synopses / Joel C. Gregory.
      p.   cm.
    Includes index.
    ISBN 1-4243-0923-9
    1. Sermons-Outlines, syllabi, etc. I. Title. II. Title: Sermon
synopses.
BV4223.G654   1992
252'.02-dc20   91-24724
                                         CIP

DEDICATION

In Honor of

Dr. Burton Patterson
Friend and Counselor

In Memory of

Dr. Ray Summers
Dr. Curtis Vaughan
Dr. Richard Cutter
Who Taught Me Exegesis

Preface

To The First Edition

This volume presents a set of sermon synopses. These are neither outlines nor manuscripts. They do represent the structure of biblical sermons of some brief expository notes suggesting the direction of the message. These synopses were not written in a vacuum nor were they originally intended for collection and publication in a single volume. Rather these were written week-by-week over a five-year period and given to the congregation as part of the Sunday bulletin. Thus, these sermon digests were born out of weekly preaching preparation and given to listeners on Sunday.

I first encountered such sermon synopses in 1970-71 when Dr. D. L. Lowrie, then pastor of North Fort Worth Baptist Church, included such condensations in the Sunday bulletin. He in turn attributed the idea to Dr. Stephen Olford, then pastor of Calvary Baptist in New York City. For years I followed the same procedure.

These outlines are obviously structural, but not arbitrarily so. I hope they represent sermons that are not only biblical in *content* but also biblical in *construction*. Not only the *sense* of the sermon but also the *shape* of the sermon should be determined by the text. The points and subpoints should show what is dominant and what is subordinate in that biblical passage. The major movements of the outline are stated in the present tense, indicating the timeless truth of the supporting passages. Most of these synopses contain only the expository element of the sermon, not the illustrations and applications which were added later to the full manuscript.

These are extended to preachers and Bible students as an additional stimulus for your own study. They are certainly not the only approach to these texts. They are offered with a prayer that they may be helpful in assisting us all to be "a mouthpiece for the text," which is preaching at its best.

Joel C. Gregory

Preface

Ten years have passed since Broadman Press printed *Gregory's Sermon Synopses: 200 Expanded Summaries.* Over that period of time I have been pleasantly surprised to discover the usefulness of these expanded summaries to preachers around the country. I have often been asked to re-publish the original volume. I express appreciation to Broadman Press for extending to me the copyright and the opportunity to present these sermon digests once again.

The passing years only strengthen the conviction that sermons both biblical in *content* and in *structure* stand the test of time. There are many kinds of Christian preaching. Devoted servants of the Word do it in various ways, as individual as their own temperaments and gifts. The abridged sermons presented here are the way I try to do it. It is not the only way.

As an addition to this re-published volume, the actual 200 messages as preached are now available in audio media formats. The interested reader may listen to these and hear the fully illustrated and applied sermon beyond these brief notes.

I am profoundly grateful to Burton H. Patterson and his foundation for his generosity in making possible this publication and the attendant audio media. These go forth with the sincere prayer that they will in some small way help future generations of preachers with the task, as well as provide a devotional thought to concerned lay readers.

Joel C. Gregory
Fort Worth
gregoryministries.org

Contents

Old
Testament
Synopses

The First Temptation — A Pattern

(Genesis 3:1-6)

As in other matters of human existence, Genesis sheds light on the first experience of temptation. Without question humankind—that means you and me—acts with a self-destructive and self-defeating impulse. From where does that come? More importantly, how can we recognize the way that impulse comes at us? The first instance of temptation provides lasting clues to the dynamics that can lead to personal disintegration. We ought to learn from our first parents something about temptation and how to avoid its devastating effects. There is a process to be observed in the first temptation. We should learn from observing that process.

Temptation Begins with Attention that Should not Be Given

Temptation begins by making something the object of attention that deserves no attention. Eve should have sensed immediately that something was out of order when a serpent spoke to her. That overturned the order of creation itself. We should recognize temptation first as that which overthrows the order, responsibility, and accountability of our lives.

We should pay no attention because of the *shrewdness* of the tempter. He is indeed "crafty" (v. 1). The word suggests that which is sly, cunning, wily, insidious, and shrewd. He is expert at the art of not appearing to be what he really is. From the first we should understand that his remarks are not what they appear to be and should be examined carefully. No mere human can or ever has resisted his shrewdness unaided. He is indeed able to turn himself into an angel of light.

We should pay no attention because of the *strategy* of the tempter. His strategy is never frontal or obvious. It is always first a sneak attack, a Trojan horse that promises a gift but holds death. He began his first temptation with a polite discussion about the nature of God, "Did God really say? . . ." It is not a denial of the truth. It is a sly and insinuating statement. He simply suggests that God may not have really meant what God actually said. "Even God Himself would not want to keep something so good as *the* tree away from someone as deserving as Adam and Eve."

Yet the tempter gives himself away. He calls the Creator "God." He does not use the word *Lord* God. To the tempter He is a remote figure not really all that interested in what Eve does with the tree in the garden. The first mistake was to pay attention to his words.

Temptation Continues with a Conversation that Should not Be Spoken

Attention became conversation. Eve moved toward the serpent's goal the very moment she began to speak with him. In His temptation, the Lord Jesus did not speak with the devil; He confronted him with the Word of God. There are some things that should never be said.

When we speak with the devil, we *minimize* God. We minimize the *goodness* of God. Eve's statement concerning God's prohibition limits the actual generosity of God. God said, "You are free to eat from any tree in the garden" (2:16). In Eve's mouth this generosity is minimized (3:2). We begin to minimize the *character* of God. Eve suddenly stops talking to the *Lord* God and uses the mere word "God," which the tempter used. By adding the words "You shall not . . . touch it (v. 3, NASB), she suggests that

God is too demanding, confining, and strict. Under the fire of temptation, you will find yourself questioning God's character if you intend to yield to the temptation. You will tell yourself, "God has no right to be so strict and so confining." We eventually minimize the *command* of God. The language of Eve in quoting God's command "You will die" softens the prohibition in the original language. It suggests some question about whether or not such a disastrous result would come from such a trivial act.

On the other hand, when you enter into a dialogue with the devil he will *criticize the command* of God. "You will not surely die." He moves from insinuation to direct assertion. Having administered the narcotic of scepticism, he puts in the knife of actual denial. God does not mean what He says, according to the devil. Then he calls into *question the character* of God. God is acting from motives of jealousy (v. 5). "God knows that life will be fuller, more independent, and even exhilarating if you will eat the fruit" (author's words).

It is only a small step then for the adversary to *compromise the truth* about God. A half-lie will serve the tempter well. "Your eyes will be opened." He suggests that they will really see what life is all about. Adam and Eve thought that would be shrewd. But instead of shrewd, they only saw that they were nude. What they saw was only their own remorse and guilt. The devil had duped them with a half-truth. They would indeed see something new. It turned out to be their own guilt.

Temptation Results in an Action that Should not Be Taken

The end of the story is almost an afterthought. The enemy had won the battle when he got the attention and conversation of Eve. The serpent withdraws and does not say another word. The actual act of taking the fruit was as good as done.

Herein rests the actual lesson. Temptation defeats us before the actual act itself if we give attention and enter into conversation. The sure defense is never to give attention to that which is outside God's order for our lives and never to enter into mental dialogue with the devil about the character and commands of God.

The words of James form the best comment on the entire story: "Each one is tempted when, by his own evil desire, he is dragged away and enticed. Then, after desire has conceived, it gives birth to sin; and sin, when it is full-grown, gives birth to death" (Jas. 1:14-15).

The Sacred Tenth: God's Perpetual Expectation
(Genesis 14:20; 28:20-22; Leviticus 27:30-33; Matthew 23:23)

Is the tithe a novelty, a modern innovation of church finance? Does it have to do with buildings and budgets, but nothing really central in the perpetual purposes of God? Is the tithe a part of Old Testament legalism that New Testament Christians should disregard? Where did the principle of the tithe begin? Does God really expect *me* to tithe? These are questions not be answered by human supposition, but by a careful scrutiny of Scripture.

The Very Earliest Men of Faith Accepted the Tithe as an Established Duty

The first categorical reference to tithing in the Bible relates to Abram (Gen. 14:20).

The great patriarch paused after victory in battle to give one-tenth to Melchizedek, the native priest of Salem (Jerusalem). Clearly Abram does not consider this an *offering*, but rather an *obligation*. This same passage contains the first temptation *not* to tithe. King Chedorlaomer invites Abram to split the spoils of battle with him. Abram refuses to give the sacred tenth to anyone but God. That Abram tithes is one of the few patriarchal acts named in the New Testament (Heb. 7:4).

Abraham lived until the boyhood of Jacob. The latter adopted Abraham's faith personally, including the practice of habitually giving God the sacred tenth (Gen. 28:20-22). It is beyond question that the tithe became the practice of the earliest men of faith.

Tithing is nowhere specifically commanded in Genesis. For that matter there is no specific command against murder or adultery, but Cain was held responsible for the former and Tamar for the latter. Abraham was given statutes, commandments, and laws (see Gen. 26:5) of which we have no record, but to which he was faithfully obedient. Tithing must have been among these commands. In fact, the ancient peoples of whom we have record *universally* practiced the tithe or more. Egyptians, Babylonians, Persians, Phoenicians, Arabians, Ethiopians, Greeks, and Romans practiced giving a tithe or more to their deities. Where did they get such an idea? Was it not that God originally spoke to the first man not only *that* we should sacrifice, but also *how much?* There is likelihood that Cain's offering was rejected because it was the wrong proportion (Heb. 11:4).

The Old Testament Law Amplifies and Continues the Practice of Tithing

The tithe is introduced in the Law of Moses as an already established practice and proportion (Lev. 27:30-33). The law spelled out that every Israelite was to bring 10 percent of all produce, both grain and fruit. Further, one out of every ten cattle born each year was to be given to God. No entire single chapter in the Law of Moses speaks of tithing. The subject is introduced incidentally, without solemn preamble. That is to say, *it was taken for granted.* What Abraham practiced and what Jacob vowed was household knowledge in Israel of the exodus and afterward.

There is strong evidence that the Old Testament called not for just one tithe, but for three during some years. Beyond the tithe for the priests, there was to be a festival tithe (Deut. 14:22-27) in which the giver participated by eating of the tithed material. Also every third year there was to be a tithe given for the poor of the land (vv. 28-29). Thus, the divine expectation for Old Testament persons could approach 30 percent some years.

Jesus Christ Called for the Tithe as Only the Beginning of Giving

Jesus specifically enforced the payment of the tithes (Matt. 23:23). Jesus did not promulgate afresh for Christians, as from a New Testament Sinai, the law against murder, adultery, or any other law. But to show the binding and spiritual nature of the Mosiac law, and its far-reaching principles, He taught that these Commandments may be broken by an angry word or a lustful look. Neither did our Lord reenact that His followers should pay a tithe. He demanded much more: "Whosoever he be of you that forsaketh not all that he hath, he cannot be my disciple" (Luke 14:33, KJV). For Him the tithe was only the bare beginning.

Jesus lived in the most tithe-conscious generation of people ever to practice the sacred tenth. The Pharisees' chief criteria for service to God was the giving of the tenth.

We should note that the Pharisees watched Jesus constantly. They accused Jesus of many things. Yet not once did they accuse Him of failing to tithe or teaching against the tithe. The Lord Jesus suffered many controversies with the Pharisees, but there was never a controversy about the tithe.

Likewise, Jesus judged the Pharisees for many things, but He never criticized them or condemned them for giving the tithe. Just the opposite is the case. The Lord Jesus commended them for giving the sacred tenth. The Lord Jesus told believers that unless our righteousness exceeds that of the scribes and the Pharisees we cannot be part of His kingdom (Matt. 5:20). In light of that, how could any Christian honestly doubt that the beginning point of giving is the tithe?

There are some issues of Christian living that need to be settled never to be changed. Surely giving God the tenth of all He gives you as the beginning point is such a commitment.

Motherhood and the Sovereignty of God
(Genesis 22—29; Exodus 2)

So much of motherhood is waiting. Mothers wait for that life which grows under their heart to be born. They wait for that little one to go to sleep. Rarely do they wait for the baby to wake up. In the most significant things that happen to a baby all a mother can do is to wait. She must wait for the child to talk, to walk, and to display that distinctive character which will mark the child as an individual.

That is to say, a great deal of motherhood is dependent on the sovereignty, providence, and timing of God. While a mother may be ceaselessly active on her child's behalf, the ultimate issues absolutely and really rest in the sovereignty of God. The Bible illustrates to us how mothers may relate to that sovereignty.

Mothers May Forget the Faithfulness of God—Rebekah

Rebekah appears on the Old Testament scene as a woman of charming, even disarming, character. Her treatment of Eliezer, Abraham's servant sent to find a wife for Isaac, revealed her as gracious and unselfish. She is a woman of assertive decision who leaves her Mesopotamian family to marry a man she has never met in a foreign culture. She is a woman of purity—this is the first great monogamous marriage of the Genesis accounts. She is a woman of prayer. She is specifically cited as the first woman to call on God (Gen. 25:22). Everything about Rebekah appears to be ideal.

The character of Rebekah suffered from one flaw. At a critical juncture, both for her family and for God's plan, she forgot the dependence of motherhood on the sovereignty of God. This lapse began with an obvious *favoritism* for one of her children over the other. While Isaac preferred Esau, she loved Jacob more. Such prejudiced motherhood inevitably leads to family tragedy. This favoritism led to *manipulation* of family life and *deception* on behalf of Jacob. Rebekah wanted the right thing, but she wanted it the wrong way. God desired Jacob to be His man of choice, but God in His sovereignty could have shaped the destiny of Jacob without the manipulation and deceit of Rebekah.

Because Rebekah could not trust the sovereignty of God, the remainder of her life was heartache. She saw strife between her children, she lost the confidence of her husband, and she even lost Jacob forever. When he returned twenty years later she was dead.

Mothers May Rely on the Faithfulness of God—Jochebed

We are told virtually nothing of this truly great "mother of Israel." Maternally and paternally she was from priestly ancestry herself. A slave woman in Egypt, she mothered three remarkable children: Aaron, the great priest; Miriam, a spiritual leader; and Moses, the incomparable. Jochebed's singular contribution was her utter trust in the sovereignty of God.

She was a woman of *perception* concerning her child. She saw that he was a goodly child (Ex. 2:2). The Hebrew word suggests that there was something remarkable about Moses from the very first. Jochebed had the spiritual vision to note the remarkable. Jochebed knew in God's providence when to *hold* her child and *when to let him go.* For three months she held him and hid him. But the time came when she had to release him for God's purposes. She suppressed her own possessive maternal love and released her son to God's plan. Here she was utterly unlike Rebekah. She perpetrated no deception. She did combine absolute faith faith with prudent provision. With motherly activity, she carefully constructed the little basket-boat.(She did not just throw Moses into the Nile and say, "God, take care of him!") But then with distinctive trust in God, she released the baby into the river worshiped by the Egyptians as a god. God could use that unlikely vehicle for His purposes.

Because she released her baby to the sovereignty of God, she also got him back in a most remarkable way. For the first seven years of his life, he was exclusively hers, even though adopted by Pharaoh's daughter. Rebekah forgot God's sovereignty and lost everything. Jochebed remembered it and won all.

A Man on the Run Wrestles with God
(Genesis 32:22-32)

Our generation lives "on the run." Jacob lived like that. He was literally born "on the run," trying to outdo his brother, Esau. He ran from Esau, his brother. He ran from Laban, his father-in-law. He was really running from himself. Yet a time came when he ran out of resources and ran into God. That night witnessed a life-changing wrestling match.

A Man on the Run Will Come to the End of His Resources

A person without resources can prevail with God in prayer, changing his nature and his situation. "Jacob was left alone" (v. 24). After a lifetime on the run, Jacob ran out of resources. In that moment, he was left alone with God. Anxious fear, darkness, loneliness confronted him. His physical situation at the Jabbok River and his family's absence underscored his loneliness. God can stop every person on the run and confront that person with his lack of resources.

A Man on the Run May Encounter God in Prevailing Prayer

A mysterious, night hour Visitor wrestled with Jacob. It is really uncertain who was wrestling with whom. Jacob wrestled with a visible manifestation of the invisible God. Jacob's redeeming character trait was an indomitable, undeniable *desire to know the blessing of God.* Jacob prevailed, but the Visitor marked Jacob with a blow to his thigh. God wanted Jacob to know that he was in the match with a power greater than Jacob that marked him for life. Jacob decidedly determined not to let go until God blessed him.

A Man on the Run May Experience a Changed Life
Through Prevailing Prayer

Jacob had to own who he really was, a trickster and deceiver (v. 27). When he had owned who he was, he could disown who he was and become someone new. God changed his name and nature, and assured him of future victory with God and man. Yet there was an element of mystery in it all beyond any human explanation (v. 29). Anyone can experience a change in nature and situation through an encounter with God in prayer.

Confrontation with God:
The Great "I AM"

(Exodus 3:1-6,14)

The whole of the religious life focuses at only one point—your personal confrontation with God as He really is. All of the other personalities, activities, emotions, and institutions of religion lose any meaning apart from confrontation with God as He really is. Surely a singular encounter with God was that of Moses on the mountain with the bush that burned without burning out. The circumstances that led Moses to that moment have their parallel in your own circumstances. Likewise, God comes to us today with the same methods He came to Moses.

The living God always takes the initiative to confront you in your life as it actually is.

Understand the Preparation for Meeting God as He Really Is

God moves your life toward a confrontation with Him. You may or may not be conscious of His invisible hand, but that hand pushes and pulls you toward Him. That hand had directed Moses toward the confrontation for eighty years. How does God prepare for The Meeting?

God prepares with *devastating events*. Forty years early Moses was expelled from the Egyptian court (2:15). He moved from the palace to the pasture, from the companionship of princes to the keeping of the sheep. One could hardly find a more devastating change of life in world history. For forty years Moses reflected on the shock, bitterness, and finality of expulsion from the Egyptian palace. The devastating event of your own life can always be God's moment.

God prepares in *isolated places*. God sent Moses "to the far side of the desert" (v. 1), literally behind the wilderness. Far beyond the camp of his clan, Moses went to new, distant, higher grazing grounds. It was a place of aloneness, silence, isolation. "Horeb" means a dry ground, desolation. Moses was in a dry, sterile, barren, bleak, rocky place. He was utterly driven to think of God alone. God meets you when life isolates you. A human loss, an illness, a move—God awaits you in the isolation of it.

God prepares in *humbling activities*. At eighty years Moses was still the shepherd of his father-in-law's flock. He did not even have land or flock of his own. Egypt faded in his memory. He felt his own life ebbing away. Dreams of achievement and leadership had long before drained away like water into the sand around him. Shock, rejection, and bitterness died in the pasture with the sheep. If God has humbled you, it is His path toward a burning encounter.

Remember that the Lord Jesus was prepared in the same way. His life began with devastating events. For thirty years He lived in an isolated place with the humble activities of a carpenter's shop. Then suddenly heaven opened and the Spirit fell.

Experience the Realization of Meeting God as He Really Is

God takes the initiative in the meeting. God does meet you when you do not expect it. Moses expected nothing that day.

God takes the initiative by *arresting* us—a thornbush, a bramble kept on burning but not being consumed. Moses knew that God had presented Himself in trees (Gen. 18:1; 12:6-7; Judg. 6:11-12; 2 Sam. 5:24) and in fire. Here is a tree that burns and in it the personal representative of God. God is always setting bushes on fire, calling you, arresting you, grabbing you. "Earth's crammed with heaven, And every common bush afire with God; But only he who sees, takes off his shoes" (Elizabeth Barrett Browning, *Aurora Leigh*).

God takes the initiative in *instructing* us. He instructs us by what we see. A bush that burns but not burns up! The bush was a humble bramble or thorn. The supernatural had entered the lowest part of the natural, and burned without destroying. This is God's way. He enters your natural life and shines. The bush is only the vehicle. This is what God does with a Moses. God will burn in Moses for the next forty years without consuming Moses. This is God's desire for you. Even though your outward person perishes, He will renew day by day.

He instructs us by what we hear. He calls us by name: "Moses, Moses." Just when we think God has forgotten our address, He summons us by name. God calls us close, but not too close: "Take off your sandals, for the place where you are standing is holy ground" (v. 5). The Hebrews took off their shoes where we would take off our hats. When God is really present there is always fellowship and fear, approach and awe. This ought to keep private devotions and church in a blaze of anticipation. There is no commonness and boredom in the presence of the holy.

Know the Identification of God as He Really Is

No moment compares with this moment. God reveals His name. The name of God is not mere identity. God's name resounds with His character, reputation, and power. Moses knew the names of the Egyptian gods. They were numerous and successful. But He is the great "I AM."

God's name means His *continuity* in history. He is the God of Moses' father, Amram. He is the God of all the patriarchs. God had not spoken as He did to Moses for 200 years since His conversation with Jacob. We deal with the same God today who addressed Abraham, Isaac, and Jacob. That means He keeps His promises, covenants, and plans.

God's name means His *activity*. Many scholars translate the name of God "I will be what I will be." This means that God is active and reveals Himself to us only in His relationship with us and His activity in our lives. The name of God is not a password to memorize or a secret word to get us into heaven. God gives His name to us in active relationship. Moses would learn for forty years who God is.

God's name means His *immediacy*. He is "I AM." He will not meet you in your past or in your future but only now, in this razor-thin moment. Unless God is known in the midst of immediate relation, He is not known.

You meet Him in Jesus Christ who said, "Before Abraham was, I am" (John 8:58, KJV).

How God Guides

(Exodus 13:17-22)

God guides. God's personal leadership belongs to biblical faith. It is the heritage of God's people. We can expect that God will give us personal leadership. Before the written Word of God came, God gave guidance through extraordinary means. Before the Holy Spirit internally indwelt every believer, God used various visible means of His guidance. We who have the written Word and the Spirit can learn principles of God's guidance from those who depended on other means.

God does give His people protective guidance which the world cannot understand.

God Protects Us from Enemies We Cannot See

God sometimes leads us the *longer way*. The obvious way to go to the promised land from Egypt was the way by the sea. Instead, God sent the people south when they needed to go northeast. God often sends His people the longer way. David went the longer way to the throne. Paul went the longer way to Rome. Why does God lead the longer way?

The longer way is sometimes the *safer way*. God knew that the Philistines lived on the short route to the promised land. God already knew that His people could not face what they did not even know was there. If they had faced the warlike Philistines, they would have turned back to Egypt (v. 17; cf. 14:10).

Why does God lead us through detours? He often does so because He knows what we are not ready to face. Even Jesus detoured away from the cross until His hour had come. If you seem to be going the long way, believe that God knows what you cannot face.

God Reminds Us of Faithfulness We Cannot Forget

God's faithfulness in the past gives us confidence for His leadership in the future. Centuries before, the Hebrew patriarch Joseph made his people promise to carry his bones with them to the promised land (Gen. 50:25-29). When they carried his bones out in the exodus, they acknowledged God's faithful accomplishment of His promises. Evidently they carried out the bones of all the rest of the patriarchs as well (Acts 7:16). Every tribe had a personal reminder of God's faithful guidance in the past.

We need to make memories of God's guidance. Your future hope for God's guidance rests on your past experience of God's faithfulness. The God who was our help in ages past is our hope for years to come.

God Leads Us with a Guidance We Cannot Explain

God guides in a *timely way*. God gave His guidance at just the moment needed. "Etham" was on the edge of the desert. They could make it to Etham without supernatural guidance. God expects us to go where we can see without demanding supernatural events. But beyond Etham there was no road to see—the treacherous desert extended to the horizon. When they needed direct divine guidance, God provided the pillar of cloud and fire.

God guides us in a mystery. The cloud was dark on one side and bright on the other (Ex. 14:20). The Egyptians saw only darkness. Israel saw the light. Always God's people can detect His guidance. The world sees nothing where we see the finger of God. God's supernatural direction is for His spiritual people. The world sees a dark cloud.

God guides us from in front (13:22). The cloud of fire was usually in front of the people. God moves us toward His future. However, there are times when God does protect us from our past (14:19). He stands between us and that which is behind us. By His presence He surrounds.

God guides us now in His word. The cloud of light is now gone. We should not look for it again. Now God's Word is the lamp and the light (Ps. 119:105). He has lodged His guidance in His word through His Spirit. His word goes before us in the future and protects us from the past. Our God guides. The Lord Jesus is both the Author and Finisher of God's guidance (Heb. 12:2).

Walking into an Impossibility
(Exodus 14:10-20)

The power of God is displayed when we move beyond our possibilities. The Hebrew slaves found themselves surrounded by the impossible. Before them was the sea, beside them was the desert, and behind them was the enemy. They faced three alternatives. They could go back to Egypt, stand still where they were, or go forward. God commanded them to walk into the impossibility.

Travis Avenue Baptist Church is at one such crossroad today. Behind us is a great history of walking forward. In front of us is one of the greater challenges in the history of our church. We must decide to walk forward into that challenge.

In the Face of an Impossibility We Can Say, "Go Back."

We may wish to go back when God has just begun to go forward. The Hebrews wanted to go back when they had only begun to go forward under the blessing of God. They thought the beginning was the end. This was the first real challenge they had faced after God delivered them.

They wanted to do the right thing the wrong way. They cried out to God, but they cried out in fear rather than faith. It was right to call on God but wrong to call on Him in fear. They did the wrong thing. They blamed their leadership. They did the unthinkable thing. They wanted to reverse God's blessings and cancel their own history. More than anything else they did the inexcusable thing. They ignored the blessings of God in the past and the providences of God they had already seen.

Travis Avenue Baptist Church has never said, "We will go back." The seventy-six years of our church's history has never witnessed a generation or a pastor who said, "Go back." If we went back, where would we go? Nowhere but decline and oblivion. We must go forward.

In the Face of an Impossibility Some Say, "Stand Still."

Some wish to go neither backward nor forward. They desire to freeze in the present. They stand in paralysis in the midst of opportunity. Moses was going in the right direction when he said, "Stand still." But not far enough. He believed in divine blessing but not strongly enough in human initiative. He believed in the divine reality but not strongly enough in human risk. He believed in divine initiative but not strongly enough in human participation.

It is never enough to stand still. Travis Avenue does not have the luxury to say we will stay where we are. Churches do not in fact stand still. They are always moving forward or starting backward. Christians do not stand still. Every day we are either higher or lower in our relationship to God.

In the Face of an Impossibility God Says, "Go Forward."

There is a divine timing in going forward. There is a time to pray but there is also a time to act. In verse 15, the Lord said to Moses, "Why are you crying out to me? Tell the Israelites to move on." The time for praying was past, the time for acting had come. There is also a time of risk. God told the Israelites to move on into the impossibility. Certainly we should not risk in an imprudent way that tests God. But risk we must. Human instruments often seem insufficient for that risk. An eighty-year-old shepherd holding out a wooden rod over a sea did not appear sufficient for the situation. But it was the rod of God. It was God who said, "Go forward."

There is a glory when God says, "Go forward." Throughout this message the emphasis rests on the glory given to God in the situation. Note verse 18 says "The Egyptians will know that I am the Lord when I gain glory through Pharaoh, his chariots and his horsemen."

There is a divine protection when God says, "Go forward." That mysterious, mystical cloud that had been in front of them moved behind them. God gave them a supernatural protection between them and everything that would harm them.

Travis Avenue Baptist Church is at a crossroads to go forward. The generations before us in this place risked much. Movement forward will give God glory.

This is also true personally. Every Christian must move forward. We can live in the faith of Paul who said, "He who has begun a good work in you will carry it on to completion" (Phil. 1:6).

When a Willing Heart Gives
(Exodus 25:1; 35:4-29; 36:3-7)

God's people normally bring their gifts with planned regularity. But on special occasions God desires a single great day of giving by His people. The gifts for constructing the tabernacle marked the first great day of giving. As we anticipate our harvest day, God can instruct us from the timeless principles behind one great day of giving.

When a Willing Heart Gives, God
Recommends the Motivation of the Givers

Worshipfulness of giving marks God's people. The "offering" indicates what a person separated from his own property and marked as sacred to God. It was called a "wave offering" (35:22) because the worshiper waved it in the air before God. It was called a "heave offering" because it was literally heaved or lifted upon the altar. Giving to God is first an act of worship.

Willingness of giving marks God's people. The single characteristic most noted in the passage is that of the people's willingness (25:1; 35:5,21,22,29). Literally, every man's heart "drove him to give." No obedience is pleasing to God unless it is voluntary (2 Cor. 9:7).

Your giving to the harvest day should be in worship and free-hearted joy.

When a Willing Heart Gives, God
Commends the Participation of the Givers

Reflectiveness marks that participation (35:20). Each person returned from the assembly to his tent to meditate on what he should give. Their liberality was premeditated, not impulsive. God desires planned giving, not impulsive.

Inclusiveness marks that participation. Second only to the freewill character of the gifts, the word emphasizes the inclusiveness of the givers and the gifts. All the people gave—the men, women, and the chief leader. All kinds of gifts were given. Some were so poor they only gave goat hair (35:23). Some were so rich they could give precious stones. It was not equal gifts, but equal sacrifice (Eph. 4:15).

When a Willing Heart Gives, God Enjoys the Lavishness of Giving

Out of eagerness, the people brought their gifts persistently, "every morning" (36:3). They brought so much that more was given than needed. Moses had to stop the offering. The people had to be restrained from giving (v. 5). This generosity often marks the willing heart (Matt. 26:7; Phil. 4:14-19).

On the Edge of Greatness

(Numbers 13—14)

God desires for every authentic church to enter greatness. Greatness means maximum service in that church's own setting. Whether or not a church enters greatness is decided in a very significant location, a place called "the edge of greatness." That edge is found at the intersection of opportunity and choice. There are more than enough biblical and modern examples of churches that faced the choice.

God's Old Testament church stood on the edge of greatness in a dramatic and unavoidable moment. Unquestionably God had brought them to that moment. Jehovah had sent the ten plagues, led them through the Red Sea and provided an exodus. God had promised them a new land. Yet at the edge of greatness they stopped believing. With overwhelming evidence of God's power behind them, they suddenly stopped believing God and pressing forward. Out of twelve spies who investigated the greatness of their tomorrow, ten said that they could not do it. This episode was recorded as an example for us (1 Cor. 10:11; Heb. 3:17-19; 4:1-11).

Travis Avenue stands at the same edge of such greatness. The evidence of our past shows God's definite leadership. We must decide whether to press on to greatness or retreat to a wilderness of mediocrity. This month of intensive emphasis will be a large part of that decision.

We Ought to Explore Greatness Carefully

God lets us look at the vision of greatness. "Send some men to explore the land . . ." (13:2). They chose representative leaders to look at the greatness God had promised. The function of leadership is to explore the vision of tomorrow and bring back a word for direction today.

We ought to explore thoroughly God's promise for greatness (14:17-22). They examined every aspect of what God had promised. They took an adequate amount of time, forty days. They saw the truth of a land filled with promise. Similarly, Travis Avenue has had years to consider all that God can do. We have seen His past faithfulness and should believe in His future provision.

Leaders ought to bring back evidence of future greatness (vv. 22-23). They brought back tangible evidence that God's promise about the future was as rich and ripe as He had said.

The leadership of Travis has carefully explored the provision that God has made for our future. In April 1987 God opened an unexpected door by providing almost a block of property for additional parking and educational space. In September 1987 the church passed a unanimous joint recommendation to seek the financing to remodel the space and claim the future. In May 1989 we will have space to reach 400 more people in Bible study. This is a step in the direction of greatness.

We Ought to Cross Over to Greatness

Everyone should see the evidence of greatness for the future. All twelve of the Hebrew spies brought back the word that the land was as good as God had said (13:27). It was undeniable that there was blessing ahead if they would cross over and take it. But at this point a difference of opinion emerged.

For many *the threat outweighs the blessing* of greatness. "But the people who live there are powerful, and the cities are fortified and very large" (v. 28). Ten came back with a bad report about the people and the situation. They saw the impossible and said the impossible. The first report is always "there are giants in the land." Mere statistics are almost always against advance. Every advance is in the face of facts why it cannot be done.

When their original negativism was not enough, they began to imagine that things were worse than they were. The land devours people, everyone is a giant, and we are grasshoppers in comparison (vv. 32-33).

The essence of their report was to postpone, hesitate, resist, wait, digress, and go back. Unbelief always waits for a more convenient season. They were all for capture, but not now. They were positive as long as they were not confronted with the immediate call to advance.

Travis Avenue could take this attitude. There are giants of economic uncertainty, future unknowns, and shadows of the undetected we cannot see. We could say that we are generally for building a great church, but not right now.

For some *the blessings outweigh the threats* (v. 30). Caleb said, "We should, . . . we can." It is not what meets the eye but the person behind the eye that counts. Caleb repeatedly said, "He will lead us, . . . he will give it to us. . . . Do not be afraid, . . . the Lord is with us" (14:8-9). Joshua and Caleb also saw the giants, but they saw God as larger than the giants. They knew that the God who led them that far would not abandon on the edge of greatness.

Travis Avenue has always been led by those who said, "We should . . . we can." This is true for our church's early history and our recent history. The mighty, specific intervention of God has led us to this moment to underwrite all He has done for us. It is for us to say, "We should . . . we can."

There Are Results When We Refuse
to Cross Over to Greatness

When a church refuses greatness, it turns on itself. Numbers 14 contains a full report of the self-destructive grumbling that characterized that Old Testament church when they refused greatness. A church either gives itself to growth, conquest, and vision or to pettiness and arguments about procedures, policies, and the preservation of the status quo.

When a church refuses greatness, it wants to go back (14:2-4). On the edge of greatness a church may decide to turn around and go back. But Thomas Wolfe's George Webber was right, "You can't go home again." Israel wanted suddenly to go back to Egypt—the good old days of slavery and brick making! But they were caught in a wilderness of wandering for forty years of lost opportunity. It demolished a generation. They murdered their own opportunity. A church does not go back "to the way it was." When a church says no to greatness, there are years of slow death and decline.

Later, the church cannot reach greatness even if it wants to (vv. 40-42). When the realization comes that greatness was missed, God's people may decide to attempt it on their own. There is a time of destiny which must be taken. If we refuse this, God does not go with us (v. 42). In our own city there are churches that missed their moment of destiny, and God no longer opens the door to the future.

The pastor is confident that Travis Avenue will choose greatness. The month of April will go far to indicate that direction. You can respond by three ways: prayer for this program; participation when you are called on to serve and work; and sacrifice when it is time to give.

What Is Success?
(Numbers 20:1-13)

Who could question that our society is obsessed with success? For centuries most people wanted simply to survive. Today we want success quickly and visibly. Yet we are haunted by the question, "Have I succeeded?" What is success? Is it achievement, acclaim, affluence? How much do you have to accumulate to be successful?

Most people would consider Moses a success. Yet at the end of his 120-year-long life he failed. He ended as a successful failure. We can learn from his final failure what does not and what does constitute a real success.

Is Success Overcoming Adversity?

We often measure successes by the amount of adversity overcome. By that measure Moses should have been successful. He overcame four kinds of adversity in the pressure cooker of leadership.

We may overcome adverse *environment*. Moses led a mass of people in the destitute desert. He had done so for thirty-eight years. The entire group lived like Bedouins in an uninhabited, hostile environment. Moses achieved in an impossible place.

We may overcome adverse *memories*. The Hebrews returned to Kadesh, the place of their failure thirty-eight years before (13:26). At that place they refused to enter the land that God had given them. The huge rock at Kadesh was a landmark of lost life, a monument to failure. Yet Moses overcame the adversity of past failure.

We may overcome adverse *emotions*. Miriam died at Kadesh. She was the sister of Moses and Aaron as well as the leading woman of the Hebrews. It was Miriam who had placed the baby Moses in the Nile and watched until he was claimed by the daughter of Pharaoh. Now she suddenly died after 119 years of companionship.

We may overcome adverse *criticism*. The people criticized Moses for the lack of water. This was unjust and unreasonable criticism. It had not been by the impulse of Moses that they enjoyed the exodus. Besides, God had met their needs for years. Moses often overcame the adversity of unjust criticism.

This experience of Moses reveals that you can overcome adversity and still fall short of God's standard for success.

Is Success Seeking God?

Surely success is found in seeking God. Moses did not retaliate against the critical people, but turned instead to seek God. There is a great contrast between the leaders and the led.

We may *seek* God immediately and reverently. Moses turned toward God with an urgency to find an answer in the crisis. In reverence he fell down before the presence of God. Such immediacy and humility are surely to be commended.

We may *see* God's presence. Moses suddenly saw the glory of the Lord. This cloud of light had occurred before in special emergencies as a token of God's presence and intention to vindicate His name (Ex. 16:10; Num. 14:10; 16:19). Moses not only sought but also saw the presence of God.

We may *hear* God. The Lord spoke a practical, specific, and hopeful word to Moses about the crisis of no water. Moses heard the word of God with a startling clarity.

Yet seeking, seeing, and hearing God does not mean success. Another Old Testament man, Saul, sought God through every means but did not find Him (1 Sam. 28:6).

Is Success Obeying God?

Outwardly Moses appeared to be successful. He acted with authority and action. He produced. There were results—water gushed out of the rock at Kadesh. Yet Moses was a successful failure. Though people could not see that, God made it clear. What was the *reason* for failure?

We fail because of an *attitude*. Moses had an attitude of distrust toward God (20:12). He did not believe that God could make water come out of the solid rock, even though God had done it before. He also failed to see how God could have mercy on the critical Hebrews.

We fail because of an *acclamation*. Moses acclaimed, "Listen, you rebels" (v. 10). This was a word of anger. God told Moses to speak to the rock, not the people. Moses' rash anger caused his failure. But it was also an acclamation of ego. The little word "we" (v. 10) supplanted God and placed attention on the action of Moses and Aaron.

We fail because of an *act*. Moses acted in disobedience which was rebellion (v. 24). He struck the rock twice when he was only supposed to speak to the rock once. He literally took matters into his own hands.

In short, Moses was a successful failure because he refused to obey God. Success is not results, but obedience to God is! The water flowed from the rock, but Moses failed. The *only* ultimate measure of success is faithful obedience to God.

The *result* of failing to obey God may be severe (v. 12). Moses was not able to lead the people into the land. He did not lose his salvation, but he did lose his big opportunity in this life. The punishment appears severe. This was his only outward sin in forty years. Yet God takes the sins of leadership very seriously. Visibility means responsibility. Success is obedience. The lack of obedience has serious consequence. Measure your success by obedience.

Temptation to Forget
(Deuteronomy 8:1-11)

"How soon they forget" is more than a proverb. Sports fans forget that a coach won last year. Children forget the sacrifices of parents. Students forget who taught them. We suffer many kinds of amnesia. We forget names, dates, places, and even the names of old friends. Fortunately, most of what we forget is not all that serious.

Forgetfulness in the spiritual realm is more serious. In Deuteronomy Moses gave his farewell words to God's people. He warned them of forgetting God's activity in their past in the affluence of their present. God sustains us when we are nobody and have nothing. Many forget Him when we are somebody and have something.

When life is very good, beware the temptation to forget God.

Beware of Forgetting God When Life Gets Good

The reality of forgetfulness is in the words, "Be careful that you do not forget the Lord your God" (v. 11). This does not refer to mere absentmindedness. Facts about God can be remembered while we forget God. Even in the midst of church the living reality of God can fade and cease to be a governing principle. Abundance blunts the edge of your awareness of God. It is the ultimate contradiction that we can forget the One who is always and everywhere present.

The reason for forgetfulness of God is the present abundance of life. We can forget Him because of the very gifts He gives us. When our hands are full, we can forget what we learned when our hands were empty. For four decades the Hebrews had wandered as nomads, like modern Bedouins. They were about to settle down in permanent locations. They would begin to accumulate. Inwardly, they would be sated with more than enough food. Outwardly, their cattle, sheep, and camels would be stouter and more powerful than those of their wandering life. They would begin to accumulate precious metals which they never had as nomads. For years as wanderers they had been on the edge of poverty and never accumulated anything. Now they would accumulate and forget God.

You can count on it. When you have little you live in dependence on God. When you have a big house, a big car, and big bank balance you can easily forget God.

The Result of Forgetting God Is Arrogant Self-Sufficiency

Spiritual forgetfulness leads to an arrogant attitude: "Your heart will become proud" (v. 14). Pride is lodged in the seat of your personality, the heart. Pride grows in the heart when you forget your past absolute dependence on God. Israel had forgotten the pit and the pathway of its past. Israel's very life had depended on God's protection and provision. God had protected Israel from the dryness and the dangers of a desert existence. He had provided for them when it appeared no provision could be made. Water and food came out of impossibility. The strength to wander came from God alone.

Most of us have an early wilderness experience. Resources are short, we live from day to day, the future is insecure. God's provision is a living reality. But then things get good. We forget that God sustained us when we had little.

Spiritual forgetfulness leads to an arrogant confession: You may say to yourself, "My power and the strength of my hands have produced this wealth for me" (v. 17). Notice that you say this "to yourself." You may still go through the motions of worshiping God and thanking Him in public, but "to yourself" you offer congratulations. You studied while others were playing, you worked while others were sleeping, you were shrewd while others were dumb, etc., etc. Outwardly, you may go through the motions of praising God, but inwardly you congratulate yourself. Your energy and your ability did it. God fades and disappears. Instead of "How Great Thou Art" you hum inwardly "How Great I Am."

The Recovery from Forgetting God Is a Deliberate Recollection

How do you get over spiritual amnesia? A deliberate effort at memory begins the recovery. Remember that God alone sustains your life (v. 18). You should sit down and if necessary write out the provisions for your life. If you will relive your life in memory, you will rediscover that it was God alone who provided when provision was needed. The central message of Deuteronomy is that God alone is the author of life's provision.

Further remember that God sustains you because of His faithfulness, not your performance. God "confirms his covenant which he swore to your forefathers" (v. 18b). God's blessings in life are the result of His own promise, not our changing performance. He blesses because He is true to His own word and name. We recover from spiritual forgetfulness when we remember that all we are and have is the result of His faithfulness to His word and covenant.

Press On!
(Joshua 1)

The Book of Joshua begins with the word "and." This implies that it continues all that God had done in the previous five biblical books. God moves forward. He is always advancing and pressing on. If we are not personally and congregationally pressing on, we are not moving with God. What God told Joshua, He tells you: "Get ready." (1:2b, NIV). God presses on.

You can press on in spite of human circumstances and in light of God's word and promise.

I. Press On in Spite of Human Circumstances.

Human leadership and companionship changes and disappears: "Moses my servant is dead" (v. 2a, NIV). When they needed their great leader most, he was gone. Nevertheless, they pressed on.

Personal disappointment delays life's greatest dreams. Joshua was eighty-five years old when he assumed leadership. He had waited in frustration for forty years. Nevertheless, he pressed on.

Application: What human circumstances keep you from pressing forward with God's will for your life? Are they more difficult than those Joshua faced?

II. Press On in Light of Divine Promises.

Draw encouragement by God's past promises to those who pressed on: "I promised Moses" (v. 3), "I swore to their forefathers" (v. 6b).

Draw encouragement by God's present assurances to those who press on: "Be strong and courageous" (v. 6a).

He gives special, personal assurances at critical times.

He gives repeated assurances because of our repeated need.

III. Press On by Careful Obedience to God's Word.

To press on requires obedience to the whole of God's word.

To press on reveals a God who blesses with success those who keep His word.

Conclusion: You only possess what you claim. Israel never claimed what God had given them. Have you claimed the fullness of life God desires to give you?

Crossing Over

(Joshua 3)

The day has come to cross over the Avenues for Advance. After five months of preparation, a day finally comes when we will all make a decision to commit or not to commit. God's people have faced other crossings over. After forty years of wandering in the wilderness, Israel faced the Jordan River at floodtide. They could either cross over to a purposeful future, or stay behind in aimlessness and futility. God's faithful people always make a positive decision to cross over into His future.

A Commitment to Cross Over Requires
a Certainty of God's Direction

When God's people cross over, they need a certain indication of His leadership. The visible presence of the ark of the covenant gave that certainty to Israel (v. 3). We need an equal certainty of God's spiritual leadership. The eight Avenues for Advance have been prayerfully and carefully considered by God's people. We feel that we have found His leadership.

We need His leadership because of the unfamiliar future: "You have never been this way before" (v. 4). A group of slaves from Egypt had wandered in the desert for forty years. They were stepping out into the unknown. They needed the certainty of divine direction to cross over into the future. We are in the same need. To make sacrificial commitments without knowing the future economy, health, or world conditions is an act of faith.

A Commitment to Cross Over Requires
an Activity of Personal Consecration

On all great and solemn occasions, God's people are to consecrate themselves. Just as a symphony needs a prelude, a mighty act of God calls for a special consecration by His people. The special manifestations of God's presence should be awaited by His people in a posture of deep humiliation, penitence, prayer, and diligent efforts to cleanse ourselves in His presence. In Joshua's day, they were to wash themselves and abstain from everything that might indispose their minds from the serious and devout attention to the miracle about to be performed on their behalf.

Tonight, we expect God to intervene in a supernatural way as His people rise up to make a commitment. We should spend these hours in special, personal prayer and examination to be ready for crossing over the Avenues for Advance.

A Commitment to Cross Over Requires
a Dependency on Divine Intervention

We can step out in that dependency. When Israel crossed over, first the leaders (v. 8) and then the people (v. 17) stepped out in the Jordan. They crossed over into the unfamiliar future with nothing but the spoken promise of God.

We all experience God's intervention (v. 16). When His people step out in faith on His word, God intervenes. He would have more to lose than His people if He failed to keep His word.

Stopping to Remember
(Joshua 4)

God's people sometimes suffer from spiritual amnesia. The psalmist complained, "They forgot what he had done, and the wonders he had shown them" (78:11). On the contrary, God expects His people to remember His mighty acts in their lives. We can easily forget the significant because of the clamor of the immediate. The same things that could cause Joshua's generation to forget could cause us to forget. The inconvenience of the moment, the pressure of the practical, and the call of the future can always create spiritual amnesia.

God desires His people to appropriately and meaningfully remember what He has done for them.

God Prescribes the Way His People Ought to Remember

God's people ought to remember inclusively. "Choose twelve men from among the people, one from each tribe" (v. 2). Twelve representing all the people of God were each to carry a stone for a monument to God's mighty acts. To remember what God has done is not just for historians. From the most recent to the eldest member of God's family, we are all to hold in memory His mighty deeds.

God's people ought to remember conspicuously, "Joshua set up at Gilgal the twelve stones they had taken out of Jordan" (v. 20). The twelve stones were caused to stand erect on a large eminence. The people of God gave a conspicuous place to the memory of what God had done for them. We ought to keep before us and near us the reminders of the mighty acts God has done.

God's people ought to remember with vividness. The stones of remembrance were taken from the place "right where the priests stood" (v. 2). They recalled with vividness the mighty act of God. When parents recounted to their children what God had done, they told it as if their children had actually been there during the act itself (v. 23). We ought to remember by creating the present power of God's past acts.

God Prescribes the Reason His People Remember

God desires His people to remember for the purpose of instruction. We are to tell His mighty acts to our children in every generation (v. 6). This includes not only what God has done in the biblical revelation, but also what He has done in our church. Rootlessness is a curse of our times. Our children will profit from knowing they are part of what God has been doing here for seventy-five years.

But our celebration of God's mighty acts also warns the enemies of His cause. The hearts of God's enemies sank when they heard of His mighty victory (5:1). To celebrate what God has done in our past warns the opponents of His kingdom that our God is a mighty God.

But beyond that, we instruct the entire earth by remembering what God has done. "He did this that all the peoples of the earth might know that the hand of the Lord is powerful and so that you might always fear the Lord your God" (4:24).

God desires His people to remember for purposes of commemoration. God has acted for the intervention and preservation of His people. He has done for them what they could never do for themselves. Beyond that, He has sustained them by repeated, mighty acts.

God desires His people to remember for the affirmation of the future. The monument of stones was placed midway between Jordan and Jericho. They placed their memory halfway between God's mighty deliverances in the past and the unknown challenges of the future. The God who had delivered at Jordan was the God who could deliver at Jericho.

That monument reminded them that there was no retreat. The God who opened the Jordan before them closed the Jordan behind them. The ultimate meaning of that memorial was a call to advance into the future, for there could be no retreat into the past.

Forever Friends

(1 Samuel 18—20; 23; 31)

What is a friend? Rollo May indicates that most people make 500 to 2,500 acquaintances each year, but have fewer than seven personal friends. Most of us have twenty to one hundred casual friends we relate to from time to time. Close friends involve associates, personal friendships, and those of whom we share mentor relationships. But beyond that are *best friends*—those with whom we share deepest feelings and hopes. Most people in one survey had four active, current intimate friends.

What are the marks of a good friendship? For most of us, an illustration is more helpful than a definition. The Bible presents the friendship of David and Jonathan. In many ways this friendship was most unlikely. David was the son of a poor shepherd. Jonathan was a prince, the son of King Saul. Saul was insanely jealous of David. David could have been a threat to Jonathan. The friendship of David and Jonathan was in the midst of romance, violence, suspicion, jealousy, retaliation, loyalty, treachery, secrets, and hideaways.

We can learn from their story that *friendships grow because of what friends are themselves and because of how they relate to those outside the friendship.*

Inside Friendships

Friendship begins with commonality. "Jonathan became one in spirit with David" (18:1). Friendship began when Jonathan felt bound to David by a common spirit. In this instance, that oneness was a shared faith that one could risk great odds because of faith that God could overcome any obstacle. The friendship began after David killed Goliath (1 Sam. 17). Jonathan in a similar way overcame great odds in battle. Lasting friendships share oneness of spirit.

Great friendships must share deeply. For some this sharing is emotional and for others it is primarily mental. Friendship listens, speaks, understands, and accepts because there is a bond. When you look for a friend, look for that bond of commonality.

Friendship continues with a *covenant.* The basic and most characteristic mark of the David-Jonathan friendship was a willingness to commit unqualified loyalty. This covenant marked the very beginning of the friendship (18:3) and was repeated (20:16,42). Renewing the covenant of their friendship was the last thing they did the final time they met (23:18). The covenant of friendship was made openly, sacrificially, repeatedly, and lastingly.

The sustaining basis for friendship is loyalty. This particularly means loyalty in the midst of adversity. "A friend loves at all times, and a brother is born for adversity" (Prov. 17:17). The basis for real friendship is not just the good times, but also the bad times. Some of Paul's loneliest words were found in 2 Timothy 4:16, "At my first defense, no one came to my support, but everyone deserted me." Paul founded numerous churches and must have had hundreds of acquaintances. Yet he had to stand alone in bad times.

Friendship grows with expressions of *concern*. This expressions of concern can take the form of *gifts* and *guidance*. We express concern through giving to friends. Jonathan shared with David gifts of prominence and practicality (18:4). He gave David his prince's robe which was a mark of prominence. He also gave his sword and bow, rare gifts of great value. Self-sacrifice is a measure of friendship. "Each of you should look not only to your own interests, but to the interests of others" (Phil. 2:4). Do you have a friend for whom you would set aside personal interest, cancel a vacation to meet a friend's deep need, or accept the care of their children temporarily or even permanently? Friendship expresses concern through gifts.

But friendship also expresses concern through *guidance*. More than once Jonathan guided David through warnings and acts of protection (19:1-2; 20:12-13). Friends help solve problems, share alternate solutions, and ask for counsel or help. "As iron sharpens iron, so one man sharpens another" (Prov. 27:17).

Friendship consoles. The highest moment of the David-Jonathan friendship is recorded in 1 Samuel 23:16, "And Saul's son Jonathan went to David at Horesh and helped him find strength in God." Friends inevitably drive you to or from God. Jonathan encouraged David by calming his fears, assuring him of a stable future, and pledging his personal faithfulness. That is not a bad definition of friendship: one who helps you find strength in God.

Outside Friendship

Friends not only relate to each other, they also relate to those outside the friendship about one another.

Good friends defend. On more than one occasion Jonathan defended David to Saul. He became his friend's advocate (19:3-7). In a tense moment, Jonathan defended David's actions, motives, and intentions. Knowing Saul's short temper, that was a courageous act, even for a son. One way to defend a friend is by never breaking confidences. Few things destroy a friendship more quickly than a broken confidence.

Good friends reconcile. Jonathan so loved David that he reconciled Saul to David (v. 6). In fact, Saul then restored David to his place at the royal court. Friends should care enough to try to heal the wounds between others. Barnabas was such a friend to Paul that he reconciled Paul to the Jerusalem Christians (Acts 9:27).

Forever Friends

For many friendship ends with death. Jonathan died (31:2) and David was never the same. Christian friends can expect something better. Peter, Andrew, James, and John, Paul and Silas and others are still friends today—2,000 years of friendship. How? They all had another Friend—the Lord Jesus Christ. When He is your Friend everyone who shares that friendship will be friends forever.

Christian friendship will deepen forever. You can spend forever knowing more and going deeper with friends when Jesus is your Friend in common.

What Is Sacrifice?

(2 Samuel 24:18-25)

For many of us it is difficult to answer the question, "What is sacrifice?" Even though sacrifice is central in the life of God's people, it has become marginal in contemporary

Christian thinking. David gave us the best definition of sacrifice in the Word: "I will not offer burnt offerings to the Lord my God which cost me nothing" (v. 25, NASB).

A sacrifice is that which costs us something in the way we live. It means giving up something I love and cherish for something I love and cherish more. Our capital campaign, Avenues for Advance, will only reach its goals as we together—all of us—reach out to touch sacrifice.

Sacrifice Begins in
the Desire to Worship God

The word of God came to David with an invitation to worship. That word designated a specific place, time, and circumstance to worship God. The place was a threshing floor in Jerusalem. The time was immediately. The circumstance was a great need in the land.

Avenues for Advance should first and last be a great act of worship to God. If it is less than that, it is not truly biblical sacrifice. Our pledges should be made in a holy, praise-filled, joyful act of worship.

Sacrifice Grows with a Refusal to Offer God
that Which Costs Me Nothing

David had the opportunity to offer to God a free, cheap, absolutely costless worship. Araunah attempted to give David the altar, the sacrifice, and even the wood to burn the sacrifice. It was a "package deal" that would allow David cheap, inexpensive worship. It has always been the temptation of God's people to give God a worship that costs them nothing. It grieves God when His people give Him the least and the worst, instead of the first and the best (Mal. 1:13-14).

In the future, everybody in our fellowship will enjoy the fruit of Avenues for Advance. Both those who sacrifice and those who give nothing will alike enjoy the use of new facilities and new ministries. The question is one of integrity and worship: "Will I allow others to sacrifice for what I will enjoy?" A good practical question to ask is this: "If everyone gave at my personal level of sacrifice, would it be worthy of God?"

Sacrifice Results in a Costly Offering
Which Pleases God

David did offer to God that which cost him something. Initially, he bought the threshing floor and the oxen for sacrifice. Ultimately, he paid a much larger price for the whole area that would become the temple (1 Chron. 21:25).

As a result of David's costly worship, the plague was averted from the land (v. 25). No one could disagree that many plagues assault our land today. To know freedom from these plagues will include sacrifice on the part of God's people at His house.

Leadership and Response

(1 Chronicles 29)

There is a proverb which goes, "He who thinketh he leadeth and nobody followeth is only taking a walk." Leadership is meaningful because people respond to a leader. In the Old Testament account of building the temple, David appears as a leader who effectively moved other leaders and followers to the task. A leader must have both a vision and a task. A vision without a task is an illusion. A task without a vision is a drudgery. But a vision coupled with a task means leadership.

Travis has a vision of serving the maximum number of people in Fort Worth and Tarrant County. This vision requires a task. Spiritual goals of the church require physical provisions for the church. *Travis Together Triumphant* gives us the challenge of leadership and response.

Leadership Calls for a Vision and a Task

We must *envision* building for God's work. David had the vision of a building that was "not for man but for the Lord God." The visionary dream of a temple for God's work fired the life and imagination of David. He was clear in his motive that the purpose of the structure was for God and not for man (v. 1). Through a providential intervention God has provided us with a block of property and a new building. God clearly intervened in the timing, personalities, and circumstances for the south education building.

We must make *provision* for the vision. Along with the vision is the task of paying for the vision. Because David wanted the vision to be reality, he made regular, planned contributions to the work (v. 2). But beyond his regular contribution he was willing to give "over and above" all that he regularly gave (v. 3). God's plan for making vision reality remains the same. We ought to give regularly the tithes that belong to God as well as our offerings. On extraordinary occasions, however, God calls us to do more in the face of need. Such giving ought to be *personal, additional,* and *devotional.* The act of giving is really the act of consecrating oneself.

Leadership Calls for Response

By definition a leader is a leader because people respond and follow. *Every level* of leadership should respond to the commitment of the principal leader. When David made his pledge to the building of the temple, the other leaders in the congregation responded. This included the heads of families, the officers, commanders, and every level of officials. Your pastor and family are committed to this program. The leaders of your church have already made a sacrificial commitment at many levels. Leaders at Travis are leading.

God's people should *respond in reaction* to their leaders' commitment. The response of all the people was one of joy and generosity when they saw their leaders give to the work. All of the people were moved to sacrificial giving in light of the leaders' example. The result was a total effort of leaders and followers which created great joy in the congregation.

Praise Results from Such Giving
in the Congregation

There is no praise in the congregation to match that which follows from supernatural giving. Such praise results in the *magnification of God* (vv. 10-13). The words of David's joyous praise-prayer still resound in our own worship. The highest days of praise Travis will ever know will come from response in sacrificial giving. Praise is not cheap. It grows loudest out of devotion that is deepest.

Such giving demonstrates *the position of humankind* (vv. 14-15). We are a *dependent, derivative,* and *disappearing* people. Even when we give we confess our humility in the face of daring to present anything back to God. We are so derivative that we can only confess, "Everything comes from you, and we have given you only what comes from your hand" (v. 14). We should also keep in mind that we are disappearing: "Our days on earth are like a shadow without hope." Giving acknowledges that we do what we can when we can.

Such giving results in a *celebration* of the Lord's presence: "They ate and drank with great joy in the presence of the Lord that day" (v. 22) On May 7 we will celebrate the victory that has come in *Travis Together Triumphant*. Those of us who have responded will celebrate the joy in God's presence. Would you not be part of that celebration?

Revival in the Temple of Your Heart
(2 Chronicles 29)

In the Old Testament God had a temple for His people. In the New Testament He has a people for His temple. Under Hezekiah a great revival took place at the temple in Jerusalem. A revival at the temple shook the nation for God. The young king gathered the people, purified the temple, and led the people in consecration to God.

The same principles can lead to personal spiritual renewal in your heart. You can experience revival in the temple of your heart.

I. Consider the Priority Revival Reveals

An experience of personal renewal for the nation and for himself became the passion of the young king (note vv. 3,17,20,36).

Personal spiritual renewal must have first place or it will have no place.

II. Consider the Adversity Revival Reveals

The place of spiritual illumination was dark

The place of prayerful intercession was silent

The place of sacrificial consecration was cold

III. Consider the Activity Revival Renews

Revival renews inward purification

Revival renews personal consecration

Revival renews spiritual exaltation

The last verse emphasizes that all this happened suddenly. There is no reason why new spiritual life cannot begin now for you.

Get the Treasure Safely Home
(Ezra 8:21-35)

Stories of capture and escape always excite interest. This interest increases when the captives escape with great treasures. The Jewish escape from Babylon is one of the most dramatic in history. Taken captive in 597 B.C., the Jews were released in groups from 538 to 458 B.C. The last group was led by Ezra, the great priest and scribe. His group escaped with an enormous treasure. They carried that treasure across 900 miles of desert for four months. Their goal was to get the treasure to God's house in Jerusalem. Upon arriving, they gave one of the greatest offerings in history.

Harvest Day marks the great yearly offering at Travis. There are instructive biblical parallels between Ezra's great offering in Jerusalem at the temple and our offering in Fort Worth at Travis Avenue. Both offerings demand preparation. In both instances God's people must protect the treasure that belongs to Him. On both occasions there is a solemn presentation in God's house. Next Sunday at Travis Avenue it is essential that we get God's treasure safely home. The work of God here depends on that.

Make Preparation to Get God's Treasure Safely Home

Our preparation begins with a recognition of God's protection. Nothing prepares us to give like a careful reflection of God's goodness. Ezra was about to make a tremendous trip across a difficult desert. He acknowledged his absolute dependence on God's protection. "The gracious hand of our God is upon everyone who looks to him" (v. 22). He recognized and renounced ultimate dependence on anyone other than God. This preparation led the people to an act of deliberate self-denial, a time of fasting. This preparation led the people to a time of intense prayer for God's guidance. The preparation to get God's treasure home rested on their past experience and future certainty of God's protection.

As you prepare for Harvest Day 1990, can you not also confess the protection of God across the year since the last Harvest Day? Could you not say with Ezra, "The hand of our God was on us, and he protected us from enemies and bandits along the way"? (v. 31). The only ultimate protection that any of us has is the protection that God gives. As you prepare to give on Harvest Day, let it be with a careful reflection on God's protection across the last year. Next Sunday we will come to God's treasury certain of His protection across the year.

Provide Protection to Get God's Treasure Safely Home

At the heart of this story is the careful provision made to protect God's treasure until it was safely home. This year God has provided for most of us some treasure. He expects us to protect that part of the treasure that is His until it is safely home on His altar. Ezra's people protected the treasure God gave them until it rested on God's altar. May we do the same with the treasure God has given us.

God does make *provision* to give His people a treasure. God enriched His captive Jewish people incredibly. Even the pagan Persians gave an offering to them (7:15-17). Added to the gifts of the Jews themselves, this made an enormous treasure. Today, who could say that God has not enriched His Baptist people? Most of us live at a far higher standard of living than our parents or grandparents did at the same age.

God makes an *evaluation* of the treasure He gives us. Crucial to this story is the careful weighing out of the treasure God gave His people. The treasure was weighed at the beginning of their journey, and it was weighed at the end of their journey (vv. 25,33). God expects us to show up at the end of the journey with the treasure He gave us at the beginning. Next Sunday we will bring our treasure to the altar. There will not be a visible pair of scales, but there will certainly be an invisible pair of scales. Jesus Himself made it clear that God will measure what we have done with our treasure (Matt. 25:19).

We have a responsibility for the *protection* of the treasure until it rests in God's house. "Guard them carefully until you weigh them out in the chambers of the house of the Lord in Jerusalem" (v. 29). What an enormous responsibility to protect a treasure across 900 miles of desert for four months. Yet God expects us to protect the treasure that belongs to Him across the miles and the months until it rests on His altar. Most of us carefully protect that part of our treasure which is due for our mortgage, car payment, and utility payment. Do we have the same sense of protection for that part of our treasure which belongs to God?

Plan the Presentation of God's Treasure When Safely Home

We should plan to present God's treasure in His house as an act of worship. "In the house of our God we weighed out the silver and gold and the sacred articles" (v. 33). After months of preparation and protection, they finally came to the moment to present God's treasure at the altar of His temple in Jerusalem. This should be a time of careful presentation. Nothing haphazard characterizes the scene. The treasure is weighed in, receipted, and acknowledged. This is a time of individual responsibility. The very names of those in the process are preserved for all time. The presentation of the treasure is a public act or worship in the house of God.

Next Sunday will be a high day of worship at Travis. By families and individuals we will bring God's treasure home. May there be nothing careless or indifferent about it. Just as they protected their treasure across the miles and the months, so should we. Next Sunday God will weigh in what He has weighed out to us. May all of us get the treasure safely home.

God Crowns a King
(Psalm 2)

Even though we live in a democracy, God intends to rule His people and the world through a King, an absolute Sovereign. In the Old Testament, God desired to rule Israel and the world through David and his heirs (2 Sam. 7:16). God wanted to rule the earth from Jerusalem through the dynasty of David. Because of His own people's failure and the world's rejection, that rule never happened.

But God's promise did not fail. In Bethlehem, the city of David, One from the family of David came to take the throne. Humankind begged for Someone greater than David or Solomon. He came in the person of Jesus Christ. His own church recognizes His reign now. Ultimately, everyone will bow to His rule.

Psalm 2 was written for the coronation of an Old Testament king, but its greater fulfillment is the coronation of the King of kings. God crowns Christ King and gives Him the nations of the world as His coronation present.

Humankind Rejects the Reign of God

What is the most apt diagnosis of the human condition? Is it poverty, lack of learning, psychological sickness? The most accurate diagnosis of the human condition is rebellion against God. The psalmist looks with astonishment as creation rebels against the Creator: "Why do the nations conspire and the peoples plot in vain?" (v. 1) He is astonished and indignant that the nations and sovereigns of the earth do not submit to God. The language depicts a kind of "United Nations Against God." It is an imaginary picture of a great crowd's tumultuous uproar. It is the picture of a huge convention to hatch plots against God.

History demonstrates this rebellion. The Old Testament world never recognized Israel's king as God's anointed ruler. At Christ's birth neither Rome nor the Jewish people accepted Him as King. Augustus, Herod the Great, Tiberius, and Pilate all failed to recognize God's King. The sum and substance of history is a revolt against God.

Today, that is still true. The rule and reign of God is not taken seriously by the peoples of the earth. Man is still "man in revolt." We still want to break the chains and throw off the fetters of God's rule (v. 3). But what is true of nations is only what is true of individuals. Do you submit to the reign and rule of God in your life? God's rule in history is not the immediate question. Do you yourself submit to His rule?

God Responds by Installing His Son as King

Human rejection does not threaten God. Mere human beings are stung by rejection. The Sovereign of all creation does not react to rejection as humans do. God "laughs, the Lord scoffs at them" (v. 4). These words do not drag God down to mere human behavior. But this lets us know that God's reaction to the rage of the nations against His rule is closer to a human laugh than anything else.

God can quickly dispatch human rejection. When rejection persists, God speaks and His Word is power. His indignation will vex, confound, and strike with terror the mere men who oppose His will. You can see this clearly when you look at the end and the last days of those who opposed the coming of the Christ.

God's only answer is His only Son. In verse 6 you would expect a great battle of God against the rebellious earth. But instead you read the edict of God: "I have installed my King on Zion, my holy hill" (v. 6). God's answer was not a great battle. His answer was the coming of a baby, an infant, the greater Son of David. When you would expect the clash weapons or a thunderbolt from heaven to vaporize a rebellious planet, God sends a baby to Bethlehem.

God's answer for your personal rebellion is His Son. He wants to come to terms with you through Jesus Christ. His invitation is "Kiss the Son" (v. 12).

God Will Give the Earth to His Kingly Son

What is the destiny of our planet? Will it collide with a meteor? Will it bomb itself into oblivion? The intention of God is to give the earth to His Son. "Ask of me, and I will make the nations your inheritance, the ends of the earth your possession" (v. 8). These words found their fulfillment in Jesus' great claim, "All authority in heaven and on earth has been given to me" (Matt. 28:18). God's promise to give the earth to His Son will find its ultimate expression in the reign of Christ over a renewed earth (Rev. 21).

The characteristic of Christ's rule will depend on our response. For those who yield He will "herd them like sheep with a crook of iron." Firm, stable, unbending lordship will mark His reign on the earth. For those who refuse to yield there will be easy, complete, irreparable destruction. They will be shattered into fragments which cannot be put back together.

God intends to give the earth to His Son as a result of our witness to all nations. When that happens, the end will come. God wants to take possession of you before He takes possession of the earth. Why not acknowledge His reign now willingly rather than later unwillingly? Our God will reign!

Faith and Fear

(Psalm 27:1-6)

Psychology Today asked 1,000 respondents what they most feared. The answers in order of frequency were: death of a loved one, serious personal illness, financial worries, nuclear war, being a crime victim, spiders, loss of a job, natural disaster, the dark, loneliness, and being unloved. Probably some of your fears are on this list.

The psalmist faced the choice of faith or fear. Psalm 27 expresses a tried faith that triumphed in spite of very real fears. Your personal faith can overcome fear when communion with God dominates your life.

Only a Personal Faith Overcomes Fear

Faith overcomes fear when God is first. You must begin with faith or fear will flourish. The psalmist begins the day with an affirmation of Jehovah God as light, salvation, and safety. Because of the priority of his praise, fear can find no place. Before fear can raise its head, the psalmist affirms that God is the light that dispels darkness and leads the way out. God is rescue in the face of all that chases him and a stronghold in view of all that endangers him. This dependence is exclusively on God. He has given up any dependence on other men or himself.

Faith overcomes fear when faith is personal. The psalmist uses five personal pronouns in verse 1. His faith is intensely personal. He did not overcome fear through understanding theology or remembering only what God had done for Abraham and Moses. God is a triple shield to him only in the personal character of his faith. Faith that is personal overcomes fear.

Faith overcomes fear when we remember past experiences. In the past your faith has overcome fear. Remember? In verse 2 the psalmist remembered that his faith had triumphed over actual threats, not paper tigers or imagined enemies. People with intense personal ill will had tried to devour him with vicious speech. In each instance they had stumbled and fallen. Most of the bad things you thought would happen did not happen, did they?

Fearless Faith Roots in a Single Desire

Are you a "one thing" person? The fearlessness of your faith will depend on the singleness of your desire. The psalmist can look into the future as well as the past and say with confidence that one thing pervades his life—a desire to commune with God. This singleness of heart provides peacefulness of heart.

Fearless faith desires communion with God: "that I may dwell in the house of the Lord all the days of my life" (v. 4a). Physically, the psalmist desired to be in God's house. David was often compelled to wander far from the tabernacle where God's physical presence dwelt. He longed to be in the house of God always. This means spiritually that he desired an intimate, inward fellowship with God. Such constant communion renews fearless faith. For us this is both localized and spiritualized. It does mean to be in the place where God's people meet when they meet. It also means that when we are away, we commune with God.

Fearless faith practices the contemplation of God. David desires an extraordinary experience of God. He desires to "behold the beauty of the Lord" (v. 4b, KJV). The phrase suggests a clinging, lingering, entranced gazing at God. How do you gaze at God? The psalmist wanted to see through all of the acts of worship to the reality behind them in the face of God. He earnestly marked everything in the worship service for what it revealed about God Himself. His faith became fearless in the communion and contemplation of God.

Fearless Faith Realizes God's Protection

God habitually hides from enemies or elevates above difficulty those whose faith is personal.

Personal faith gives a hiding place. Everyone has to retreat in order to survive, even the Lord Jesus. The psalmist speaks of hiding in God's house, sanctuary, tabernacle, and tent. These images speak of God as our host and protector. Psalm 23:5 expresses the same reality: "You [spread] a table [for] me in the presence of my enemies."

Personal faith elevates us above the difficulty: "He shall set me high upon a rock. And now my head shall be lifted up above my enemies." (27:5-6, NKJV). The psalmist describes a sheltering asylum on a hill where God makes him inaccessible to dangers which are far beneath him. Fearless faith can elevate you above the fray.

This is but an echo of that great shout of Romans 8:37: "In all these things we are more than conquerors through him who loved us." It will either be faith or fear.

Guilt Can Go — Now!
(Psalm 32:1-5; 1 John 2:1)

Where can guilt go? How do you dispose of the residue of past failure? If left alone, guilt can become insomnia, outbursts, free-floating anxiety, criticism of others, and physical disease. The Christian faith must deal effectively with guilt if Christianity is effective in human life in any way. The good news of the gospel is this: God's forgiveness is a bigger event than your guilt. The Bible presents an extreme case of guilt in the life of David. If God can deal with this, He can deal with anything. Guilt can go if you tell it like it is and turn to Jesus Christ as your Advocate.

Guilt Can Go If You Tell It Like It Is

The way up and out of guilt is to tell the story to God just like it is. We often deny, hide, refuse, or cover up before God. Relief comes from telling it to God like it is. David spent a year in silence—speechless and mute before God. When he came to himself he made a threefold confession. It touched on three dimensions of his guilt.

Godwardly, we have rebelled. The word "transgressions" (v. 1) means rebellion, revolt, or acts of sedition against the government of God. In secular language, it referred to a break in relationship between two parties. David broke God's law, violated his own conscience, and betrayed other people. But the first step up and out of guilt was to relate guilt to God, not to other people.

Manwardly, we have missed the mark. We must admit that we have deflected our aim, erred from our own standards. The shepherd boy David never intended to do what the king David did. The author of the twenty-third Psalm hardly expected to have to write the thirty-second Psalm. He had missed the goal that he had set for his own life.

Inwardly, there is something twisted that needs to be straightened out. At the level of doing, we rebel and miss the mark. But that is not the deepest truth about us. There is something askew that needs to be set straight. There is something warped that needs to be unwarped. David had to admit what he *was*, not just what he *did*.

The moment we make this three-dimensional confession, we experience the pardon of God. Guilt can go. The confession must be made sincerely by those in whose spirit there is no deceit.

Guilt Will Deal with You If You Do Not Deal with Guilt

Dr. Tournier expressed, after years of practice, that many of the physical symptoms he saw in his patients resulted from suppressed guilt from years before. David said the same thing more eloquently three thousand years earlier. He noted that psychologically and physically guilt would have destroyed him had he not told it to God like it was.

Psychologically, guilt makes the conscience roar. David expressed that his conscience was "roaring all . . . day long" (v. 3, KJV). The word refers to the ravenous roar of the leaping lion. The shepherd David knew the blood-chilling reality of that roar. All day long his conscience roared at him.

Physically, guilt can affect the body. "When I kept silent, my bones wasted away" (v. 3). The framework of his body was racked, shaken, and the seat of his strength seemed to disintegrate. He was fatigued and listless with no sense of direction or purpose.

No one can argue that guilt exacts a great price in human thought and physical life. It can make people self-destructive in ways they do not even recognize. Deal with guilt before guilt deals with you.

Turn to Jesus Christ as Your Advocate

We know something better than David knew. He looked back to animal sacrifices and a temple. We look back to Calvary and a Risen Lord. That Lord is now our great Advocate.

We have an Advocate *presently.* He is right now at the right hand of the Father in heaven. We do not have to worry about the immediate availability of His help. Whether our guilt was caused ten years ago or yesterday, He is even this moment at the right hand of God.

We have an Advocate *positionally.* Jesus Christ is in that face-to-face access to the Father which enables Him to speak for us in our time of need. Our own sin would shut us out from the presence of the Holy One. Our Lord Jesus is never outside the immediate presence of God Himself.

We have an Advocate *powerfully.* Because His name is Jesus, He is a sympathetic Advocate. Jesus is a friend to sinners in this age. But because His name is Christ, He is a sinless, powerful Advocate. Because He has no sin of His own, He stands in the Father's presence as my substitute.

You can tell it like it is and turn to Jesus Christ as your Advocate this very moment. Guilt can go.

Out of Your Impossible Situation
(Psalm 40)

You probably believe that God can bring you out of a difficult situation. Do you truly trust that God can bring you out of an impossible situation? The psalmist didn't. In fact, his own efforts only proved the final futility of the problem. But God intervened, and the psalmist responded to God's intervention with a fresh sense of praise and a new demonstration of obedience.

By asking God alone to act, you can find a way out of your impossibility.

God Delivers from an Impossible Situation

The words present a memorable picture of *human helplessness:* "He lifted me out of the slimy pit, out of the mud and mire" (v. 2). The words picture a deep pit where even deeper waters resound from a horrible cavern further below. Such pits were used as dungeons (Jer. 38:6), pitfalls for wild beasts (Ps. 7:15), or could even refer to a grave (28:1). The emphasis rests on the roaring, resounding noise of the place as well as its depth. What was worse, the bottom of the pit was like the muck of filthy mire. The more the psalmist struggled to get out, the deeper he sank into the bog at the bottom.

What kind of experience led the psalmist to express himself this way? It may have been a military defeat, the opposition of wicked people, sickness, or the impossible situation created by personal sin in his life. Perhaps it is best that we do not know. We can then identify with the psalmist in our own impossible situation.

There is an equally impressive statement of *divine intervention.* Suddenly, God moves into the difficulty and the entire situation changes. From the instability of the bog beneath he suddenly finds sure footing on stable ground. God not only gave him present safety but also future stability. A new life opened up before him immediately after a threat that would have ended life.

How do you find such an experience. The secret is in verse 1: "I *waited* patiently for the Lord; he turned to me and heard my cry" (v. 1, author's italics). There is an emphatic repetition in the original language: "I waited, yea, I waited." The resounding of the words indicates a total reliance on God alone to extricate him. This also suggests an exclusive waiting on God: "I simply waited; I did nothing but wait." God may place you in a situation where only a divine act can deliver you from the impossibility. The opposite of waiting on God is to fret, be angry, and to take things into your own hands (Ps. 37:7).

You Can Respond Appropriately
to God's Delivery

You can respond first with *fresh praise* to God: "he put a new song in my mouth" (v. 3). How long has it been since you had something fresh about which to praise God? God had done such a dramatic new thing in his life that none of the old psalms would do. He wrote a new victory hymn celebrating God's recent deliverance in his life. The emphasis rests on the new quality of the song, not just its recent composition. Part of the reason for this new song was the impact of God's intervention on those who observed the psalmist's life: "Many will see and fear and put their trust in the Lord" (v. 3). God's act will compel the attention of the bystanders to the power of God. Does anything in your life do that?

You can respond with a *new obedience.* The psalmist struggled with how to express gratitude toward such a delivering God. He weighed all of the outward religious rituals of his day. Animal sacrifices, meal offerings of fine flour, burnt offerings indicating total dedication, and sin offerings propitiating God all presented themselves as possible ways to indicate gratitude toward God. But there must be more.

God does not want ritual, but reality. He desires harmony *with* Him rather than ceremony performed *for* Him. So the psalmist expresses that he has heard God: "my ears you have pierced" (v. 6). This unusual phrase meant that God had broken through at a new level of speaking to the inward person. The result of that is an immediate sense of obedience to the will of God: "Then I said, 'Here I am—I have come'" (v. 7). These are the characteristic words of a servant who comes immediately to do the will of the master.

When will we learn that God wants obedience and reality above all else? The only real response to God's intervention in your life is to hear and obey. All else is ritual. When you do so, you will have a fresh song for God to sing tomorrow.

Escape Despair Now!
(Psalms 42—43)

The old spiritual says, "Sometimes I'm up, Sometimes I'm down, standin' in the need of prayer." In these psalms the psalmist expresses three times that he is "down." If you have never been down, you do not share the experience of Moses, David, Jeremiah, Jonah, Paul—even Jesus. Psalms 42—43 are one unit of experience. The writer is down because he is far away from the place where he meets God and faces the taunts of unbelievers who chant that God has abandoned him. The whole is filled with the tension of despair fighting with faith.

The psalmist finds a way out of despair. He calls on past memories of God's faithfulness, present gleams of God's presence, and expects the future active intervention of God. You can escape despair now.

Escape Begins When You
Remember Past Encounters with God

You may indeed experience *present depression*. The psalmist is depressed because of both inward and outward circumstances. *Inwardly*, he is thirsty for God. He is away from the place where he meets God and cannot go back. He may have been exiled or simply sick and could not go to the temple. His thirst reminds him of the hind that languishes by a dry river course, expecting but not finding living water. He thirst for nothing less than absolute reality of God as He really is. He is down because he cannot find the place to meet God.

Outwardly, he is depressed because unbelievers taunt him, "Where is your God?" (42:3) His inward emptiness is worsened by the jeers of the unbelieving world outside of him. Although he thirsts for God, his tears are all that he tastes. Are you down because God seems distant and the unbelieving world does not understand or sympathize with you?

A believer can remember *past celebration*. Do you not remember when God was present and life was a joy? The psalmist remembered earlier days when he went three times a year with the dense crowd of pilgrims to the worship festivals in Jerusalem. These were times of ceaseless joy and elation. Suddenly, he remembers that in the past God had been real and present. This abates his despair. Can you not remember times when God was so near that nothing was closer? These can sustain you when He seems far and others do not understand.

Escape Continues When You
Experience the Present Faithfulness of God

Once again, the psalmist turns to *present tribulation*. That tribulation is expressed in terms of *distance* and *difficulty*. You may feel *distant* from all that is nurturing and sustaining. The writer is far away from church, home, family, and friends. He is somewhere in the far north of the Holy Land where the Jordan has its sources near Mount Hermon. He acutely feels this alienation. When we are alone we are often down. Added to that he feels deeply his *difficulties*. He was in an area where cataracts and waterfalls sounded on both sides of a deep valley. These roaring waters only reminded him of the difficulties that seemed to swallow him (v. 7). The roar of waters without him reminded him of the difficulties within him. Isn't despair just like that? Whatever you see when you are down reminds you that you are down.

Yet you can experience *present elation*. In the midst of it all, there are glimpses of God's loyal love throughout the day. After such days the psalmist spends the night thankful for God's loyal love. Your present experience with God is not all despair. If you will reflect, there are tokens of God's faithfulness all around. These present gleams of glory in the midst of gloom should help you out of despair.

Escape Arrives When You
Expect God's Future Intervention

Memory of past encounters and looking at present mercies are not enough to escape despair. Both of these activities only turn you in on yourself. Real escape comes when you turn out in active seeking of God's intervention.

The whole mood changes when the psalmist says, "Vindicate, . . . rescue. . . . send forth your light and your truth" (43:1,3). As he begins speaking to God rather than to himself, the whole outlook changes. He had been talking about God behind God's back. Now he turns in positive petition to God. He calls for God's active intervention. Everything begins to change. He promises to go to God's altar and expects joy and delight when he arrives there (v. 4). What made the difference? He stopped talking to himself and began talking to God. Further, he expected that God was already in the process of lifting him up and out.

If you are down today, tell God. Stop talking to your own soul and look beyond yourself to His active intervention. Recover the active expectation that God indeed will act for you. Then you will no longer have to thirst for God. You will discover the truth of Jesus, "Whoever believes in me, as the Scripture has said, streams of living water will flow from within him" (John 7:38). You can drink from a source that the psalmist could not even imagine. Drink from that living water now and escape despair.

God Our Refuge

(Psalm 46)

Recent world crises would make anyone ask, "Is this a safe place to live anymore?" Yes, but only if God is your Refuge and Strength. The psalmist watched God deliver Jerusalem from a devastating crisis. God's help came at the last possible moment, but exactly the right time.

God gives His people refuge when they stand still and appropriate His inner resources.

I. God Gives Refuge When Life Comes Apart (46:1-3)

Sometimes everything *does* turn upside down (vv. 2-3).

Only God Elohim can undergird your life when that happens (v. 1).

God specializes in making Himself accessible in life's narrow, hard places (v. 1).

Remember, even the storms belong to Him as well as the calms (vv. 1-3).

II. God Gives Resources When Life Comes Apart (46:4-7)

As the noisy world threatens, the believer has a quiet inner resource (v. 4).

Man's power *is* loud; God's omnipotence is silent.

God's help appears at precisely the right time (v. 4).

> Not *before* you know that only He can help

> Not *after* it is too late

III. You Can Experience God's Refuge and Resource By Personal Decision (vv. 10-11)

This decision requires that you stop, cease, get quiet, and reflect (v. 10).

This decision gives you numberless spiritual resources (v. 11).

You cannot deserve this; you can only experience it (the God of Jacob: if He could help Jacob He can help you!).

When You Want to Run Away from It All
(Psalm 55)

Have you ever wanted to run away from it all? Do you want to escape from the pressure and problems of your life? Would you like to hide somewhere so that no one can find you? If so, you are not alone. The psalmist, a great man with a greater devotion to God, felt the same way. This psalm may reflect the experience of David when his son Absalom rebelled against him (2 Sam. 15—18). In this experience of betrayal and pain, the old king longed to escape from the situation. He found that he could escape—he could flee to God. When life closes in around you, you can turn to God for support.

Understand the Reasons Why You Wish to Escape

When we face difficulty, it may come from ourselves or from others. It may be because of disloyalty to God or because of loyalty to His cause. Sometimes, as with David, the reasons are mingled.

Inwardly, we may wish to escape our emotions. David confessed that he was troubled by his thoughts. It reflects a man who was restless with distraction (v. 2). In addition, he is distraught or disquieted. His mind felt the confusion that characterizes a demoralized army. A quaking, aching, disquieting, throbbing fear seized him (vv. 4-5). He literally wanted to run away from the way he felt internally.

Outwardly, we may wish to escape opposition. Most of us know what it is to be opposed in some way. Someone threatens us, dislikes us, or desires to hurt us. David had to deal with three levels of opposition that were very real to him. He knew personal opposition. Both the words and the stares of his personal enemies stung him (v. 3). He heard the voice of his enemies insulting and threatening. Whoever said, "Sticks and stones may break my bones, but words will never hurt me," may have been deaf. He knew impersonal opposition. The psalmist is afraid of the unknown in the chaos of crime that characterized the city around him: "I see violence and strife in the city" (v. 9). We too know what it is to live in a place where impersonal but very real danger can strike at any time. But most devastating of all, he knew the sting of betrayal (vv. 12-14). He might have been able to handle it better if an old enemy had hurt him. But instead, one of his closest friends, an equal, a comrade, turned against him. They had confidential conversation in private and companionship in worship in public.

You may not face all the same reasons the psalmist faced, but you probably have faced some of the reasons he desired to escape. How do you respond?

Understand the Response When You Desire to Escape

When life is too much we do sometimes want to run away from it all. The psalmist longingly looked at a dove flying above him. He wishes that he could wing his way to a cleft in the rock of some inaccessible place, far from the things that threaten him. Or he imagines himself wandering off into the desert wasteland where he could quickly hide from any violent storm.

There have been other spiritual giants who had the urge to escape. For some it has been wishful. Jeremiah cried out, "O that I had in the desert a lodging place for travelers, so that I might leave my people and go away from them" (Jer. 9:2). For others the desire to escape has been actual. Elijah ran all of the way to Mount Horeb on the Sinai peninsula in order to escape the consequences of his loyalty to God (1 Kings 19:3ff.).

Escape is easy, but not usually noble. Security is not always found in solitude. Wickedness can overtake us in the wilderness. Personal demons can spring alongside us to the place of escape. We may find our old nemesis welcoming us in the what we thought was the safe haven of escape. What then is the answer?

Appropriate the Resource When You Desire to Escape

You can escape. Such escape does not come by running away from reality but by running toward reality. You can escape to God. This can be your confession (v. 16). In the midst of all that threatened him and caused him to want to run, he called out to the convenant God, Jehovah. He called out to God three times per day, systematically (v. 17). Our God is a God who acts. God hears, intervenes, and truly rescues. The very nature of God is to intervene and rescue. At the very beginning David pleaded with God not to ignore him. God will not act like an unmerciful person who turns away from misfortune he does not want to relieve.

This confession leads the psalmist to an admonition for us. We can cast our cares upon Jehovah. Whatever your problem, your appointed lot, whether you created it or it was given to you—it can be cast onto the Lord (v. 22). God will sustain, nourish, uphold, and support you. This does not promise that God will carry it away, but that He will sustain you so that you do not fall under the weight of the problem.

Actually, there is no place to escape our problems. But we can escape to God. That is running toward reality, not away from it. Why not run to Him today? Our Lord Jesus put it better than the psalmist ever thought: "Come to me, all you who are weary and burdened, and I will give you rest. Take my yoke upon you and learn of me" (Matt. 11:28).

Obsessed with God: A Psalm for a New Year*
(Psalm 63)

Do you have an obsession? Does something compel you daily in all of life? The psalmist expresses an obsession with meeting and knowing God. Psalm 63 has been called the "Soul of the Psalms." The earliest church sang it every morning. It is our psalm for a new year.

Sometimes circumstances leave us with nothing in life but God alone. David had been betrayed by his own son, exiled from his throne, and humiliated in the desert. Out of that experience, he expressed his desire for God alone. In the new year, every believer should crave a relationship with the living God.

Begin the New Year Seeking God

Do you have a passion for God? David reveals and overwhelming passion for God Himself. We should mold our approach to God after that of David; he sought God not for anything God could do for him, but for the worth of God Himself.

Seek God with *intensity*. "Earnestly I seek you" (v. 1) combines thoughts of earliness and eagerness in the quest for God. David's words "thirst" and "long" suggest a condition just short of fainting for the presence of God. Is there anything approaching the intensity of David in your quest for God?

Seek God with *totality*. David speaks of "soul" and "body" belonging to his craving for God. Taken together, he means his whole being, his total self. There is nothing about us that should know satisfaction short of God. Our emotions, reason, will, and the physical body through which they act, should all crave the living God.

Seek God out of *necessity*, "in a dry and weary land where there is no water" (v. 1). David considered himself like a desert in need of water from God. The greatest necessity of our life is confrontation with God.

Begin the New Year Remembering God

Remember God in *worshipfulness*. "I have seen you in the sanctuary and beheld your power and glory" (v. 2). We need high moments in God's sanctuary which we can recall in life's later low moments. Exiled and alone, David could remember gazing on the things of God in the Jerusalem sanctuary. Such "sanctuary memories" sustained him in the desert.

Remember God in *wakefulness*. "On my bed I remember you; I think of you through the watches of the night" (v. 6). At night, when sleep fails or fear stalks, we should remember God. What do you do with insomnia or sudden awakening in the night? David became so engrossed with the thoughts of God's goodness that he recalled them throughout the night. The night as well as the day ought to belong to Him.

Begin the New Year Praising God

Reasons abound for the praise of God. We can praise God because of His *affection*. It is literally "better than life" (v. 3). We can praise God because of the sense of spiritual *satisfaction* in spiritual life. Spiritually, we have been satisfied with a rich and sumptuous feast, like eating succulent fat meat (v. 5). We can praise God for His *protection*. We enjoy a living protection of One who really responds to our needs, like living under the shadow of mighty wings (v. 7). We have a strong protection of the Almighty hand holding us even as we cling to Him (v. 8).

Responses announce the praise of God. Repeatedly, David emphasizes the *vocal* dimension of praise to God. Singing, shouting, and lauding the goodness of God with our lips is appropriate response.

There is also a *physical* dimension in our praise to God. "In your name I will lift up my hands" (v. 4). This is the outward symbol of an uplifted heart. The inwardness of spiritual feeling must be completed by outward expression in physical action. "I will therefore that men pray every where, lifting up holy hands" (1 Tim. 2:8, KJV).

There is every reason to begin the new year obsessed with God Himself. Surely we desire God to bless our church, families, and work. But first, we must seek Him for what He is in Himself. *Two slightly different sermons on Psalm 63.

God Is All You Have

(Psalm 63)

Sometimes God is all in the world you have. When this happens, you need to be obsessed with God alone. The psalmist expresses an obsession with meeting and knowing God. Psalm 63 has been called the "Soul of the Psalms." The earliest church sang it every morning. It would be good for us to do the same.

Sometimes circumstances leave us with nothing in life but God alone. David had been betrayed by his own son, exiled from his throne, and humiliated in the desert. Out of that experience he expressed his desire for God alone. Every believer should crave such a relationship with the living God.

When God Is All You Have, Seek God

Do you have a passion for God? David reveals an overwhelming passion for God Himself. We should mold our approach to God after that of David; he sought God not for anything God could do for him, but for the worth of God Himself.

Seek God with *intensity*. "Earnestly I seek you" (v. 1) combines thoughts of earliness and eagerness in the quest for God. David's words "thirst" and "long" suggest a condition just short of fainting for the presence of God. Is there anything approaching the intensity of David in your quest for God?

Seek God with *totality*. David speaks of "soul" and "body" belonging to his craving for God. Taken together, he means his whole being, his total self. There is nothing about us that should know satisfaction short of God. Our emotions, reason, will, and the physical body through which they act should all crave the living God.

Seek God out of *necessity*, "in a dry and weary land where there is no water." David considered himself like a desert in the need of water from God. The greatest necessity of our life is confrontation with God.

When God Is All You Have, Remember God

Remember God in *worshipfulness*. "I have seen you in the sanctuary and beheld your power and your glory" (v. 2). We need high moments in God's sanctuary which we can recall in life's later low moments. Exiled and alone, David could remember gazing on the things of God in the Jerusalem sanctuary. Such "sanctuary memories" sustained him in the desert.

Remember God in *wakefulness*. "On my bed I remember you; I think of you through the watches of the night" (v. 6). At night when sleep fails or fear stalks, we should remember God. What do you do with insomnia or sudden awakening in the night? David became so engrossed with the thoughts of God's goodness that he recalled them throughout the night. The night as well as the day ought to belong to Him.

When God Is All You Have, Praise God

Reasons abound for the praise of God. We can praise God because of his affection. It is literally "better than life" (v. 3). We can praise God because of the sense of spiritual satisfaction in spiritual life. Spiritually, we have been satisfied with a rich and sumptuous feast, like eating succulent fat meat (v. 5). We can praise God for His protection. We enjoy a living protection of One who really responds to our needs, like living under the shadow of mighty wings (v. 7). We have a strong protection of the Almighty hand holding us even as we cling to Him (v. 8).

Responses announce the praise of God. Repeatedly David emphasizes the vocal dimension of praise to God. Singing, shouting, and lauding the goodness of God with our lips is appropriate response.

There is also a physical dimension in our praise to God. "In your name I will lift up my hands" (v. 4). This is the outward symbol of an uplifted heart. The inwardness of spiritual feeling must be completed by outward expression physical action. "I will therefore that men pray every where lifting up holy hands" (1 Tim. 2:8, KJV).

There is every reason to be obsessed with God Himself when God is all you have. First we must seek Him for what He is in Himself. God and God alone deserves the universe's throne. He also deserves the throne of your life.

Finding the Faith that Defeats Doubt
(Psalm 73)

Your neighbor who never enters a church or gives a dime to God's work receives a promotion and big raise. You go to church three times a week and support God's work sacrificially and are passed over for promotion. Your coworker laughs at God and ridicules the faith yet is as healthy as a horse. You live for God and stay sick. These undeniable realities about life can become the seedbed of real doubt about God's existence or goodness.

An unknown psalmist had struggled with that doubt. He begins his song with a conclusion: "[Nevertheless] God is good." The conclusion at the beginning of Psalm 73 implies a previous struggle of soul. The psalmist had asked himself the question: "Is it worth holding onto the belief that God is really good?" He found the answer. Or more correctly, the answer found him. Human observation creates doubt, but divine revelation renews faith.

Doubt Springs from the Observation of Life

Your *reaction* to life may cut the ground out from under your faith. The psalmist confessed that faith had slipped and he had lost his footing in life (v. 1). It frightened him to feel the very foundation of life slipping away from beneath his feet. Why would God's person feel such instability? The undeniable facts of human life threatened his faith. The warm flush of envy filled his face when he considered the prosperity of those who lived without God. Any believer who honestly looks at life has faced this contradiction. The godless do very well in the world.

This comes from the *observation* of life. The unbelievers do prosper more than God's people. *Outwardly*, they seem to be exempt from the struggles of ordinary people. *Physically*, they look better than God's people. Their bodies are sleek and strong and stylish. They seem to be exempt from the problems that plague most people. Beyond that, they are arrogant about their obvious superiority. They wear pride like a necklace (v. 6). *Inwardly*, their "fat hearts" look through evil eyes and their mind is a fountain that never ceases to flow with selfish schemes. *Verbally*, they speak as if they were gods in their own world. They act as if the whole earth belonged to them and disparage everything and everybody (v. 9).

What galls is the popularity of the godless. *Influentially,* they lead the masses to drink up their words and ways like a thirsty person drinks water (v. 11). The obvious prosperity of the godless leads the masses to question whether God has any knowledge of the individual person's life at all. Indeed, the fortune of the wicked causes many to question whether there is a God who knows everything.

What the psalmist saw is true to life as we know it. This leads to a desperate *conclusion.* It does not pay to serve God. What good does it do to keep ourselves outwardly and inwardly pure? We who believe receive blow after blow from life while unbelievers waltz their way from success to success. This is the point where faith can collapse unless there is an answer.

Faith Comes from the Revelation of God

Restoration of faith *begins* with our influence on God's people. When faith is about to slip, anything God uses to restore it is good. The psalmist caught himself in the fall when he thought of the influence of his cynicism would have on God's people. He wanted to parade his perplexities and declare his doubts, but this would treacherously undercut God's people. He stopped in the downward slide when he thought of the church. He did not want to hurt God's church.

Restoration of faith *happens* when we meet God. The psalmist tried to penetrate the mystery and it was too much for him (v. 16). The great turning point from doubt to faith came when he went to the place where he met God: "I entered the sanctuary of God; then I understood their final destiny" (v. 17). In the quiet place of worship a revelation from God crashed into his life. His whole value system was reversed. He looked at the life of the godless from the standpoint of the end. Their life was really like the phantom of a dream that cannot be remembered the next morning (v. 20). That is, he completely changed his mind about what was actually real. A moment before, the wealth, glitter, and proud pomp of the godless appeared eternal. Now it all disappears in a new vision of God.

Restoration of faith *leads* to a confession. *Negatively,* we may think more like a beast than a person. The psalmist confessed that he had reacted with no more faith than a hippopotamus! In the presence of God he had experienced a reversal of values so radically that it could be compared to a beast suddenly thinking like a human being. But he does not grovel in the negative.

Positively, we must affirm some things about God and ourselves. We must affirm that God is present, even in our doubts. He protects us and provides direction for us when we are about to slip. Suddenly, the thought of God fills every horizon. The Real One replaces the apparently real. We may make a great affirmation about ourselves: God is all we want in heaven or on earth. The psalmist's raging, doubting ego disappears. His superficial evaluation of the godless vanishes. Regardless of how little he has or is, God fills every horizon.

He still looks at reality. His flesh and heart—his whole life—may dissolve and disappear. Suffering is still real, but God is more real. Though he himself should disappear, he is confident of life in God. Now God and His people appear to be permanent and prosperous. The godless vanish. He found a new way of looking at life when he went to the house of God. Have you?

Longing for the Lord
(Psalm 84)

Do you ever remember feeling homesick? To be away from home in a strange place can create yearnings for the familiar and the friendly. The psalmist had been away from the place where he usually met with God. He expresses the longing in his heart to come back to that place where he and God could meet. He acknowledges that such a return is a process, a pilgrimage. There are obstacles to overcome in the return to the place where we can meet with God. But if you desire to do so you can return to Him. You can confess that time with Him is better than any other time. When you desire to return to the place where you meet God, faith overcomes every obstacle until you arrive.

Longing Begins with a Desire for the Place to Meet God

Do you have an ardent desire to find the place where you meet God? Longing for God begins with a yearning to recover the place where you last experienced Him. For some reason the psalmist has been away from the place where He usually met God, the temple. Although we no longer meet God at a temple, we can spiritually identify with his desire to return to the place of conversation with the living God. The words are almost those of a love poem: "How lovely is your dwelling place" (v. 1).

Longing for God creates an *intensity* of spirit. The very words express the passion of this person seeking God. He yearns in the sense that he literally grows pale with expectancy. He faints and is consumed with a desire to find God. Indeed, his inward longing becomes a loud cry for God. The totality of his person is involved: soul, heart, and flesh. You have right now just as much of God as you intensely want. "Draw near to God and He will draw near to you" (Jas. 4:8, NASB).

Longing for God reflects an *integrity* of intention. The psalmist wants nothing less than the living God. Although he wants to go to the temple, it is only a means to the end of meeting God. He is not longing for the house of God as much as for the God whose house it is. We do not come or give to the church as the end in itself. All of its organization is worse than nothing if it does not lead us to the living God. Travis is a travesty if the means becomes the end. We should be here not to run a vast institution but to meet the living God.

Longing for God reveals an *intimacy* of desire. Lovers envy anything that is near the one loved. The psalmist envies the sparrows that build their nests in the temple complex. Such inconsequential creatures find a place near God. He longs to be as close to God as such mere birds nesting in the temple. We should desire a closeness and intimacy with God that matches this beautiful desire.

Longing Continues with the Discovery of
the Process to Meet God

To walk with God is a journey, a pilgrimage. Those who really set their hearts on God must be ready for the journey. The psalm has a beatitude for those who have set their hearts on such a pilgrimage. On the journey to God you overcome obstacles in the way.

Longing for God *transforms barren places*. Every moment on the way is not a moment of light and joy. There are dry, arid places. In the literal journey to the temple the pilgrims passed through the "Valley of Baca." This refers to a waterless, barren valley on the road to Jerusalem. Yet in this terrible wilderness they dug down to find water in the desert. If you walk with God you will have the faith that dares to dig blessings out of hardships. But along with this personal initiative you will find the sudden blessings which God alone can provide: "the autumn rains also cover it with pools" (v. 6). After dry times in life suddenly the showers of blessing fall with living water. In your journey with God there will be obstacles interrupted by blessings.

Longing for God *experiences renewed resources:* "they go down from strength to strength" (v. 7). Instead of fainting in the journey, you can gain fresh strength the closer you are to the presence of God. In life's process we slow down mentally and physically. But in the spiritual dimension the closer to the goal the stronger you can be. We are changed from one degree of glory to the next (2 Cor. 3:18).

Longing Results in the Direct Presence of God Himself

Your yearning for the divine will not be disappointed. No basic hunger in human life is unmet by God. One who has the ambition to know God (vv. 1-4) and takes the journey to approach God (vv. 5-8) will experience arrival with God (vv. 9-12).

The direct presence of God may be expressed by a *contrast*. Time in God's presence is better than any other time: "Better is one day in your courts than a thousand elsewhere." Can you honestly confess that time with God is qualitatively better than any other time? The place of God's presence is better than any other place: "I would rather be a doorkeeper in the house of my God than dwell in the tents of the wicked" (v. 10). In his own world the psalmist would rather humbly lie down at the threshold of the temple than live a sumptuous life with the scoffing wicked. The lowest place with God is better than the highest place with wicked humans. How would you rather spend your time and at what place?

The direct presence of God may be expressed by a *confession*. You can confess that God is your Provider and Protector. God is indeed Provider. Here alone in the Old Testament is God called "a sun" (v. 11). The sun communicates itself in life, heat, and energy. It is new every morning and yet the same. God provides with the same qualities as the sun. God also protects. He is our shield. He stands for all that protects and renders foes inaccessible.

Your longing for God can lead to the confession that God is everything you need. Begin the journey, overcome the obstacles, and encounter the Presence!

God's Protection in a Dangerous World
(Psalm 91)

Any assessment of our world marks it as an increasingly dangerous place to live. What kind of certainty can characterize the life of believers? The psalmist confessed his faith that God does protect. Psalm 91 is an expansion of Paul's great cry, "If God is for us, who can be against us?" (Rom. 8:31).

God promises His sheltering protection from all kinds and times of danger until He fulfills His will in your life.

God Promises Sheltering, Covering Protection
Based on His Very Nature

God provides protection *comprehensively* by many means. He protects by providing secret shelter (vv. 1-2), by covering with His wings (v. 4), and by angelic intervention (v. 11). God provides protection certainly because of His own nature. He is the God "Most High" so that danger cannot touch Him (v. 1), and He is "God Jehovah" so that danger cannot outlast Him (v. 2). Make personal your confession of faith in His protection as did the psalmist: "He is *my* God" (v. 2).

God Protects from All Kinds and
All Times of Danger

God protects from all *kinds* of danger (vv. 3,5,6,13): Secret, hidden, insidious dangers; open, manifest, obvious dangers; natural, threatening, powerful dangers; supernatural, overwhelming dangers.

God protects from all *times* of danger (vv. 5-6): Danger hidden under the darkness of night; danger obvious in the midst of days.

God protects from all *circumstances* of danger (vv. 7-8): When danger and judgment come to others, God preserves His faithful people.

You are invincible until your life's duty is done.

God Confirms His Protection by
the Very Integrity of His Name

Our protection does not depend upon our own steadfastness, but God's intention to preserve the power and majesty of His name.

A Psalm for Thanksgiving
(Psalm 100)

This is the only psalm with the original title indicating a psalm of thanksgiving. Its five verses ring out with the universality and gladness of gratitude towards God. It is one of a series of psalms beginning with Psalm 93 which emphasize "The Lord Reigns." This song was sung at the gates of the temple itself by those who longed to express to God their gratitude. There are several imperatives in the psalm—things you can do to express thanks to God. There are also seven descriptions of the joyful praise we can give Him. The psalm resounds with two ringing calls to praise, each followed by the reason we should give God the praise. Let us offer such glad thanks to God in this season of gratitude.

Thank God for His Relationship to His People

There is a **call to praise:** "Shout for joy to the Lord" (v. 1). This has the blast of a trumpet about it. It is the equivalent of a fanfare accompanied with shouts of homage to a king (95:1; 98:6). The **emotion** of this praise is to be joy. Joy is the aim, the motive, and the spirit of the praise given to God. The *direction* of this praise is to God Himself. We are not making a noise to impress the church or one another. The actual direction of our gratitude should focus on God Himself. There is a longing for an *inclusion* in this thanksgiving of "all the earth." There is to be no one who sits mute and silent. It is God's intention that every voice in each nation one day thunder back to Him His praise.

This call to praise refuses to divide worship from service. This first service we owe to God is worship. Both prayer and activity go stale in isolation. We serve Him when we come before Him with thanks. There are times for minor keys and low notes, but thanksgiving is not one of them. Every note in this psalm is one of unabated joy.

There is the **content of praise**. The praise of thanksgiving is the very nature and person of God Himself: "Know that the Lord is God." Thanksgiving is the actual acknowledgment that God alone is God. Human self-assurance and independence vanish in the face of this confession. Everything human takes its proper place in the face of this one confession. Because of this, we thank God for His *creation*—we are His because He made us. We thank God for His *redemption*—we are His people. We thank God for His *protection*—the sheep of His pasture. The focus of this Thanksgiving season should not be first the obvious material benefits, but the person and nature of God Himself.

Thank God for His Revelation of His Character

There is again a **call to praise**. "Enter his gates with thanksgiving" (v. 4). The psalmist pictures a throng of people pressing into the temple through its massive gates. As they enter, he calls them to shout words of thanksgiving. The accompaniment of every right approach to God should be the attitude of gratitude. It is to be the background music of every other request and petition in His presence. The Christian not only comes to the outer courts of a visible temple, but we can stand in the holy of holies itself because of the new and living way of Christ. Our thanksgiving penetrates where the psalmist could never imagine.

There is again the **content of praise**. We praise God because of His nature. His very essence is only and always that which is good. He is what James 1:17 claimed Him to be, a Father of lights from whom only good and perfect things come to us. But the faithfulness of His love is not based on some emotional whim. To know God is to know One who is in covenant with us. He does not love us with some arbitrary mood of a heavenly despot. His love is based on His own nature which never changes. This is the basis of gratitude indeed. I may change but He never does.

With this background, why not make this Thanksgiving a time for genuine expression of joyful gratitude to God? Thank Him for the persons, provisions, institutions, and groups that bless you. Do it this week with urgency and daily. Do it at God's house and your house. Do it out loud and verbally. Do it musically. Write down a letter to the Lord expressing your gratitude and read it to high heaven above. Make the words of this psalm your words.

Praise God
(Psalm 103)

Psalms sing to the soul. The very soul of music is the music in the soul. Psalm 103 rings out the praises of God without interruption. Although the words belong to the Old Testament, the music belongs to the New Testament. There is not one jarring note in this song of praise. Whereas Psalm 102 is filled with complaint and petition, Psalm 103 rings out only praise and affirmation. The circles of praise ever enlarge. The individual begins with personal praise (vv. 1-5). He then enlarges on the grounds that Israel has for national praise (vv. 6-14). There is finally a call for universal praise from every created thing (vv. 20-22). The psalmist eagerly invites you to sing a song of a forgiven soul.

Praise God with the Priority of Praise

The priority for praise is *personal*. Twice the psalmist exhorts himself for praise: "Praise the Lord, O my soul" (vv. 1,22). Praise is not our natural response. It must be excited, aroused, and stimulated within. Regardless of how we feel or what others do, it is our duty and responsibility to praise God. We know that the psalmist was a passionate praiser of God. If someone such as he had to goad himself to praise, how much more do we.

The priority for praise is *total*. He speaks to his own soul. This is the *ego* of the psalmist speaking to his total being. It is a dialogue within himself. All of us carry on inward conversations. What should be the subject? The praise of God. We should praise God with all that is within us. Every faculty, capacity, and inclination must be given over to the affirmation of God.

The priority for praise is *unforgetful*. We are not to forget any of God's acts performed for our benefit, His deeds of loving-kindness. There is a great inclusiveness here: *all* of me is to praise *all* that He has done. That is enough challenge for a lifetime of praise. We tend to forget God's goodness and remember our own griefs and complaints. What is the "all" that we are to remember? He gives us a series of images.

We thank God for the *law court* of heaven: He "forgives all your sins" (v. 3). This is the fountain from which all else flows and the greatest cause for praise. Praise God for the *hospital of heaven:* He "heals all [your] diseases" (v. 3). This is sometimes immediate (2 Sam. 12:13) and always ultimate (Rom. 8:23). We praise God in the *slave market:* He "redeems [your life] from the pit" (v. 4). We have been bought back from the grave itself. All of the above would be enough, but God takes us to the *throne room* where He weaves us crowns of loyal love, the *banquet room* where He fills us with satisfaction, and finally to the *mountaintop* where our vitality is renewed like that of the eagle. These are all of His benefits, none of which we should forget and for all of which we should offer Him praise.

Praise God for the Reality of Forgiveness

Forgiveness is the *divine revelation* of God from the beginning. The psalmist looks back to what God revealed of Himself to Moses in the past. Moses asked to know the ways of God (Ex. 33:13). In response God passed before Moses proclaiming His basic attributes (34:6). These attributes are named in our psalm: compassionate, gracious, slow to anger, abounding in love (v. 8).

Forgiveness is the *actual operation* of God in our experience. God does indeed drop His case against us. "He will not always accuse" (v. 9). On Calvary God ceased to press His suit against you. He is not like a person who harbors a grudge looking for the opportunity of revenge. He does not try to balance the books against you (v. 10). Who could deny the truth that God has not dealt with us as He might?

Forgiveness is the *immeasurable separation* of God from our sins. God's love is like Himself—infinite. The psalmist stretches language to its capacity to measure the divine geometry of forgiveness. The height is as high as the heavens, the breadth as far as east is from the west. Others saw that God casts sin into the depths (Mic. 7:9) and goes to the length of casting it to the back of His presence (Isa. 38:17).

Forgiveness is the *fatherly invitation* of God to His family. No infinite distances express the grace of God as does the intimacy of family. The Lord has compassion on His children better than the best of human fathers. Whether you look back to history, inward to personal experience, upward to the heavens, or homeward to the Father, every horizon is filled with praise for the God who forgives.

Praise God for the Eternity of His Love

One ground for the fatherly love of God is His knowledge of our own mortality and frailty. God knows our mortality. His knowledge is personal. He Himself knows as no other how we are formed. He made us. His knowledge is historical. He was present and personally responsible when He fashioned us from the dust (Gen. 2:7). The Everlasting

One understands in a way we cannot what it means to face death and the grave. God does have compassion on such frail, mortal people as we are.

He knows the brevity of our vitality: "As for man, his days are like grass." He knows the vanity of our beauty: "he flourishes like a flower of the field" (v. 15). He knows the anonymity of our memory: "its place remembers it no more" (v. 16). Our weakness, frailty, and brevity of life call out divine mercy.

In contrast to all of this is the eternity of God's love: "from everlasting to everlasting the Lord's love is with those who fear him" (v. 17). Join with all creation forever to praise the eternal One!

God Does Rescue
(Psalm 107:1-32)

God does rescue from helplessness. Our psalm more than states this. Psalm 107 gives four vivid pictures of the conditions from which God can rescue. These pictures are those of travelers who are lost, prisoners who are trapped, invalids who are weak, and sailors about to sink in a storm. Taken together these pictures present four situations of human helplessness. The promise of God is clear. To those who call out of helplessness He will give help.

You should not think that your situation is beyond God's help. God can respond with the resources necessary to reverse your helpless situation.

God Does Rescue from Helplessness

God rescues from *aimlessness*. "Some wandered in desert wastelands" (v. 4). A lost caravan of desperate people in the trackless wasteland paints a picture of life with no certain aim. Such lost travelers have no stability. They face the lack of resources to sustain life that comes from such a condition: hunger, thirst, and loss of life. Some people simply grope their way through a pointless existence with no direction. Instability, insecurity, and lack of sustaining relationships mark them. God can replace this with direction.

God rescues from *confinement*. Those lost in a desert are in too wide a world. Others are trapped in too narrow a world. "Some sat in darkness and the deepest gloom, prisoners suffering in iron chains" (v. 10). Ancient prisons were unlighted vaults. Those who rebel against God find themselves in darkness, confinement, and exhausting circumstances. Aimlessness may not be on purpose, but the confinement that comes from rebellion is deliberate. God can release from confinement.

God rescues from *foolishness*. "Some became fools through their rebellious ways" (v. 17). This pictures spiritual invalids who reached their condition because of rebellion. They suffer the physical impact of spiritual disobedience. Loss of appetite causes them to languish near the doors of death. This was the earlier experience of the psalmist (Ps. 32:3-4). God can heal this with His Word.

God rescues from *powerlessness*. "Others went out on the sea in ships" (v. 23). The Hebrews were not a seagoing people. The tiny ships they had hugged the coast itself. A raging sea painted the picture of absolute powerlessness. "They reeled and staggered like drunken men; they were at their wits' end" (v. 27). We can be rocked by situations we never created but which threaten to sink our very lives.

Together these four pictures show the range of human helplessness. Sometimes we are victims of our own folly. At other times we are carried away by vast forces we did not cause.

God Rescues at Our Insistent Call

In each of the four situations the helpless ones found the same remedy. "Then they cried out to the Lord in their trouble, and he delivered them from their distress" (v. 6, see also vv. 13,19,28). With an intensity they made an outcry. This was not directed in terror toward the situation but in faith toward the living God. They cried out because they were in trouble, literally in the "straits." They were in narrow, restricting, confining circumstances that hedged them in on every side. God's reaction was to rescue them from their misfortunes.

This means that God does not say, "Stew in your own juice." This means that God will never respond, "You made your own bed—lie in it." When we lack wisdom to face the testing times of life, God gives it to us generously and He does not upbraid us for our own helplessness (Jas. 1:6).

God Reverses Our Helpless Situation

God reverses aimlessness with new *direction*. For those who are lost in the desert God "led them by a straight way to a city where they could settle" (v. 7). Anything else would be little more than first aid. God can give stability and permanence to lives that had no direction or aim.

God reverses confinement with *freedom*. God breaks the chains that bind, cuts through bars of iron and floods life with the light of freedom. The first sermon of our Lord indicated His entire ministry would be one of release from confinement (Luke 4:18ff.).

God reverses foolishness with the *healing* of His word (v. 20). For those who suffer the physical and emotional weakness that comes with foolish sin, God makes whole with His word. Instead of languishing in weakness, they will "tell of his works with songs of joy" (v. 22).

God reverses powerlessness with the assertion of His *power*. "He stilled the storm to a whisper; the waves of the sea were hushed" (v. 29). We know this through our Lord Jesus Christ who said over the Sea of Galilee, "Peace be still," and there was immediate calm. With a single word all was well.

Our God does rescue. Your situation is by no means beyond the reach of His mighty power. What He's done for others, He will do for you.

The Prediction of the King
(Psalm 110)

The coming of God's Messiah-King was predicted in the psalms. Many of the psalms foreshadow the coming of that King. Two of the psalms directly predict the coming of that King, Psalms 2 and 110. Psalm 110 is a direct prediction of the coming Christ. Nothing about David or any of the kings that followed him in Israel could have fulfilled the prediction of Psalm 110. It is purely prophecy concerning the coming Christ. We do not have to doubt the direct application of this psalm to Jesus Christ. Jesus Himself interpreted the psalm and applied it to Himself (Mark 12:35-37). This psalm is the most quoted in the New Testament. At least twenty-five times these words are referred to the Lord Jesus. God did predict the coming of His King.

God Promises to Send a King

David overheard a conversation in heaven. That is the substance of Psalm 110:1. The Lord Jehovah promised the Lord Jesus Christ that He would reign. As a third party David, the greatest king of Israel, heard this promise. He recorded what he heard as a matter of prophecy.

This promise concerns the person of the King. He is greater than the greatest of the kings of Israel. Peter clearly said this in Acts 2:34. He will be the epitome of the royal, the regal, and the ideal king. He is greater than any heavenly being. No celestial creature excels His greatness (Heb. 1:13).

This promise concerns the power of the King. God has exalted him as ruler and sovereign. As awfully as man rejected Him, God has exalted Him (Acts 5:30). He reigns now as Savior and Intercessor (Rom. 8:34).

This promise concerns the position of the King. He is now seated at the right hand of God. This is the place of honor and the place which indicates the completion of his task. Other priests stand daily. He is seated because he has offered the once-and-for-all sacrifice (Heb. 10:11ff.).

This promise concerns the realm of this King. His rule is absolutely at one with the rule of God. The scepter of God's strength, power, and might also belongs to Him. He will rule in the very midst of those who are His foes. He will exercise sovereignty in the midst of those who are His enemies. He will literally march forth through the ranks of His enemies.

This promise addresses the followers of the King. They will be joyful volunteers. He will not draft or conscript His followers. Fresh youth will constantly join the ranks of those who follow after His leadership (v. 3).

God Promises to Send a Bridge Builder

The predicted King will join together the role of king and priest. God has sworn and will not change His mind that He will send one who combines the powers of a great ruler with a great bridge builder to God. The Latin word for "priest" is *pontifex*. The word itself means a bridge builder. A priest is one who builds bridges between God and man.

The origin of this King-Priest is mysterious. He is compared to that Old Testament king-priest Melchizedek (Gen. 14:18-20; Heb. 5:5-10; 6:19 to 7:28). He is an eternal priest without predecessor and follower. He is the final bridge builder between God and man.

This King-Priest will conquer all of His enemies and build a worldwide kingdom (vv. 5-6). With His volunteer followers, He will wage a war of righteousness until the whole earth belongs to His Kingdom. He will pause to refresh Himself along with His followers, but then He will continue unabated until all belong to His kingdom (v. 7).

If the greatest king who ever lived called Him Lord, would you not call Him Lord? Why not volunteer for His army today and be a victor then?

Living Before the One Who Knows

(Psalm 139)

God knows you totally and is always there. The psalmist was both comforted and disturbed by that most basic truth. That God knows me through and through is fearful when I live with guilt and sin. That God knows me totally is comforting when I live in His grace through Christ. Either way, He is the "Hound of Heaven," who is always there and always knows.

God Knows You with a Total Knowledge

The emphasis and stress rests on God exclusively, not man. The great "I AM" is the one who knows you.

God knows you with *intensity*. His knowledge is not passive. It is searching, penetrating, and disturbing. He searches you with a minute examination. He discerns you like a man sifting grain (v. 3). He hems you in like a besieging army (v. 5). His knowledge of you is active.

God knows you *comprehensively*. He knows both the active and also the passive side of your life. Your daily habits are open to Him. In activity we forget Him, but He always knows us.

God knows you *mentally*. He knows a thought from a distance (v. 2). The great space between heaven and earth does not deter His knowledge. Before you can firm up what you are saying, God knows every word (v. 4).

Reflect carefully on your typical day in light of God's knowledge of your words and deeds.

You Cannot Escape the God Who Knows You

There is no *place* of escape. There is no height so high or depth so low that He is not already there. God in Christ has invaded even the unseen world of the dead (1 Pet. 3). There is no direction, east or west, up or down, to escape Him.

There is no *speed* of escape. If you could travel at the speed of light (v. 9), you would only meet the God who created light.

There is no *circumstance* of escape. Men hide from one another in darkness (vv. 11-12). To God the very darkness is like light.

Do you seek escape from God by workaholism, substance abuse, or hedonism?

You Should Respond with All Awe and Submission

The appropriate response to God is one of *awe*. We should be baffled by His knowledge that is inaccessible (v. 6). The appropriate response to God is one of *submission* (vv. 22-24). The psalmist invites God to know him, to reveal His deepest secrets to him, and to lead him to everlasting life.

The God who knows you invites you to "be honest to God."

Cornered and Alone
(Psalm 142)

Ultimately, we will all face a situation where we are cornered and alone. We will be hemmed in, and it will appear that nobody cares. On a small scale we face this kind of situation many times. On a large scale we will face this situation in a few great crises of life. King Saul unjustifiably chased David and threatened his existence. Eight psalms are attributed to David during this distress. This psalm claims to be written from the cave where David was hiding (1 Sam. 22—24). He was literally and figuratively cornered and alone. We can learn some valuable lessons from this sincere psalm.

When you are cornered and alone, audibly turn to God as your only ultimate resource.

Cornered and Alone, There Is a Petition in Your Prayer

Such praying ought to be a *vocalization*. There is a time when for relief you should "cry aloud" to God. With this voice, and not merely in silent prayer, the psalmist called to God for relief. Audible prayer in itself soothes and strengthens. Most prayer in the Bible was audible prayer. The psalmist uttered his "complaint," that which distracted him and troubled him and made him restless. He poured it out at God's feet like liquid. Prayer would be more relief for many of us if it was audible, actually uttered.

Such prayer has a definite *direction*. The weight rests on the direction of the prayer: "to the Lord, . . . to the Lord. . . . before him; before him" (vv. 1-2). This repetition emphasizes the target of the prayer. This man is utterly alone and cries only to God. Most of us spend our crises muttering to ourselves or complaining to others. Relief comes when the actual direction of our prayer is God Himself.

Urgency of such praying grows out of *exhaustion*. The psalmist was ready to give up; he was out of inward resources to face the pressure. He felt like Jonah, swallowed by the situation (Jonah 2:7). This dwindling energy caused him to turn to the only Source. There comes that time when only waiting on Jehovah renews our strength (Isa. 40:31).

The relief of an *affirmation* grows out of such prayer: "It is you who know my way" (v. 3a). This is the first light to shine into the cave! God and God alone is intimately acquainted with the past and future path of the psalmist. There are perils in the path, but God knows every step. The Lord Jesus went through the same exhaustion of spirit followed by affirmation. On the cross He first cried "Why have you forsaken me?" (Matt. 27:47; Mark 15:34), only to follow with the triumphant "It is finished" (John 19:30).

Cornered and Alone, There Is Pressure on Your Path

We will someday walk through deliberate *danger,* "men have hidden a snare" (v. 3b). The psalmist had no choice; he must walk that way. He had no choice but to walk the path where there is danger; circumstances had hemmed him in. Sometimes we have to walk a dangerous path not of our choice. Every step seems like a trap. Jesus encountered this throughout His ministry.

Such danger may also be a time of *desolation*. There is no one at his right side. The right was the place open to attack and the place usually taken by a helper and advocate. Even God cannot find anyone to stand with this abandoned person. Someday in most lives there comes a moment of total isolation; no one stands alongside. We spend our lives relying on family, friendship, colleagues, networks, and our own clever resourcefulness. One day nothing is there. This is a providence of God. It forces us to turn to Him alone.

The presence of such danger and desertion can leave us desolate in our spirit. The psalmist decides that no one cares about him, looks after his interest, or befriends him. All around him is only a void. His lonely soul faces nothing but an empty universe where he seems at the whim of the fates.

In the face of all of this, the psalmist makes a *decision* of faith. He deliberately decides that God is his only refuge and portion. The cry "You are, . . . my portion" (v. 5) is the breakthrough of faith. What if he stands alone? What if he perishes in the cave? He can call Jehovah His God. In the face of all evidence to the contrary, he shouts out in faith. Faith is always in the presence of evidence to the contrary. Otherwise it is not really faith. Christian lives and great churches are built in the face of evidence to the contrary.

Cornered and Alone, There Is Promise in Your Praise

At the end, faith breaks through. Faith climbs out of the cave. Faith reaches a new summit. The psalmist stands on a mountain and sees something entirely different from his circumstances. Suddenly, crowded around him are the people of God in tender sympathy. Instead of being alone, he sees the time when he will stand with God's people worshiping and praising. All of this is because of God's goodness.

Faith literally enabled him to see the invisible and the future (Heb. 11:1-2). His circumstances will be entirely different because of God's faithfulness. He is no unrealistic optimist. There are foes too strong for him and there are snares set to trap him. In faith, he sees that God will overcome.

Jesus said it best: "In the world you will have tribulation; but be of good cheer, I have overcome the world" (John 16:33, NKJV).

God's Ideal Mother
(Proverbs 31)

What woman would not like her husband to say, "My wife is a rare find"? This confession is not based on external, superficial characteristics but on the intuitive perception that this woman is a woman of character. Do you want to be a rare find? Look at the character described here.

Her Character Supports Her Relationship to Her Family

Her husband can trust her. He has confidence in her abilities and judgment and has no reason to change his mind. There is a Gibraltar-like steadfastness in her life that leaves him with no distrust. He need not worry that every evening he will come home to a threatening, unsettling situation. Out of this profound trust, her husband quarries the inner strength to be a man of accomplishment. "Her husband is known in the gates" (v. 23, KJV). The proverb suggests that a man's wife is the chief source of his own significance and self-worth.

Her family senses her domestic concern. She has her finger on the pulse beat of her household (v. 27). She does not mind finding or taking the extra time needed to demonstrate interest in the domestic (v. 15). She uses resources to bring beauty and variety to her home. She uses imagination and is prepared to experiment (v. 14). Her household is not the perimeter of her life. She has other horizons in life, but not to the exclusion of the domestic.

She will have the praise of those who know her best (v. 28). It is a small thing if those who know us least are those who praise us most. This woman has the praise of her husband and children, the most important of all.

Her Life Reflects Interest Beyond Her Family

By no means is the domestic the end of her interest. She enjoys the exhilaration of creativity (v. 13). The biblical woman is not riveted to a mop handle or a diaper pail. This woman knows unfettered artistic freedom. She works with her hands.

She is a business woman (v. 16-17). Good judgment and acumen, financial independence, and the trust of her husband characterize this woman. The sense of weariness that comes from indolence is foreign to her. She is an enterprising woman with that which is hers.

She is socially responsible (v. 20). Her interest extends beyond the circle of her own family. She does not have a domestic tunnel vision which sees nothing beyond the household routine. Because of this she is sought as a sympathetic and gracious counselor (v. 26). Wisdom becomes an artesian well springing up within her. Any woman who embodies the traits of this proverb will become sought after by many friends who want the secret of her life.

Her Life Reflects Awareness of Her Own Worth

This woman is not unaware of the high esteem she has in the eyes of her husband and children. She knows that "her children arise and call her blessed; her husband also, and he praises her" (v. 28). She reflects this sense of self-worth in the clothing that she wears (v. 22). The Bible takes it for granted that a woman's self-worth is expressed in the way she clothes and carries herself. This true worth is established in her inner relationship with God (v. 30). She is an independent individual in her own right, not merely an appendage to her husband (v. 31). She does not have to fawn, flirt, or posture herself for praise. "Her own works praise her in the gates" (KJV). She laughs at the future (v. 25). Time is not the great enemy of this woman.

How should you react to this picture? No woman may embody all of this ideal portrait. But every Christian woman should say, "I will do what I can." This will bring the praise of God and of man.

The Expectant Lord
(Isaiah 5:1-7; Luke 13:6-9)

Are you interested in vineyards? The Lord must be. He repeatedly uses the vintage and the vineyard as emblems of His people. After the flood, Noah planted a vine, symbolic of a new age. The spies of Moses returned from Canaan with the grapes of Eschol, symbolic of the promise of the land. The prophets refer to God's people in the imagery of the vineyard. Jesus' first miracle was to reproduce what only a vineyard can do, turn water into wine. Jesus warned that His message was new wine that could not be placed into old skins. Throughout Scripture the vine and the grape symbolize God's expectations for His people.

Isaiah dramatically seized on this image to dramatize God's expectations for a mature, productive, fruitful people.

The Lord Provides Generously for a Fruitful People

Isaiah assumes the role of a folksinger. He sings a song about the vineyard of an unidentified Friend. Every conceivable provision has been undertaken to ensure that this vineyard produces the highest quality vintage. The vineyard is planted on a very fruitful hill, literally "a horn of fatness." This Owner tediously removed the unwanted stones. The Hebrew indicates that he provided it with the finest grapes grown in Syria. Customarily, a crude hut was constructed to keep watch over a vineyard. The Owner built a great tower, not only for protection but for pleasure of observation over the growing vineyard. The Owner even excavated a vat for the new wine out of the solid stone nearby. Nothing was wanting; nothing was spared.

Isaiah's parable originally applied to the nation of Israel. It cannot be applied to the United States for we are not God's covenant people, any more than Luxembourg or Liechtenstein. The *church* is now the vineyard. No provision has been left wanting for God's church, for God's staunch people, and, most pointedly, for our congregation. We are provided with more resources for fruitfulness than any generation of believers before us.

The Lord Waits Patiently for a Fruitful People

Having made every provision, the Lord had every expectation for a fruitful people. The fruit that the Lord expected is noted in the application of the parable, verse 7. The Lord looked for the inward attribute of "righteousness" manifested in the outward demonstration of "justice." Instead, His vineyard yielded the acrid and bitter grapes of oppression and the hollow cry of the abused poor.

Each individual inhabitant (v. 3) of Jerusalem is invited to give his judgment on the vineyard. Unwittingly, like David before Nathan, their judgment is a judgment on themselves. Did the Lord omit anything necessary for fruitfulness? Did the vineyard not in fact bring forth bitter grapes? Their very silence renders the verdict.

How long has God patiently waited upon you to become fruitful? Has he really omitted anything from your life that would be necessary? Nothing in all of His universe delights Him unless His people are fruitful. The stars in their orbits, the oceans in their immensity, and the sun in its intensity are nothing to God compared to the delight He has in the fruitfulness of His people.

The Lord Judges Ultimately a Fruitless People

The clear implication is that God builds a hedge of protection around His people while He awaits their fruitfulness. But verse 5 indicates a time when God irrevocably removes that hedge. Like domestic and wild animals running amok over what was once a carefully manicured vineyard, so would the nations trample over Israel. Our Lord Jesus in Luke 13:8 becomes the Vinedresser who pleads for one more year on behalf of His people. Jesus tells the story of a man who planted a fig tree. It was placed in the choicest location of attention, a vineyard. The owner looked for fruit for three years, more than adequate time to produce fruit. When it had no fruit, the owner wanted to cut it down. The vinedresser, a symbol of the Lord Jesus, pleaded for one more year that it bear fruit. Our Lord intercedes with the Father for our fruitfulness. He expects and provides for the best. He Himself is the Vine, our great Supply (John 15:5). Could this be our year?

Confrontation with God:
High and Exalted
(Isaiah 6:1-8)

"The chief end of man is to glorify God and to enjoy Him forever." The purpose of a believing, faithful life is the expectation of the vision of God. "Blessed are the pure in heart; for they shall see God" (Matt. 5:8, KJV). The expectation of every believer is that we shall see the King someday. The invisible God we serve will be gazed at in His glory.

In the past God gave us a preview of what we shall spend eternity viewing. One such preview was given to the prophet Isaiah about 740 B.C. While he was at God's house, the building vanished and he saw God as He is. We only see ourselves as we are when we see God as He is.

The Vision of God Reveals His Glory

The occasion of seeing God is often a crisis. "King Uzziah died." This king reigned fifty-two years. His significant reign enlarged the nation to its greatest extent. After his death the nation declined. His death marked a personal and national crisis. God emptied an earthly throne in order that Isaiah could see His eternal throne. God comes to us at life's critical passages. When a chair on earth is empty, we see the throne in heaven more clearly.

The manifestation of God defies human description. Scripture clearly and repeatedly states that no one can see God at any time (Ex. 19:21; 20:19; 33:20; John 1:18; 1 Tim. 6:16). God is pure Spirit and therefore invisible. Yet Jacob said "I have seen God face to face" (Gen. 32:30, KJV) and Isaiah says, "I saw the Lord." We must understand that God adapts Himself to a form mere humans can see. That form is the Lord Jesus. John 12:41 makes it clear that the human form and glory that Isaiah saw was the Lord Jesus.

The manifestation of God may take place at His earthly house. Whether temple or church, the most likely place to see God is at the place of worship. Isaiah must have been at the Jerusalem temple when God broke in with this vision. He went to church and really saw God.

The vision of God emphasizes His position and His praise. His position is one of elevation, "high and exalted." This emphasizes His power towering above all earthly powers. This defines His elevated separation above all that is human and creaturely. We ought to dwell on His sublime elevation.

His praise comes in both action and confession from sublime heavenly beings. The seraphim are named only here in the Scripture. Their very name means "burning ones." They are personal beings with faces, feet, and the capacity to speak. They must be terrible and splendid to see. Their action is one of humility, activity, and availability. Their humility is expressed in covering their faces and feet. Their activity for God is ceaseless—they always hover with their wings in His presence. Their activity is without ceasing to praise and serve God.

Their confession is the holiness of God. Never stopping, they cry back and forth in choirs, "Holy, holy, holy." The very word suggests the divine perfection that separates God from creation. The threefold repetition suggests the three Persons of the Holy Trinity.

We should join with them now for believers shall be with them forever. How do we do on earth now what they do in heaven? We meditate deeply on the attributes of God Himself. We live a life of truly humble service to our King.

The Reaction of Man Reveals Our Need

There is a universal reaction to the praise of God. The very threshold and foundations of the eternal temple shake with the reverberation of praise. Like a mighty organ shaking a cathedral, all creation vibrates with the praise of God. A mysterious vapor or cloud of smoke adds to the mystery of the scene.

There is a personal reaction to the vision of God. The exclamation is one of "Woe." When mere humans see God as He is, they expect calamity is about to fall. Isaiah felt as if he were about to dissolve, be cut off completely from existence. When we see God we are driven to confession. That confession concentrated on the area of speech for Isaiah. He feels deeply flawed before God in the area of His speech. He recognizes this not only about Himself but about all others around Him.

Have you experienced God? Such an experience will definitely lead to a confession of your own need for cleansing.

There is a heavenly reaction to the need of man. That reaction comes at divine initiative. With the nod from God, one of the fiery ones takes a hot stone from the altar and touches Isaiah's lips. Note well that cleansing comes from a place of sacrifice at the initiative of God. We know what Isaiah did not know—that place would be the altar of

Calvary with God's own Son giving His blood. No seraph touched us with a hot stone; Jesus cleansed us with His blood.

God wants us to know that we are forgiven. Isaiah was shown by deed and informed by word that God forgave and cleansed him. The messenger informed Isaiah that both his sin and the resulting sin of guilt had been covered—"your sin atoned for" (v. 7). Atonement means that my sin is so covered by sacrifice that God no longer can even see it. What peace and well-being that brings. By deed and by word the Lord Jesus died on the cross and gives you His word of honor that He cleanses and purifies.

The Decision of Man Volunteers to Serve

You can never be the same after such an experience with God. Isaiah has a radical change of insight and a new freedom. He becomes a glad volunteer to take the word of God. He is not drafted. He eagerly steps forward to take the word about a holy God who makes a way for man to stand in His presence without fear and guilt. Have you volunteered?

Battles and Babies:
Fear and Faith
(Isaiah 7:1-17)

What is the answer to man's battles? Christmas reminds us that God's baby is the answer to all man's battles. Isaiah 7; 9; and 11 predicted a coming, mysterious Somebody who would be the ultimate answer to all man's fearful battles. That coming Somebody would be God's baby, Immanuel, God with us (v. 14).

Man's Battles Bring Fear

What does a prophetic word from 2,700 years ago say about our world at Christmas 1986? It is filled with peculiar names from faraway places, yet it says much in every way.

Like Isaiah's times, our generation also lives with the *fear of disaster*. Isaiah's tiny nation, Judah, was faced with war from two powerful nations to the north, Syria and Israel. The modern equivalent would be twenty divisions of Russian soldiers camped just over the Canadian border!

With the ever-increasing threats to peace in 1986, it should be of comfort that Isaiah's first promise of the coming Christ was spoken in days looming with disaster. Anytime we fear men's battles, the ultimate answer is God's baby.

Like Isaiah's times, our generation *fears inadequate defenses*. Isaiah found the political leadership of his times anxiously examining the defenses of the country (v. 3). They were asking if they could withstand a siege that cut them off from their water supply. How much this is like Christmas 1986. The more things change, the more things stay the same. We, too, are concerned about the ultimate defense of our nation and ourselves.

For these fears, Isaiah had a word for those whose ultimate trust is in God. When we trust God, we can find that He is the Preserver of courage, the Disposer of adversaries (v. 4), and the Designer of destinies (vv. 8-9). But there is a worse fear than the fear of disaster.

The ultimate ground of all fear is the *fear of unbelief*. Our world and Isaiah's is troubled because there is no relief without belief: "If you do not stand firm in your faith, you will not stand at all" (v. 9). God wants our belief as the only relief from fear. He will do anything He can to assist our belief (v. 11). His ultimate assistance to our faith is the sign of Immanuel: "This will be a sign to you: You will find a baby wrapped in strips of cloth and lying in a manger" (Luke 2:12).

God's Baby Brings Faith

The answer that God gives to man's battles is astounding: He confronts our *battles* with *His Baby*. Isaiah 7:14 foresaw a coming birth that would promise God alone can and will save His people. The only ultimate security is not in man's battles but in God's promised Baby. While Syrians and Israelites marched 2,700 years ago and while Russians and Iranians march today, God's response is the same. The ultimate outcome will not be with man's marchings but with God's Messiah.

God's cradled Christ is more than a sufficient answer to man's crying crisis. While others stand with the fear of Ahaz in the face of man's battles, let us stand with Isaiah looking toward God's Baby, the Christ, Immanuel, God with us.

The Prince of the Four Names
(Isaiah 9:1-7)

Eight hundred years before He came, the prophet looked for a coming Somebody. In Isaiah's seventh chapter, He is a baby more potent than all man's battles. Here He is the Prince of the Four Names. He will be *Wonderful* in that His person and His performance excite amazement. He will be *Counselor* in His office as the ultimate administrator of God's truth and the fountain of all wisdom. He will be the *Father of Eternity* as the One who made it and gives eternal life. His principality will be one of peace. He is in summation the *Mighty God*.

Isaiah could not know all this meant. Just as an astronomer knows there must be another planet, although he has never trained his telescope on it, so Isaiah knew of His coming. What blessings will mark it?

He Brings Hope to the Hopeless

He will come to darkness, remoteness, and rejectedness to turn them into light, access, and acceptance. For Isaiah, the northern tribes of Zebulun and Naphtali represented all that was obscure, exposed, degraded, remote, and marginal. Far from capital and temple, that district was cursed with the intermingling of Jew and Gentile. It was in Isaiah's generation the last place on earth to expect the most significant event in man's history. In fact, Jesus was reared in Nazareth of the tribe of Zebulun.

The Prince of the Four Names brought hope to the most hopeless place both in anticipation and in fulfillment. What could be more hopeless than an unmarried, teenage mother laden with child turned away from the only accommodation? What more hopeless congregation than shepherds? What more hopeless future than an infant chased by a tyrant? The whole of the Christmas message in anticipation and in fact speaks of God's absolute ability to bring hope out of the hopeless. You believe the very fact of Christmas if you consider your own situation to be hopeless.

He Brings Peace to the Peaceless

The announcement of His birth is accompanied with the promise of universal peace both in Isaiah and in Luke. Says the prophet, "Every warrior's boot used in battle and every garment rolled in blood will be destined for burning" (v. 5). From the first fore-gleam of His coming the Prince of Four Names holds the only hope for peace. His coming will end the *need* of war for there is a way to peace. His coming will end the *noise* of war for angels sing of something better if benighted men can hear. His coming will end the *knowledge* of war for its implements are to be burnt. Hard beside the cra-dled Christ, Isaiah would see a terrible conflagration—the burning of the instruments of war. The coming of Christ means the rejection of the instruments of war. While we parade them and put them in museums, Isaiah says, "These are destined for burning, will be fuel for the fire" (v. 5).

He Brings Government to the Ungovernable

Everywhere we encounter this coming Somebody He will be Governor, Ruler, the ultimate King. His government will be *personal* for it is "unto us." Other governments of men are remote. God wishes to bring His government to us, as near as the breath of life. That we might be linked with the administration and the Administrator of the universe is the message of Christmas. His government is to be *perceptible*. "The government shall be upon his shoulder" (v. 6, KJV). He will be *seen* to wear the robe and insignia of government. In His first advent, He was the Ruler who served, and His government was not visible except to His own. In His next advent, He will be the Servant Who Rules, and all will know that the government is upon His shoulder. His government is to be *perpetual*, "there shall be no end." All men's government ends in time and space; it runs out of time and territory. His will expand in space and time forever. His government is to be *purposeful*, "with judgment and with justice." Men seek power for power's sake; He will be granted power for justice's sake.

The cynic looking at the world in 1987 would laugh this promise to scorn. But the fulfillment of this promise is not left to the cynic. It is not even dependent on the believer. "The zeal of the Lord of hosts will perform this" (v. 7, KJV). Nothing else but the zeal of Jehovah could do it. God's intense honor for His own name will see that this promise inaugurated in the first advent will be consummated in the second. It is as certain as God.

A Prophet Looks at the Manger
(Isaiah 11)

We all know the warm circle of faces gathered around the manger of Jesus. Joseph, Mary, shepherds, and wise men are part of the Christmas scene. But we should remem-ber that there are other faces around the manger, those of the Hebrew prophets. At least six of them are quoted in the stories of Jesus' birth. Among them, Isaiah more than any other foresaw a definite coming, Somebody who would restore hope. When you look toward the manger with Isaiah, you, too, can recover his hope through the charac-ter of the Christ.

You See Hope Out of Helplessness at the Manger

Isaiah had both insight and foresight. He had the insight that the mighty Davidic dynasty would fall. It would become as hopeless as the rotting stump of a hewn-down tree (v. 1). Yet he also had a positive foresight. Out of this deteriorated stump would someday come a new tender shoot of life.

At just the darkest moment, hope did come out of hopelessness. Mary and Joseph, obscure, unknown descendants of David, suddenly became heirs of Isaiah's hope. Their situation was the most unlikely conceivable, yet out of it God brought the hope of the world.

Are you living with only the stump of a crushed dream? God can bring hope to you through faith in Christ.

You See the Character of the Christ at the Manger

Seven hundred years before Christ came, Isaiah anticipated the character of the coming Christ. He would bear a unique relationship to the Spirit of Jehovah. The coming Christ would have faculties of perception, practical application, and insight into the character of God. Further, he would identify with the poor and the meek (v. 4).

What Isaiah could not know, we do know. The same Spirit that rested on Him reproduces the same character in us.

You See the Ultimate Impact of the Christ at the Manger

The coming Christ will bring a revolution in relationships. That which is by nature violent, severe, and oppressive will be changed. That was foreseen by Isaiah, symbolized at the manger, realized in the Christian, and universalized at the second coming.

Isaiah saw 700 years before the birth of Christ that He would draw all people to himself. What began when shepherds and wise men came to His manger will end when every knee bows before Him.

Why not bow before Him now and let Him bring a revolution in your relationships?

Soaring on Eagles' Wings
(Isaiah 40:28-31)

Are you running on empty? Are you weary—tired all of the time? Do you go to bed tired, get up tired, and run tired all day? Have you become quiet, sullen, or even withdrawn? Does God seem remote, disinterested, and the Bible make little sense? If these things are true of you, there is a word about soaring above it all from the prophet Isaiah.

Isaiah's generation faced devastating days. They would be carried away to be refugees. They would live in exile. In this experience, they would emotionally and spiritually cave in. They burned out centuries before anyone spoke of burnout. The prophet gives a way out of such emptiness. A confident waiting on God exchanges our emptiness for His soaring strength.

Strength Begins with a Description of God

Recovery of strength does not begin with focus on the human situation, but rather on divine adequacy. There are some things believers ought already to know. Isaiah reminds us with a double question. "Do you not know" by repeated experiences with God? "Have you not heard" from the declaration of His Word? There are four attributes of God that are foundation stones for the life of that source. We should begin with the divine adequacy, not the human deficiency.

We should understand the *eternity* of God. God was before time and after time (Ps. 90:2). For God beginning, succession, and end are not three but one, not separate as a first, a second, and a third occasion, but one simultaneous occasion as beginning, middle, and end. God possesses a complete, interminable life. Time does not apply to

God. The question "How old is God?" simply does not apply. He is no older now than a year ago, because infinity plus one is no more than infinity.

We should think about the *infinity* of God: "The Creator of the ends of the earth." With God the question of location simply does not apply. There is no boundary to His presence. There is no place where He cannot be equally found. God cannot be plotted by a set of coordinates. He is everywhere and at all times.

We should be encouraged by the *inexhaustibility* of God. God is incapable of fatigue or feebleness. There is no diminishing the divine energy. There is no slacking of the divine vitality. Here is an absolute difference between human and divine. While we grow weary, He never loses power.

We should accept the *inscrutability* of God: "His understanding no one can fathom." God's discernment and insight are unsearchable, unfathomable, and beyond scrutiny. You cannot search through or explore God's understanding (Rom. 11:33-36).

We should dwell on these aspects of God. To love God with all our heart means we reflect on these mind-boggling truths. How does this help me? Because He is timeless, He can help me in my little time. Because He is beyond space, He can help me in my little place. Because He is inexhaustible, He can help me in my exhaustion.

Strength Continues in the Situation of People

After Isaiah has looked at God, he considers the needs of people. He confronts the *reality of our need for strength.* God is the solitary source of strength. He alone gives strength to the weary. All inner resources come from Him. God is the sufficient source for strength. He multiplies abundantly the strength of those who are weak, who have no vigor, and who faint.

He confronts *the reason we need strength.* The choicest among us will hit the wall and need His strength, no less the weakest among us. "Youths" refers to those choicest and most energetic who were chosen for athletic or military service. Even the strongest stumble, exhausted from depletion of strength or overexertion. We should recognize that no one will be immune from needing Jehovah's strength.

Strength Arrives in the Appropriation of God

We find strength in the *waiting:* "those who hope in the Lord." Waiters on the Lord are those who believe God can deliver and who wait for Him to bring His promise to fulfillment. Waiting is not passive, but is an active and vigilant exercise which absorbs the power of God.

We discover strength in *exchanging.* "Renew" suggests the exchange of our spentness for His fullness, our depletion for His donation of new strength. Like children bringing a deflated toy to a Father, we wait for the breath of God to fill us again.

We discover that His strength leads to *overcoming.* Some will soar like eagles. The word refers to the golden eagle. The bird has been a symbol of imperial power since Babylonian times. The golden eagle has a wing span of eight feet and lives up to thirty years in the wild. God grants to His waiting people longevity of strength for the duration.

That longevity is appropriate for the life situation. For those with a race to run, He rescues us from weariness. For those whose daily life is a weary walk, He frees us from faintness. He matches the strength of His resources to the level of our need.

Why not appropriate this promise beginning today? Submit yourself to wait quietly before the Lord, infused with the strength inherent in the energy of His might.

Majesty and Mercy
(Isaiah 40)

We worship a God of majesty who is also a God of mercy. On earth, we seldom find great power and great compassion together. Where there is majesty, there is seldom mercy. God revealed to Isaiah that at the same time He is majestic and kingly, He is also the God of personal mercy and renewal. When you worship the God of majesty, you also meet the God of mercy.

The God of all creation offers renewal to those who faithfully wait on His power.

I. The God of Majesty Confronts Us in His Power (40:12-17)

He reveals His power in the magnitude of His operations.

The oceans

The heavens

The mountains

He reveals His power in the massiveness of His intelligence.

He reveals His power in the might of His sovereignty over the nations.

He reveals His power in the measurements of His worship.

II. The God of Mercy Renews Us in His Compassion (40:28-31)

He gives His majestic power to fainting men and women.

The choicest and strongest among us will one day need that power. We will faint sometime in life's struggles.

Those that wait upon the Lord will find their weakness exchanged for His strength.

God will give to you strength adequate for your needs, not more or less. He does not chain eagles to the ground, nor does He make plodders fly higher than they can go.

God's Initiative in Your Forgiveness
(Isaiah 43:25; 44:22)

The pardon for our sin is a double necessity. It is necessary for us and it is necessary for God. Forgiveness is what we need in order to live. Forgiveness is what God needs in order for us to stand in His presence. For God, sin must be removed from us or we must be removed from His presence. Outside the New Testament no one states the grace of God more clearly than Isaiah. "I, even I, am he who blots out your transgressions, for my own sake, and remembers your sins no more." "I have swept away your offenses like a cloud, your sins like the morning mist. Return to me, for I have redeemed you." The ultimate grounds of our pardon is God's initiative. The reason for forgiveness rests not in us but in Him.

God's Action in Forgiving You

Forgiveness rests on *God's initiation*. We stand forgiven because He took the first step. He is *sovereign* in this initiative: "I, even I, am he. . . ." The threefold repetition of God's name points to His lordly, kingly decision. God did not have to forgive sin. In His majesty He chose to do so. My pardon rests on a decision in Him, not in me. He is *unilateral* in this decision. He decided to forgive when we were not even seeking forgiveness. In its beginning the decision to forgive is entirely one-sided. God's decision to forgive is *unmerited* by us. His people refuse to give Him worship or prayer (43:22-24). In spite of this rebellion, God decides to forgive.

Forgiveness rests on *God's motivation:* "for my own sake." God's motivation in forgiveness is entirely *personal,* it is first for His own sake. The motive for forgiveness rests entirely in Himself. The movement of His love toward us began in Him, not in us. It stands written, Not to us, not to us, O Lord, . . . but to your name be the glory" (Ps. 115:1). The sole motive for God's patience and endurance rests in His respect for His own name. He will not let His own name be defamed by the way He treats His own people (Isa. 48:11).

Far from making God seem selfish, this is the most *beneficial* ground for our pardon. If our forgiveness rested on anything within us, it could have never been. If God's continuing pardon rooted in my consistency, performance or merit He could never pardon me. He does it for the name of His dear Son, Jesus.

God's Method in Forgiving You

God forgives by *removing*. This removing is like the eradication of something that is written and the dissipation of a cloud in the sky. God erases from His book the writing that is against us and God sweeps out of the sky the cloud that stands between Him and us.

God erases from His book. There are books in heaven (Rev. 20:12). Whether or not there is a literal library, there is most certainly a record. The whole of God's Word informs us that we will meet that record. It will be read in the presence of God and perhaps others. We are writing an autobiography in the presence of God. How does God forgive? He promises to erase from His book. When He forgives He removes the record. In Christ Jesus He canceled the writing that was against us by nailing it to the cross of Christ (Col. 2:14). Life's ledger is more than balanced by what Christ did.

God sweeps away the cloud between us and Him. Satan seduces us into sin. Then he convinces us that our sins can never be forgiven. They are so dense and dark, says he, that they can never be caused to vanish. Yet God can deal with sins like the wind removing a cloud from the sky. Because of God's gracious acts, our sins are as temporary as mist, vapor, or fog. The remains of sin are transitory. Do not make unmovable what God can move away! The heavy cloud of a morning looks like forever; the sun will burn it off before noon. Let the Son remove the cloud.

God forgives by *forgetting*. He "remembers your sins no more." When forgiven, your sins are no longer in God's mind. They are rendered to oblivion. This means that God does not meditate on your sins. We brood over wrongs done to us. We nurse them. Indignation turns to fury which becomes the desire to retaliate. God is not like that. He does not upbraid us for our sins. He does not drag them up to remind us. No one can call them to His attention. Sometimes we forget a wrong done to us only to have it brought up by another and it suddenly revives with all of its pain. God cannot be reminded of our sins which He erases and forgets. What is even better, He treats us generously. A mere human may look you in the eye and tell you he forgives you. But in his eyes are a contradiction. God not only forgets, He restores us to a place of honor. Look at Peter. The denier of Christ becomes the preacher of Pentecost. God not only forgets, He honors us.

How does God do this? He paid the price of a *ransom*. "Return to me, for I have [ransomed] you" (44:22). It is not until Isaiah 53 that we understand the cost to God in order to forgive with justice. "The Lord has laid on him the iniquity of us all" (v. 6). What Isaiah saw only dimly, we see totally in Calvary.

The Suffering Servant Substitute
(Isaiah 53:1-6)

Has history ever been written in advance? Those who believe biblical prophecy say, "Yes." Centuries before the Lord Jesus' ministry Isaiah foresaw a coming Somebody whom the prophet called "The Servant of Jehovah." He described this Somebody in Isaiah 42; 49—50; and 53. We know that this Somebody is Jesus.

It should strengthen our faith that the meaning of the Lord Jesus' life was foreseen seven hundred years before He came. Isaiah looked forward to the same great truth we see by looking back. God sent a suffering Substitute for our sin. These words from Isaiah 53 concentrate on the beginning of the Lord's life and the very ending on the cross.

The Prophet Considers the Beginning of the Lord's Life

The prophet begins with an *exclamation*: "Who has believed our message?" He is surprised at the scant, small response to the report he brings. Relatively few people believe the story of the Suffering Substitute. A small group sees "the arm of the Lord" (v. 1), the strength of Jehovah God, displayed in the Suffering One. Yet the truth never depends on the number of people who believe it. Regardless of the rejection of this report, it stands true.

The prophet continues with an *explanation* about the origins of the Suffering Servant's life. The coming Servant will have an *unlikely origin*. He will be like a twig or sucker in comparison to great trees. In His own time and place He will appear negligible. He will be "like a root out of dry ground." Like a shrub in arid soil, the conditions of His early life will be unfavorable. Consider the family, locality, and history of the Lord Jesus? He came from the nobodies who lived nowhere, but He saves the world.

The coming Servant will have an *unlikely appearance*. There is "nothing in his appearance that we should desire him" (v. 2). Both outwardly and inwardly, the first impression of the Lord would not compel belief. Only for those who see God in Him will His word bring life. Only God creates the faith that sees the Servant the act of God to save life. Do you see in the Lord Jesus Christ the One can rescue you?

The Prophet Considers the Means of the Lord's Work

The prophet Isaiah leaps as it were from Nazareth to the cross. Centuries before the cross Isaiah stands before the cross to consider the reaction to and the reason for the cross.

The prophet considers the *reaction to the cross*. The reaction of others is one of rejection. The One on the cross is despised. He is both shunned and shunning others in shame. He is the One from whom people turn and avert their faces. People even fear lest His gaze contaminate them. The reaction of the One on the cross is a reaction of sorrow and suffering. The words reflect the pain and sickness that relates to leprosy. The Servant on the cross carries with Him the sum total of sickening pain related to sin.

The prophet considers the *reason for the cross*. This is the heart of Isaiah 53 and the work of the Lord Jesus. "Surely he took our infirmities and carried our sorrows." The Servant came to be a Substitute. The great contrast is between "he" and "our." Nothing was wrong with Him. Everything was wrong with us. Yet we had a false estimate of Him. "We considered him stricken by God" (v. 4). Jesus Christ is the misunderstood One. That is part of His own suffering. We should understand that He is our Substitute.

The Prophet Considers the Meaning of the Lord's Work

Isaiah saw that the Servant came to take penalty and provide the remedy for our sin. He considers *the severity of the penalty:* "he was pierced, . . . he was crushed" (v. 5). The image changes from One sick because of sin (v. 3) to One Who takes into Himself violence because of sin. The Lord Jesus not only felt the sickening suffering sin brings all of His life, but at the end was pierced through and crushed on Calvary for the penalty of sin.

Beyond the penalty, there is *the reality of the remedy*. This is the grace of God too good to imagine. The chastising punishment that fell on Him actually gives me peace. Every blow that landed on the Lord Jesus cries out "Peace, peace" to my own heart. In an incredible trade-off, the gaping welts left on His back are the very things that completely heal me. His stripes are my salvation. His pain is my peace. He is both penalty and remedy.

The *necessity of Calvary* rests in what we are: "We all like sheep have gone astray" (v. 6). Only after we see the Servant can we see ourselves for what we really are—straying out of our own stupidity, nearsightedness, willfulness. This is true of us "all." There is not one of us to help the rest of us other than the Suffering Servant. Yet God caused the twistedness of us all to fall upon Him.

Your only hope is the Substitute. You may be outwardly righteous or openly sinful. Your only hope before God is to come to the Substitute. He is the Wounded Healer.

Finding Forgiveness
(Isaiah 55:6-9)

If you ask God for forgiveness, can you be sure that He grants it? What are the qualities to which God responds? With what urgency should you seek Him? This passage presents one of the great assurances in the Bible that God *does* hear and respond to sincere request for forgiveness.

Seek the Lord with an Intense Priority

Seek the Lord *actively*. Isaiah 55:6 speaks of the pursuit of God as primary, not secondary. It is a pursuit actively, not passively. To pursue God is to allow nothing to stand in the way of that pursuit. It is literally not a trivial pursuit. The word "seek" originally pointed to a deliberate treading or stepping toward God in prayer and sacrifice. Another prophet of repentance spoke, "You will seek me and find me when you seek me with all your heart" (Jer. 29:13).

Seek the Lord *urgently*. Our seeking must be "while he may be found . . . while He is near." God is not always equally accessible. God would not be God if He were no more than a cosmic houseboy to be summoned at our whim. There are moments of time and windows of opportunity when we must seek God. Second Corinthians 6:2 insists, "now is the time of God's favor." Jesus warned His disciples of the urgency for decision now: "You are going to have the light just a little while longer. Walk while you have the light, before darkness overtakes you" (John 12:35). There is a critical, spiritual moment when the wind blows and the tide comes in. That moment must be grasped.

Seek the Lord with a Positive Expectancy

We may believe with security that God will have mercy, that He will pardon. What are the conditions of that pardon?

Pardon relates to the sincerity of the seeker. *Outwardly,* the seeker must lay aside an habitual course of sinful living. Repentance is the missing note in much modern, Christian proclamation. *Inwardly,* there must be a radical change in disposition. External reformation without internal purification is not enough. When we come to God, or come *back* to God, there must be a radical sincerity that embraces both the outwardness of visible life and the inwardness of the unseen disposition.

Pardon relates to the certainty of salvation. The very act of turning to God is an expression of His mercy. His grace met us more than halfway, or we would never have returned. But God's pardon is not scant, stingy, or begrudging. "He will freely pardon." God delights to multiply and make great His pardon when we come with radical repentance: "Where sin abounded, grace did much more abound" (Rom. 5:20, KJV).

Seek the Lord with an Assured Certainty

God's forgiveness is *better* than mere man can imagine. "For my thoughts are not your thoughts, neither are your ways My ways, declares the Lord" (v. 8). To guilty humanity, the reality of absolute forgiveness appears impossible. The narrow confines of guilt-ridden minds cannot imagine the goodness of God. The Lord assures us that He is indeed better than we can imagine, as the heaven is high above the earth.

God's forgiveness is more *certain* than man can imagine. Isaiah 55:8-9 provides us an assurance that God's purposes and promises are irrevocable. It is a universal and timeless principle that He will forgive. "He who is the Glory of Israel does not lie or change his mind for he is not a man, that he should change His mind. (1 Sam. 15:29). The assurance of your forgiveness rests in the character of God Himself. To be God, He must stand true to His promise. You can be sure of seeking and finding forgiveness.

God and the Gods
(Jeremiah 10:1-16)

When we lose the consciousness of God we do not lose the need of God. When we lose the vision of God, we do not lose the necessity of God. We must create a god when we lose the God who created us. Man is ultimately either a God worshiper or a god maker.

The form of idols changes but the central significance never changes. Idolatry is not an Old Testament issue only. Everywhere the claims of God are avoided, idolatry manifests itself. The idols of power, sensuality, and self-gratification have borne many names but remain the same. Are you worshiping God or the gods?

The Origin of an Idol

Anything handmade or manmade that becomes the ultimate concern of life is an idol. The prophet chronicles the *origination* of an idol (v. 3). An idol always reflects the elements of the earth, finite, material—a piece of wood. Idols come from the earth beneath a man and pull him down to their own level. The *beautification* of an idol is a matter of deception only. Idols are gods by disguise only! When a man worships a handmade god he must continually disguise it or it will be seen for what it is, a piece of wood. The *stabilization* of an idol is illusory. Instead of stabilizing a man it must be stabilized by a man: "they fasten it with a hammer and nails" (v. 4). The living God carries you; you must carry an idol.

In contrast to this, God is the Maker, not the made; the Framer, not the one who framed (v. 12). Men's idols are boringly the same—wealth, power, sensuality. Of God it may be said, "There is no one like you." If the one you worship bores you, it is an idol, not the living God.

The Nature of an Idol

When men worship gods created in man's image, what kind of gods do they worship? First, they are *contemptible*, "like a scarecrow in a melon patch" (v. 5). What satire! Men who worship the work of their own hands even ultimately come to hold their gods in contempt. In contrast, the living God will always be due reverence (v. 7). Men never discover the grounds for contempt in Him.

Man-made gods are *immobile*: "they must be carried because they cannot walk" (v. 5). When you manufacture your own god, it becomes a burden that you have to carry. Man-made becomes a burden, not a burden bearer. Sensuality becomes a weight, not a help in the way. The biblical God moves and acts. He carries His people; He does not have to be carried by them.

Most sadly, manufactured gods are *unhelpful*. They cannot speak, they cannot bless, and they cannot even curse. When a man turns to them in the great griefs and disappointments of life, their instruction is no better than the wood they are made of (v. 8). You ask and they do not answer. You cry and they do not speak. In life's terrible hours manmade gods are more terribly silent. In contrast, the living God is the special possession of His own people (v. 16). He hears, blesses, and, in disobedience, curses.

The Worth of an Idol

The ultimate worth of such gods is summarized in one word, *emptiness*. Repeatedly the prophet calls them vain, vaporous, frauds (v. 14), and nonentities. They are breathless, unlike the God who moves the winds of the storm. When you turn to them, there is nothing. Concerning your gods you must say with Ecclesiastes, "Vanity of vanities; all is vanity" (1:2, KJV). An empty god means an empty life.

That further means their *deceptiveness*, "the objects of mockery." Although idols cannot bless or help, they can most certainly mock. In the hour of great need, man-made gods laugh and sneer. They leer at us with their own impotence, the court jesters of our empty heavens.

They will be disclosed in their own *temporariness*, "when their judgment comes, they will perish" (v. 15). Unlike the eternal God, man's concocted deities are under a death sentence. The terrible possibility is that when you make your own god, he may die before you do. Men who worship wealth become jaded as their god disappoints them and they go out into despair. Men who worship the sensual find that age cools the faggots of lust and their god dies before they do. Where is Baal today? The old idol is an object of idle curiosity.

The final word is this: All substitutes for God are less than the men who make them. Did your God make you, or did you make your god?

Whom Do You Trust?
(Jeremiah 17:5-10)

On the first Sunday of a new decade, we would do well to face the most basic of questions. Where does your ultimate trust rest? There are two places to deposit your ultimate confidence. You may place your ultimate trust in human beings. You may put your ultimate trust in God. When you trust the one, you do not place trust in the other.

Jeremiah waged an inner battle and conducted a debate with himself at the point of ultimate trust. Would he rely on humankind or on God and God alone? The heart and soul of Jeremiah's prophecy turns on the question: "Do I ultimately rely on God or human cleverness?"

Your well-being depends on your total trust in God, not in yourself, your family, your vocation, or your network.

Ultimate Reliance on Mere Humans Curses Life

Life can indeed be lived under a curse that blasts life. This is the Word of the eternal One. He does not desire to curse life. Yet life that places reliance on mere humans inherently curses itself.

The *reason* for life that curses itself is misplaced trust (v. 5). When a mere person places ultimate reliance on man as man, that person relies on mere dust. The Hebrew word for trust indicates throwing oneself forward toward an object in order to rest on it. When you trust humans you lean on dust (Gen. 3:19). The life that habitually trusts human strength will be desperately disappointed. We chose between the "arm of God" or "the arm of flesh." God rescues us repeatedly with His invisible but mighty arm (Ex. 6:6). When we lean on any human arm, we lean on flesh that will collapse as weak and perishable.

Where is your confidence? If life falls apart, to what do you turn? Ultimately, nothing in the human dimension is adequate. Your own mind, body or appearance will change. Your family, vocation, or network will desert you. If your ultimate reliance is on any of these, you live under a curse.

The *result* of life under a curse is despair. When you fail to trust God alone, life is diminished, deprived, and deserted. Jeremiah uses poetic language to describe the man who refuses to trust God. He tells us what the man is, what he misses, and where he dwells.

Refusal to trust God alone *diminishes* life. "He will be like a bush in the wastelands." A barren bush, a dry scrub, a stunted shrub in a wilderness! Such bushes were stripped naked and bare by the desert goats. The person who refuses to trust God ekes out an existence in a barren life.

Refusal to trust God alone *deprives* life. "He will not see prosperity when it comes." The person who refuses to trust God alone has no eye for the good when it comes. Misery in the midst of prosperity characterizes the affluent life that does not trust God alone.

Refusal to trust God means a *deserted* life. "He will dwell in the parched places of the desert" (v. 6). Life that refuses trust in God means life in a parched, stony wasteland, uninhabitable and isolated. The person who refuses trust in God is terribly and finally alone with his own inadequacy.

Ultimate Reliance on God Blesses Life

Life can and should be lived under the blessing of God. When you place your total confidence in God, there are resources, responses, and reaction that give well-being.

Life that trusts God alone finds *faithful resources*. "He will be like a tree planted by the water." What a contrast with life like a shrub in the desert! Trust in God alone means available resources, regardless of external circumstances. Such resources are hidden. They belong to the wellsprings of life that only God can give (Ps. 42:1; 46:4; John 7:39, KJV). God's resources are abundant. The plural word "waterbrooks" suggests more than one stream of resource. Best of all, these resources for life are independent of our inhuman environment. When drought comes, the stream still flows.

Life that trusts God alone makes *vital responses:* "that sends out its roots by the stream." There is vigor and vitality in God and God alone. This life is not passive. It actively and energetically thrusts out its roots deeper and deeper into the great Source. While life without God dwarfs, withers, and retreats, life in God grows.

Life that trusts God alone demonstrates *stable reactions*. In adversity "It does not fear when heat comes." When the heat is on, this life stands stable. In insufficiency "it has no worry in a year of drought" (v. 8). When all outside resources dry up, there is stability because this life is sustained by an inner secret.

Only God Can Reveal to You Where Your Reliance Rests

How do I know whether my ultimate trust rests in God or humans? Only God can reveal that to me.

You cannot know your own heart. By *description* "the heart is deceitful above all things." There is a crookedness and twistedness in the human heart. Our own heart deliberately dogs our own heels in order to betray us. By *diagnosis* the heart is "beyond cure." The human heart at its best is dangerously sick. The diagnosis is "terminal." Unaided by God, our response to our own heart must be despair: "Who can know it?" (v. 9, NKJV). No one can fathom the secrets or pierce the darkness of his own heart. This is especially true in the question of our ultimate trust. Only God can tell you who you really trust.

Your hope rests in this. God does know your heart (v. 10). God and God alone explores your heart, probes your mind, and assays your emotions. God has the clue to the maze and can descend into the dark cavern of our inward life. Be still before God. He will reveal to you the basis of your trust. He will draw to Himself and deposit your trust on Himself.

A Future and a Hope with God
(Jeremiah 32)

The confident believer can believe in the darkest times that there is a future and a hope with God. In apparently hopeless circumstances, Jeremiah affirmed a future and a hope with God. He shows us how to do the same thing.

The Believer Looks Realistically at the Future

The believer is not a dark pessimist, or a Pollyanna optimist, but a believing realist. The text gives great detail to show how hopeless things looked in 587 B.C., religiously, financially, internationally, nationally, and personally. The confident believer does not hope because he shuts his eyes to the way things really are.

The Believer Confidently Expects a Hopeful Future

In dark days, Jeremiah had a pious premonition that God was up to something hopeful. He listened for a word of hope from God. That word came in the midst of his everyday affairs. We learn how to express hope from Jeremiah.

We should express hope tangibly and sacrificially, obviously and memorably.

God Positively Confirms the Believer's Future

We have a definite, historical demonstration that Jeremiah's hope was well-founded. Seventy years after his words of hope in the midst of hopelessness, the people came back to the city. The walls, the temple, and the homes were rebuilt.

Our hope is also well-founded on the open and empty tomb of Christ.

The Indestructible Word
(Jeremiah 36)

Why do we have the words of the Bible? We have them only because God has undertaken to see that His Word will not be destroyed. Jehoiakim, the vile puppet king, sought to destroy both the message and the messenger. Always, the Word of God has been under threat of destruction. Critics without and within the church, political and religious, assault both physically and mentally—and still the Word of God stands. This chapter presents changeless truths about the eternal preservation of God's Word.

Revelation of the Word of God

The text leaves no room for doubt concerning the absolute divine inspiration of Jeremiah's prophecy. God says, "Take a scroll and write on it all the words I have spoken to you" (v. 2). The words of Jeremiah's prophecy are veritably the words of God Himself. This text clearly teaches that God reveals Himself in words, men record those words, and those words, once recorded, are the object of divine protection forever. The text does not teach that Jeremiah's prophecy is a *reaction* to the Word of God. It *is* the Word of God. Jeremiah received the words of God Himself. This is so much so that the prophet could say to his scribe: "Jeremiah dictated all the words the Lord had spoken to him" (v. 4).

Reaction to the Word of God

The passage is a timeless demonstration of people's reaction to the Word of God. The Word of God was spoken to them in a time of *peril*. The armies of Babylon were literally at their doorstep. Further, it was spoken *prominently* in the temple and *persistently* by God's man. This chapter records three times of proclamation in a single day. Nevertheless, the people's reactions differed. The common people heard the Word with total *indifference*. The responsible people heard the Word of God with *conviction*. The king heard the Word of God with *angry rejection*. One evidence of the Bible's inspiration is that it contains within itself the timeless reactions of men to its own words.

Rejection of the Word of God

Men seek to destroy the Word by *physical destruction* of the Word itself (v. 23). Seated by a brazier of coals in his winter palace, the king cut the Word with a knife and burned it in a fire. From the days of Diocletian, through the life of Wycliffe, until the fading communist regimes of today, there has scarcely been a time when the Word of God was not the object of physical attack. Still it stands.

Men seek to destroy the Word of God through *spiritual disregard* (v. 24). "The king and all of his attendants . . . showed no fear." The Word that caused the king's officials to tremble meant nothing to the king. We, too, may be guilty of using the penknife of disregard. When we choose to believe some passages and not others, follow radical criticism wherever it leads, and subject the Word of God to our own interpretive bias, we join with Jehoiakim.

Men seek to destroy the Word of God by *destruction of the messengers* (v. 26). From the days of Jeremiah and Baruch to the death of Wycliffe translator, Chet Bitterman, in Colombia, men seek to destroy the Word by destroying those that bring it. Then and now, it is a doomed tactic.

Renewal of the Word of God

The renewal of the Word of God is *divinely assured* (v. 28). Immediately after the king acted to destroy the Word of God, God acted to renew it. Moses may break the tablets of stone, but God renews His commands.

The renewal of the Word of God is *divinely enhanced*. The Word of God renewed became larger and fuller (v. 31). God will do to Jehoiakim what the king had done to the Word of God. The renewal of God's Word is increased in the enlargement of God's Word. When God's words came to Jeremiah the second time, "many similar words were added to them" (v. 32). Far from diminishing the Word of God, the rage of Jehoiakim gave occasion for even more oracles from God to be preserved. Like embers spread by those seeking to quench a flame, strike at the Word of God, and it will only burn more brightly in more places than ever before!

A Wheel Within a Wheel:
The God Who Is Everywhere
(Ezekiel 1:1-28)

What is God like in Himself? Is He a celestial policeman out to arrest sinners? Is He an indulgent grandfather who chuckles through eternity? Is He an oblong blur or a computer? J. B. Phillips said, "Your God is too small." He may also be too local and too limited.

We do not discover God by thinking about God. God reveals Himself or we would never know Him. Ezekiel's vision of God exceeds in length and detail from all others in the Bible. In a summer storm while he was a refugee in Babylon (Iraq), Ezekiel had the grandest vision of God in the Bible. He saw God on a chariot-throne. God is on a throne because He rules all. God's throne is on a chariot because God pervades all things. The vision is progressive, developmental. It begins with the lowest, earthliest aspects of God's power and moves up to the highest, heavenly aspects of God's person.

This vision reveals the inadequacy of all human language and pictures to speak of God. Fifteen times in this vision Ezekiel indicates that God "looks like" what he describes. He struggles with language to say what language cannot say. This passage is so potent that Jews were not supposed to read it until they were thirty!

God presents Himself as the eternal Ruler whose power and presence penetrate every circumstance.

Circumstances of Loss Prepare Us to Meet God

Most of us meet God as He really is out of our own human frailty in the midst of change and loss. By his thirtieth year Ezekiel had lost the location, vocation, and companion of his life.

We meet God when *location* changes. In 597 B.C., the prophet was taken from Jerusalem to the refugee colony in Babylon, seven hundred miles east across the desert. There he lived by an irrigation canal on top of a mound of ruined ancient cities. He dwelt in a mud brick house far from home. When we change locations in life we can know that God is there.

We can meet God when *vocation* changes. Ezekiel was a priest. He had spent five years preparing for the priesthood when he was suddenly uprooted from the temple and the temple was later destroyed. Instead of a priest in Jerusalem, he felt like a nobody in the refugee camp. Often change or loss of vocation leaves us vulnerable and open to a vision of God.

We can meet God in the loss of *companion*. Ezekiel's wife also died (24:18). He seemed to be stripped of everything. He was alone, without job or wife in a foreign land.

At just this time God came to him. A violent July storm swept across the plains of Babylon. Looking at the natural storm, Ezekiel had a supernatural vision. If you are experiencing life's losses, you too can by faith encounter God Himself.

God Reveals Himself as the Supreme Lord of Creation

God is *omnipotent*. All creation reflects His powerful purpose. God's all-powerfulness in nature is symbolized by the four living creatures (1:5-14). These creatures show God's power in its entirety. Each has four faces. The human face represents God's most exalted creation. The lion's face stands for the most exalted wild beast, as does the ox and the eagle the most exalted domestic and flying creation. Together they stand for God's power in all nature. The numeral "4" in the Bible stands for completeness in all the earth. The creatures represent God's activity in nature; their wings move them with energy. These creatures represent God's energy in nature. They move straight ahead with intensity of purpose (v. 9) and spiritual energy like fire (v. 13).

These creatures support the throne of God and He expresses His will through them. God is alive and has life in Himself. He does not need anything in nature. He rules above creation on His throne.

God is *omnipresent*. He penetrates all creation with His presence. God's chariot-throne is on mysterious wheels (vv. 15-18). These wheels intersect at right angles. This was the prophet's way of saying that the throne of God can move in any direction effortlessly. The whole of God's chariot-throne moves in any direction without the wheels ever turning.

In human language what better way could Ezekiel say that God's presence is everywhere? Contrary to all human laws of motion, God's presence is effortlessly present in unity at all places. Like Ezekiel, we may connect God with a particular geographical location. If things do not go well, we are tempted to think that God is not there. God is not localized. You never leave Him behind. He is already at your destination waiting for you.

God is *omniscient*. He knows all things. The wheels of His chariot-throne are "full of eyes." Although this sounds grotesque, it presents the reality that God sees all. The eyes of the Lord are in every place, keeping watch on the evil and the good (Prov. 15:3). We are completely transparent. God sees all and knows all. He has all information. He never revises or experiences surprises.

Do you grasp the implications of this for your life? Your personal circumstances never overcome the power of God. The movements of your life never take you away from God. The moments of your life are never beyond the view of God.

God Reveals Himself as the Holy One—Absolutely Different

God reveals His *separation*. The "otherness" of God is revealed in sight, sound, and symbol.

In sight, the throne of God is set on a firm foundation above the creation. The word suggests a flat surface of ice or crystal. In sound, the wings of the creatures emphasize the separation of God. They sound like the rushing of cataracts, the marching of an army.

In symbol, the holiness of God is presented with reluctance, reticence, and reverence. God's dominion is described as One who sits on a throne. That throne sits on a lustrous, marble floor. The description of the form of the One enthroned hides as much as it reveals (v. 27). From the waist up He looks like a contained fire, a hidden mystery. From the waist down, He looks like burning fire. Around His throne is a rainbow, the sign of covenant. He never changes His promises.

Man responds to God's revelation with *submission* and with God's *affirmation*. Ezekiel falls down as if dead at this awesome sight (v. 28). Yet God responds with affirmation (2:1-2). He does not want to overpower us with fear, but fill us with His Spirit and life.

Does not this vision make you happy that God revealed Himself in His Son, the Lord Jesus Christ? This presentation of God is almost too much. In Jesus God put on human flesh and walked among us. We know Him in a way Ezekiel could never imagine. Yet this vision shows us what He is in Himself.

God and the Kingdoms of Man
(Daniel 2:31-49)

Consideration about our national destiny dominates many discussions during this fall's political activities. Concerned Christians believe that the last word about national destiny is not in the hands of men of state but in the hands of God. Does the Bible give us evidence concerning the ultimate outcome of men's kingdoms? Daniel indicates that it does. Although Daniel's visions do not provide us with finely tuned detail, they do give us firm orientation as to God's intention. Daniel does give us an understanding of the future. He does give us stability in the present. He does give us certainty about ultimate destiny.

God's Description of Man's Political Kingdoms

Our passage relates the dream of Nebuchadnezzar, ruler of the first great, cohesive world empire. He has dreamed of a colossal statue, metallic, bright, and terrifying. It is left to God's man Daniel to tell the man of state what his dream was and what it meant.

There is an emphasis on the *composition* of the statue. The movement in the statue is one of degradation, disintegration, downwardness, deterioration. This is true *anatomically*—the image moves down from the nobility of the head to the humility of the feet. This is true *metallically*. The image moves from fine gold to iron mixed with brittle clay. The silver chest and arms represent the Medo-Persian Empire. The bronze anatomy represents the great Greek Empire reaching its height under Alexander the Great. Yet there is no progress. There is downwardness. There is no cohesion. The history of nations is not evolution; it is devolution.

Stress must be placed on the *origination* of the statue. The statue represents that which is artificial, man-made, handmade. As such it is a fitting representative of the kingdoms of men. They are human in their origination. Nebuchadnezzar or Cyrus or Alexander or Caesar carved their kingdoms out of human flesh and blood. But when God sets up His kingdom it is from "a stone cut . . . without hands" (v. 44, KJV).

As to their *duration*, the kingdoms of men devour and replace one another. The Babylonian Empire (605-539 B.C.) was swallowed by the Medo-Persian Empire (539-331 B.C.). That in turn was swallowed by the Greek Empire (331-146 B.C.). That in turn was swallowed by Roman rule for 500 years. In blood and gore human kingdoms swallowed one another. That never changes.

God's Destruction of Man's Political Kingdoms

Suddenly, it is all over. "A stone was cut out without hands" (v. 34, KJV). This mysterious, majestic, mobile stone smites the statue on its feet. God's mighty act will strike man's pretensions of political greatness. God's destruction will be *total*. The empires of man will be crushed to pieces, all of them together. God's destruction will be *instant*. When God smites, it will not just be process, it will be instant impact. God's destruction of man's pretension will be absolute. Every element of human civilization from the brittle clay to the finest gold will be gone with the wind, like the chaff from the threshing floor.

God's Declaration of an Eternal Kingdom

All of this is a prelude to the *inauguration* of God's kingdom "In the days of these kings shall the God of heaven set up a kingdom" (v. 44, KJV). Unlike human kingdoms, the *origination* of this kingdom is superhuman and supernatural. It is the stone cut without hands (Matt. 21:44). In its *duration* it is eternal. Man's kingdoms conquer and swallow up one another. God's kingdom will never be vanquished. That kingdom was inaugurated in the ministry of Jesus of Nazareth. It will be consummated when He comes to reign as Lord of all lords and King of all kings. What Nebuchadnezzar acknowledged (v. 47) all the world will one day acknowledge. God's people must not substitute any merely political message for the triumphant declaration of this ultimate kingdom.

How God Humbles the Proud*
(Daniel 4)

How does God respond to human pride? We may gain insight for our own lives from His dealings with Nebuchadnezzar, proud king of Babylon. This chapter is unique in all Scripture for containing the imperial decree of a pagan king. This is Nebuchadnezzar's own testimony. From his dream of a great tree and its destruction we learn how God responds to human pride.

Human Pride

Virtually every shade of pride is reflected in the experience of Nebuchadnezzar. He demonstrates the pride of *engrossment* (vv. 4,29-30). "Is this not the great Babylon I have built?" He is like all those who are totally preoccupied with their own personal kingdoms to the neglect of God! Witness in his life the pride of *establishment* (vv. 10,22) Just as a massive tree stands in lonely loftiness, so Nebuchadnezzar towered above all men in the stability of his kingdom. Men assert their pride when they think too much of their own human stability. Added to this is the pride of *enlargement* (vv. 11,22). Even as Nebuchadnezzar watched all that he was doing grew and expanded. It is a rare man who can overcome pride as his accomplishments grow. All of these other occasions of pride were joined by the pride of *enhancement* (v. 12). All that Nebuchadnezzar did had about it a health and brightness that was unsurpassed. His very presence betokened the exquisite and the luxuriant. When a man is so graced he may easily be proud. In his relationship to others there is exhibited the pride of *endowment* (v. 12). All the known world depended on Nebuchadnezzar for protection and nourishment. Whenever a man harbors those beneath him who are dependent for life and protection he may become proud of his very responsibilities.

Those qualities which provoked Nebuchadnezzar's pride abide in every generation as temptations to hurtful and obnoxious pride before God.

Divine Judgment

It is axiomatic in scripture that God will judge pride. It is not a matter *if* God will do so, but *when* God will do so. Certain factors in God's judgment on pride are exhibited in Nebuchadnezzar's experience.

God's judgment is *appropriate in its announcement* (vv. 14,31). God judges human pride in a way that is unmistakable. When the word of God came to Nebuchadnezzar, the decision was already made and the source of judgment was undoubtedly God himself. In just the hour that Nebuchadnezzar most luxuriated in his power God spoke.

God's judgment may be *total in its abasement*. When God deals with the man of pride that man is first *diminished* (v. 14). One word from God can cut a man down to human size. Such a one when judged may also be *deserted* (v. 14) and *deranged* (v. 15). The most devastating judgment of God on Nebuchadnezzar is to witness the great king *dehumanized* (vv. 16,25,33). Nebuchadnezzar would not only live *where* the animals lived but he would live *as* an animal. Nebuchadnezzar's pride evidently deranged his mind until suddenly it broke. He went from the palace to the pasture. It is a matter of encouragement that God's judgment on pride is *delineated* (v. 16). God wishes to judge a man only so long as necessary to bring repentance.

God's judgment is *purposeful in its accomplishment*. The desire of the living God is to teach all men His absolute sovereignty and His divine mercy (vv. 17,25,32). The judgment of God is not a blind rage; it is a purposeful discipline. Therefore the judgment of God is *merciful in its accompaniment*. If Nebuchadnezzar will repent, God will temper His judgment (vv. 26,27). Judgment is God's "strange" work. He delights in mercy.

Redemptive Repentance

The pathway to wholeness begins with *resignation to divine sovereignty* (v. 34). It was when Nebuchadnezzar lifted up his eyes to heaven that healing began in his proud life. Immediately after that there is a restoration of human *rationality* (v. 34). Nebuchadnezzar's understanding returned when in humility he looked up to almighty God. The insanity that characterizes proud leaders in this present age will be healed only when they too look up. This led to a *recognition of divine eternity* (v. 34). In contrast to the transient and temporary kingdom of Babylon, Nebuchadnezzar recognized the eternal kingdom of God. Pride always ends when a man recognizes fully his own mortality. In it all there is a beautiful *realization of divine equity* (v. 36). After the judgment of God, Nebuchadnezzar was more brilliant in his rule and more prosperous in his kingdom than ever. In his great mercy God does not wish to crush the proud man but to redeem him.

God Versus Pride
(Daniel 4)

It is a basic, biblical axiom that God sets His face against pride. It is a deadly sin. The Word reveals a dramatic confrontation between God and the pride of Nebuchadnezzar, the arrogant king of Babylon. The king gave his own testimony concerning the power of God to confront and humble the proud. What you see on a *grand* scale with Nebuchadnezzar may happen on a small scale with anyone.

God always confronts the proud and ultimately brings them to the place of humility.

I. The Word of God Reveals the Roots of Human Pride

Nebuchadnezzar demonstrates every hue in the rainbow of pride. Engrossment with personal accomplishment causes pride (vv. 4,30). The enlargement of one's endeavors can cause arrogance (v. 11). It is a rare individual who can watch the growth of all he touches and remain *humble*. The enhancement of one's life with beauty may cause haughtiness. Even the ability to endow others with good things may lead to pride (v. 12).

II. The Word of God Reveals Judgment on Human Pride

God's judgment against pride is appropriate in its announcement. God may speak judgment by a dream (v. 5), a delegate (v. 13), a declaration (v. 19), or from heaven itself. God knows how to speak to the proud person's heart, to find a crack in his armor.

God's judgment may be total in its abasement. A proud man may be diminished, deserted, and even dehumanized (v. 33). God can deal with pride in an absolute totality of overwhelming judgment.

God's judgment is purposeful in its accomplishment. God desires to bring the proud person to a point of confession and redemption (v. 17).

III. The Word of God Reveals His Mercy
After Repentance from Pride

The proud person can find a way back to God. There must be a resignation to divine sovereignty (v. 34). That will result in a restoration of human rationality. There will then be a confession of divine eternity, that God reigns forever. At the end, there will be a demonstration of divine equity (v. 36). God does not desire to crush even the proud person, but to redeem. *Two slightly different sermons on Daniel 4.

The Road Back Home
(Hosea 14)

Most of us enjoy stories of reunion. We like to hear that people got back together. In our hearts there is a desire for reconciliation. This is the timeless appeal of the most unusual Old Testament prophet, Hosea. Hosea watched his wife Gomer leave him and publicly humiliate him. He exhausted all of his resources in the successful attempt to reclaim her. Through his own experience, Hosea learned that there is no length to which God will not go to recover relationship with His people.

A loving God receives you unconditionally when you return on His terms.

God Actively Longs for You to Return

Hosea 14 is one of the great passages in the Word concerning *return* to God. Hosea used the word *return* fifteen times in his prophecy. It is the major call of the book. The word simply means a radical reorientation of life back toward God. The whole of Hosea is the call of love that simply wants a chance. God cries throughout the book: "The door is opened from my side; come back."

Understand that this call comes after God's people had already experienced disastrous disobedience: "Your sins have been your downfall!" (v. 1). Hosea is not a warning to somebody about to slip. Hosea speaks to those who had already stumbled. Everything was already lost, broken, and devastated. Yet God said, "Come back and we will begin again." All of the time you are running away from Him, He is running after you.

God Specifically Instructs You How to Return

God wants a *real conversation* with you: "Take words with you" (v. 2). In today's language, Hosea tells us to have a real conversation with God again. In fact, he gives us the very words to say. It is as if Hosea said, "Now repeat after me." They had been away from God so long that they did not know what to say.

We stop conversation with God when we substitute *ritual for reality,* the mechanics of a dead religion for the meaning of a living faith. This is a major theme of Hosea: "For I desire mercy, not sacrifice, and acknowledgment of God rather than burnt offerings" (6:6). They had even substituted contribution to God for conversation with God. God wants the "fruit of our lips," a sacrifice of real conversation with Him. We can lose the reality of conversation with God in the midst of religious rituals.

Out of that real talk with God ought to come some *renunciations.* We cannot own what we ought to be until we disown what we must not be. We must renounce ultimate dependence upon every external resource except God: "Assyria cannot save us." We cannot give to anyone else the dependence that belongs to God alone. We must renounce dependence upon every internal resource except God: "We will not mount warhorses." Israel had become confident in her own internal resources, even when they were pitifully weak in the face of her pressures. We must renounce every idol: "We will never again say, 'Our gods' to what our own hands have made" (v. 3). In every life there is a ruling passion, a mainspring to the personality. That must be God alone.

God Abundantly Restores You When You Return

He restores you graciously. He can heal the spiritual disease, not merely treat the symptoms. God promises to heal waywardness. We have a tendency toward rebellion that is self-destructive. God promises to touch us at the deepest point of our will and make us radically different. God receives you spontaneously without any further demands or conditions: "I will love them freely."

God restores you to wholeness. He does this by giving back vitality where there is no life: "I will be like the dew to Israel." The dew in Israel was mysterious yet trustworthy. During the long, rainless summers only the dew watered the vegetation. God can renew vitality in the spiritual life in the same way.

He gives back beauty where there was ugliness: "He will blossom like the lily" (v. 5).

The word refers to the miracle of new life in unlikely places. This was a flower that grew in the desert valley among thornbushes. In an unlikely place God can give life.

He gives back stability where there is instability: "Like a cedar of Lebanon he will send down his roots" (v. 6). Your life needs not only the beauty God can give, but the stability that only He can give.

He refreshes you in all the seasons of life. "I am like [an evergreen]" (v. 8). With the changing seasons, the evergreen always shows the presence of life. God is like that. When you come back, His love is always in season, always fresh. Gomer found that the love of Hosea was like that. So is the love of God for those who take the road back home.

Come Back Now

(Joel 2:12-14)

Have you been away? You can come back to God. Our spiritual adversary uses sinister methods. He will alienate you from God, then tell you that you have gone too far. The prophet Joel told of a judgment that was already moving toward God's alienated people. It was in the form of a devastating locust plague. That day was immediately upon the people: "The day of the Lord is great; it is dreadful. Who can endure it?" (v. 11)

Yet even at the last moment, you can return. God cries, "Even now, . . . return to me" (v. 12). When you have been away from God for so long that judgment seems immediate, you can return. You can return not because of your nature but because of the character and conduct of God.

Return to God with an Inward Intensity

The Bible abounds with invitations to return to God. It is really the theme of the Book. To return means a total reorientation of life toward God. Moses predicted that God's people would abandon Him, then return (Deut. 30:2,10). Solomon prayed at the temple dedication that the people would return to God (1 Kings 8:48). Amos declared that God judges in order that His people return (4:6-11). The entire Book of Hosea is one long call for Israel to return to God (14:1-2). We can return even when we have greatly revolted (Isa. 31:6). Jesus' favorite parable related the return of a son (Luke 15:11-32). At all times God desires your return.

Return to God is not a casual matter. Return requires an *intense inwardness:* "with all your heart." This phrase indicates the entire force of your moral purpose. The biblical heart is not only the organ of affection, but of intellect, resolve, and moral purpose. Return to God cannot be a laid-back, mellow matter.

That return requires *inward reality* and not just outward ceremony: "rend your heart and not your garments" (v. 13). In the biblical world to tear one's garments expressed exceptional emotion on the occasion of overwhelming misfortune. Jacob tore his garments when he thought his son Joseph was slain (Gen. 37:34). Joshua and Caleb tore their clothes at the lost opportunity to enter the promised land (Num. 14:6). David and all his army tore their clothes when they heard of the death of Saul and Jonathan (2 Sam. 1:11). To rip one's garments is an impressive act of intensity, but the prophet calls for more intensity than that. We must rend our hard hearts and crack them open so God can penetrate them. God returns to a broken and crushed heart (Ps. 51:17).

Yet there is also an *outwardness* in returning to God: "fasting and weeping and mourning" (v. 12). Any real return to God will express itself outwardly. Fasting is a voluntary abstention from food and physical relations in order to express self-abasement and sorrow for sin. We have lost something because we no longer fast. Return to God does express itself in emotional outlets appropriate to our own personality.

James 4:7-10 gives us the same steps to come back to God. Outwardness and inwardness characterize any return to God.

Return to God Because of Divine Integrity

The reason for our hope when we return to God is the consistency of the divine character. Our hope does not rest in our own intensity but in divine integrity.

You can count on *God's character* when you return. Four aspects of God's character encourage you to return. God is gracious. This is one of His earliest self-disclosures (Ex. 34:6-7). God's graciousness means the complete goodwill of a superior person who condescends to a lesser person.

God is *compassionate*. The word suggests a fatherly or motherly care extended to one who is helpless and endangered. God has a tender regard to one who needs to return.

God is slow to *anger*. The word beautifully suggests one who takes a long breath in order to postpone and place at a distance any anger. God restrains His anger toward sin in order to give time to return.

God is abounding in love. This points to many concrete deeds of voluntary kindness in our life in order to keep faith with us and renew His covenant with us. When you leave God, you must trample underfoot mountains of His kindness. Jonah discovered these aspects of God's character in the return of Nineveh to the living God (Jonah 4:2).

You can count on *God's conduct* when you return: "He relents from sending calamity" (v. 13). When man repents, God relents. This is a mystery to mere humans. God can intend with all His might to send personal judgment. Yet when man repents, God relents (Jonah 3:10; Jer. 18:7-8; Amos 7:3,6). Although we cannot explain this change in God's mind, it can be a personal reality.

But not only does God relent, He also restores blessings (v. 14). The locust judgment would leave a scorched earth. When Joel's generation returned to God, there would be a new fertility and abundance. God does not desire a mere neutrality in His relationship with you. He wants an abundant life (John 10:10). You can come back, but do so now.

At Ease in Zion

(Amos 6)

On national holidays Christians ought to be patriotic, but not in a heedless manner. The United States is not God's chosen people. Only Israel in the Old Testament and the worldwide church in the New Testament era are God's chosen people. Nevertheless, our government embodies more biblical principles than many others. Abraham Lincoln may have been right when he called America "the last, best hope of the earth" and her people the "almost chosen people."

Amos has a word for us this July Fourth. To the extent our nation reflects the people of God, to that extent Amos's word applies to us. His word is not a comforting word but a sobering word. He spoke to Israel forty years before her history ended. He warns us against the heedless security in the face of God's certain judgment.

Misplaced Trust Gives a False Security

An entire nation can be recklessly at ease. Amos' generation lived in contentment with a shallow optimism founded on a false sense of security. This baseless, false security extended from the first citizens of the nation to the rank and file of the population. The nation founded after the exodus had only forty years remaining. Yet they were a group of people who lived in carefree arrogance.

We may place the trust that belongs to God alone in our own way of life. Amos indicts those "who feel secure on Mount Samaria" (v. 1). Forty times the same word is used for the trust that belongs to God alone. We may habitually put our ultimate confidence in our own way of life rather than in God. This happens when we trust our government, economic system, military complex, educational system, or social system with the trust that belongs to God alone.

While bragging about our own country, we should consider the destiny of other nations. Calneh, Hamath, and Gath (v. 2) were once great nations felled by the same enemy approaching Israel. During the 212 years of United States history, other mighty powers have fallen because of the same sins of our country. Patriotism must be informed with the reality that God does not play favorites.

False Security Leads to Indulgent Living

We may fight off thoughts of judgment by an indulgent life-style. Verses 4-6 are unlike anything else in the prophets. They picture a society consumed with self-indulgence. Amos gives a panorama of a life of luxury to the point of brutishness, an animalistic approach to life. Every item in the list represents what had once been available only to royalty but now is available to everyone. That generation reclined on beds of ivory. They draped themselves across couches, sprawled in a stupor, unable to control their limbs. They ate the choicest lambs out of the flock—only the very choicest veal would satisfy their voracious appetites. They amused themselves by extemporizing musical stringed instruments. The Hebrew word suggests the howling screeching quality of their songs. (I am reminded of Aleksandr Solzhenitsyn's indictment that the Western soul is shriveled by intolerable music.) They drank their wine not in goblets, but in large bowls. They anointed themselves with ointments of the chiefest kinds.

No one or two of these items is in itself worthy of condemnation. The picture is one of unbridled luxury that has tenderized the moral muscle of society. The awful irony of their position is that they do not see the wound in their midst. Immersed in the vortex of pleasure, they do not see the flagrant sore in the mind of their society.

No Nation Can Win Making Odds with God

You do not gamble with God and win. Verse 12 asks if the absurd can happen. Verse 12 also states that the absurd did happen. Some used common sense in the natural realm and refused wisdom in the spiritual area. The Hebrews had turned the world upside down morally and claimed they could not fall off. They could not say that and neither can the United States.

How should an American Christian celebrate the national holiday? We should celebrate with patriotism and pride, but that is not enough. Christians must also celebrate with repentance and prayer. We must place that trust in God alone which belongs to Him, not in our own way of life. Our only security must be that which comes from God alone not from a groundless reliance upon our own way of life.

Praying for Our Nation
(Amos 7:1-9; 8:1-2)

Our great national holiday ought to raise the question, "What can I do for my country?" Christians should vote, pay taxes, and serve. But what is the unique contribution of Christians to the nation? Amos would say, "Plead with God to forgive and cease from judgment." Christians should pray for those in governmental authority (1 Tim. 2:2). Beyond that Christians may see the looming possibility of God's judgment and plead with Him to forgive and stop.

Amos was a rural shepherd who lived in isolation. He was a layman, not a priest or a figure of the religious establishment. God showed Amos His intent to judge finally and absolutely the ten northern tribes of Israel. Amos begged God to forgive and cease. Because of one layman's prayer God averted judgment. Today we, too, may beg God to relent from judging our nation. What is the nature and content of such prayer?

How Should We Pray for Our Nation?

Such prayer begins when we see what others do not see. —God always takes some of His own into His inner counsel so they can see and hear what is hidden to others. God caused Amos to see two disasters before they happened. He saw a plague of locusts being formed in a larval stage. Such a plague was the unstoppable agricultural disaster in the ancient world. Amos also saw a "judgment by fire" (v. 4), something like a flash fire that scorched the earth and even the hidden springs beneath.

Amos saw clearly the threats to the nation. Do we? Does our church live with any sense that we are a nation under threat? Or would we rather not see that? God needs a few who live with the discomfort of seeing the threat. This means we must get beyond rush, hurry, and superficiality.

Intercession continues as we understand the crisis. —Amos saw that national survival was threatened. A ravenous, dreadful plague of locusts destroyed the nation's food supply. Locusts ate all herbage—seeds, vines, and fruits. That meant total oblivion. A flash fire of drought only doubled the crisis. For the deep artesian sources of water to disappear meant extinction. Is there any reason to believe America faces an unprecedented crisis for survival? God may show this to some of us and call us to intercede.

Intercession for the nation often comes at the most critical moment. — Amos prayed as the locust plague was coming to devour the second crop of grain. The king got the first harvest of the year for himself. After the latter rain in April the farmer got the second harvest of seed grain, food, and hay. Following that there were six months of absolute drought with no hope for harvest. To lose the second harvest was to lose all. Amos prayed at the most critical moment for God to forstall judgment.

You may know this for certain. Some day some generation of praying American Christians will plead with God before the final crisis. Who knows when that generation will pray?

What Should We Pray for Our Nation?

Intercession comes with the appropriate attitude: "Sovereign Lord" (vv. 2,5). When we plead with God for national survival we are dealing with the supreme sovereign, exalted potentate of all, the one who has always disposed of the nations of the world and their rulers. When we beg for the nation we come with an unusual sense of God's awesome lordship over history. At the same time, we come on the basis of our own personal relationship to God. The Hebrew text says, "My God." When we pray for the nation we hold in tension the loftiness of God and our own personal relationship with Him.

Intercession comes with appropriate content.—It simply represents our "requests" to God. Amos prayed for God to forgive, to cleanse the people even in the absence of their repentance. When Amos saw the judgment by fire he simply called out for God to cease, to stop.

Our prayers for the nation do not have to be lengthy, but they should be intense. Jesus raised Lazarus with a few words. Our prayers should give a *reason* for God to cease judgment. "How can Jacob survive? He is so small!" (vv. 2,5). We should plead with God on the basis of hopelessness, helplessness, littleness, the inability to recover that characterizes a people under His judgment. We seldom go wrong pleading with God for His compassion.

It helps us plead with God not to judge when we think in terms of individuals. It is easier to pray for "Jacob" than for the nation "Israel." When you plead for the nation think of your own friends, family, and neighbors being spared from national judgment.

How Does God Respond to Our Intercession?

God may relent from what He actually intended to do.—This is a mystery, but nonetheless a reality. God does relent (vv. 3,6). The word means a change in mind because God is deeply moved. God turns away from an earlier decision because our appeal matters. The word actually suggests someone who sighs deeply or groans while changing the mind. The God of the Bible is not an inflexible machine. He personally responds in a dynamic dialogue with those who pray. The word simply reveals this too often to ignore. When Abraham pleaded for Sodom, God changed His mind (Gen. 18:22-32). When Moses prayed for the survival of Israel after their decision at Kadesh-Barnea, God changed His mind (Num. 14:11-20). In the days of Jeremiah, God stated as a principle that He may change His purpose for a nation from good to evil or evil to good (Jer. 18:1-10). God changed His intent to destroy the city of Nineveh (Jonah 3:10). God may change His intent when we pray for Him to do so. He is not a rigid, cold, calculating computer.

There comes a time when God cannot relent.—Amos saw a vision of God holding a plumb line (vv. 7-8). In this vision God asks Amos what the prophet sees. The prophet confesses a single word, "plumb line." This indicates that God has taken the final measure of the nation and will no longer bypass judgment. The same thing is indicated by a division of a basket of summer fruit (8:1-2). The nation is now ripe for the judgment of God. There is a time to intercede. But there is also a time when intercession is too late.

God has never told anyone as a matter of record to stop interceding for America. We are still living in the days of God's mercy. It is a sobering thing to recognize that Israel as a nation lasted from 922 to 722 B.C., 200 years. God has given us more time than that. We, His people, should make the national holiday a time of intercession.

A Purse with Holes in It
(Haggai 1:1-11)

Does it appear that you can never get ahead? You work so hard, but what you have seems to disappear? Indeed, even what you buy seems to disappoint you? Haggai's generation felt the same way. It was as if they had "a purse with holes in it" (v. 6). Two times Haggai gave God's command: "Give careful thought to your ways (vv. 5,7). Because they failed to invest in the work of God, their entire life-style seemed futile.

If your life has stopped paying dividends, consider investing in the work of God.

Recognize the Procrastination
When Life Stops Paying Dividends

Recognize the reality of procrastination in your spiritual life. "These people say, 'The time has not yet come for the Lord's house to be built'" (v. 2). Fifteen years earlier, they had just stopped. They worshiped in ruins and rubble for fifteen years! They admitted that the house of God ought to be built, but just not now.

Recognize the real reason for procrastination in your spiritual life. Haggai noted that God's people lived in "paneled houses" (v. 3), while God's house rested in ruins. Evidently, they had taken the very cedar brought for the new temple and used it to cover their own houses. Although there was not time to sacrifice for God's house, they had plenty of time to sacrifice for their own.

Realize the relevance for Travis Avenue. The time has come. We have not chosen the time, the time has chosen us. We cannot say that the time has not yet come. It is here. The question facing us is the same as that of Haggai: will we use our resources for God or for ourselves?

Remember the Futility
When Life Stops Paying Dividends

Reflect carefully on your way of life. Four times Haggai called his generation to careful reflection on their ways (vv. 5,7; 2:15,18). If they would only stop and reflect, they would see the emptiness of life that neglected the work of God.

Remember critically your way of life. Haggai's generation experienced futility, hopelessness, and meaninglessness because they did not invest in God's work. Their planting, eating, drinking, clothing, and earning was a drudgery with no meaning or purpose. "You earn wages, only to put them in a purse with holes in it" (v. 6). They had high expectations of life, but were disappointed again and again (v. 9). Life seemed fruitless, wearisome, vexing, and hopeless.

Can you really say that you enjoy what you have? If you are not investing in God's work, you will never enjoy it.

Renew the Activity that Makes Life Pay Dividends

There is a simple practicality in the life that pays dividends. "Go up into the mountains and bring down timber and build the house." When God's people set their hearts on building God's house, life begins to pay dividends again.

There is a purpose in the activity, so that God "may take pleasure in it and be honored" (v. 8). When the goal of your life becomes building for the pleasure and honor of God, real meaning comes back. The way to repair a purse with holes in it is to invest in the work of God.

New
Testament
Synopses

The Forgotten Man of Christmas
(Matthew 1—2)

The forgotten man of Christmas is Joseph. He never speaks in the Bible. One called him "Joseph the silent." He is usually relegated to the role of an extra in the Christmas story. That should not be. Even though Joseph was remarkably simple, he was simply remarkable.

Joseph demonstrates to us all the consequences and influence of obedience to the word of God.

The Forgotten Man of Christmas
Demonstrates Obedience to God, Regardless

We can obey God with immediacy. Zacharias denied the command of God. Mary doubted the command of God. Joseph simply obeyed. He woke up from his dream and married Mary. Nothing pleases God like obedience.

We can obey God in painful circumstances. Joseph's obedience came in the midst of betrothal to a pregnant woman. The rabbis demanded that such a woman be put away. Yet Joseph obeyed when it hurt.

We can obey God in spite of fear. Joseph felt terror at the holy thing God was doing. God told him "Do not be afraid" (1:20). We can obey God even while going forward in fear.

We can obey God by staking everything on His word alone. Even though Joseph had no New Testament, he staked his future on the word of God.

The Forgotten Man of Christmas
Demonstrates the Consequences of Obedience

Obedience to God always has immediate personal consequences. Joseph "took Mary home as his wife. But he had no union with her until she gave birth to a son" (1:25). Joseph was probably a young man. The immediate consequence of his obedience was to live with Mary in chastity until she gave birth. He watched her, protected her, but did not touch her.

Obedience to God sets the course for a lifetime of consequences. The trip to Bethlehem, the flight to Egypt, the running from Herod's family, looking for Jesus at the temple, and many other consequences came from the initial decision of obedience.

There is no obedience to the word and will of God without consequences.

The Forgotten Man of Christmas
Demonstrates the Influence of Obedience

Your obedience always influences how others think about God. When Jesus called God "Abba, Father" he was reflecting his relationship to Joseph. When the hero in the parable of the prodigal son was the father, we see a reflection of Joseph.

Your obedience influences how others yield to the will of God. When Jesus prayed, "Not my will, but thine," He was reflecting what He saw in the life of Joseph who had obeyed years before, regardless of the consequences.

Emmanuel
(Matthew 1:23)

Someone noted that there are 365 names in the Bible for our **Lord Jesus Christ**.

No one name can do justice to what He is. **Emmanuel,** God with us, is particularly His name for Christmas.

I. Emmanuel—God as He Really Is with Us as We Really Are

The *eternal* God with us in our little moment.

The *omnipresent* God with us in our little place.

The *all-knowing* God with us in our ignorance.

The *all-powerful* God with us in our weakness.

The *invisible* God made visible.

God in *His* holiness with us in our sin.

II. Emmanuel—The Greatest Comfort

A comfort for all people.

A comfort for all people at every moment.

A God who is absolutely approachable.

III. Emmanuel—The Great Rejection

"He came unto his own, and his own received him not" (John 1:11, KJV).

Matthew's Gospel ends with the promise: "Lo, I am with you alway" (28:20, KJV).

The New Testament ends with the promise: "The tabernacle of God is with men" (Rev. 21:3, KJV).

The Cradle and the Cross: Changeless Responses
(Matthew 2:1-12)

Reactions to Jesus Christ have timelessly remained the same in every epoch of man's response to the good news. The faces we see around the cradle are also the faces we see around the cross. Nowhere may the sameness of man's reaction to the Christ be more dramatically seen than in contrasting His first week and His last week, His cradle and His cross.

The cradle and the cross represent the two points of His greatest weakness, His manifest impotence. From the cradle He grew in the strength and His Divine manhood until the moment He surrendered it on the cross, and once again became as weak as the One in the cradle. Yet, nowhere in His ministry did He more surely shake the world than in those two moments of His greatest manifest weakness. For it was in those two moments of His apparent weakness that kings were shaken, the holy city was shaken, the heavens were shaken, and God Himself intervened. How may we compare these two divine moments?

Witness the Timelessness of
Human Reaction to the Christ

Around His cradle, Herod and all Jerusalem with Him were troubled (v. 3). What a paradox that a raging tyrant shakes at an impotent infant! Yet at the last, another Herod and all Jerusalem were also shaken by the crucified Christ. What a paradox that a Man nailed to a tree and bleeding away His life should terrify a city and trouble its rulers. "Because the foolishness of God is wiser than men; and the weakness of God is stronger than men" (1 Cor. 1:25, KJV).

In the cradle of Christ and at the cross of Christ, there is the same sequence: revelation, proclamation, and twofold reaction (acceptance and homage, or rejection and persecution). God reveals Himself in a cross, angels proclaim a resurrection, fisherfolk believe while kings and priests reject. Those who are nigh were really far off. Those who were far off were really nigh. The paradox of God, the great reversal of God, the unfathomable wisdom of God. See it in the cradle! See it in the cross! "God chose the foolish things of the world that he might put to shame them that are wise; and God chose the weak things of the world that he might put to shame the things that are strong" (v. 27, ASV).

Wonder at the Cosmic Disruption
Because of the Christ

Reaction to the Christ in His cradle and on His cross was not limited to the human sphere. Both events were marked by two profound cosmic disruptions. In each case, there was a disruption on the earth and a disjunction in the heavens. At His conception, there occurred the mysterious moving of the Holy Spirit over the womb of Mary. A quite physical miracle. At His crucifixion, there was a quaking of the earth (Matt. 27:51-54). A notably demonstrable physical miracle. At His birth, there occurred a singular phenomenon in the sky, a new light. At His crucifixion, there occurred a striking disjunction of the heavens—darkness in the midst of the day. He lives and there is light; He died and there is darkness. Among the first to come to Him were Gentile Magi drawn by the light of the star. Among the first to respond to the cross was the Gentile centurion drawn by the shaking of the earth. How sovereign God is! When His own people will not respond, He can shake the earth or move the stars to draw men to Christ.

Why this cosmic upheaval at His birth and at His cross? Because those two moments will have ultimate implications for the farthest reaches of the universe. "The creation itself also shall be delivered from the bondage of corruption into the liberty of the glory of the children of God" (Rom. 8:21, ASV). Shakings of the earth and changes in the heavens were only premonitions of that time when all the universe will be changed at His appearing.

Witness to the Divine Intervention
for the Christ

In the crucifixion, Jesus dies but is brought back to life through the resurrection. In the cradle, Jesus is taking away to another land but returns. In each instance, God has confounded the kings and the rulers who assembled against Him and His Messiah (Ps. 2:2). God will yet intervene once more for the Christ. Then it will be the cradle, the cross, and the crown!

Standing with Us
(Matthew 3:13-17)

The public ministry of Jesus began with His immersion in the Jordan by John the Baptist. No meeting between two men ever did more to change history. In His baptism, Christ stands with us in our need, but He stands above us in His uniqueness.

In His Baptism, Christ Stands with Us in Our Need

The baptism of John the Baptist was one of repentance because of sin. As such, it was a baptism that Jesus did not need. Why did He submit Himself to an act designated for sinners?

Jesus voluntarily chose to stand in solidarity with sinners. He identified Himself with the people He came to save. His baptism was an act of loving communion with us in our misery. The Sinless One chose to put Himself alongside the sinful ones.

Jesus still stands with us in our need. His example ought to motivate us to stand with other sinners in their need.

In His Baptism, Christ Stands for Us as Our Substitute

The exchange between Jesus and John (vv. 14-15) clearly states the sinlessness of Jesus. John stated his own unworthiness in the face of Jesus' character. Jesus did not disagree with John. Jesus never demonstrated a sense of personal sin.

As the Sinless One, Jesus stood in the waters of baptism for us. He clearly connected His baptism with His death on the cross: "I have a baptism to be baptized with; and how I am straitened till it be accomplished!" (Luke 12:50, KJV). When He emerged out of the water, it was a prophecy of the resurrection. He went into the water for us, just as He died for us.

In His Baptism, Christ Stands Above Us as Son of God

Three dramatic events immediately following the baptism of Jesus place Him above the human race as the Son of God. No other baptism ever witnessed these events.

Jesus' baptism opens the heavens. Instead of being a wall, heaven becomes an open door between God and man.

Jesus' baptism reveals the Holy Spirit. The Spirit of creation (Gen. 1:2) abides on Jesus as He recreates humanity.

Jesus' baptism resumes the voice of God. God speaks again after centuries of silence. He tells us that the baptism of Jesus is a coronation of a King and the ordination of a Suffering Servant. All of us should echo that voice.

Tested in the Wilderness
(Matthew 4:1-11)

In the wilderness, Jesus took the conflict into the enemy camp. Jesus' friends considered the wilderness the very turf of evil itself. Whereas Adam fell to temptation in a perfect place, Jesus overcame temptation in a horrible place. In His victory there are two levels of truth: unique and universal. Because Jesus was Son of God and Savior, the temptations are unique. Because He is Perfect Man, they are universal. In Christ, we win over every level of temptation.

In Christ, We Win Over Temptation of the Shortcut

A shortcut, a sidetrack, from the way of the Suffering Servant belongs to the unique- · ness of the first temptation. If Jesus could turn stones to bread, He could feed the mob and be hailed as Messiah.

The temptation to take the convenient shortcut is universal. Satan always suggests that a legitimate craving be satisfied in an illegitimate way. He always whispers that the privilege of a Son is that of selfish gratification rather than responsible living.

In Christ, We Win Over the Temptation of the Spectacular

The uniqueness of the second temptation rests in the appeal to dazzle, to sweep off the feet with the unusual. If Jesus could miraculously float into the temple court, He could be hailed as the Messiah at the beginning of His ministry. He could avoid rejection, betrayal, and Calvary.

The universality of this temptation is the desire to take fast track of the spectacular rather than the long march of daily trust.

In Christ, We Win Over the Temptation of Power

The uniqueness of the third temptation rested in its bald-faced appeal for Christ to join the powers of the age. Rome owned all power: money, politics, culture, connections. Why try to conquer the world with a gaggle of Galilean peasants? It was the temptation to go along in order to get along.

The universality of this temptation belongs to our obsession with power. Religious people are not immune. The way of the clenched fist always seems simpler and quicker than the long march of the faithful servant.

The Only Reliable Deposit Insurance
(Matthew 6:19-21)

Jesus did not oppose your having a treasure. Indeed, He recognized that you must have a treasure. He does give direction about the only secure place to deposit your treasure. Only treasures deposited in heaven are ultimately secure. You choose to deposit your treasure where it will certainly perish or where it will definitely endure. By "treasure" Jesus did not mean a great hoard of wealth. In His world a "treasure" was a margin, anything left over beyond subsistence.

The Sermon on the Mount gives the character of those who are entering Christ's kingdom. Those who enter His kingdom place their treasure in His kingdom's work.

You Can Never Have a Secure Treasure on Earth

Our Lord begins with a prohibition. "Do not store up for yourselves treasures on earth" (v. 19). He discourages an attitude He already detected. Jesus is not against treasures. He does prohibit His people from storing up on earth treasures that are only for themselves.

He further gives an explanation. As Son of God and Lord of the church He does not have to explain His commands, but He also knows our natural covetousness, and He gives the reason. Every earthly treasure is transient. In that primitive, simple society there were no banks, safes, or police. Treasure was kept at home in the form of garments, foodstuff, and precious metals. Each of these had its own enemy. Some of these enemies were impersonal. Moths ate garments that were heirlooms. Blight could consume stored foodstuffs. Corrosion could cause precious metal to vanish. Other enemies were personal. Thieves could dig through the mud walls of their homes and steal their treasures. Although the treasures in Jesus' day were different, the truth remains the same. No treasure on earth is safe.

These words call for a qualification. Jesus does not prohibit our saving or planning in a prudent way. God gives the power to give wealth (Deut. 8:18). Abraham, Job, and David were obviously wealthy men. God expects us to save (Prov. 21:20). He even directs us to the ant who knows how to set aside for the future (6:6-8). Parents should provide for their children (2 Cor. 12:14). What Jesus forbids in this passage is giving primary intensity and centrality to treasures on earth. He excludes that excessive, insatiable desire to have more than enough. He calls on us to govern our treasure, not be governed by our treasure. Elsewhere He said, "Labour not for the meat which perisheth" (John 6:27, KJV).

You Can Have a Treasure in Heaven

Jesus points to a reality. You can have a treasure in heaven. His command is to start now investing in a heavenly treasure. How can you have a treasure in heaven? You cannot launch your money into space or have an armored car deliver it to the pearly gates today! You deposit your treasure in heaven by the right use of your possessions on earth. You can invest in this age in such a way that you meet the investment in the age to come. You deposit treasure in heaven when you support those who are in need (Luke 12:33-34). Even the cup of water given in Jesus' name builds heavenly treasure (Matt. 10:42). The way you use earthly treasure actually creates a firmer foundation for the life beyond this life (1 Tim. 6:18-19). In fact, you can so use your money in this world that when you reach the next world those who benefitted by your money will be there to greet you (Luke 16:9). That is, you deposit your treasure in heaven by placing it into the lives of those who are going there.

Our Lord gives a reason for investment in heavenly treasure. It alone is a secure treasure. None of the impersonal or personal enemies that threaten earthly treasures can threaten heavenly treasure. In heaven the market never varies and the value of the dollar never changes. Only the things you invest in God's work will meet you in heaven. You will meet your personal giving record in the presence of God.

Your Heart Follows Your Treasure

No one had the insight that Jesus had into the human heart. The ultimate reason for putting your treasure in God's work has to do with the location of your heart. "For where your treasure is, there your heart will be also," (v. 21). Jesus assumes that everyone has a treasure. He also knows that your heart will be where your treasure is. Just as a sunflower follows the sun or a compass needle follows a magnet, your heart will follow your treasure.

The biblical "heart" represents the very center of your personality—intellectually, emotionally, and your will. Our heart goes where our money goes. When you invest all your money in the things of this world, your heart will be captured by this world. When you put your money in the work of God, your heart will be captured by the things of God. Would you like to have your heart in the work of our church? Put your treasure here and your heart will be here. Those care most who invest most in the work of God through His church.

One out of six verses in the Gospels deals with your relationship to money. You handle money more than any other commodity of life. When you face God you will give account for your stewardship of money. Be sure you have a safe deposit.

Winning Over Worry
(Matthew 6:25-34)

Have you ever kept a worry log? It would be interesting to note for seven days everything about which you worry. One thing would quickly appear. Most human worries center around what we will eat, or drink, or put on. Jesus does not intend that His people be overcome with such worries.

You can stop worrying about life's lower anxieties when you give yourself to life's greatest concern, the kingdom of God.

I. Stop Worrying About the Secular Trinity (6:25-32)

What you eat, drink, or put on.

A. Heed the command—do not be distracted about the basics of life.

B. Analyze the argument—God's greater gifts always include the lesser.

Look at the birds—worry is unnecessary.

Look at yourself—worry is unavailing.

Look at the flowers—worry is unbecoming.

II. Stop Worrying About Future Uncertainty (6:34)

You can master the demons of worry if you confine them to today.

When is what you worry about going to happen? Almost always tomorrow.

This philosophy of life worked for Jesus. Humanly speaking, He had more about which to worry than anyone in history, yet He walked without worry.

III. Stop Worrying by Substituting the Great Concern Above All Others (6:33)

This is a command, not an option.

This is a continual way of life for the Christian, a habit.

The substitution of greater concern excludes the lesser concerns.

Before You Judge
(Matthew 7:1-6)

Jesus calls for the highest moral standard imaginable in His sermon. How shall we react to those who do not meet that standard? The natural tendency is to act with criticism. The disciples' mandate is to refrain from judgment until I have first judged myself. Before you judge, there are words you should remember.

Remember the Prohibition Against Judgment

We must know the *definition* of the judgment Christ prohibits. He does not prohibit the judicial process of the courts. That the Christian is to respect (Rom. 13). Neither does He prohibit the discerning use of our moral capacities. We must react to the impure, the immoral, and the unjust. He Himself did so. What He does prohibit is the censorious, harsh, self-congratulatory seeking of faults in others. He condemns the attitude that is judgmental. The character of His followers is not to be marked by a judgmental spirit. He Himself did not judge when He might have done so (John 8). He did not judge you when He might have done so.

We must know the *motivation* that keeps us from judging. As we judge, so shall we be judged. That is true on the human level. Haman is always hung on his own gallows. If you usurp the prerogative of God, your fellows will expect you to be as consistent as God. But Jesus' reference is primarily to God's judgment. At the final court, our own judgment will be conditioned by our attitude toward others. If we have been generous, we will find generosity. If we have been harshly critical, we shall find scrupulous examination by Him who knows how to do it best. His Beatitude reminds us that if we are merciful, we shall receive mercy. His prayer reminds us that we will be forgiven only as we forgive. You will meet what you have been at the judgment.

Remember the Admonition for Judgment

Jesus does not tell us to exercise no judgment. He does remind us that *examination of self is always prior*. The humorous exaggeration between a speck of dust and a plank of wood contrasts those who judge the trivial in others while neglecting the tremendous in their own lives. Jesus labels this as hypocrisy. The fault is not in our inability to see ourselves, but our unwillingness to see ourselves.

Confrontation with a brother then becomes possible. First judge yourselves; then confront your brother. I am my brother's keeper. Nowhere did Jesus say to leave sin neglected in the life of a brother. Just as a splinter in the eye can be irritating and dangerous, sin in the life of my brother can be spiritually blinding to him. When I have *first* dealt with sin in my own life, I am to turn to him in a spirit of grace and help (Gal. 6). We are not to accuse our brother, but neither are we to excuse our brother.

Remember the Concession About Judgment

Moral discrimination is necessary. Saints are not simpletons. To refrain from a judgmental spirit is not to refrain from moral discriminations. The prohibition against judgment is not an excuse for moral laziness.

Christ reminds you of your *possession*. You possess a treasure. He calls it "that which is holy, . . . pearls" (v. 6, KJV). Your experience of God's kingdom and grace is nothing less than a priceless treasure.

Christ reminds you of your *caution*. The world may not respect your treasure. No wise man parades his most treasured possessions indiscriminately before all men. Some men live on the moral level of dogs and swine. To the Jews, those brute beasts represented all that was unclean and loathed. The wild scavenger dogs cannot even appreciate the food you throw them. Swine would think that pearls were peas. They would trample your treasure and then turn on you! There is a time to refrain from speaking of holy things. You are to judge when that time is at hand. There is even a time to shake the dust off your feet and go on (Acts 13). The message is as simple as it is necessary: judge yourself, restore your brother, and respect your treasure.

Good News/Bad News: Mission America
(Matthew 9:35-38)

The Lord Jesus desires to pass through America. He sees our nation as we are—harrassed like a hunted animal and helpless with exhaustion. He gazes at the potential for abundant spiritual response, yet He assesses the paucity of spiritual workers. He feels for America a compassion that moves Him inwardly to the core. His solution—out of the deepest desire we are to plead God the Proprietor of the harvest to thrust out workers into America.

The Lord Jesus Passes Through America

The good news is that Jesus always desires to go throughout the land. This was His habit then in Galilee (4:23; 9:35) and today in America. He desires to go through America teaching where God's people gather, heralding the reign of God, and making people whole.

The bad news is that there are 22,000 sites for new churches/missions which will not have them unless we pray and provide.

The Lord Jesus Feels for America

The good news is that the Lord Jesus sees our nation as we really are, and He feels our national pain.

The bad news is that we are a harrassed people, driven, hunted sheep vexed and torn.

We are an exhausted people and the pursuits of our life have dropped us in our tracks and scattered us.

The Lord Jesus Prays for America

The good news is that the harvest is abundant in America. There is an abundance of human life right now responsive to the Lord of the harvest. The Lord of the harvest will send out workers in response to our genuine request.

The bad news is that the workers are few. What avails the abundant harvest if we lack laborers?

Christ Calls Us to Rest
(Matthew 11:28-30)

The Lord Jesus is the inexhaustible Person. Only He can stand before all times and places with an offer to give everyone who comes to Him rest. We can hardly sustain ourselves and those who need us. For us the weariness of sustaining one other in deep need depletes. Unlike us, Jesus offers a river of rest that runs ever afresh from its high-land sources. His offer never diminishes or abates. The more He gives rest the more He seems to have to give.

Jesus offers us the initial rest of salvation. We can never rest until we know for certain that guilt and alienation from God have been removed. But beyond that, Jesus gives us the rest we find in discipleship. There is a deeper rest beyond the initial rest. That is the rest of wearing His yoke. Jesus offers initial and continual rest to all who come to Him.

Jesus Offers Rest in Salvation

Every religious movement and each spiritual leader offers rest. Even philosophical schools claim to give satisfaction from the tensions of life. Towering over them all, Jesus promises rest to everyone weary of the struggle for meaningful existence.

Jesus offers His rest in a great *invitation*: "Come to me. . . ." His word is both a command that pushes us and an invitation that draws us. This is an invitation from Jesus' sovereignty. Only Jesus has the royal authority to command us to approach Him. Consider how absurd these words would sound from anyone else. His words ring with an urgency. It could be translated "Hither to me, now." Life traps us in a bog of sloth. Unless Christ crisply calls us up and out, we sink. Our Lord's invitation is to a personality, not just a theology. He does not call us to an institution, organization, ceremony, or ritual. He calls us to Himself. Two verses reverberate with the personal pronouns *me, I, my*. Rest comes only from the person of Christ.

Jesus offers rest specifically to *those invited*, those who are actively toiling and those passively loaded down in life. Besides those who live on the merely animal level, most experience the toil and weight of life. In our toil we seek fulfillment in human work. But work becomes labor and labor becomes toil. Beyond our jobs, there is a lacerating toil to find meaning in human existence. On top of this, we passively bear the loads of life. The loads include the religious expectations placed on us by others. Religion can place burden on our relief (Matt. 23:4), while others command from you what they themselves cannot perform (Acts 15:10). Jesus invites those who are exhausted in the rat race of religion and bent over with the dead weight of impossible expectations.

Jesus' *intention* is indeed spiritual rest. The source of this rest is personal, "I [myself] will give you rest" (v. 28). Spiritual rest does not come from reflection, ritual, or religious activity. Rest comes from the Person of Jesus Christ. In that regard His rest is contrasted with the promises of others. Unlike the Pharisees, He can give the power to be and to do what He requires. Christians experience rest-in-relationship.

The significance of His rest is that of pause, recovery, refreshment. Christ gives rest from guilt, disfavor with God, and bondage to our own lusts. His cross rests us from guilt. His righteousness attributed to us rests us from disfavor with God. His life in us releases us from bondage to desire.

Jesus Offers Rest in Submission

Beyond the initial rest of salvation, there is a deeper rest in submission. At the beginning of the Christian life we experience recovery. Under the continuing lordship of Christ, we enter into deep rest. We discover the paradox—Christ places a yoke on us that lifts us up.

We should face the *necessity* of a yoke. Absolute freedom is absolute illusion. To be "free" in such a way is to experience the bondage of self-absorption, live life on the level of mere self-satisfaction. That is a yoke that chafes and drags down. You will wear a yoke—your own, someone else's, or the yoke of Christ.

We may experience the *superiority* of Jesus' yoke. By Jesus' time, the word "yoke" was already a common term for discipline, obligation, instruction. To wear Jesus' yoke means to learn from Him, to become His disciple. This learning has to do with His Person, learning about Him from the Gospels and experiencing Him in the circumstances of daily life. Self-satisfaction and self-delusion harness us with a yoke that exhausts. Jesus places on us a yoke that lifts us up. It is like harnessing yourself in a hang glider—a moment of weight and then the strange unseen uplift.

There is a simplicity in Jesus' yoke. That simplicity is one of method and manner. He is gentle and mild. Compared to the unapproachable, hard, and haughty teachers that sometimes represented God, Jesus receives us with meekness. He is not proud, impulsive, ambitious, or desiring dominion over the minds of people. This is not merely true of the external demeanor of Jesus, but pierces to His very heart. Some may assume an attitude of humility. He is the very essence of it.

The significance of the rest resides in its quality. His easy yoke and light burden gives rest to the soul. The cry of the Old Testament was, "Ask where the good way is, and, . . . you will find rest for your souls" (Jer. 6:16). This great invitation to rest preceded the cross. Jesus does not tell us how He will provide the rest. We see that in His death, resurrection, and presence (Rom. 5:1; 8:1). It is enough that He promises. When we know the who, we need not wonder about the how.

Present Imitation—Future Separation
(Matthew 13:24-30,36-43)

Everyone knows that the church contains the real thing and imitation, genuine Christians and those who are not. How did this happen? What should be our reaction?

Jesus knew there would be mixed conditions in His church. They already existed during His ministry. Christians cannot separate the imitation from the genuine in this age, but God will make that separation in the age to come.

The Reign of God in His Church Includes
Both Authentic and Imitation Christianity

The Son of man (Jesus) sows only genuine Christians in His church. The field belongs to the Lord. The seed that He sows is excellent. He cannot be blamed for the mixed conditions in His church.

The Enemy (the Evil One) sows imitations in the church. He does this secretly. He also does it harmfully. The tares or darnel weed are not only useless but also poisonous. The Enemy does this intimately. The tares are sown through and through the wheat.

The difference becomes apparent at the time of expected maturity. Tares and wheat cannot now be distinguished at first. But when the grain ripens, the difference becomes apparent.

The Reign of God Prohibits a Separation Now

The servants of the Lord often want to make that separation now. This is a natural reaction of those devoted to the Lord and His church.

The Lord explains why the separation cannot be made now. The imitation cannot be removed without also harming the authentic, genuine Christian (v. 29). The Lord did not say that you cannot tell the difference. The Lord did say that you cannot now make the separation.

This does not prohibit church discipline. The pastor and leaders of the church should do all in their power to maintain a pure church. Nevertheless, with every effort made, we can never in this age totally purify the church. The Enemy works secretly, and you cannot tell the difference at first.

The Reign of God Ensures a Separation Later

That separation will be made at the end of this age. Only at the end of the present church age will the separation between the imitation and the authentic Christian be made.

The administration of that separation will be by those qualified to make it. "The angels" have always been God's administrators of judgment. They rejoice at the beginning of every Christian life (Luke 15:7) and eagerly watch the things of salvation (1 Pet. 1:12). They are qualified to make that ultimate separation.

The destination of that separation will be appropriate. There will be a destination of judgment for imitation Christians. The words speak of punishment and regret. There will be a destination of glory for authentic believers. That destination will include a protection and an illumination. "The righteous will shine like the sun" (v. 43). This suggests that they may have been overlooked in this age, but in the age to come they will appear brilliant in their genuineness.

Treasure Hunt—Finders and Seekers
(Matthew 13:44-46)

Most enjoy a treasure hunt. Some are surprised by treasure, while others actively seek it. Jesus compared the rule of God in personal life to finding treasure. Some are surprised by finding the rule of God in their life. Others seek the highest good in life and find the rule of God. Whether you are a surprised finder or a serious seeker, you must risk everything for a unique opportunity of knowing God's rule in your life.

Each of Jesus' parables presents a past picture and tells a timeless truth. Look at the picture and learn the truth.

Some Find God's Rule in Life as an Unexpected Treasure

The parable presents a past picture. A poor day laborer plows the field of another man. Suddenly, he finds a treasure trove. Though rare today, such finds were very common in biblical lands. Invasions, revolutions, and natural calamities caused people to bury wealth. There were no banks. When the owner perished, no one knew where the treasure was buried. The common laborer took legitimate, legal steps to secure the field. He sold everything he had to buy the field. This was a good investment, for he only paid for the field, and got the treasure as an extra grace. His motivation was one of joy, transported by wealth beyond dreams.

The parable tells a timeless truth. Many find the rule of God in their life without seeking it. They are surprised by joy. The woman of Samaria suddenly finding living water (John 4) or the jailer of Philippi suddenly finding real security (Acts 16) represent the type.

To most, the kingdom of God is a hidden reality. Like a dull day laborer, they plow through life not expecting more than eating, sleeping, working, and dying. Some suddenly strike the treasure!

The discovery calls for total investment motivated by joy. Impelled by sheer joy, we gladly invest everything to know the rule of God in life. It is an investment joyfully made, with no sense of sacrifice (Phil. 3:8ff.).

Others Seek the Highest Good in Life and Find God's Rule

The parable presents a past picture. The merchant is a traveling wholesaler looking for precious pearls. Whereas there were many day laborers plowing fields, this man represents a relative rarity. He went to the Indian Ocean seeking pearls from the pearl fishers. Suddenly, he found the pearl of all pearls. At once he took advantage of this unique opportunity. He went quickly and immediately sold everything he had. That is, he not only traded his entire stock of other pearls, but divested himself of all else. He was not a collector but a dealer. He knew that this was a good investment. The day laborer was surprised by a treasure. The pearl merchant was successful after a long search.

The parable tells a timeless truth. Many search for the highest good in life—meaning, purpose, reality. After a long, such search, they finally find it in Christ. Apollos was such a man (Acts 19). When that moment comes, there must be the immediate risk of total investment to grasp the unique opportunity. Sadly, many would rather clutch paste pearls.

Both Finders and Seekers Must Risk
the Unique Opportunity

The similarity between the finder and the seeker outweighs the difference. When each discovers the power of Christ and His presence, it is a moment to risk everything for a once-in-a-lifetime opportunity. This was central to Jesus' teaching. It is exactly the opposite of those excuses at the parable of the banquet (Matt. 22:5). So urgent is His call that we are to cut off hands (5:29), let the dead bury their dead (8:2), leave parents (10:37) and follow Him. This is no lame, same, tame Savior calling us to a modernized, trivialized religion. This is the treasure hunt. Risk now!

The Bridge Over Troubled Waters
(Matthew 14:22-33)

After Jesus fed the 5,000, the mob wanted to take Him by force and make Him king (John 6:15). This was a real temptation for Jesus and the twelve to avoid the cross and seize the crown. Masterfully and urgently, Jesus forced the disciples to leave, and He, Himself, dispersed the militant mob. "He went up to a mountain apart to pray . . . he was there alone" (v. 23, KJV). Even Jesus had to have isolation and solitude to avoid temptation and know God's will.

While the Lord was hidden from view on the mountain above, His disciples struggled with difficulty on the sea below. Then, and now, Christ discloses Himself to us in our difficulty, and shares with us His dominion over difficulty.

Our Difficulty Provides Christ's Opportunity

Obedience to Christ often creates difficulty. "Jesus made the disciples get into the boat and go on ahead of him" (v. 22). At His insistence, they obeyed, embarking across the sea. Their very obedience to Christ placed them in difficulty. Faithfulness brings no immunity from difficulty. It almost ensures it. To follow Christ in this age guarantees storms. This storm at sea was preparatory. Peter and the others would spend a lifetime in storms because of obedience to Him.

In difficulty we lose sight of Him, but He never loses sight of us. When we cannot see Him, He always sees us. Christ was hidden on the mountain above, while His disciples faced difficulty below. He prayed on firm ground, while they sailed on uncertain waters. Truly, He had stilled a storm already, before their very eyes (8:23-27). But that was in the day, and He was in the boat. Now, it was night, and He was absent. This, too, was preparatory. Christ would ascend on high to the right hand of the Father. We no longer see Him visibly. In difficulty He sees us and comes to us.

Divine delays in difficulty are always purposeful (v. 25). The disciples struggled to exhaustion all night, but Christ did not come until the fourth watch (3:00-6:00 a.m.). He waited until they understood the full force of the storm and the futility of their un-aided effort. Then He intervened. In your life He is waiting until you and everyone around knows that only He can act in a delivering way.

Christ's Divinity Discloses Itself in Our Difficulty

Christ discloses His divinity decisively in our difficulty. Do you wish to know the Deity of Christ as the real fact in personal experience? You meet it in your difficulty. Christ walking on the waters of difficulty reveals His divinity. In the Old Testament record only God could tame the sea. God walks on the sea as an opposing power or a defeated enemy where no one else is able to walk (Job 9:8). The psalmist confesses, "Through the sea was your way, and your path through many waters" (77:19). At the end of the storm, the disciples worshiped Jesus and confessed, "Truly you are the Son of God" (v. 33).

We may not recognize Christ's help when it comes (v. 27). The disciples thought they had seen a phantasm or an apparition, the unreal presence of a living or dead person. Further, "He would have passed them by" if they had not called on Him (Mark 6:48, KJV). If it were not for His grace, we would not even recognize Him in our difficulty.

Christ always reveals Himself to us personally in difficulty (v. 27). They recognized both His voice and its content. He gives us a word of affirmation: "Take courage!" He gives us a word of identification: "It is I." He gives us a word of prohibition: "Don't be afraid." When you listen, you know He is there in troubled waters.

Our Difficulty Provides Our Opportunity

Christ calls us to share His dominion over difficulty. When Peter wanted to share Christ's power over troubled water, Christ gladly said, "Come" (v. 29). Our Lord invites us to share in His victory over everything that vexes us.

We do share Christ's victory over difficulty unless faith fails. What Christ commands, He enables. Peter walked on the water toward Jesus. Yet, faith failed at the very finish. He was almost touching Jesus when faith failed. While doing the greater thing (walking on water) he was unnerved by the little thing (the blowing wind).

When faith fails in difficulty, Christ furnishes new faith. "Immediately Jesus reached out His hand and caught him" (v. 31). The touch of Christ recreates, restores, and renews failing faith. Christ has brought you this far above troubled waters to abandon you. When faith fails on troubled waters, He always furnishes new faith. He did that more than once for Peter. He always does that for us.

The Great Confession *
(Matthew 16:13-20)

Sometimes the apparent insignificance of a place contradicts the significance of what happened there. Such is the case with Caesarea Philippi. That remote site on the other side of the globe witnessed the Great Confession concerning Jesus Christ. There Simon Peter testified, "You are the Christ, the Son of the Living God" (v. 16). This confession was not made at Rome because it does not need man's political endorsement for its power. It was not made at Athens because it does not need man's academic certification to be true. It was not made at Jerusalem because it does not need the stamp of established religion. Only God can reveal to the individual the truth of the Great Confession.

The Question Posed

Jesus begins with a request for the *popular opinion* concerning Him. That question may have been either educational or informational in its nature. He asked the question in terms of His favorite self-designation, "Son of Man." "Who do people say the Son of Man is?" (v. 13). That title minimized who He was rather than advertised who He was. You find "a son of man" in Daniel 7:13, a figure of humiliation who is exalted into God's presence. The question of Jesus' identity touches today with a new force. More has been written about Jesus in the last twenty years than the previous two thousand.

Popular opinion about Jesus changes little. Some base their belief on *superstition*— "John the Baptist." Herod thought Jesus was a resurrection or reincarnation of the Baptist (Matt. 14:1). Some deal with Jesus by categorizing Him with others rather than recognizing Him as unique. Some base their answer on *misinterpretation*—"Elijah." The last words of the Old Testament indicated that Elijah would return before the Day of the Lord. Some quickly applied those words to Jesus, even though He Himself applied them to John the Baptist (Matt. 11:14). Others based their opinion on mere human *observation*—"Jeremiah or one of the prophets." They saw in Jesus some of the characteristics of other great Jewish preachers. In each instance the people stopped short of the full confession and surrender to Jesus Christ.

Jesus continued with a request for the disciples' *personal confession*. Jesus is not concerned with popular opinion. He is concerned with the adequacy of His church's confession. Is it accurate, authentic, biblical?

The Affirmation Given

The Great Confession represents a *culmination* of other confessions. Preliminary confessions had been made earlier in Jesus' ministry. The first days that His followers spent with Him they confessed that He was the Messiah, King of Israel, and Son of God (John 1:41,45,49). What then made the great confession *great?* It was great because it was born out of the personal experience and observation of the disciples. Our greatest confession about Christ ought always to be our latest confession about Christ. We ought to know more the longer we walk with Him.

The Great Confession represents a new *comprehension* about Christ. He is not only the Jewish Messiah, but He is the universal Son of God. The Jews expected a human Messiah. There was no expectation that the Messiah would be God-man, very God, invested with the Godhead Himself. This was the flash of revelation that moved Peter beyond anything before confessed—He is the Son of the living God.

Peter made that confession at a location which recognized other gods. Near that site were the worship of nature gods and human gods. In the face of all other gods, Peter confessed Christ as the Son of the living God.

The Foundation Acknowledged

On the bedrock of the confession of Christ's Godhead, Jesus Christ builds His church. The erection of the church begins with Peter's confession of the messiahship and Deity of Jesus Christ. The first layer of that foundation is the apostles and prophets (Eph. 2:20). Jesus builds His church on the bedrock of their confession.

Since that time He continues to build His church out of living stones (1 Pet. 2:4-5). Every believer coming into contact with the great Foundation Stone comes to life as a living stone, part of the universal church that God is building through the ages. When the last living stone has been added, He who is the Foundation Stone and the Cornerstone will become the Capstone.

We must turn the Great Confession into our confession. It must move from the second person—"You are the Christ"—to the third person—"He is the Christ." On Sunday we confess to Jesus our belief, "You are the Christ." But every other day we must confess to the world outside, "He is Christ." *Two slightly different sermons on Matthew 16:13-20.

The Great Confession
(Matthew 16:13-20)

The Christian believes one great something about the Person of Jesus Christ—He is the promised Messiah and the divine Son of God. That great confession was first made by Simon Peter in a remote area of the northern Holy Land. Caesarea Philippi was marked by the worship of nature gods and human beings. In this setting six months before the cross Peter confessed that Jesus Christ is the Son of the living God. Every genuine Christian must make this confession. The church is built on the substance of this profession—the Godhead of Jesus Christ.

The Great Confession Begins with
the Rejection of Inadequate Views

Jesus asked the great question, "Who do people say the Son of Man is?" The title "Son of Man" was Jesus' favorite self-designation. It roots in the vision of Daniel 7:13 where a divine man comes with the clouds of heaven into the presence of the Ancient of Days. God gives to that divine man authority, glory, and sovereign power. Jesus wanted to know if His generation understood Him in that light. This question may have been educational, to lead the disciples to a deeper knowledge of Him. Or the question may have been informational, He was really seeking to know from them what others were saying.

Their response indicates the inadequate views of any generation concerning the person of Jesus Christ. Some responded on the level of superstition, "Some say John the Baptist." Herod himself feared that John had risen from the dead (Matt. 14:1). These views were on the level of mere superstition. Others saw a reduplication of what God had done before. Elijah was supposed to return before the end (Mal. 4:5-6). Some Jewish traditions stated that Jeremiah would return before the end. Others in Jesus' generation were less sure than that. They saw in Him only "one of the prophets."

In each instance they tried to account for Jesus Christ by previous categories of what God had done. The lesson of the great confession is that He is truly incomparable.

The Great Confession Continues with
the Affirmation of an Accurate View

Jesus sharply sets the popular view of Himself over against the view of the disciples: "You yourselves, in contrast to the others, who are you saying I am?"

When the disciples initially met Jesus they had a preliminary confession of faith based on immediate impact. Andrew had said, "We have found the Messiah." Nathaniel had confessed that Jesus was "the Son of God, the King of Israel" (John 1:41,49). Now after two years of watching His words and works what will their confession be?

Peter speaks for the group or with the assent of the group: "You are the Christ, the Son of the living God" (v. 16). This confession identifies Christ as the expected Jewish Messiah. But it goes beyond that expectation. Peter confesses the divinity of Jesus Christ. It was Jesus' claim to divinity that aroused the popular fury (John 8:58-59), and led to the final confrontation with the religious establishment (Matt. 26:64-65).

These words are followed by the only instance in which Jesus ever called an individual "Blessed." This joyful congratulation to Peter has definite grounds. No mere human insight enabled Peter to see in Jesus of Nazareth the Son of God. It was a direct, divine revelation. It always is.

The Great Confession Provides
the Foundation for the Church

This confession determines the nature of the church. Jesus came not only to teach a doctrine but to found a society, an organism, the church. That church would be the congregation of the faithful throughout the world under Christ as the Head.

The foundation of the church is the confession of the Godhead of its Lord. In a historical sense the church is built on the foundation of the apostles and the prophets (Eph. 2:20). In an eternal sense it is built on Christ Himself (2 Cor. 3:11). But here the foundation of the church in the world is the confession that Jesus Christ is the Messiah, the Son of God.

The Builder of the church is Christ Himself. "I will build my church." Wherever the true church truly grows, it is the work of Christ Himself. That true fellowship will be invincible: "the gates of Hades will not overcome it" (v. 18). Nothing in the unseen world will ever undermine God's intention in His church.

Jesus at that time warned the disciples not to tell anyone that He was Christ (v. 20). That is not the case today. We are to go everywhere telling everyone that Jesus is the Christ. Our entire life is to be the Great Confession.

The Crisis of the Christ
(Matthew 16:13-20)

This time marks the crisis of the public ministry of the Christ. "From this time many of His disciples turned back and no longer followed him" (John 6:66). Six months before the cross, no class of people understood the message or mission of Jesus. Thus, Jesus took the twelve to Caesarea Philippi—a safe, pleasant, isolated area in the far north. He intended to see whether they understood and would commit to Him.

Short of the cross and resurrection, no other event in Jesus' ministry stands on equal ground with this episode. It reveals the insufficiency of all human speculation about Christ and the necessity of divine revelation to know Christ. God lays the foundation for His church in the divine revelation concerning Jesus Christ.

I. This Crisis Reveals the Insufficiency of Human Speculation About Jesus Christ (vv. 13-14)

The *critical question* of life concerns the Christ: "Who do people say the Son of Man is?" Jesus asked this question for information, affirmation, and education. He did not use His supernatural powers for information when natural inquiry would suffice. At that lonely moment, He sought the affirmation of His closest followers. He intended their education by contrasting the popular confession with the disciple's question.

The **inadequacy of speculation** characterizes the crowd. Then and now, the mass of people know only insufficient speculation about Jesus Christ. There are some earmarks of human speculation in the answers given by the first followers of Jesus.

Some see in Christ a mere **repetition** of what God has done before. Unaided human opinion cannot see a wholly, new departure in Jesus Christ. He was like John the Baptist in His mysterious birth and call for repentance. He was like Elijah in His confrontation with religious leaders. He was like Jeremiah in His personal grief over religious barrenness and hypocrisy. Because of that, people have seen in Jesus no more than another religious leader. Human speculation about Christ always places Him in an insufficient category.

Some see in Christ a **reduction** of what God has done before. For some, He was "one of the prophets" (v. 14). The language suggests a class of people who see in Christ no more than one in a long succession of religious spokespersons. In His own lifetime, people saw in Him only "Joseph's son." Some even identified Him with a demon. Mere human reflection on Christ never discovers who He is.

II. The Sufficiency of Divine Revelation About Jesus Christ (vv. 15-17)

There is only one acceptable identification of Jesus Christ: "You are the Christ, the Son of the living God" (v. 16). Peter identified Jesus of Nazareth with the promised, predicted, and expected, anointed Messiah of the Old Testament. But Peter went beyond that. He said something about the Messiah that no Old Testament Hebrew ever confessed or expected. Peter confessed the Godhead of the Messiah, the Deity of Jesus Christ. This is especially significant in light of the surroundings. The most ancient worship of nature gods and the most recent worship of Caesar surrounded the location of this confession.

There is only one **source for this revelation** about Jesus Christ. Humanity in its feebleness, weakness, fallibility, and fragility ("flesh and blood" v. 17, KJV) can never make this discovery or confession about Christ. There is nothing in human reason, education, tradition, or observation that would compel one to confess this about Jesus of Nazareth.

Every confession of Jesus Christ is an act of God invading and illuminating the mind of the confessor. God, Himself, lifts the veil and parts the curtain, or you cannot grasp or confess the God head of Jesus Christ. In that sense, you do not "decide to become a Christian." No one can come to me unless the Father who sent me draws him" (John 6:44).

III. The Permanency of the Foundation of Jesus Christ (vv. 18-19)

Those confessing the Godhead of Jesus Christ constitute the foundation of His church. The person and truth about Jesus Christ is the only adequate foundation for His church. The first layers of the foundation are the apostles and the prophets (Eph. 2:20). Luther: "All Christians are Peters on account of the confession Peter here makes, which is the rock on which Peter and all Peters are built."

Christ's relationship to His church is one of **construction**. "I will build my church." We do not build His true church. Men may build large, ecclesiastical organizations on the basis of human attraction, but only Jesus Christ builds His church.

Christ's relationship to His church is one of **possession:** "My church. . . ." The only owner of the local church or the whole assembly of all believers in the earth is Jesus Christ, not a pastor, board, or denomination.

Christ's relationship through His church is one of **confrontation:** "the gates of [hell] will not overcome it" (v. 18). The unseen world of death and the grave swallow every generation, but they will never swallow the church of a living Lord.

Transformation: His Reality—My Possibility
(Matthew 17:1-8)

Transformation is both the history of the Christ and the possibility for the believer. The transfiguration was a unique event of revelation concerning the nature of Jesus Christ. But the transfiguration is a prediction concerning the possibility of every Christian. What happened to Christ on that mountain can happen progressively and ultimately to every Christian. Let us look at the transfiguration from both perspectives. The transfiguration reveals the Deity of Jesus Christ and the ultimate possibility for every Christian.

In the Transfiguration the Deity of Christ
Shines Out Through His Humanity

Certain circumstances enable us to see more of Christ. Prepared observers in a prayerful place are most likely to see Christ most clearly. Jesus took the inner circle—Peter, James, and John. These three had seen Him most clearly, so they were chosen to see Him most fully. These three were called aside two other times. They saw Jesus superior to death (Mark 5:37-43) and saw Him yield to death (Matt. 26:37). Only those prepared by past intimacy will see more of Christ. Also, they were isolated and alone in a place of prayer and solitude (Luke 9:28). The fullest vision of Christ comes only to those who go with Him into the place of isolation, solitude, and prayer.

The content of the transfiguration itself gives a past revelation about Christ and the future possibility of the Christian. In the past revelation, Christ "was transfigured" (v. 2). The word distinctly refers to an inward change which radiates from the inside to the outside. It is a change not in the superficial, but in the essential. The change touched both His appearance and His apparel. Moses' face had reflected the glory of God (Ex. 34). Jesus' face radiated the glory of God. God gives us "the light of the knowledge of the glory of God in the face of Christ" (2 Cor. 4:6). In this, we see not only Jesus' Deity, but God's original intention for humanity.

The content of the transfiguration shows us our future possibility. Looking toward Jesus by faith, we "are being transformed into his likeness with ever-increasing glory, which comes from the Lord" (2 Cor. 3:18). Even in this life, we are to experience a transfiguration that radiates and reveals itself. Ultimately "the righteous will shine like the sun in the kingdom of their Father" (Matt. 13:43). Our destiny will be a radiant, luminous kingdom of light where we will "share in the inheritance of the saints in the kingdom of light" (Col. 1:12).

We would do well to ask where we are in the personal process of transfiguration. Every authentic Christian should show evidence of transforming change.

In the Transfiguration, the Necessity of the Cross
Appears to Humanity

Just as Jesus was transfigured, there appeared two titanic figures from the Old Testament, Moses and Elijah, representing the law and the prophets. What is their significance?

There is an affirmation of the cross. This is a heavenly "summit conference" concerning the cross. Luke states explicitly that "they spoke about His departure, which He was about to bring to fulfillment at Jerusalem" (9:31). For Jesus, it was a conversation of affirmation and encouragement. Moses and Elijah represent the saints of the ages urging Christ on to His final work.

There is an attempted interruption of the cross. Peter's petty parentheses (v. 4) would have kept them on the mountain in the glory of it all. Like all of us, Peter wanted nothing to do with the cross that awaited below. Yet down we must all go to see human sorrow and sin (v. 15), to witness distressing unbelief (v. 17), and to set out for the cross that awaits.

A present perversion of Christianity would keep us on the mountain in the glory without the valley and the cross. "Health and wealth" theology wants all mountaintop and no valley. No cross, no crown.

In the Transfiguration, the Finality of the Christ Appears to Humanity

The acts of God point to the finality of the Christ. A bright cloud revealing the presence of God enfolded them. It is the same bright cloud of the Old Testament which revealed the visible presence of the invisible God (Ex. 24:15-18; 40:35). Such a token most clearly indicated the divine pleasure with the moment. Out of the cloud came a voice. That voice insisted to the disciples, "Listen to him!" (v. 5). Listen to Him when He speaks of the cross, the way of suffering, the necessity of Calvary. Listen to Him more than to Moses and Elijah. Listen to Him and not to Peter. Listen to Him! That voice thunders down the ages to this very morning. "Listen to him!"

The acts of Christ reveal His own finality. "When they looked up, they saw no one except Jesus (v. 8). Moses and the law were gone; they had done their work. Elijah and the prophets were gone; they had done their work. There stands Jesus alone, above all, preeminent. May we also look up day by day and see Jesus only. When life is done and we walk through the fear of death, we then feel His touch and look up to see Jesus only!

A Wanting World – A Weakened Church
(Matthew 17:14-20)

What happens when the church cannot produce? A church can have words without works, promises without performance, a reputation for power without a demonstration of power. Matthew, Mark, and Luke each record a failure in faith immediately following the transfiguration of Jesus. While their Master was gloriously changed on Mount Hermon above, the disciples disastrously failed in the valley below. Representing an absentee Lord, they failed.

We too represent in our church an absentee Lord. The world brings its desperate needs to us and asks, "Can you help?" The church fails to help human hurts because faith fails.

Failures in Faith Embarrass the Cause of Christ

Hurting humanity expects the church to help. The father of an epileptic boy represents all who come to Christ's church desperate for help. The nine failing disciples remind us of the church which does not have the faith to make a difference.

The adversaries of Christ's church criticize failures in faith. Mark 9:14 notes the presence of cynical scribes who ridiculed the disciples before the mob because of their failure in faith. When our faith fails we give cause to the critics of Christ.

Disciples are embarrassed by failures in faith. In the face of critics and the watching crowd the nine disciples could not produce. By implication the failure of the disciples was the failure of their Master. We stand today embarrassed by the inability to make a dent in the hurts of helpless humanity.

The helpless remain unhelped when faith fails. There is hardly a sadder picture in the New Testament than this frantic father whose last hope for help was Jesus Christ. His only son was seized by evil and thrown into places of danger and threat. Our world is seized by life-destroying forces that only Christ can change. Christ Himself is doubted when our faith fails and we cannot heal the hurt.

The Fault for Failure in Faith Rests with the Disciples

A failure in faith is the fundamental failure in discipleship. When Christ cried out "O unbelieving and perverse generation" (v. 17), He did not exclude the disciples from that cry. Unbelief twists, warps, and contorts the world in which we live. The nine disciples had embodied the very perverse unbelief that characterized the world at large. Rather than change the unbelief of the world, they had joined the world in unbelief.

Failure in faith gives personal pain to Jesus Christ. His words reveal that the disciple's failure to connect with His power in simple trust pained Him as much as a personal insult. Christ was pained by the absence of trust more than all else.

Merely mechanical ministry results in failed faith. Christ had earlier commissioned the twelve to do the very thing they here failed to do (10:8). They could not simply go through the motions, repeat the ritual, and make any difference. Life-changing service must continually call down the resources of Christ if it makes any difference at all.

Restoration of Faith Requires a Recognition of Failure and a Request for Instruction

The disciples wisely approached Jesus in private to ask why their ministry failed. We would do well to take our failures in faith to Christ for His correction.

A minute faith can work a great miracle. The mustard seed grew from the smallest seed to the largest garden shrub. Evidently the faith of the disciples had grown small indeed if it was not even the size of a mustard seed! We fail not because of the strength of the opposition but because of the smallness of faith.

Small faith can move the immovable. "To move a mountain" was proverbial for overcoming great difficulty. Elsewhere Jesus stated that faith could uproot what appeared to be permanently rooted.

Who May Say, "I Am the Greatest"?
(Matthew 18:1-4; Mark 9:33-36)

Who is the greatest person in our church? You would probably nominate someone with ability, gifts, visibility, or strong personal appeal. Our Lord does not choose that way. For Him, the greatest person is "the very last, and the servant of all" (Mark 9:35).

Questions of precedence and rank were extremely important in both Jesus' world and are in ours. The disciples expected that He would begin a temporal kingdom with higher and lower officials. They wanted to be the greatest in that kind of kingdom.

Christ confronts and contradicts every human standard for greatness.

Disagreement About Greatness Disrupts Christ's Disciples

Disagreements about greatness can erupt when we compare the gifts and blessings of God. Some are blessed by God with circumstances others do not enjoy. The inner circle—Peter, James, John—had witnessed the transfiguration. Peter had been singled out repeatedly for recognition and blessing. The disciples probably argued about the exact order in which they first followed Jesus (John 1). When you focus on God's gifts to others rather than your own call to servanthood, you will disagree about greatness.

Christ quickly discerns such disagreements. Our pettiness is not hidden from Christ. Although Christ may have overheard their argument, Luke suggests that He knew their hearts supernaturally. Christ knows the smallness of our thoughts. When He revealed His knowledge to the twelve, they were abashed and silenced (Mark 9:34). Would we argue about who is the greatest among us if Christ actually sat in our midst?

Disagreements about greatness contradict the Christian call. This ugly eruption about rank and preeminence exploded after our Lord's announcement of His cross and the call for all disciples to carry a cross (Matt. 16:24). People on the way to execution seldom argue about human greatness. We are to live with that perspective.

Disagreements about greatness tend to endure. When you become obsessed with thoughts of your own greatness, you face a lifelong conflict. The argument about greatness among the twelve continued until the end (Matt. 20:20). Argument about greatness is a danger that can disrupt any fellowship.

Christ Confronts and Corrects Confusion About Greatness

Confusion about greatness calls for a radical reversal of values. Those who argue about greatness must "turn" (Matt. 18:3). We are headed in the wrong direction when debate about "first place" characterizes us. While the twelve argued about greatness in the kingdom, Jesus informed them that they could not even enter the kingdom until they humbled themselves. Willingness to consider myself little because I am indeed little, is the requirement for mere entrance into His kingdom, not to mention greatness in it.

Confusion about greatness calls for a radical reversal in roles. "If anyone wants to be first he must be the very last, and the servant of all" (Mark 9:35). The word "servant" emphasizes one who performs lowly, personal service for another. That was the last thing on the disciples' minds! Jesus repeatedly emphasized this same truth (Mark 10:43; Matt. 20:26-27; 23:8-11; Luke 14:11; 18:14; 22:26). The sheer repetition of this teaching indicates the weight He gives to servanthood as the pathway to greatness. We stoop to conquer. The way down is the way up in His reign.

Christ Dramatically Demonstrates the Nature
of Greatness in His Kingdom

Greatness in Christ's Kingdom is that of a confiding, trusting, docile, humble, simple child. To be called, led, and loved as a child marks greatness under Christ. To possess nothing and need everything, to earn nothing and receive everything, characterizes a little child.

When Jesus called, the little child came without pride in its own response. When

Jesus called, the little child did not say, "What an excellent child I am." The little child felt itself loved without reflecting on its own loveliness.

We must beg Christ for the grace to have the child heart. Only such belong to the kingdom.

Personal Influence – Beware!

(Matthew 18:6-14)

Strong influences bombard our lives on every side. Media, peers, Madison Avenue, and music all bend our minds. Every one of us lives in a sphere of our personal influence over others. Jesus warned in explicit terms of the danger inherent in our influence on others, as well as influences on us. Every believer must live with discipline in the face of the dangers of influence.

Jesus Warns About the Danger of Influence on Other Believers

The *designation* of Christians is "little ones." This does not refer to babies or children. At the point of personal trust, every believer is the same, like a little child. However sophisticated the professional, worldly-wise the business person, or brilliant the theologian, each must come to the same trust in God of a little boy or girl.

The *destruction* of a Christian results from negative influence. The warning rests on "tripping" another Christian into sin. The suggestion is that of a baited trap, set with the premeditated intent to entrap. Every single "one" of the believers is of ultimate value and must never be the object of our negative influence.

The *destiny* of one who so trips a believer into spiritual destruction is terrible. Actually, Jesus contrasted two terrible destinies, one preferable to the other. The thought of being weighted with a huge millstone and dropped into the open sea would strike terror into anyone. Yet, that is preferable to the destiny awaiting those who deliberately trip Christ's little ones.

Jesus Calls for the Discipline of Influence on Ourselves

We discipline our bodies in the face of temptation. Our organs of mobility (hands, feet) may take us toward sin. Our organs of perception (the eyes) may dwell on objects of sin. To refuse to discipline is to invite spiritual disaster. We are to deal with the first line of resistance, not the last avenue of escape.

Cutting off limbs and gouging out eyes are extreme cases not likely to occur. If the only alternative one faced was habitual sin or amputation, the latter would be better. But that is not the only alternative for a believer. We may discipline ourselves into subjection (1 Cor. 9:26-27). Jesus is comparing two courses of action to make a strong point. Actually, a blind person can lust and a footless person can move toward sin. The only course open is dedicated discipline empowered by Christ.

Jesus Presents the Dignity of Every Humble Believer

Every humble believer is the object of angelic observation (v. 10). Angels minister to God for the benefit of the saved (Heb. 1:14). They protect God's servant in danger and difficulty (Ps. 91:11; Matt. 4:6). In some way they observe our worship, and our conduct in worship should respect their observation.

Every humble believer is the object of divine preservation (vv. 12-14). There is a further reason why we should do no harm to childlike believers. A single, humble believer may seem insignificant and unimportant. Not so, says our Lord. The Father Himself takes pains to preserve every single one. We should discipline our influence with a sense of the dignity of every humble believer.

Controversial Generosity
(Matthew 20:1-15)

What is the kingdom of God like? It is like the controversial generosity of an eccentric vineyard owner! Perhaps the most puzzling of all parables, this parable of controversial generosity has been called the "Wallflower of the Parables." Yet it speaks to the very heart of Jesus' self-understanding and mission.

A remote and an immediate context frames this parable. Jesus' running battle with the Pharisees over table fellowship with sinners is the deep background. Harlots and bums invade God's kingdom at the eleventh hour, while the Pharisees have served all day. The immediate context is Peter's understandable but mercenary question: "We have forsaken all and followed thee; what shall we have therefore?" (Matt. 19:27, KJV) This question betrays a calculating approach toward service.

This parable answers both the Pharisees and Peter. Let God be as good and merciful as He really is, and celebrate that goodness with trust.

God Sovereignly Calls Us to His Kingdom

Sheer sovereignty animates the householder in relation to his vineyard. He calls whom he wishes, how he wishes, and when he wishes. Some he calls at dawn, some at 9:00, 12:00, and 3:00 respectively. In astonishing sovereignty he even calls some to work at the hour of 5:00, the last working hour. In all of this he acts at his good pleasure. This parable is saturated with the sovereignty of God—His sovereign call and His sovereign right to be generous and merciful.

Men may react differently to that sovereign call. The first group to be called haggle and bargain with the householder. They evidence a mercenary spirit that will surface later. The other groups called later simply trust the goodness of the lord who calls them to work. We may likewise react differently to the call of God. Some respond in trust and some with calculating motives.

God Sovereignly Rewards Us in His Kingdom

The householder is outrageously and controversially generous. He pays all the same, regardless of the work done. It is not, as some suggest, that the later workers had worked harder than the earlier. This destroys the intent of the parable. The intent is to demonstrate the sovereign goodness of God. It is simply the fact that we all come into the kingdom at different times. Jews came before Gentiles. Some of us came as children; others have come in the eleventh hour of a life long spent. God's reward is the same for us all.

The mumbling, grumbling twelve-hour men of the parable betray a wrong spirit. They have served on a *quid quo pro*, tit-for-tat basis. They evidence the same spirit that discolored the elder brother of the prodigal son. They are self-conscious and calculating. The proper spirit for kingdom service is not to let the left hand know what the right hand is doing. That is, the sheer joy of working in the vineyard of the generous King is enough.

God Sovereignly Instructs Us About His Kingdom

His justice and goodness questioned, the lord of the vineyard does not explain or defend himself. He speaks in sheer sovereignty, just as he calls in sheer freedom. What he does do is point to the spiritual defect in his detractors. "Is thine eye evil, because I am good?" (v. 15). The detractors from his generosity will not let him be as good as he wants to be. May we learn from them, and let Him be the controversially generous and merciful Lord!

Spiritual Ambition
(Matthew 20:20-28)

There is a real possibility of misunderstanding our Master at the point of spiritual greatness. In the context of our passage, Jesus had just predicted His own crucifixion for the third time (Matt. 20:17-19). James, John, and the twelve misunderstood Jesus and His intention. While He was predicting His passion, they were plotting their position. Jesus took this occasion to explain true spiritual greatness. Greatness in Christ's kingdom depends on sharing His suffering and His servanthood.

Jesus Does Not Reject Spiritual Ambition

We may approach Christ with our spiritual ambition. Nowhere in this passage does He reject the idea of spiritual ambition. James and John came on the wrong grounds of ambition. They had been among the first four to follow Jesus. They had been on the mountain of transfiguration. Their mother, Salome, was probably a sister to Mary, the mother of Jesus. They advanced these grounds for greatness.

We may misunderstand spiritual ambition. James and John did not grasp the nature of greatness or the norm for greatness in Christ's kingdom. They did not understand the nature of greatness. They envisioned an earthly kingdom in an elaborate throne room, with prime ministers seated around Christ. Actually, He would come into His kingdom on a cross, surrounded by two thieves. They did not understand the norm for greatness. Christ does not give greatness in His kingdom as an arbitrary favor, as if He were an Eastern king making sovereign decisions. Greatness in Christ's kingdom is not donated, but earned by suffering and service.

Jesus, however, does not reject this request. He does redirect their spiritual ambition.

Jesus Does Correct Spiritual Ambition

Jesus corrects spiritual ambition with gentleness. This is the kind of mistake that comes only from those who believe. James and John did believe that Jesus was the Christ, and that He would have a worldwide kingdom. Because of that, He treated their misunderstanding with gentleness.

Jesus corrects spiritual ambition with thoroughness. He gives a thorough definition, prediction, and clarification to the disciples. To be great in His kingdom is to share His "cup." The word "cup" refers to His ordeal or His destiny in suffering servanthood.

Jesus makes a prediction about greatness in His kingdom. James and John would drink His "cup." James was martyred in A.D. 44, by Herod Agrippa, the first to drink Jesus' "cup."

John would outlive all of the original apostles and be the last to drink the cup of suffering on Patmos.

Jesus gives a thorough clarification of greatness. Greatness in His kingdom is not based on favoritism, but fitness. God has already prepared a place for those fit to be greatest in the kingdom.

Jesus Does Direct Spiritual Ambition

How we react to the ambitions of others reveals more about us than it does about them. Boiling indignation characterized the twelve when they heard the request of James and John (v. 24). They were, in reality, no better than James and John in their ambitions. Christ's disciples rejected the secular model of greatness. Secular greatness depends on those "who lord over it" and "play the tyrant." Power and pressure exerted from above characterize the world's greatness.

Christ's disciples embraced the servant model of greatness. The world must be transformed not by power from above, but by service from beneath.

For Christ, the great man does not sit atop lesser men, but he carries lesser men on his back. For Christ, the higher the dignity, the lower the servitude. He is His own best example (v. 28).

There are seats close to Christ in the kingdom. We should have ambition to sit in those seats, but we must drink His "cup" and employ His model for greatness in order to fulfill spiritual ambition.

The Final Week:
The Presentation of the King
(Matthew 21:1-9)

The word *king* actually means "one who is able." Until the last week of His ministry, Jesus rejected the title "King." He always was King in the profoundest sense, for preeminently He is the One who is able. If you are a Christian, you have acknowledged this and staked your eternal welfare on that great fact.

Jesus presents Himself as King to every man and in every generation. There are some timeless truths about His kingliness. The same Christ who entered Jerusalem in a triumphal procession, enters the lowly heart of believer on the same principles. What are they?

The King Prepares

As Jesus prepared His final appeal, everything about Him speaks of a Sovereign who has a firm grip on the help of time and steers a certain course. His hour has come. He prepares with *regal authority*. His preparation displays a sense of command: "go, . . . find, . . . bring" (v. 2). For the only time in the Gospels, He calls Himself "Lord" (v. 3). The moment to openly demonstrate His messianic secret, His hidden identity, is finally at hand.

He prepares with *profound symbolism*. Other prophets had dramatized their messages in Jerusalem. Now, the object of their prophecies will dramatize His message. In solemnity, He rides a young animal never before ridden. This was the prerogative of a king. Solomon, the lesser son of David, rode a donkey to his coronation. Now, the greater Son of David does the same. The lowly ass is the burden bearer of the East (the horse is the beast of war). Other kings burden their subjects. This King bears the burdens of His subjects!

He prepares with *prophetic consciousness*. Jesus makes His own a prophecy written five centuries before (Zech. 9:9). The context of the prophet spoke of a coming King who would be rejected. The peculiar quality of His kingdom is to be *meekness*. The

Hebrew word means, literally, "One who does not resist." Jesus will no more force Himself on you than He did on Jerusalem. He presents Himself as the humble King, and then awaits your decision.

The King Receives

This is a strange King, and a still stranger parade. Kings' mounts were often covered with splendid clothes. This King rides on peasants's shirts. Most subjects die for their king; this King dies for His subjects. His court is little children, shouting "Hosanna." His soldiers arm themselves with palm branches. How strange to the Romans visiting the city. A King honored with old clothes and broken trees!

Most of the crowd spread their garments (v. 8). But not all. There were still men talking about the price of wheat, and women gossiping about the neighborhood. The world shook and changed that day, and some never knew it. Josephus says there were three million people in Jerusalem at Passover. The great majority of them never saw and never knew and never cared. Has this changed?

What a strange army this King has. It is an army that cries out words of peace. *Hosanna* literally means "save now." That was precisely what He could *not* do. He could not save as a royal king riding into the city. He could only save as a bloody King on a crossly throne. Jesus saw beyond the strewn garments to soldiers gambling for His garment. He saw beyond the strewn branches to the awaiting tree. Did His eyes bedew themselves with tears as He heard the "Hosannas" echo against the walls of Pilate's fortress? Other words will echo there on Friday. The crowd can change its shout.

The King Explains

Rebuked by Pharisees for receiving these praises (Luke 19:39), Jesus clarifies His situation. It would be necessary that the very stones cry out if men did not. This was His hour. The city will think it rejects Him, but in reality, He will reject the city. "You did not know the time of your visitation" (v. 44, NKJV). Do you?

Jesus Christ Versus Religion that Forgets Its Purpose
(Matthew 21:10-17)

Jesus came proclaiming the kingdom of God, and this proclamation of necessity confronted and alienated the religious establishment of His day. Religion, particularly the Christian faith, may be institutional in either a good or a bad sense. Christianity is institutional in a good sense when its institutions are prophetically alive and instantly alert to God's presence. Christianity is institutional in the bad sense when it simply absorbs its culture, becomes an entrenched establishment, and perpetuates itself.

The first time He came to Jerusalem, Jesus had pointedly confronted establishment religion. His cleansing of the temple dramatically demonstrates God's reaction to cultural, merely institutional, establishment religion. Christ comes again to His temple, the church, to cleanse and to challenge. What are some marks of establishment religion?

Religion Can Forget Its Own Purpose

Both John and the Synoptics connect Jesus' act of cleansing the temple with His first visit to Jerusalem. It was protest at first sight. Jesus passed by many *good* things that could have been done in Jerusalem to do the *best* thing, set His Father's house in order.

The Old Testament ends with the promise that the Messiah will come suddenly to His temple (Mal. 3:1). Jesus identified with that prophetic tradition.

Jesus found the outer court of the temple occupied by the "Bazaars of Annas," a fraudulent con game, a tourist trap for the rural pilgrims. Most grievous was the fact that these "money changers" had set up shop in the one place set aside for Gentile worship, the outer court. Those responsible for the temple had forgotten its purpose—a place where needy worshipers meet God. Jesus challenges them with their own Scripture, particularly Isaiah 56. The ancient prophet had predicted a day when the deformed and the sons of the stranger would all have a part in God's house. Jesus Himself heralds that day. These warnings are a word to us when we make central that which should be peripheral, and peripheral that which should be central.

Christ Can Restore Purpose to Religion

For a golden hour, the temple in Jerusalem became what God intended it to be. With money scattered on the floor, tables overturned, and animals bleating in the confusion, the Son of God becomes the center of His temple. What a picture! It was truly springtime in the temple. The face, a moment ago hard with indignation, is now radiant with compassion, as the temple becomes a place of healing for the blind and the lame. The little children gather about Him to say, "Hosanna to the Son of David!" They look in wonderment at the Godlike face of the Christ, and then on the healed sufferers. At least for a moment, God's temple was what the Father had intended: a place for instruction and healing for *all* men.

The sensitive church must ever ask Christ to come and to cleanse. No body of Christ will ever be ineffective in worship and witness if it can pray daily, "Lord, come and cleanse Your temple again."

Religion Can Become Indignant in the Presence of the Christ

The reaction of the religious establishment was indignation (v. 15). They found no fault in clinking coins and the bleating of nasty animals at the House of God, but they could not stand the cries of happy children. But, Jesus sees in these children the New Israel of God. "The very stones will cry out if necessary." God *will* always have a people. May we always be that people.

Truth or Consequences
(Matthew 21:23-32)

Many refuse to acknowledge the truth about Jesus because they fear the consequences. Events from the last Tuesday of Jesus' public ministry reveal this in a striking way. Two days earlier, the city had hailed Him as King. One day before, He had forcefully reformed the temple. This day, He was teaching in the temple porch, as if He were Owner! All this was too much for the religious professionals. They sent a formal delegation of clergy and laity to challenge Jesus' credentials. Jesus' response revealed their incompetence to judge spiritual authority. The authority of Jesus always puzzles unbelief, but you must act urgently now on what you know.

Jesus' Authority Puzzles Unbelievers

The authority of Jesus Christ does not fit into any known categories of human authority. The nature and source of His authority mystifies unbelief.

The *nature* of Jesus' authority puzzles unbelief. "By what authority are you doing these things?" Jesus had entered the city as a King, reformed the temple, and was teaching as if He owned the place. The authorities demanded to know what right and the power that went with it to enable Him to do these things. What kind of authority does Jesus have? Physical, moral, ecclesiastical, political, spiritual? The authority of Jesus transcends every human category.

The *source* of Jesus' authority puzzles unbelief. "Who gave You this authority?" The religious establishment gave accreditation to all religious teachers. Jesus amazed the people "because He taught as one who had authority, and not as their teachers of the law" (Matt. 7:29). There was a reality about Jesus' teaching that broke every category.

Non-Christians cannot explain Jesus on the basis of any known authority. You can only accept Him as Lord in His uniqueness, not explain Him.

Unbelievers Lack Competence to
Understand Jesus' Authority

Jesus answered their question with a counterquestion. This was not an evasion, but an accepted pattern of religious debate. His question revealed their incompetence to understand any religious authority. If you refuse to act on what you **do** know, you will be given no more light.

Jesus responds with simplicity. They asked Him two questions. He asked them one — from where did John the Baptist's authority come, from God or from man? The Baptist's movement had been the largest intervention with God in 300 years. If the religious leaders could recognize God at all, they should have seen Him in the Baptist's movement.

Unbelief reacts with duplicity. Unbelief refuses to tell the truth because it fears the consequences. If they admitted John the Baptist was from God, they revealed their own inconsistency. They neither believed John nor what he said about Jesus (John 3:25-30). If they denied the Baptist's divine origin, they feared the crowd. The millions in Jerusalem at Passover were easily inflamed.

Most people know the truth about Jesus. They simply do not want to face the consequences of commitment to Him.

Unbelievers Must Act Now on What They Do Know

Jesus refuses to give more of Himself to those who refuse to act on what they already know. The cowardly confession, "We don't know" (v. 27), unmasked the religious leaders. They professed incompetence to decide the greatest religious question of their lifetime. None are so blind as those who will not see.

Jesus bluntly told them that those they considered scum would come to Him before they would. Every word shouts with urgency, "Come now!" God will not give you more than enough evidence. If you do not come on the basis of what you **do** know, you will never know enough to come.

Come to the Banquet
(Matthew 22:1-14)

The rule of God in life is a great *feast*, not a sad fast. The kingdom of God is often compared to a wedding feast. In Jesus' world this was an occasion of joy and significance. The feast lasted for seven days. The significance of the wedding for a king's son is even greater. The king recognized the son as heir to the throne at the wedding feast. In every generation, God gives a wedding feast and invites all to come. The feast recognizes the royalty of His Son, our Lord Jesus. Some do come. Many refuse to come. But God's grace will ultimately draw a large number to that eternal celebration.

God gives a gracious invitation to come to His Son, but He examines those who do come.

The King Extends His Invitation Graciously

The King extends His invitation *initially*. In Jesus' world there were two invitations to a banquet. The initial invitation was days before. The immediate invitation was given when the banquet was ready, for there were no timepieces. Here the King calls those who were already called.

Historically, God invited the Jews to His kingdom through the prophets who told of the good time coming. That was the advance invitation. Immediately God called the Jews through John the Baptist and Jesus' own ministry. But they *refused* to come.

Personally, God calls each of us initially and immediately. Everything about our lives is part of our call toward Him. Many of us, however, refuse that initial and immediate call.

The King extends His invitation persistently. An ordinary king would have been insulted. This King is one of grace and mercy who gives repeated calls to come. He renews His call by stressing the *urgency*. Everything is ready (v. 4). He commends His call by stressing the *excellency* of the feast. The choicest food is waiting and prepared (v. 4). This King has prepared such a feast as only a King could prepare.

Historically, God persisted in His appeal to the Jews. Following the crucifixion of Jesus, the apostles repeated the invitation to the Jews. They enlarged it and pressed it persistently.

Personally, has not God done the same for you? Through life's ups and downs, sermons, churches, and Christian friends He has appealed for you to come.

Many reject the invitation of the King. Some reject the invitation through *indifference*. They simply make light of it and go to their other interests. Others reject the invitation with *viciousness*. They violently reject the messengers and their message. There is a limit to the grace of the King. Judgment has the last word on those who reject His gracious offer (v. 7).

The King Enlarges His Invitation Generously

If you do not accept the King's invitation, others will. The grace of God will not be defeated. He will gather a great people. Whether or not you come, others will.

The King enlarges the *scope* of His invitation. He sends His servants to the "street corners." This refers to the terminal ends of the roads that bring people from far and near. He extends His invitation where the maximum numbers of people may hear and respond. *Historically*, when the Jews of Jerusalem rejected the gospel, He extended it to the entire world. *Personally*, when you reject the gospel He can extend it to the others who will respond.

The King enlarged the *recipients* of His invitation. At first He offered it to the respectable and the righteous. When they refused, He invited all indiscriminately, "both good and bad" (v. 10). Historically, when the outwardly religious Jews rejected the gospel, the apostles took it to the pagan Gentiles who responded with joy. God will find a way to see that His feast is full. When the Old World was weary with the gospel it moved to a new world. Now the gospel moves toward the Third World. God will have a people.

The King Examines Those Invited

The supreme moment comes when the King enters to view those gathered at the banquet. It is a moment of joy and privilege for all. One must note the reality of the examination. The King did not come looking for an unprepared guest. He could not help but see that there was one, but only one.

The reason for the King's examination is obvious. One must be attired appropriately at a king's feast. Most believe that the king provided the garments he required. This was often a custom in the ancient world, especially when guests were quickly brought in from the streets. Certainly God provides the covering of righteousness which we need to attend His final feast.

The reaction of the unprepared guest is instructive. He is simply speechless. Nothing can be said when the grace of the King provides what the law of the King demands. Those not prepared to stand in God's presence will have nothing to say.

The result of the examination is to be sent outside the feast (v. 13). From the brightness of the King's feast to the darkness outside is a striking contrast.

Come to the feast with the garment the King provides.

Between Now and Then
(Matthew 24:1-14)

Tuesday of Jesus' final week of public ministry was a day of controversy and teaching. It was the last day of public ministry to the crowds. The single largest block of Jesus' teaching that Tuesday concerned the judgment of Jerusalem and His second coming. The disciples asked, "When shall these things be?" (v. 3, KJV) It was difficult for them to imagine the destruction of Jerusalem as a separate event from the end of the age.

Matthew 24 is one of the difficult passages in the Gospels. While we may debate the details, it is difficult to miss the main point. Christ describes the problems of the entire age while waiting for the second coming. He also challenges us with the program for the age.

Christ Warns Us About the Problems of This Age

Jesus first warns against deception. The message begins with the words, "Watch out" (v. 4). That which we are to watch for is deception. The most important factor in this age is to avoid deception. The word deception means "to wander off course."

The specific object of our watchfulness is those who claim, "I am the Christ." He means those who pretend to have the authority and the power that belong to Christ alone. He does not mean they will openly make the claim. Those who reject the true Christ leave themselves open to every false Christ.

Jesus warns against the depression that characterizes this age. "See to it that you are not alarmed" (v. 6). The word describes hysterical behavior that issues in crying aloud. He names some depressing things that will not be the sign of the end of the age, but of the entire age before Christ comes.

First, the history of the age will be a history of war. The study of man is the study of war, or the preparation for war. No war or rumor of war is the sign of the immediate end.

This age will be characterized by famine and disease. We should seek to relieve these (Matt. 25). But, their widespread presence is not an immediate sign of the end. They are symptoms of the entire age while waiting for the end.

Unusual physical phenomena are not to cause depression about the end. "Earthquakes" stand for any unusual physical phenomena. These will belong to the entire age of the church. We live in an age when all such things are part of a divine necessity (v. 6). They signal the beginning of such an age, not the end (v. 8).

Jesus warns about the declension that will characterize this age. There will be a falling away from apparent faithfulness by those who claim to belong to Him. There will be two reasons from outside the church why people will fall away. There will be persecution because of His name. The world will never be friendly to the people of the gospel. This will cause some to fall away. There will be lawlessness in the world at large, rebellion against all order. This will cool the *agape* of the fellowship one for another.

There will be two reasons from within for the declension of Christians. There will be disloyalty within. Christians will hand one another over to persecution. There will be deception from within. False prophets will deceive many within the community of faith. Was not Jesus right? Has not this characterized the twenty centuries since He spoke these words?

"He who stands firm to the end will be saved" (v. 13). In the midst of deception, depression, and declension, the one who endures with triumphant fortitude shows the mark of saving faith.

Christ Challenges Us with the Program for This Age

"This gospel of the kingdom will be preached in the whole world as a testimony to all nations, and then the end will come" (v. 14). Although we should do all we can to relieve the problems of this age, these problems will ultimately rest beyond our power to control. Rather than speculate about the problems, we are to be people of the divine program. The good news about the reign of God in Christ is to be taken to every nation in the earth. When all people have heard the gospel, then the end will come. People cannot build the kingdom of God by human effort. But, we can bring back the king by a worldwide effort of witness and evangelism. Christianity has always been at its best when that is its motivation. Not speculation but proclamation should characterize us as we look toward the end.

The Watchword Is "Watch"
(Matthew 25:1-13)

The very last public teaching of Jesus called for watchfulness in light of His coming again. On the Mount of Olives, He closed His three-year teaching career with three parables, all of which call for a singular attitude—"Watch!" The parable of the wise and foolish virgins applies to all professing Christians of all times. We will meet God in the condition in which we are at the moment of death or at Christ's return.

This story reflects ancient Jewish wedding customs. A group of the bride's friends waited along the route from her house to the groom's house. They joined the wedding procession with torchlights when it passed nearby. But this story also tells a timeless, spiritual truth. It reveals the condition of Christendom at the end. Some who profess Christ have made real preparation to meet Him. Others will be surprised in the moment of truth. The moral is clear: Be ready to meet life's decisive, spiritual moments.

Vigilant Preparation Marks Spiritual Wisdom

Jesus identifies the principal distinction among professing believers as the "wise" and the "unwise." All had lamps, and all expected to meet the bridegroom. Outwardly, there appeared to be no difference. All may appear to have an outer form of Christianity and profess expectation to meet Christ when He comes.

Jesus makes a basic distinction. Some were sensible and others were senseless. Some were prudent and others were imprudent. That basic distinction decided their fate. Some had oil. They were not wise because they had oil; they had oil because their lives had a deeper wisdom. Although there will not be an equal number of wise and foolish in that day, there will be a large number of surprises.

The foolish ignore preparation for life's decisive, spiritual moment. Some took no oil. It was an ancient custom to use torches consisting of a ceramic bowl filled with rags on top a stick. Wise waiters took a jar of oil to replenish the small amount in the torch. Otherwise, they did not have resources for a long wait with a sudden ending. There is a timeless, spiritual truth implied. Oil represents everything required in a lifetime of preparation to meet Christ. Be supplied for the long wait!

The wise make preparation for life's decisive, spiritual moment. The wise took oil with them. In the ancient world, small vessels were carried with extra olive oil. It was inconvenient, but proved to make all the difference. As a timeless truth, believers must be supplied with that oil. There is a suggestion here about a container, contents, and conflagration. The container is the believer, the content is the inner resources of the spiritual life, and the conflagration is the shining testimony that results. The implication is that people will act in their spiritual life with a lack of preparation that would never characterize their material life.

Sudden Intervention Marks Christ's Return

Christ teaches that His return will be marked by delay. In biblical times, the wedding procession was often delayed by bargaining over the gifts exchanged between the families. Waiting for a bridegroom actually happened as described. But, beyond this literal fact is Christ's clear teaching that His return would be after delay. The fact that all ten maidens slept may suggest the reality of death as we all wait. It certainly means that those with preparation may wait with security while those without preparation sleep foolishly.

Christ teaches that His return will be marked by a sudden desire for preparation. A vivid cry will mark the moment of His return (24:30-31). It will be self-evident that it is happening. Each had to make individual preparation for that moment, for all then "trimmed their [wicks]." That refers to everything that makes the light bright and beautiful.

The foolish then found the stark reality of no preparation. They asked for a transfer of what cannot be transferred. The wise were not selfish in refusing to give of their own oil. Spiritual character cannot be transferred, even if we would. Preparation is a quality of life, not a quantity that can be shared. Nothing makes up for unreadiness at the critical moment. Self-preparation at the last moment is impossible. At the end, there will be a great desire for preparation to meet the Coming One, but only those already prepared will be ready.

Final Exclusion Marks the Unprepared

The prepared are included eternally, while the unprepared are excluded eternally. God's grace is vast in its extent, but has a definite limit. An adulterous and murderous David can come in, a thief on the cross can come in, a cursing Peter can come in—all may come while the door is open. But, the door will be shut and none will enter.

Urgent, anxious pleading will not change that situation. What pleading preparation will do must be done now. There is nothing more final than the verdict of the Bridegroom, "I do not even recognize them" (v. 12). Come while the door is open (Rev. 3:20).

The watchword is "Watch!" This refers to everything that makes us ready to meet Christ. To be heedful, vigilant, and intense is the mark of that readiness. It does not mean a feverish activity as much as a long march of deliberate faithfulness. Our Lord's final public word is "Watch!"

Great Chapters for Greater Living: Take a Risk
(Matthew 25:14-30)

As generations go, ours is less inclined toward risk than many. It seems to be a time when many play it safe, hedge their bets, and cover their tracks. We do a great deal of looking with very little leaping.

Christ is the great "Caller to Risk." The One who told fishermen to drop their nets and follow Him always calls us toward risk. Christ expects those who claim to follow Him to risk the very stuff of life for His sake.

Risk Participating in What Christ Is Doing Rather Than Observing

The central character of this parable is a typical watcher, spectator, observer, and nonparticipant. He does nothing rather than something. Jesus reserved some of His harshest judgments for this one who was prudent but useless. Failure to risk, warps your perspective on God and your fellow servants. As God moves through our church in unusual ways, what is your level of risk?

Risk Doing Something for Christ Rather Than Doing Nothing

The riskless man of this parable was doing nothing out of the ordinary for his day. What he did would have been considered common, prudent behavior. Jesus never promised that following Him would lead to life lived on the principle "safety first." Where are you moving away from the common, routine, and expected to risk the unusual for Christ?

Risk Accepting Responsibility Rather Than Placing Blame

Eventually, God will reveal to everyone the level of risk they have lived:

"After a long time the master of those servants returned" (v. 19). Some try to shift the blame from themselves to God or others for failing to risk in Christ's service. All those who risk belong to the same order of heroes in God's sight. God has already tilted the game of life in favor of those who risk in His service. There is a personal threshold of risk that God wills for you to cross.

Authority in Word and in Deed
(Mark 1:21-28)

Jesus demonstrates a perfect authority both in word and deed. Some speak with authority, but there is no matching performance. Others act with authority, but their words are their undoing. Our Lord began and continued His ministry with a balance in authority between word and deed.

Christ Demonstrates His Authority in Word

On the day of worship, Christ entered the synagogue. Although the Son of God, He sensed the need for corporate worship and fellowship with the people of God. There He demonstrated His authority.

An authentic encounter with Jesus' authority will leave you *astonished* (v. 22). The expression means that which strikes one out of his senses with fear, wonder, or joy.

The biblical *definition* of Jesus' authority is "to compel one to decision." When Jesus is heard, His authority has the capacity to compel decision about His person and claims.

The *question* about Jesus' authority is not the fact or impact of His authority, but rather its source. The source of His authority was not in His content or style, but in His commitment to the cross. Concerning His own life He claimed: "I have authority to lay it down and I have authority to take it up again" (John 10:18).

Have you had a personal confrontation with the authority of Christ?

Christ Demonstrates His Authority in Deed

Although many contemporaries minimize the power or possibility of the demonic, the characteristic act of Christ in Mark's Gospel is the exorcism of demons. Although much is not clear to us about the demonic, three things are certain.

The demonic senses the *ultimate threat* to its very existence in the person of Christ (v. 24). Even the approach of Christ rocks the kingdom of evil with fear.

The demonic has *supernatural knowledge* of the person of Christ. It knows His name, point of origin, and essence (v. 24).

Jesus approaches the demonic with an authority unlike anyone else (v. 27). He deals with evil in brevity, power, and dignity. We may not understand how the demonic operates today. But we certainly know this: the power of evil in our lives is beyond the power of man as a man. You and I need the authority of Christ.

When Religion Raises the Roof
(Mark 2:1-12)

Some passages can lose their vitality through years of familiarity. These four men carrying their friend to Jesus echo in our earliest memories of Sunday School stories. Yet we need to take another, closer look. These four men are carrying more truth than we might think.

Just as the paralyzed man got up and walked, let the truth walk in your life. Jesus always acts with an urgent priority to make us spiritually whole.

When Religion Raises the Roof, an Urgency Defines the Moment

When Christ is present and available, the moment is urgent. Jesus came and went from Capernaum, and now He was back again.

Christ will always receive you, but He is not always equally available in power and presence. When desperate need is present, the moment is urgent. Desperate need clarifies and simplifies; get the need to Jesus any way possible.

Urgency reveals character by response. The owner of the house found urgency for

Jesus *costs*. The onlookers found urgency *excites*. The critics found urgency *irritates*. Christ found urgency *interrupts*. But urgent faith found the answer.

When Religion Raises the Roof, Priority Dominates the Moment

For Jesus, *spiritualities* always take precedence over *materialities*. Spiritual wholeness even takes precedence over physical wholeness. Everyone else saw a man who needed physical freedom—Jesus saw a man who needed spiritual freedom.

There is a relationship between sin and sickness: (1) My sin may lead to my sickness; (2) Your sin may lead to my sickness; (3) Being a part of a sinful race always leads to sickness and death (Rom. 6:23). Jesus desires first to heal from sin. He does heal sickness, sometimes immediately, but always ultimately.

When Religion Raises the Roof, a Clarity Reveals the Moment

Jesus always makes visible the invisible. To say, "Your sins are forgiven," is invisible. To say, "Take up your mat and walk" is visible.

Jesus did the visible, physical thing to reveal the invisible, spiritual thing.

When forgiveness comes, you see the wholeness—Christ always reveals in the way we get up and walk.

Encounter with Jesus: Three Kinds of Folks at Church
(Mark 3:1-6)

Not everyone who shows up at church comes for the same reason. We all know that. When the Lord Jesus comes to church, He comes to confront those here for the wrong reason and to help those who came for the right reason. The presence of Jesus means both conflict and healing. Mark 2:1 to 3:6 finds Jesus in constant conflict with the religious establishment. The religious establishment cared more for institutions than for persons. Jesus cared more for persons than for institutions. Jesus comes to get God's healing grace to people. Religious establishments always tend to protect their power, keep their traditions, and control the situation.

Jesus confronts meaningless religious tradition but gives wholeness to those who admit their own disability.

Some Come to Church Aware of Personal Disability

Some of us come with an acute consciousness of personal *disability*. The man with a shriveled hand stands for all of us who come here withered in ourselves. He had not always been this way. The words suggest that this was not congenital. Through a terrifying process he had watched his hand retract and shrink. Tradition says he was a stonemason, ruined for life. Some of us know what it means to watch ourselves decay and not be able to stop it.

We may come to church in *passivity*. This man is silent and passive throughout the story. He says nothing and does nothing without being told. He has lost initiative in life. He sits and watches. Some here today are paralyzed to speak or act in the spiritual realm. We just wait.

We may come to church in *expectancy*. He must have held some vague, half-conceived notion that the only place he would actually find help was in God's house. He was there with hope, however small.

We may expect to receive *mercy*. He did receive mercy. God gave him back his wholeness. This was altogether unrequested and undeserved. There was no more merit in him than in thousands of others with such disability. God acted in grace and sovereignty. That is the only reason that any of us are whole.

Others Come to Church Projecting Personal Superiority

Some come to church only with the insight that they are superior to the others present. The Pharisees were the power people who kept the traditions and retained the rituals. Their driving motive was to protect and control their power and position.

We may come to church with the *wrong motive*. We may come more for the institution than for people. The Pharisees placed tradition above compassion. Their motive went wrong with their whole viewpoint: God was interested more in outward ritual than inward reality. This motivated them to do anything to kill Jesus (v. 6). He embodied a total threat to their whole world. They lived for legalism. Jesus lives for liberty.

When we come to church with the wrong motive, it leads to the *wrong method*. We come to make observations rather than receive grace: "they watched him [Jesus] closely" (v. 2). They came to church to see that everything was done "right."

They comprised "The Way We Always Do It Here Committee." Out of their observations they came to question: "Is it lawful to heal on the Sabbath [day]?" (Matt. 12:10). Listen to how someone talks about church. Are they always carping about "the way things are done around here" or are they ever rejoicing that God did something here?

The wrong method leads to the *wrong message*. How little can we do here instead of how much? Church becomes confining rather than freeing, restricting rather than liberating, limiting rather than enlarging.

The greatest sin our church can commit is to do anything to keep the grace of God from meeting human need.

Jesus Comes to Church to Make Us Whole and Set Us Free

Jesus does come to church, even when we do not deserve it. Where His word is expounded He comes to meet with us. Even though the teaching was poor, He got little out of the message, knew much more than the preacher, and was not Himself wanted—He still went to church!

Jesus comes to church *confrontively*. Be careful before you gush, "How great it would be if Jesus came to church." Jesus comes to church with question and observation. He questions whether we really understand God's intent for church. Are we here to guard the rules or to heal withered people (v. 4)? He comes to make observation: "He looked around at them." Mark often regards this searching glance of Jesus at friend and foe. We would do well to remember as we meet that He still looks around at us.

Jesus comes to church *emotionally*. He can come to church with anger and sorrow. His anger is not vindictive. He hates legalism but loves legalists. He is angry when He sees an entire institution forget why it exists, to make withered people whole. Yet He always mixes anger with even deeper sorrow: "deeply distressed at their stubborn hearts. . . ." He actually feels sorry for those who live with the self-imposed misery of spiritual callousness. Legalism makes unhappy people.

Jesus can make us whole at church. Jesus *confronts our impossibility*. He asked this man to do precisely what the man could not do, "Stretch out your hand." His power pours into our impossible situation after our obedience.

Jesus *demonstrates His potency:* "his hand was completely restored" (v. 5). Jesus restores without a word or a touch. By sheer power of His will He makes whole. He can do that today from the right hand of God as easily as He did so in the synagogue.

Jesus answers empty discussion with powerful action. Which crowd do you belong to at church today?

Jesus' Kingdom Will Come
(Mark 4)

The central teaching of Jesus is the coming kingdom of God. Today we speak more of personal salvation and less of God's kingdom than did Jesus. In Jesus Christ the reign and rule of God broke into history in a final, decisive way. Jesus talked about the reign of God in simple parables. Some understood His stories; some did not. To understand Jesus' stories, you need a relationship with the storyteller.

The three stories of Mark 4 contrast the apparent insignificance of Jesus' kingdom at its beginning with the conquering triumph of the kingdom at its end. These three parables answer the anxiety of Jesus' followers in every era concerning the growth of His influence. His word falls on such unpromising ground, the growth of his kingdom seems so uncommonly slow, and the number of His disciples seems so insignificant.

In the face of this, Jesus gives us the great assurance that His kingdom will indeed come.

The Kingdom Triumphs in Spite of Discouraging Response

Someone pointed to the apparent failure of Jesus' words with so many of His hearers. He was not succeeding with many people. Both His friends and enemies were wondering out loud, "Does God work like this?" In response, Jesus told the parable of the sower (vv. 13-20).

This parable is not about bad soils or futile sowing. How often has it been implied that Christian work fails three out of four times on the basis of this parable! How clumsy the farmer in this parable appears—sowing on paths, rocks, and thorns! A significant detail throws light on this story: in Palestine the farmer sows before he plows. He would plow all seeds under the soil. The emphasis rests on the joyous confidence that there would be an abundant harvest in the face of every difficulty.

In Palestine a tenfold return on seed sown was considered extraordinary, a sevenfold return was routine. Here the response is incredible—thirty, sixty, one hundredfold. In spite of all stony, rocky, thorny opposition, there will be an incredible response to the gospel of Jesus.

We should take hope from this in Christian endeavor. Around the world today there is amazing response to the gospel. The slow response in secular America is not the response in Africa, South America, or Russia. The field of the kingdom is the world, and there is a great harvest.

The Kingdom Triumphs in Irresistible Power

The kingdom of Jesus appears weak in contrast to the world's armies. The Zealots of Jesus' day urged armed revolt against the Romans in order to bring God's kingdom. Jesus' program appeared pale compared to theirs. In response, Jesus told the story of the seed growing spontaneously (vv. 26-29).

The message of the gospel is not as weak as it appears. The strong emphasis rests on the irresistible, germinal power in the seed. The seed grows *automate* of itself. This word *automatic* is found only one place else in the New Testament. There is an irresistible growth in the seed. The farmer can watch the process carefree, confident of the harvest to come. The harvest comes in spite of human passivity. The farmer is not unconcerned, but he does go to sleep. The farmer is interested and he is an instrument, but he is not the cause of the growth. Ultimately, the kingdom does not depend on my ability or inability, my will or my act. How ridiculous for the farmer to dig the seed up to see if it sprouted!

There is an irresistible, germinal power in that seed which is the gospel. It bears fruit *automate,* spontaneously. The kingdom of God will grow because of the power inherent in its message.

The Kingdom Moves From Insignificance to Dominance

Jesus' contemporaries expected the kingdom to come with a noisy, political victory by Israel. Israel would become the political center of the world. How different from all expectations were the microscopic, ragtag bands that followed Jesus. In the parable of the mustard seed (vv. 30-34) the emphasis rests on the two ends of the process of sowing. How small was the beginning. The mustard seed was the smallest thing the human eye could see. Yet it grew to become one of the largest of the garden shrubs. It could reach a height of eight to ten feet.

This parable is a simple word of encouragement. The band around Jesus appeared impossibly small. His methods of teaching and healing were not the weapons the Messiah was expected to use. Yet He dared to state that His kingdom would surpass all the nations of the world in glory. Like a great tree, His kingdom would become a sanctuary for all men everywhere.

The kingdom of God is coming, in spite of its apparent smallness. Are you part of that kingdom?

Legion

(Mark 5)

By giving us the extreme case of Legion, Mark assures us that we all fall within the boundary of Christ's caring power. Immediately after taming a wild sea, Christ tames a wild man. This is not just a tall tale. Legion is the picture of Satan's finished product, the destruction of the image of God in man. The power of Christ triumphed in the case of Legion. Legion is any of us, all of us.

Legion Faces Jesus

Legion faces Jesus as a rejected man. He was probably rejected from childhood and by the whole community. He was rejected by his past that haunted him and by the diagnosis of those around him. Finally he rejected himself in despair. The door by which the demonic entered his life was rejection.

Legion was the object of negative solutions. His keepers could do nothing but confine and restrict him. There has been little improvement on this approach. For life's worst cases, we still offer only negative and confining solutions.

Legion faces Jesus as a divided man. Part of him wants to fall down before Christ and worship. Another part of him desires to run from Christ. Legion both hated and loved himself as he was. This is the problem of all of us.

Jesus Faces Legion

Jesus faces Legion as an accepting person. This is noted in the simple asking for a name. Jesus asked Legion his name so that Legion could own who he was. You cannot disown what you have become until you own what you have become. Legion had to admit that he was full of division, which his name suggests.

Jesus gave Legion a positive solution. Calmly, Jesus says, "Be gone!" As the evil element in Legion's life frightened the swine, they jumped into the sea. Legion needed to see that. He needed to know that God's forgiveness was as big an event as his sin. Often we make sin and guilt a bigger event than the grace of God's forgiveness.

Jesus faces Legion as a whole person. Because of Christ's power, a divided man became whole. Yet, when Legion became whole, the people around him were more afraid of him than when he was a divided demoniac. They invited Jesus to leave out of the fear of His wholeness.

Christ does not come to make us "a little better." He comes with awesome power to restore life to its wholeness. That part of Legion that wanted to come to Jesus ultimately overcame that part which wanted to run from Jesus. What about you?

Encounter with Jesus: One Out of the Crowd

(Mark 5:24-34)

There is more than one way to touch the Lord Jesus. Some touch Him superficially. He has always drawn a crowd where He is really present. In that crowd some touch Him inadvertently and some out of mere curiosity. Jesus does not release His power to the merely curious. There is a profoundly personal touch that does contact the healing power of the Lord Jesus. That touch recognizes personal hopelessness and rests everything on His power to make whole.

Out of the suffocating crush of a crowd one desperate woman touched Jesus. He was on His way to help someone else. He always is. Yet we can stop Him with the touch of faith and be healed ourselves. You can come to Jesus with your hopeless situation and touch Him in a way that heals.

You Can Touch Jesus in a Hopeless Situation

Longstanding problems appear to defy solution and discourage us by their very duration. We can touch Jesus with our *perpetual problems*. This woman had endured twelve years of personal and shameful difficulty. Her loss of life blood may have been constant or intermittent. If it came and went, her hopes were raised and then dashed. Her condition is both revealed and concealed. We cannot be certain what it was other than that it was always a shameful threat. It wasted her health, wealth, and rendered her socially outcast.

We can touch Jesus with our *painful problems*. This woman suffered many different things, even from those who were supposed to be healing her. She suffered physically and economically. She spent everything she had looking for help. Some of us know what it is to try everything available for spiritual and emotional relief while finding nothing.

We can touch Jesus with our *pointless problems*. In all her trying she was not helped even at one point. In fact, things only got worse instead of better. The very effort tired her and complicated her condition.

Can you identify with her in the spiritual realm? Many fight long-term battles with stubborn, relentless inclinations, passions, obsessions, fears, anxieties, and guilt. They suffer the pain of mental anguish internally while having to act normally externally. And it all seems pointless. No amount of personal resolution, counsel from friends, or religious activity changes anything. You can approach and touch Jesus from that very situation.

You Can Touch Jesus with a Sufficient but Imperfect Faith

You can touch Jesus with an *imperfect faith*. The only fitness He requires is to feel your need of Him. This woman's faith was inadequate because it was both silent and superstitious. She thought she could come to Jesus hidden in the crowd and from behind Him so He would never know what happened. Faith must confess Him. Her faith was also superstitious. She actually touched a tassel of Jesus' robe, thinking that His personal power charged His garments with magical potency. Yet Jesus did honor her faith. We cannot wait for more knowledge, perfect understanding, or theological insight before we come to Him. The best faith is imperfect. It is not perfect faith but its perfect object, the Lord Jesus, that makes whole.

We can touch Jesus with an imperfect but *sufficient faith*. We must come to Him with the personal persuasion, "If I just touch his clothes, I will be healed" (v. 28). This woman did believe in the personal power of Jesus, although she believed it was in His robe rather than His personal interest in her. The whole of the gospel can be summed up in the desire to touch Him and be made whole.

An imperfect but sufficient faith is *rewarded*. It is rewarded in *fact*. Immediately this woman was well. The flow of blood stopped on the spot. But also she was made well in *feeling:* "she felt in her body that she was freed from her suffering" (v. 29). She not only was well, she knew that she was well. She realized inwardly that she was permanently healed and profoundly healed, not only from the symptoms but also from the disease causing them.

Jesus not only wants you to be spiritually whole, but to know it—to know that the threatening failure of yesterday will never return.

Jesus Responds to a Believing Touch

Jesus distinguishes between *superficial and meaningful touches*. Scholars debate whether this cure was voluntary or involuntary on Jesus' part, whether He knew the woman's condition in advance or not. We cannot settle this. We can know that Jesus is so filled with power to make whole that any touch of personal faith is powerfully rewarded. We must understand the difference between the superficial and meaningful touch. There is always a crowd at church around the name of Jesus. But simply touching the church building, the pew, the activities, and the traditions is not to touch the Lord Jesus Himself. It is not to touch things connected with Him but to touch Him that makes the difference.

Jesus desires that we *confess Him* when He makes us whole. Jesus looks for our response. He does not desire to save us from ourselves by an impersonal religious transaction. He desires a permanent relationship with those whom He heals. We cannot steal healing behind His back and go away without Him.

We may fear public confession of Christ. This woman feared to identify herself because of her natural inclination. She had a disease that brought her personal shame. Notice that Jesus did not ask her or desire her to state what was wrong with her—He simply wanted her to confess that He had healed her.

The Lord Jesus *confirms our wholeness when we confess Him*. His public confession won His confirmation: "Your faith has healed you." Hidden discipleship lacks that assurance. But He gave her even more. "Go into peace" [Shalom]" (v. 34). He sent her out with total, personal well-being. He will do the same for you if you touch Him by faith and confess openly His healing.

Courage. Rise, He Calls!
(Mark 10:46-52)

Mark records this as the last miracle of Jesus before the cross. That Jesus would hear, stop, and meet an individual need while contemplating His cross arrests us. The very reason for His cross is to address our individual need and to change our individual life. The famous story of Bartimaeus should not be embalmed in our memory but embodied in our life. We should not come to respect an old story but to realize a present possibility. The Lord Jesus still hears and responds to real need with an immediate, powerful word.

You Must Acknowledge Your Real Need

He calls you to acknowledge your real problem. Bartimaeus had the great physical impairment of blindness and the grave personal peril of beggary. He was blind, broke, and bewildered. He had dual hopelessness, twin troubles, and double despair. This story means nothing unless we say, "Move over Bartimaeus. Is there room for me on the Jericho road?" We must admit that we cannot see what ultimately matters. We must also admit that we have spent the stuff of life on our own obsessions, cravings, longings, and compulsions until we are spiritually broke.

He calls us regardless of our partial perspective. Bartimaeus did not have perfect faith or understanding. His recognition of Jesus as "Son of David" (vv. 47-48) identifies Him as no more than a good Israelite from David's ancestry. But he did recognize in Jesus the One of sympathy who responds to an appeal for mercy. Many who never contact Christ plead an inadequate understanding or weak faith. You do not have to be a theologian or a saint to contact Jesus Christ. If that were so, few would ever touch Him.

He calls us through persistence. Bartimaeus had one remarkable, life-changing hope—a persistence that would not be denied. He made himself a nuisance! He did so in the face of everyone who would keep him away from the Christ. Jesus both in His teaching and His practice rewards perseverance. No secular physical achievement happens without perseverance.

Jesus Individually Meets Your Real Need

Jesus hears the one among the many. Amidst the babble of voices, the confusion of conversations, and the footfalls Jesus Christ heard one voice. Our hope yet rests in this today. In the vastness of this universe and in the bigness of this congregation He still responds to the individual human life.

Jesus Christ alone has the right to call for courage. In the New Testament seven times there is a call for courage. The other six times are on the lips of Jesus. Here the call to courage is on the lips of the emissaries of Jesus. No human can ultimately give you courage. We are all in the same dilemma. But when the Risen Christ calls for courage, He creates the courage for which He calls.

Jesus Christ meets you at the point of actual need. He does this by making you face and articulate your need. The blind man had to say, "That I might receive my sight" (v. 51, KJV). We have to own what we are before we can disown what we are. After we articulate, we must act. There was a moment when the man had to stand, walk, and act on the fact that he could now see. Do not blame God for failing to intervene in your life when you will not act in the presence of His power. His power operates simultaneously with your rising to grasp it.

Jesus Acts with an Immediate Power
While Calling for an Ultimate Commitment

The Lord Jesus acts with an immediate power. Once the need was acknowledged, the actual healing is almost an afterthought. Jesus did not touch him or even mention the miracle. The need was acknowledged and the deed was done! The difficulty is never with His power. It works quickly and immediately. Lazarus was raised with a sentence. The sea was stilled with a word. The same Lord acts the same today. We admit our need, act on His power, and one of His words makes us whole.

The Lord calls for an ultimate commitment. "Immediately he received his sight and followed Jesus along the road" (v. 52). That is to say, Bartimaeus became a disciple. Jesus Christ does not dispense doses of life to those who intend no commitment. Casual Christianity causes no change in life. Had Bartimaeus returned to his seat of beggary he would have been doubly blind, a dog returned to his own vomit. Those who enter Jesus actually follow His way ultimately.

Today is not a rehearsal. If He calls, rise and follow.

The Necessity for Fruitfulness
(Mark 11:12-14,19-22)

Sometimes it is necessary to act out a message rather than to speak it. When words have not made the proper impression, deeds may leave an unforgettable lesson. The Old Testament prophets acted out their message when words no longer worked (Jer. 13:1-11; Ezek. 3:1-11). On the last Monday of His public ministry, Jesus withered a fruitless fig tree. He did so to make dramatic His judgment on a fruitless people. Our Lord hopes for fruitfulness, but He judges a fruitless people.

Our Lord Expects Fruitfulness From His Disciples

Like Jesus' spoken parables, this dramatic act moves on two levels, physical and spiritual. Physically, Jesus hungered for food. The reason may have been His early rising for prayer (Mark 1:35). He had used His strength in a night of spiritual wrestling. He may have had a scanty, hurried breakfast, as he hurried to Jerusalem and His work of cleansing the temple. The reality of this hunger shows His humanity in the midst of His divinity. The same human Lord who could hunger for breakfast a moment later can wither a tree with a word in His divinity.

Spiritually, Jesus hungers for fruit on the part of His people. The expectation of God has always been for fruit. He planted His people as a vineyard in order to bear fruit (Isa. 5). Then He expected fruit from Israel. Now He expects fruit from His church. That fruit is expressed in character at the level of being (Gal. 5:19-22). That fruit is expressed in conduct at the level of acting (Matt. 23:23). He expects that fruit from every individual branch or believer (John 15).

Our Lord Judges Fruitlessness in His Disciples

Our Lord observes the profession of fruitfulness. On the physical level, Jesus saw the full foliage of a single fig tree on the roadside. The key to the entire story rests on a single fact: figs appear before or along with leaves on such trees. The leaves were a promise of the fruit. Spiritually, this was the condition of Israel. The temple, priesthood, sacrificial system, and whole way of life presented the picture of a holy people. But just beneath the surface, there was no reality behind the ritual. The same can be true today behind the life of a church or an individual Christian.

Our Lord observes the absence of fruit. On inspection, Jesus found that the tree was pretentious but barren. It was a tree of promise without performance. Ultimately, the discerning eye of Jesus detects the presence or absence of authentic fruit in the life of every disciple. Jude spoke of members of the church that are "clouds without rain, blown along by the wind; autumn trees without fruit and uprooted—twice dead" (v. 12).

Our Lord confirms a fruitless condition. This is the last of the eighteen miracles recorded in Mark. It is the only totally destructive miracle of Jesus. One should note that He performed His only totally destructive miracle on a mere tree, not on a human being. This was not a fit of anger on Jesus' part. It was a deliberate act to leave a dramatic reminder that fruitlessness can expect His judgment. He simply confirmed the tree in the condition that already existed. This ultimately happened to Israel in the judgment that came under Rome in A.D. 70. It can happen to any church that leaves its first love (Rev. 2:5). Ultimately it is the judgment of a fruitless believer (John 15:6).

There is a prevention for fruitlessness. It is a life of faith and prayer (11:22-25). Watching out for life's inwardness and reality of the spiritual is the prevention of spiritual barrenness.

Encounter with Jesus: Watching at the Temple
(Mark 12:41-44)

What did Jesus do as the last act of public ministry? He sat down in a special "pew" and watched the offering at God's house. On the last day of His public ministry He taught at the temple (11:27; 12:35). Even though the house of God was imperfect, He was there. He confronted its leaders. He cleansed its courts. But the very last thing He did was watch and instruct concerning our giving to God's work. Then and now the Lord Jesus watches our offering and teaches us what is truly great giving.

The Lord Jesus Watches Us as We Give to God's Treasury

There is a treasury in God's house. This is not an innovation, an imposition, or something alien to the purpose of God's house. In the Court of the Women at the Jewish temple there were no less than thirteen treasuries. Each was labeled for a specific purpose. Jesus commended this; He did not condemn it. When God's people cease to give, they cease to live. Money is condensed life, pent-up energy. When we give money, we give life to God. Biblical worship includes God's treasury as much or more as sermons and songs.

The Lord Jesus watches the treasury. The last act of Jesus' three-year ministry was to sit down and watch people as they gave at God's house. He had profound interest in how and what the people were giving.

The Lord Jesus watches how we give *continually*. The very word suggests not only that He carefully but also that He continually watched as people gave. He watched every gift and every giver. Jesus Christ is "the same yesterday, today, and forever." We may rest assured that He still watches the treasury of His church. When we give it is His gaze that really matters. It is not how you look at your gift, but how He looks at your gift that really matters.

The Lord Jesus watches how we give *discerningly*. He carefully evaluates as we give. He individualizes us as we give. Fifteen thousand people could fit into the Court of the Women where the treasury was located. At Passover there were mobs of people attempting to give. Jesus distinguished three groups: the crowd, the rich, and the widow. He saw each group and He studied each individual. You do not fade into the crowd at offering time. He looks and He knows.

When we give, we give to Him. We do not give to a "budget" or a human organization. Our giving is to Him. Our gifts are the very best test of our devotion to Him.

The Lord Jesus Assesses Us as We Give to God's Treasury

The Lord assesses our circumstances. That day He individually focused on one giver. He focused on her uniqueness, her resourcelessness, and her aloneness. She was unique. There were many rich, but only one such widow. She was without resources. The word "poor" indicates a cringing beggar, not just a pauper. She was alone. The biblical widow had no government agency or community fund to help her. Jesus always knows the circumstances out of which we give. To some that is an encouragement. He knows that you would give Him everything if you had it. To others it is profoundly disturbing to think that He knows what we give. We live in luxury, indulge ourselves lavishly, and give next to nothing to His work.

The Lord assesses our contributions. This woman gave two "leptons." The word refers to the smallest Greek coin that was minted out of copper. It was worth only 1/128th of a day's working wage. She had two and could have kept one. She gave both of them, leaving nothing for her next meal. Jesus did not run up to her and stop her. He knew the truth, "It is more blessed to give than to receive" (Acts 20:35). He knew what she knew: the Father would care for her. The Lord assesses our contribution in light of our circumstances every time we give.

The Lord Teaches Us as We Give to God's Treasury

Out of the crowd at the temple, the Lord Jesus called His disciples to Him for special instruction. Who should listen to this word today? Disciples should listen. He is calling you to hear this. You categorize yourself by how you listen.

The Lord makes a *surprising evaluation* of our giving. This poor widow had given more than all of the others put together. He counts the offering differently. She gave more because of her motive. But in fact, she gave more in real money. The story of this woman has motivated millions to give for 2,000 years. She indeed gave more!

The Lord gives an *instructive explanation* about our giving. Who gives the biggest gift? Some give out of their surplus, their overflow, their abundance. These never touch the nerve of sacrifice. They live, eat, dress, and drive the same as they would if they had not given.

She gave out of her poverty, need, and deficiency. It was an act of actual self-denial. The affluent gave what they did not need. She gave what was less than she needed. Jesus reveals this principle: God measures your gift not in net dollars but in relationship to all that you have.

Beneath all of this is the *basic motivation* in life. Do you trust God to care for you if you care for His church? This woman loved God's house and work. She gave everything to support it because she trusted God to care for her. Deficient giving is never a money problem; it is a trust problem. How can you trust God to save you eternally if you cannot trust Him to care for your needs in time? This woman's giving was like the cross. After Jesus commented on her giving all, He went out and did the same on Calvary.

On Harvest Day who will be the biggest giver? The one who gives like this woman— out of a motive of trust and in relationship to all of what she had.

Signs of the Times: Problems and Possibilities
(Mark 13:1-13)

Recent events in the Middle East call our attention to a biblical reality. Both the beginning and end of recorded history center in that area, according to biblical prophecy. Even a superficial reading of the Bible would indicate that the decisive and final events of time will in some way be connected with events in that part of the world. How are we to weigh present events in light of biblical belief?

Our Lord always give us a sufficient word. He does not tell us everything, but He tells us enough. He predicted that some of the problems of today would characterize the entire age until He comes. He told us specifically what our responsibility should be during this age. In an age of deception, disruption, and persecution, we must take the gospel to everyone and see that we stand firm.

Christ Demonstrates the Difficulties of This Age

Jesus predicts the difficulties that will characterize the entire age until His coming. These realities will not be peculiar to any part of that age, but will be part of the entire age.

Jesus warns against *deception*. His first words are "Watch out that no one deceives you" (v. 5). Be forewarned. This age is one of spiritual counterfeits and misinformation. Many will wander off course because of this deception. Specifically, those will deceive who say, "I am he" (v. 6). Some will openly claim to be Christ and others will claim the powers that belong only to the Christ. We are to be spiritually on guard throughout this age for those who make claims to be the Christ.

Jesus warns against *disruption*. The entire age will be characterized by national, physical, and social disruption. The Christian is never to be alarmed (v. 7). The entire age will be characterized by wars and rumors of wars, wars near and remote, wars actual and threatened. The history of the age will be the history of war. No single war indicates the end or the absence of the end. Every war should remind us there will be an end.

There will be further physical disruptions of earthquakes and famines. These seismic events will characterize the age as we wait for His coming. No one of them indicates the end or the absence of the end. All physical disruptions should remind us of the ultimate disruption—God will end history in the coming of the Christ.

Jesus warns about *persecution*. We are to be on guard because persecution will come. This persecution will be local, regional, and national (v. 9). The tension that Christ brings will invade families. It will lead to betrayal in life's most intimate relationships. All of this indicates that Jesus foresaw a considerable passage of time before He returns.

The entire age waiting for Jesus to return will be characterized by deception, disruption, and persecution. Our responsibility is to watch and be on guard. The world will never be friendly to the people of the gospel.

Christ Demonstrates Our Responsibility in This Age

As individual believers, there is little we can do about the difficulties of the age. We must pay attention to the two things that we can do.

We must pay attention to *proclamation:* "the gospel must first be preached to all nations" (v. 10). Before the King comes, the gospel must be proclaimed everywhere in the world. It is proclamation, not speculation, that brings back the King. Do you wish the soon-coming of the Lord Jesus? He will come when the message is taken everywhere. Many people waste energy on speculation about the end. Only worldwide proclamation hastens the return of the King.

We must pay attention to *perseverance:* "he who stands firm to the end will be saved" (v. 13). A faith that lasts will be the virtue of those who truly await the return of the King and the end of this age. We cannot puzzle out the meaning of every war and earthquake. We can see to it in faith and commitment that we ourselves persevere, that we endure until the end.

Whether or not we are alive at the end of the world, each of our earthly lives must come to an end. Are you ready to meet the Christ? Is your commitment to the proclamation of the gospel and perseverance in Christian service such as will please Him? We should focus on what we can change, ourselves.

Extravagant for the Lord's Sake
(Mark 14:3-9)

We do not normally relate the word *extravagant* and the Lord Jesus Christ. He lived a simple life with the bare essentials. Yet at the appropriate moment He commended an extravagant gift on His behalf. This account is recorded by Matthew, Mark, and John. This extravagant gift so impressed the Lord Jesus that He promised the giver, Mary of Bethany, universal and unending commemoration.

There are times when extravagance is appropriate for our care of Christ's body on earth, the church. Most of the time our tithes and offerings are appropriate gifts. But at critical times we should give out of spontaneous love in a way that does not calculate.

Sometimes the Cause of Christ Calls for Extravagance

There are occasions when we should meet to show gratitude to the Lord Jesus. Such an occasion was held in the home of Simon the Leper. It was a banquet of thanksgiving for Jesus' healing of Simon's leprosy. The meal probably honored Jesus for the resurrection of Lazarus as well. There were plenty of people to show Jesus their gratitude. At least fifteen men plus Mary and Martha gathered for the evening. Yet one present showed a lavish expression of gratitude.

Such gratitude offers to Jesus something that is of ultimate *value*. Mary offered to Jesus a Roman pound of pure nard. This aromatic perfume comes from the dried root of a Himalayan plant. It represents something rare that was treasured for years, held back for just the right occasion. Is it not appropriate that today we give to Jesus something we treasure and have retained for one of life's rare occasions?

Such an extravagant gift may be *unrepeatable*. An alabaster jar of translucent stone held the perfume. The lid of such a jar was crushed or broken only once, and everything within had to be used at that time, and never again. At this time in our Christian life and Travis Avenue's history many of us need to open up treasured things and give them in a one-time-only act of lavish generosity.

Such extravagant giving may be *risky*. In Jewish culture of Jesus' day a woman seldom did what Mary dared to do. She entered a room of men, anointed Jesus' head and feet (John), and put on a public display of her loving gratitude. The disciples did not understand and criticized her. Not everyone in our family, friends, or observers will understand a lavish thing for Jesus, but He does.

Such extravagant giving relies more on *devotion* than *calculation*. Mary of Bethany did not calculate. Her heart moved her to a self-forgetful act of unrepeatable generosity. The beauty of her act is the spontaneity of it. Is there ever a time when your love for the Lord Jesus moved beyond careful calculation and became an instant of such devotion?

Such Extravagance Can Create Misunderstanding

Some respond with *indignation* in the face of such extravagance. Even the disciples by their looks and remarks muttered their disapproval. They were simple people and the very act did not square with what they knew of Jesus Himself. Yet there was a deeper cause. Their indignation grew out of the roots of their own littleness and covetousness. How do you react to the generous acts of others on behalf of Christ's church? Is it with envy, indifference, hostility, or the desire to emulate what they have done?

The root of such indignation is an attitude of *calculation*. The nard perfume could have been sold for the equivalent of a year's wages. It could have fed 300 people for a day or one person for 300 days. They considered its use on Jesus a waste. It is true that we always have to calculate, to plan, to be rational. But there are also times when our giving needs to move beyond calculation to expression of gratitude that cannot be counted.

The Lord Jesus Commends Such Extravagance

The Lord Jesus accepted this act as what was due to Him. In this is an explicit claim to His own divinity. Jesus speaks in defense of all those who are appropriately extravagant for Him.

Jesus commends the *beauty* of extravagance for His sake. "She has done a beautiful thing to me" (v. 6). He calls the act a thing of self-evident moral beauty which does not need defense, no less criticism. Rather than depreciate what she did, the others should have seen the beauty in it. When we spontaneously give without calculation there is a beauty in it that speaks for itself.

Jesus acknowledges the *timeliness* in extravagant giving. The opportunity for ministry to His body would be impossible in a few days. Other opportunities for generosity would always be present. For us it is different. We are the ones who are running out of time. Consider how you will reflect on your giving in the last days of your life. Your church stands at a critical and 'historical moment in need of your support. This time will not return again.

Jesus unfolds the *implication* of extravagant giving. She did more than she knew. She had anointed His body for burial. She did not know this. Whenever we give extravagantly for the cause of Christ we do not foresee all the consequences. The provision of facilities for a great biblical and evangelistic church has consequences beyond what anyone can foresee. Thousands will benefit in the untold years ahead because some of us were extravagant to make provision today.

Faces Around the Manger: Mary
(Luke 1)

Protestants have been reluctant to speak of Mary. She is the victim of circumstances that have obscured her real character. The Roman Church has made her the divine queen of heaven and, in the process, virtually canceled her humanity. On the other hand, we have emphasized her humanity to the extent that we have feared to speak of her as part of God's redemptive intention.

Phillips Brooks's hymn, "O Little Town of Bethlehem," notes that "The hopes and fears of all the years Are met in thee tonight." This is even more true of Mary, mother of our Lord. Our hopes and fears are all reflected in her response to God's act of grace.

Mary Maintains the Continuity of God's Purposes

The opening chapters of Luke's Gospel read more like the Old Testament than the New. We move in the midst of that remnant that represents the very best of the Old Testament. Critical of the Pharisees, we often forget that the best of the Old Testament religion produced a people "agog" for the coming of the gospel.

The poetic songs of Mary are alive with Scripture, saturated with the Old Testament. There are reflections of 1 and 2 Samuel, Psalms, Job, Isaiah, Genesis, and Micah in her Magnificat. She takes up themes from Sara, wife of Abraham, and Hannah, mother of Samuel. Additionally, prophecy had stopped with that of Malachi; Mary is involved in its renewal at the birth of Jesus. Mary seems to be connected to the house of King David. Mary is living proof of God's capacity to sustain His purposes across the ages.

Mary Models the Mosaic of Human Response

All of us respond differently to God's purposes. Mary mirrors our responses. Seven times Mary speaks in the Gospels, and then she is silent. Her first word is a question of confusion, "How shall this be?" (Luke 1:34, KJV). Mary raised the first objection to the incarnation. Her second word is an affirmation of submission, "Behold, the handmaid of the Lord" (v. 38, KJV). Next, there is the word of communication and compassion. She visits her kinswoman, Elizabeth, to share in the joy that only one woman may communicate to another. We do not know what she said, but the impact of the incarnation on her life was to turn her in service to another. There is then a word of jubilation as she pours herself into the praise of the Magnificat. After twelve years of silence, there is the word of consternation, "Son, why hast thou thus dealt with us?" (Luke 2:48, KJV) She did not always understand the purposes of the One who had grown beneath her heart. There is the word of intercession, "They have no wine" (John 2:3, KJV). She recognized in Him the One who could redeem any situation. Finally, there is the word of commendation, "Whatsoever he saith unto you, do it" (v. 5). She is the one who presents Him on the occasion of His first demonstration of superhuman authority.

Mary Manifests the Fragility of God's People

Mary is not only the obedient maiden; she is not only the sorrowing mother. She is also one who does not understand what God's purposes are, who intervenes when she ought to keep silent, who interferes and tries to thwart the purposes of God, who pleads the ties of filial affection when she should learn faith. And that is what we are like. We are not only faithful; we are faithless. We are obedient and interfering, perceptive and opaque, faithful and contradictory. Mary confesses that she is not worthy to be chosen of God. That is not false humility, it is the truth of every human being's situation before

God. Mary is inspiration and encouragement that people such as we are can be taken up into God's purpose, *iustus et peccator simul* (Luther).

Virgin Birth and New Birth
(Luke 1:26-37)

The Gospels witness and the ancient creeds confess that Jesus Christ was born of a virgin by the miraculous intervention of the Holy Spirit. Mary, the mother of Jesus, gave birth to the Christ without any human sexual encounter, and Jesus had no human father. In this way God made a new beginning in human history. God Himself originated a particular human life—Jesus of Nazareth—by a new act of creation. Jesus Christ did not arise out of the continuity of human history, but God came to the rescue by creating a new person.

In a truly related way, one becomes a Christian by the operation of the Holy Spirit in the new birth. The same God who can create by a virgin birth can intervene in human life today with a new birth. The same Holy Spirit operates in both realms.

A Virgin Conceived and Gave Birth to Jesus Christ

There is an *affirmation* of Scripture. Luke takes pains to state three times that Mary was a virgin. She had never known human sexual relations. He places obvious stress on this fact. His generation knew the facts of life as well as our generation. The first readers of this understood it in the same way we understand it. There is a confirmation of this in Matthew's account written from the perspective of Joseph: "before they came together she was found to be with child through the Holy Spirit" (Matt. 1:18).

There is an *expectation* of prophecy. Matthew 1:22-23 makes clear that the birth of Jesus to a virgin was in direct fulfillment of an earlier prophecy from Isaiah 7:14: "The virgin will be with child and will give birth to a son, and will call him Immanuel." We cannot gainsay the apostolic witness of prophecy that the virgin birth of Jesus was predicted by Isaiah.

There is the *confirmation* of tradition. Jewish wedding customs called for a period of betrothal. This took place at an extremely early age by our culture, at the age of twelve or twelve and one-half years. The interval between betrothal and marriage was one year. The betrothed woman who committed adultery was subject to death (Deut. 22:23-24). Mary found herself in her expectant condition on the penalty of death.

There is the *confirmation* of other passages. Several passages imply that there was rumor or gossip concerning the parentage of Jesus Christ. Mark 6:3 curiously calls Him the son of Mary, not mentioning any human father. In John 8:41 His opponents virtually accuse Him of illegitimacy. It is of interest that there is diverse testimony from mutually hostile witnesses. The church confesses that Jesus was born of a virgin. Jews assert that Jesus was the offspring of Mary and some man other than Joseph. Both agree that Joseph was not the father of Jesus.

The new birth of a Christian is equally without human causation and just as mysterious. When we become children of God we are born "not of natural descent, nor of human decision or a husband's will, but born of God" (John 1:13). The new birth not less than the virgin birth is the sheer act of God.

Mary Raised the First Question About the Virgin Birth

The first *question* about the virgin birth came from Mary. It is the obvious question, "How will this be?" (v. 34a) This may be an involuntary expression of amazement, a gasp of astonishment. She does not doubt the possibility, only the mode. She joins with this question a simple affirmation, "I know not a man" (v. 34b, KJV). The word "know" is the Semitic idiom for sexual intercourse. The word "man" is the generic word which refers to any man, Joseph or anyone else. It is the honest protest of a young woman who knows herself to be pure and does not expect to have a child by any other than the normal processes of human conception.

The *explanation* comes from the messenger of God. The birth will be totally an *activity* of the Holy Spirit. By a separate act of revelation her betrothed Joseph was also told that the conception was due to the activity of the Holy Spirit (Matt. 1:18,20). It was thought that the Spirit had been inactive for several centuries since the closure of the Old Testament. Now the work of the Spirit begins again.

There will be an *immediacy* of action: "The Holy Spirit will come upon you. . . ." The language implies a proximity, a closeness, not a distance. There are no sexual overtones in this operation of the Spirit. By an act of God similar to creation (Gen. 1:2) the Spirit will bring about a conception. This results in the beautiful description that "the power of the Most High will overshadow you" (v. 35). This is a direct reference to the cloud of God's bright glory hanging over the tabernacle tent in the Exodus (Ex. 40:34-38). That cloud of glory represented divine presence and power. In the same way, the presence and power of God acted in the womb of the virgin. The conception was immediate and at that very moment of announcement.

There is a *sufficiency* of action. As a direct result of this operation by the Holy Spirit the one born of Mary is holy in the absolute sense of harmless, undefiled, and separate from sinners (Heb. 7:26). He did not sin (1 Pet. 2:22). He was born without the seminal overhang of the entire race that causes us to sin. Yet at the same time He was born of a woman, very flesh of our very flesh (Gal. 4:4).

This shows that at the deepest level God's redemption of His creation was by grace alone. Our humanity, represented by Mary, does nothing but just accept—and even the acceptance is God's gift. Our fallen humanity's role is strictly limited. All of our pride and self-reliant humanity is to be set aside. We are simply made the receptacle of God's gift.

The new birth in Christ is the same. We submit ourselves to the operation of God's Spirit. The Spirit does in our lives what we could never originate or create ourselves. It is a direct, immediate, and creative act of God. The same God who could empower a virgin birth can likewise give you new birth.

Mary's Song

(Luke 1:46-56)

On the surface Mary's song does not seem to be a revolutionary document. Yet one called her song "the most revolutionary document in the world." Mary sings of a revolution as quiet as it is certain, as inward as it is radical, as spiritual as it is durable.

You can experience that revolution in your life.

I. Mary Sings of a Revolution in the Fulfilment of Scripture

Mary's song answers the cry of expectant womanhood.

Mary's song answers the cry of the oppressed.

Mary's song answers the cry of those who believe even though they do not understand.

Mary's song reminds us that the God who *did* remember His promise is the God who *will* remember His promise.

II. Mary Sings of a Spiritual Revolution

React to what God is doing in your life.
    Devotionally
    Emotionally
    Confessionally
Reflect on what God is doing.
    In the past.
    In the future.
Relate God to yourself in Mary's song.

III. Mary Sings of a Revolution in the Direction of History

Paradox of the proud—God uses those of low estate, but scatters the proud.
Paradox of the powerful—He puts down potentates from their thrones.
Paradox of privilege—Those who are full, He dismisses. Those who are empty, He fills.

Applications:

Weigh the devotion of Mary against your own private devotion this Christmas.
Reflect on the impact of Christ in today's world of the proud and powerful.

Waiting for Christmas
(Luke 2:22-35)

We know the impatient difficulty that children have waiting for Christmas. There was one man who waited for Christmas with more expectancy than any other. He was an old man named Simeon. Simeon shows that God has a people prepared even in the worst of circumstances. The story of Jesus' birth shows that when religious leaders and institutions are corrupt, God still has a quiet people prepared for His coming. The characters of Luke 1 and 2—Elizabeth and Zechariah, Simeon and Anna, Joseph and Mary—reminds us that God will always have a faithful people, even in the worst of times.

Simeon shows us how to prepare our hearts for Christmas. We prepare for Christmas with integrity of heart and understanding of mind. There are certain things we should *be* and some things we should *know* as we wait for Christmas.

The Character of Those Who Wait for Christmas

Most of the people missed the significant events of that first Christmas. The political and religious leaders did not even know what was happening. Many in our city will altogether miss the significance of Christmas. Simeon was one of the few who saw and understood the mighty act of God that first Christmas. What characterized him?

Wait for Christmas with *integrity*. Simeon was "righteous and devout." With reference to God's will, there was reverence, devotion, and care about spiritual duties. No one sees Christmas who does not guard the integrity of his life. Only those whose hearts are right with God will see and sense the significance of Christmas.

Wait for Christmas with *intensity*. Simeon was "waiting for the consolation of Israel." A fierce intensity of expectation characterized Simeon. He lived daily in a white heat of expectancy that God was about to intervene. We experience as much of God as we intensely expect to experience. Christmastime ought to be a time to evaluate our spiritual expectancy.

Wait for Christmas with *inspiration*. The most critical aspect of Simeon's character was his relationship to the Holy Spirit. "The Holy Spirit was upon him" (v. 25) in an abiding communion with God. The Holy Spirit had given him a revelation—that he would not die until he had seen the Messiah. The Holy Spirit gave him a direction: "Moved by the Spirit, he went into the temple courts" (v. 27). The first Christmas was marked by a renewal of activity on the part of the Spirit of God. Every Christmas ought to be marked by a renewal of the Spirit in our lives.

The Comfort of Those Who Wait for Christmas

A sense of comfort and well-being characterizes those ready for the significance of Christmas. That comfort comes from our relationship to Christ.

Comfort comes in our *reception* of Christ. "Simeon took Him in his arms and praised God" (v. 28). In a literal sense, Simeon was the first person on record to receive Christ. Moved by the Spirit, he came at exactly the right time to precisely the right place. Many parents were bringing their infants to the temple for the act of presentation. Nothing physical or dramatic caused Mary, Joseph, and Jesus to stand out from the crowd. Yet Simeon unerringly found his way to the Christ. Has God led you to His Christ? The Holy Spirit is able to bring you to that precise time and place where your life intersects with His. The very same Spirit that drew Simeon draws you this Christmas.

Comfort comes from our *satisfaction* with Christ. Simeon expressed total fulfillment of life when he saw the Christ (v. 29). His words reflect a servant who had been posted by his master to wait for a certain event. When that event has happened, the tired servant asks to be dismissed. Simeon discovered absolute contentment and total well-being in seeing and receiving Christ. Do you face this Christmas with a sense of well-being and contentment in your life? Only seeing and receiving Christ gives that.

The Concern of Those Who Wait for Christmas

Christmas gives us a comfort, but it also gives our life an ultimate concern and mission.

Christmas concerns the *certainty* of God's faithfulness. He is a God who keeps His promise (v. 29). Our entire relationship to God depends on His faithfulness to His promises. In the coming of Christ we see that God does keep His promises. At least seventy-three specific promises written in the Old Testament were fulfilled in the coming of the Messiah at Christmas. We may be sure that the God who kept His promises in the past is the God who will keep His promises in the future.

Christmas concerns the *universality* of God's salvation. The old Jew, Simeon, proclaimed that the baby he held was a "light for revelation to the Gentiles" (v. 32). He saw that what happened in Jerusalem that day was for the entire planet. A piercing light flashes in every direction from that awesome moment. The very fact you are here today is proof of that. After this prophecy by Simeon, wise men from the East came to bow before the infant Christ. The Christian world mission cannot be separated from

Christmas. It is news too good to keep. By prayer and by gift we must send that light.

Setting the Captives Free
(Luke 4:16-30)

Jesus comes to announce liberty and not captivity for all people. In His first formal public message at His hometown He proclaimed a new freedom.

Jesus Announces Liberty for All Captives

He gives liberty to those who recognize their helpless dependence on God. He gives new insight to those who cannot see and new freedom to spiritual prisoners. He lifts burdens that crush. He announces the critical time of God's liberation.

You May Miss His Liberty By Failure to Recognize Him

Some do not recognize Jesus because of familiarity, and some do not recognize Him because of His inclusive ministry. You can experience the freedom that Christ gives. Do not let overfamiliarity with His message keep you from experiencing its power.

Encounter with Jesus:
A Marvelous Faith
(Luke 7:2-10)

What impresses the Lord Jesus? In the Gospel record He is unimpressed by everything that impresses us. Position, power, wealth, talent, and human achievement impressed Him not at all. The only thing that impressed Him was the presence or absence of faith. On two occasions we are told that Jesus marveled with surprise. He marveled at the absence of faith where we would have expected it to be present (Mark 6:6). Yet in the unlikely person of a pagan military soldier He marveled at the presence of faith where we would expect it to be absent (Luke 7:9).

Would you like to impress the Lord Jesus to the point of amazement? You can impress Him only by your faith in His word and power. Even an unlikely outsider can impress Jesus with a humble faith in His word and power.

Jesus Marvels at the Presence of Faith in an Unlikely Person

Some people seem more likely to have faith than others. Those who grow up as "insiders," church people from church families, would seem to be more likely to have faith. Yet sometimes "outsiders" demonstrate more surprising faith. The centurion in this story is an "outsider."

He was an outsider religiously, racially, and politically. Religiously, he was a Gentile, with no deep background in the acts and words of God. Racially, he was non-Jewish, a Roman or a Greek. Politically, he was a soldier working for Herod Antipas, a hated puppet ruler over the Jews. In every sense this man was an unlikely outsider at the point of faith. Yet he demonstrates a quality of faith that surprised Jesus Himself.

Do you feel like an outsider concerning religion? You can nevertheless have a faith that amazes the Lord Jesus.

Jesus Marvels at the Nature of Faith in an Unlikely Person

What is the nature of faith that gives Jesus a pleasant surprise? There are some identifying marks of the faith that amaze Jesus and win His approval.

Such faith grows in a soft and loving heart. Hard, cynical people seldom manifest faith. This centurion demonstrated the heart of faith in unlikely objects of love. He loved his slave. This was rare. His slave was honored, revered, held dear and precious. Further, he loved his natural enemies, the Jews. He loved them to the point that he built a synagogue out of his own resources. This was an incredible act for a Gentile. Faith grows in softened hearts. Beware of hardness towards people. It kills faith.

Such faith demonstrates humility. This military officer did not consider himself worthy to approach Jesus. He sent a delegation of seven to ten Jewish elders on his behalf. He dropped all personal claim on Jesus as an officer and a Jewish benefactor. Further, he stopped Jesus from coming into his home. He shows a moving humility. The Lord Jesus responds to the humble spirit that makes no claims but simply trusts.

Such faith gives spiritual insight. This soldier understood what it meant to be under authority and in authority (v. 8). As the centurion reflected on his own limited human authority, he formed an opinion about Jesus' divine authority. He confessed that Jesus had at His command incredible, invisible spiritual authority. All that Jesus had to do was say the word and his servant would be healed. He showed insight into the spiritual authority and the power of Jesus' word. Would you like to impress Jesus? Then demonstrate your trust in His authority and His word alone.

Jesus Responds to Faith in an Unlikely Person

Jesus marvels at faith alone (v. 9). Others said that this man was worthy (v. 4). This man said of himself that he was not worthy (v. 6). The only estimate that counts is that of Jesus. He approved the man because of his faith. Whereas the Jews commended his love and his gifts, Jesus commended his faith. Our Lord looks for one thing, simple trust in His authority and His power. Only faith impresses the Lord Jesus.

Jesus responds to faith alone. "The men who had been sent returned to the house and found the servant well" (v. 10). Jesus did even more than the centurion expected. The centurion expected that Jesus must speak a word. Evidently Jesus healed the slave at a distance by the unspoken power of Jesus' will to make whole. Jesus did more than simply cure the threatening disease. Luke uses a word which means that the man became completely well in every way.

This story has a special meaning to all of us who have never seen the Lord Jesus in the flesh. The centurion never saw Jesus. At a distance he made an appeal. At a distance Jesus made his servant whole. We too never see the Lord Jesus physically. We too must trust the word and authority of One about Whom we have heard but Whom we have not yet seen. "Blessed are those who have not seen and yet have believed" (John 20:29).

Encounter with Jesus:
Guess Who's Coming to Dinner
(Luke 7:36-50)

We relate to and react to the Lord Jesus on the basis of our personal need and gratitude for Him. Those who feel no need have little gratitude. Those who feel great need demonstrate greater gratitude. You can evaluate your experience with Jesus by the spontaneous love you demonstrate toward Him. Everyone forgiven by the Lord Jesus demonstrates his/her forgiveness in open gratitude.

We Contact Jesus with Personal Sufficiency or Personal Need

Some contact Jesus who feel no personal need. Such only want to have a curious look at Him. Simon the Pharisee invited Jesus to his dinner out of curiosity at best or hostility at worst. Yet the Lord Jesus takes any opening we give Him. Out of supreme personal security He will be entertained by anyone who wants to consider Him. He has nothing to prove.

Some approach Jesus with a deep sense of personal need. Sinful failures are always welcome. The anonymous woman surprised everyone by approaching Jesus. It was not unusual for outsiders to watch Eastern banquets. It was unusual for a fallen woman to approach a famous rabbi. This woman was the notorious sinner in that city. Yet she knew where to find the Lord Jesus. Do the sinful failures in our city think they could find Jesus at our church?

The Lord Jesus wants our uninhibited gratitude. He always accepts the loving thanks of those He saves. This woman entered the dinner and stood behind Jesus, hesitating to act. She suddenly burst into tears. She expressed her gratitude to Jesus in three ways. She reacted **emotionally.** Her tears fell like rain on Jesus' feet. She reacted **demonstratively.** She untied her hair (considered shameful in public) and wiped His feet. She also repeatedly and fervently kissed His feet. She reacted **substantially.** She poured out on Him the most valuable thing she possessed. She had earned the perfume by and used it in her immoral life. She now gives it to Jesus.

The Jesus of the Gospels is approachable. Do sinners want to approach us? We represent Him. All that any of us can do is express our overwhelming gratitude for what He has done for us.

We May Misunderstand the Acceptance That Jesus Gives

He who sees like a Pharisee does not see Jesus at all.

Spiritual self-sufficiency cannot comprehend Jesus. "If this man were a prophet, he would know who is touching him and what kind of woman she is—that she is a sinner" (v. 39). Simon the Pharisee thought the woman would infect Jesus with sin rather than Jesus cover the woman with holiness. "If Jesus did not know that woman, He lacked discernment. If He did know her, He lacked holiness." Simon was wrong. Jesus knew the woman, her faith, and her new life. He also knew Simon.

Only through Jesus can we understand unconditional acceptance. The little "Parable of the Two Debtors" presents God as the creditor, I as the debtor, sin as the debt. We do not have it in our power to pay God what we owe Him. He forgives us the entire debt freely as a gift. The more I feel He has forgiven me, the more I will love God. If I feel no need of forgiveness, I will feel no love. If I feel overwhelmed by God's forgiveness, I will love Him the more.

Simon felt no need and insulted Jesus. The woman knew His abounding grace and lavished love on Jesus.

We May Judge Ourselves by Our Response to Jesus

Do we respond to Jesus as the Friend to whom we owe everything? We can contrast two abiding attitudes toward the Lord Jesus by the reactions of Simon and the woman.

Are we considerate toward the Lord Jesus? Simon did not even give Jesus the customary washing of the feet that was done for every friend in the Holy Land. The woman washed Jesus' feet with her own tears. Do we even consider the Lord Jesus in our actions and reactions toward Him?

Do we express our friendship to Jesus? Simon did not give Jesus the customary sign of friendship in that culture, a kiss on the face. The woman repeatedly kissed Jesus' feet. In so doing, she showed true friendship. She was a better host than the host himself.

Do we give our best to the Lord Jesus? Simon did not anoint His head with inexpensive olive oil, a tradition for a distinguished guest. The woman poured out the most expensive perfume from a container that could not be replaced.

In short, does our love demonstrate the fact we have indeed been forgiven. Consideration, friendship, and our best given to Jesus demonstrate our love. Jesus confirms what had already happened when He exclaims, "Your sins are forgiven. . . . go in peace" (vv. 48-50).

The only peace to be found is at Jesus' feet. Would you join this woman there? An attitude of proud self-sufficiency stands aloof and never hears His word of peace. An attitude of humble need finds His love and His best gift, peace with God.

Grounds for Gratitude
(Luke 7:36-50)

What actually motivates persons toward gratitude? According to Jesus, we feel gratitude when we truly sense we have been forgiven. When we feel no need for forgiveness, we demonstrate no gratitude. How much gratitude we feel is a good index to how much of God's forgiveness we have experienced.

Luke alone gives the striking contrast of ingratitude and gratitude demonstrated at the house of Simon the Pharisee. The story presupposes that Jesus had spoken about God's forgiveness, and was invited to Simon's house for a banquet. The interruption of the banquet by a notorious sinner sets the stage for Jesus' teaching about gratitude as it relates to forgiveness. Those who most know forgiveness, most express gratitude.

Ingratitude Roots in No Sense of Need

Simon the Pharisee models the absence of felt need for the grace of God. His attitudes toward Jesus present a timeless portrait of ingratitude.

Ingratitude reacts to Christ with an incorrect motivation. Curiosity without commitment never results in gratitude toward Christ. At best, Simon had invited Jesus out of curiosity. At worst, Simon desired to entrap Jesus. Nothing about Simon's reaction to Christ reveals any sense of personal need for Christ's message of forgiveness. An attitude of indifferent detachment toward Christ yields no sense of gratitude.

Ingratitude reacts to Christ with an inaccurate evaluation. A cold, calculating self-righteousness cannot evaluate the mission and message of Jesus. Simon calculated that Jesus could not be God's prophet because He let a sinner touch Him. Jesus was the prophet of God just because He did let sinners touch Him.

Ingratitude reacts to Christ with an inappropriate reception. A detached and aloof attitude toward Christ reveals no sense of gratitude. Simon did not even offer to Christ the most common courtesies of hospitality (vv. 44-46).

In spite of our rank ingratitude, Christ still tries to find an opening with us. Jesus Christ sought to touch Simon's life even though Simon's motivation, evaluation, and reception were all wrong.

Gratitude Roots in a Deep Sense of Need

The sinful woman models the presence of deeply felt need for the grace of God. Because she felt that need, she expressed gratitude toward Christ.

Authentic gratitude expresses itself spontaneously. A spirit of thankfulness does not have to be pushed or promoted. She spontaneously came into the banquet room to express her gratitude. The customs of that day enabled uninvited guests to do so.

Authentic gratitude expresses itself demonstratively. True thankfulness must express itself outwardly. Although she had not intended to do so, she began to weep at the feet of Jesus. She was not ashamed to demonstrate the depth of her thanksgiving.

Authentic gratitude expresses itself humbly. A true sense of lowliness marks authentic thanksgiving. For a woman to unbind her hair publicly in that culture indicated the deepest sense of personal humiliation and self-effacement.

Authentic gratitude expresses itself sacrificially. The alabaster container of perfume had been used by or earned from her life of sin. In pouring it out on Jesus' feet, she expressed gratitude by giving the best that she had.

When we deeply feel our need for Jesus' grace, we will openly express our gratitude for that grace.

Gratitude Marks Those Who Discover Needs Met in Christ

The little parable of the two debtors teaches that those most express grateful love who most know forgiveness. Verse 47 has always troubled sincere readers of Scripture. Jesus means, "God must have forgiven her sins, many as they are, since she displays such deep thankfulness; he to whom God forgives little shows little thankfulness."

Who will be most grateful this Thanksgiving? The person who most deeply feels the experience of Christ's forgiveness will be the most grateful. The person who shows no gratitude shows no evidence of experiencing that grace. Great grace gives great gratitude.

The Good Samaritan
(Luke 10:25-37)

"Who is my neighbor?" The question both then and now provokes debate and uneasiness. In Jesus' world the religious often debated the limits of neighborliness, the Pharisees, rabbis, Essenes, and common people drawing the line at different places. Today, the question is even more difficult than in Jesus' world. Modern mobility makes thousands of people we see only for a fleeting, few moments our neighbor. We walk by them at a mall, sit next to them in an airplane, or jostle against them at a football game. Modern media makes the question even more difficult. At our dinner table we are instantly aware of starving people in Ethiopia. There seem to be endless claims with no boundary.

The motive in which we ask the question is as important as the answer. "He wanted to justify himself" (v. 29). The expert in the Old Testament law desired to *limit* his responsibility rather than *define* his responsibility. He was more interested in theological speculation than in practical application. Where and how do we meet our neighbor?

We Meet Our Neighbor in the Troubled One
Immediately Before Us

The road to Jericho reaches all the way to Fort Worth. The ancient road from Jerusalem down to Jericho was seventeen miles long. Highway robbers lived in caves along the road. The road has been a place of danger right up to this very moment. That reminds us that it is a road anyone can travel, anytime, anywhere. The hapless traveler was suddenly surrounded by vicious thieves. They took what he had, stripped him of his clothes, and beat him as he attempted to defend himself. The story Jesus told probably represents an historical event.

Who is my neighbor, the one near me? It is the specific, troubled individual who is unavoidably before me alone. No one else is there to help. I must step *to* him, or *around* him, but he is unavoidably there before me alone. No one can be neighbor to everybody, but anyone should be neighbor in this instance.

We Can Avoid Our Neighbor Even in the Name of Religion

Two religious professionals walked by the wounded neighbor. The priest belonged to the elite of the religious professionals. The Levite belonged to the lesser group who did the heavy work of skinning sacrifices and cleaning up the leftovers. Evidently, Jesus saw two levels of callousness in their respective attitudes. The priest walked by on the "other side." The language suggested that the Levite came and looked carefully, but decided to go on after his careful inspection.

The religious law forbade touching a corpse for such religious professionals. This may have been the motivation, but they seem to be going away from the temple back to Jericho. Religious busyness often tramples right over human need. Formalism, ritualism, and institutionalism can drive religious machinery right over hurting people in the name of religion itself.

An Unlikely Person Often Cares More Than Anyone Else

Those who first heard Jesus' story would have expected the third character to be a righteous fellow-countryman. Instead it was a despised half-breed, a Samaritan. It is difficult to reproduce in 1986 the shock of Jesus' story in the first century. The Samaritans had desecrated the Jewish temple by spreading dead persons' bones throughout. In turn, the Jew cursed the Samaritan, considered his food as swine's flesh, and was told to suffer rather than receive help from a Samaritan.

Help for the one immediately before me alone ought to be personal, particular, the total. The Samaritan did not report it to a committee, he did it himself. The detail of the story indicates the particular, and meticulous care he gave. His willingness to pay for future accommodations indicates the ripe totality of his personal care. He did not hand the future to somebody else, he took responsibility himself.

No one can do this for everybody. But those who claim to have eternal life had better be doing it for somebody.

Distraction or Devotion?
(Luke 10:38-42)

Our service for the Lord Jesus either grows out of personal devotion or will lead to a disturbing distraction. Mary and Martha for all time represent the contrast between devotion to Christ and distraction in the service of Christ.

Four months before the cross, Jesus stopped at the home of Martha and Mary. Jesus Himself needed a safe house, friendship, a place to retire. So do we all, if we serve Him effectively. Luke alone tells us this story. Jesus receives the quiet, personal devotion of Mary and corrects the distracted service of Martha. Service grows from personal devotion to the Lord Jesus or it leads to the distraction of the servant.

Service Without Devotion Leads to Distraction

Distraction does not imply a lack of love for the Lord Jesus. Martha indeed loved Jesus. She met Jesus in the village. She gladly welcomed Him under her roof, even though that could mean danger for her because of His disfavor with the powerful. Martha did not love Him *less;* she simply did not love Him *best.*

Many of us serve Him and love Him, but not the best way. When there is work for Him without personal devotion to Him, we cannot love Him best. He does not desire what we do *for* Him in the absence of time *with* Him.

Distraction does dominate work without worship, service without devotion. "Martha was distracted" (v. 40). She was dragged in many directions, pulled apart, drawn hither and thither. There must have been concern about the room, the table, the meal, and the guests. This was all because of the many services she wanted to render Jesus. What a contrast is Mary, composed at Jesus' feet. Mary was not unconcerned about the details. Mary also welcomed Jesus, provided for Jesus. But Mary sat composed at Jesus' feet, seeking Him before serving Him further.

Distraction without devotion demonstrates itself in certain responses.

Distraction leads to the *interruption* of the Lord Jesus. Martha suddenly came up to Jesus, stepped in front of Him, and with a petulant outburst interrupted Him. Working without worship can cause us to interrupt Jesus' plan for our lives and for others. When we serve Him without seeking His face we can actually block what He really wants to be doing in our life, our church, and our world.

Distraction leads to *accusation.* Martha accused both the Lord and Mary. She accused the Lord of not caring about her service and Mary of abandoning her without help. Simply grinding out Christian work without personal devotion to Christ causes us to become bitter towards God ("He doesn't care") and towards other Christian servants ("they don't do enough").

Distraction leads to *domination.* Martha wanted to dominate the Lord and Mary. She desired Christ to tell Mary what to do; and she told Him that in Mary's presence! Service without devotion leads to power games, manipulation, and demand.

We should pay close attention to Jesus' evaluation of work without worship. *Inwardly,* it leads to *division.* "Worried" means to be divided, partitioned, fragmented (v. 41). The Word sets human anxiety over against divine providence: "Cast all your anxiety upon him because he cares for you" (1 Pet. 5:7).

Outwardly, such service leads to *disturbance.* Without seeking Jesus' face, our service becomes agitated, bustling, and troubling. There is no poise, composure, or peace.

Devotion Before Service Leads to Commendation

In contrast to the divided and distracted demeanor of Martha stands the simple devotion of Mary. Mary sat still at the feet of Jesus and listened to His word. This is indeed the one thing we hear about Mary. The picture of Mary for time and eternity is the devotion of presence and attention to the Lord.

There is the *devotion of presence.* Mary sat beside Jesus at His feet, the position of a disciple. While Martha was pulled apart in different directions, Mary sat in composure before the Lord Jesus. All effective and lasting Christian service comes from this. Those who wait on His presence renew strength (Isa. 40:31).

There is the *devotion of attention*. Mary habitually and continually listened to His word. The mark of a disciple is devotion to the word of the Master. All busyness without this attentiveness burns out. This is the one thing that is better than all other things.

Consider the Lord's evaluation of such devotion.

Such devotion is *the single necessity:* "only one thing is needed." Out of that one thing grows all else. "Seek first the kingdom of God, . . . and all these things [services, preparations, activities] shall be added unto you" (Matt. 6:33, KJV). Actually, Jesus speaks on two levels. At the lower level He suggests that only one dish, one simple item would have sufficed to feed Him. At the higher level He speaks of the singular need for time in His presence listening to His Word.

Sometimes our service to Christ can be an imposition on Christ rather than the intention of Christ. He expects no more service than that which flows out of a living, personal devotional relationship with Him.

Such devotion is *a chosen priority*. "Mary has chosen what is better." In one great instant act Mary chose the better. We should not live on the level of compulsive activity but on the level of chosen priority, to seek the Lord in worship before work.

Such devotion has *a promised durability:* "it will not be taken away from her" (v. 42). Only the experience of the presence and Word of Christ lasts forever. Every other work will stop. Tongues are silenced, pens are stilled, steps are halted. Fellowship with Jesus lasts now and forever.

Weather-Wise, but Otherwise
(Luke 12:49-59)

We have enjoyed a delightful change in weather that has occasioned much comment. Jesus' generation was likewise preoccupied with the weather. In our text, He repeats, in essence, two of the popular weather proverbs in the English-speaking world: "Sky red in the morning is a sailor's sure warning" and "Sky red at night is a sailor's delight."

There is nothing wrong with discerning the weather or making proverbs about it. Jesus fingered His generation's problem: They were weather-wise, but otherwise spiritually ignorant. *They could discern that which was not of ultimate significance, but they could not discern that which was of supreme importance, His presence and His claims.* His words also arrest and address us.

We Are Obsessed with Discerning Things
that Do Not Ultimately Matter

It took little wisdom to be a weatherman in Jesus' time. A cloud over the western Mediterranean was a sure sign of rain to come. A south wind disturbing the branches of the trees presaged the coming of a scorching day. Such weather telling was the preoccupation of the common people. It was done with confidence and success. The problem was the people's lack of discernment in the area that mattered *most*, the presence of Christ and the spiritual crisis He brings.

Are we not like these people? We fill our days and occupy our evenings judging and remarking on things that do not ultimately matter. Great spiritual crises burn before us, but we choose to give ourselves to the trivial. The demand to be people of ultimate concerns is too high and too heavy.

We Lack Discernment in the One Thing That Does Matter

Jesus indicts His generation because they are undiscerning of the one thing that does matter, His person, words and works. While His generation spoke of rain and wind, He was beginning the reign of God and the wind of judgment. The realm of their failure to discern was *the time*. The word Jesus used indicates a time of particular significance, a time laden with destiny, a moment of opportunity that would never be recovered. Like Nero, they fiddled with the inconsequential while their world burned around them. Any time Christ confronts us the moments are momentous.

He leaves no question as to the cause of their sloth and inaction. They are *hypocrites*. They professed to be unable to interpret *signs* such as the birth, preaching, and death of the Baptist, and the preaching and miracles of Jesus. But their weather interest proved they could be intelligent enough where their worldly interests were concerned. Every man *can* discern the significance of Christ. His truths are self-evident and transparent. His claims burn before our eyes and roar in our ears. Jesus nails every man to the final responsibility of accepting or rejecting His claims. The implication is that anyone who can discern a change in the weather has the capacity to confront and decide about Him.

Act Quickly to Discern What Is Really Significant

This little saying about the payment of debts appears to be altogether out of place and unrelated to what precedes. In reality, it most definitely speaks to the question at hand. When one discerns the critical nature of Christ's claims, he should act like a man who will either pay immediately or go to prison for life. The present is a period of crisis in which decisions of ultimate spiritual concern are demanded from every person. Act as urgently as a man would who was on trial for life. Discern the times!

Come at All Cost, but Count the Cost
(Luke 14:25-35)

The presence of Jesus always attracted great crowds. The curious, the excited, and the merely bored followed Him. In Luke 14, Jesus turned suddenly toward the crowd walking behind Him. He was walking toward a cross, and they did not understand the implication of following Him. Three times he told them of those who "cannot be My disciple." He obviously wanted quality more than quantity. He warned them that following Him is a life of repudiation and renunciation. He gave two unforgettable illustrations of the cost to a Christian in building and battling. Come at all cost, but count the cost.

Authentic Discipleship Always Costs (vv. 25-27)

Discipleship costs in *relationships*. Jesus refuses discipleship to anyone unwilling to "hate" life's closest relationships. Jesus did not mind using bold, striking language. He knew well enough we would dilute it and qualify it! Matthew stated the same principle positively: whoever loves life's closest relationships more than Christ is not worthy of Christ (Matt. 10:37). Jesus Himself paid this price (12:46-50). He predicted that His followers would face division in life's closest ties in order to follow Him (Luke 12:52-53). He also predicted a compensation beyond all imagination for those willing to follow (Matt. 19:29).

Following Jesus is not always incompatible with the claims of life's closest and dearest. But when it is, the disciple has already made the choice. In the disciple's love for Jesus, every other claim is subordinate.

Discipleship costs *renunciation*. The "hate" extends to one's own life itself. In comparison to the claims of Christ, our very existence becomes hateful. To take up our cross puts us in the position of those already condemned to die, those who regard life in this world as over. It is a mentality of martyrdom (Rev. 12:11). To settle this settles all else.

Building a Disciple's Life Costs (vv. 28-30)

Building a disciple's life costs in *consideration*. A man wishing to build a tower (a farm building, watchtower) must "sit down" to count the cost. This indicates serious consideration and deliberate calculation. The decision to follow Jesus must be made positively, but it must be made thoughtfully.

This consideration must be made in light of the ultimate *evaluation*. A builder who begins but only lays a foundation is subject to ridicule and then shame. The same is true of the disciple who starts but cannot continue the Christian way.

Battling in a Disciple's Life Costs (vv. 31-32)

Battling in a disciple's life also calls for careful consideration. Jesus portrays the odds as "two-for-one." Each of His men must be as strong as two of the enemy. Positively, the Christian life is a construction. Negatively, the Christian life is a destruction—a battle against all that stands in the way of God's will for life. We must give careful consideration to the resources both for building and battling.

The battle is also subject to an *evaluation*. The person who cannot summon the resources to win the battle must face the shame of permanent surrender, defeat at the hands of a stronger enemy. Jesus does not here indicate that we should surrender in life, but rather that we should be sure to have the resources not to surrender!

Our Lord wants builders and battlers. This word does not mean "Count the cost, and refuse to follow." Come to Christ at all cost, but count the cost.

Joy in Finding

(Luke 15:1-10)

What is God like? Once you accept the existence of God, that becomes life's biggest question. The Greek philosophers thought He was apathetic. The Romans thought He was an overblown person with outsized human failures. Some followers of Moses saw Him as the great Lawgiver, full of demand. Nowhere did Jesus more clearly answer the question than Luke 15. Jesus gives three pictures of God.

God seeks that which is lost. God's greatest joy is in finding that which is lost. If we are like God, we do the same.

Jesus Does Attract the Lost

There are two very different reactions to the same Jesus. The irreligious are drawn to Him and the outwardly religious are put off by Him.

Jesus attracts the irreligious to Himself. The central characteristic of Jesus' ministry was His appeal to the abhorrent, repulsive, despised, and branded of His age. They came to Him continually. More and more of them came, one group after the next. These were not Jesus "groupies" seeking to be close to a great man. He really had an affinity for the irreligious and they felt it in their hearts. In this regard Jesus stands unique among all biblical figures. The lost wanted to be near Him. Do they want to be near you and me?

Jesus repels the merely religious from Himself. The Pharisees were a 6,000 member layman's league dedicated to outward piety and purity. When they saw Jesus' attraction of the irreligious they continually and persistently muttered their disgust. In strongly derisive terms they judged Jesus by the company He kept. He responded that He was guilty as accused.

In these parables our Lord wants us to understand that God is like this, Jesus is like this, and those who follow Him should be like this. Our God seeks and joyfully recovers that which is lost.

We Need to Affirm the Lostness of Our City

Jesus did not here denounce His detractors with anger. He reasoned with them from their own experience. Granted that they would leave the flock to find one lost sheep, should not He take extraordinary measures to find one lost person? He also helps us understand what it means to be lost.

Some are lost through *heedlessness*. A sheep does not willfully separate from the flock. Through helplessness and mere stupidity a sheep does get separated from the flock. In the evening the shepherd counts the sheep before enclosing them for the night. If the shepherd misses one, he will go to search for it. Even though it is only one out of one hundred, the shepherd will seek the sheep. God seeks us when we are lost due to our own stupidity or helplessness.

Some are lost through *carelessness*. Jesus intends a contrast here. The contrast is between a man seeking and a woman, outdoors and indoors, a living sheep and an inanimate coin. A coin is lost through no fault of its own but through the carelessness of another. The coin in question was part of a headdress worn by Hebrew woman. All was marred because the coin was gone. The coin was lost through the carelessness of the women. When we are lost through the carelessness of others, God still seeks us.

Both parables point out the value to God of the one. Whether one out of one hundred or one out of ten, the individual does matter. God seeks the one that is lost. So should we.

We Need to Search for the Lost in Our City

Rescue requires *thoroughness*. The shepherd leaves the ninety-nine to look through the night for the one. Imagination can see him seeking through the crags and dunes of the Judean wilderness. In her peasant's house the woman lights a candle and sweeps the dark floor listening for the tinkle of the precious coin. None of this was convenient. The church that loves Jesus does not live for convenience. It raises dust and difficulty to look for that which is lost.

Rescue requires *tenderness*. The shepherd carries the sheep home on his shoulders. Early Christian art concentrated on this theme. A lost sheep often will refuse to stand or walk. The shepherd did not drive or even lead the sheep. He carried the sheep. God is like that with the lost, and so should we be.

Rescue results in *joyfulness*. This is the primary emphasis of these twin parables. There is great joy in the finding. There is shared joy in the finding. Both the shepherd and the woman call a feast to share the joy. There is no joy like the joy of going with God after the lost. Jesus drops the picture of the parables and speaks of heavenly reality as He Himself knows it to be from experience. Joy in the presence of angels includes God and all the saints in heaven. The eternal world does not rejoice at the secular achievements of man. The eternal world does not even exult in many of the activities of the church. But a single lost person found results in triumphant joy in the world of the eternal.

With whom do you identify in these stories? Are you the lost coin or sheep? Then let God find you. Are you the shepherd or the woman, seeking the lost as God seeks them? Are you the Pharisee grumbling because there is an emphasis on evangelism and going after specific lost individuals? This parable is a mirror, and we can all see ourselves in it somewhere.

Leaving Home
(Luke 15:11-19)

Most of us do not think our autobiography will ever be published. Actually, it has been. This story is the mirror which reflects the image of us all. Luke 15 gives three parables nowhere else recorded. The most memorable of these is about the boy who left home and came back when he remembered the Father. The occasion of this story was criticism by Jesus' religious enemies that all the sinners continually were being drawn to drink in His words. What they considered a shame Jesus wore as a badge of honor. This story was more than enough reply to them.

We shall look at this in three sermons. Today's message tells the story of going away from the point of the son. What happens when you leave the Father's home?

We Leave Home When We Think That Life
Is Getting Away from the Father

All of us make the decision that *the essence of life is getting away from the Father*. That means that the essence of life suddenly becomes *immediacy of fulfillment*. I want it all *now*. This boy about seventeen wanted his share of the family estate. Eve wanted it all now in the garden. We want it all now. But beyond that, getting away from the Father means *a totality of possession*. I want it *all* now. This particular demand left room for no more resources in the future. We leave the Father when we make such a demand.

The essence of getting away from the Father is an *urgency of independence* from the Father: 'Not long after that. . . .' There is a kind of hellish haste or ruinous rush about getting away from the Father. It is hard to live in a twilight zone only half there and half gone. This leads inevitably to the *desirability of distance:* "set off for a distant country" (v. 13). The very energy of life seems to be at stake in getting as far away from the Father's eye, care, and protection as possible.

The beginning of all alienation from God, others, and ourselves is the insanity that life is worth living only by leaving home, putting distance between ourselves and the Father.

We Then Hit the Reality of Life Away from the Father

Life away from the Father *begins* with a frenzy of vitality. What he had quickly gathered together he quickly scattered apart. At this point the boy's life looked like vitality, energy, and desirability. Beneath it all there was a ruinous recklessness and extravagance that depleted all of life's capital resources. Life away from the Father always begins with busy vitality. Jesus does not give the details of the boy's sin. Jesus did not want to give any reality to what is always unreal. It is the Bermuda Triangle of existence. It has no reality.

Life away from the Father *continues* with the loss of all resources. He wasted everything that he had. We spend up the stuff of life running away from the Father. Time, emotional energy, willpower—all are burned up while we do not even know it. Suddenly there is a total lack of resources inside or outside of us. There is a famine in the whole extent of the land, nowhere to turn to in all the landscape. But worse than that, we feel the worm of want eating our insides for the first time.

Life away from the Father *ends* with degrading despair. The boy who wanted to be independent has to "glue" himself to a repulsive Gentile foreigner. His independence from the Father has led to the most humiliating dependence on a stranger who did not even want him. He did the most hated thing his race could do—feed pigs. Could anything be worse than that? Yes. He envied the very swine as they ate the carob beans. He wanted to stuff his own belly with the worst imaginable food for a human. But he did not have a single friend to give him the worst to eat.

Running away from the Father leaves us to fill our lives with anything to stop the shouting, screaming rage of the emptiness within. We can fill that emptiness with all kinds of good things—housework, yardwork, churchwork, busy work. We may fill it with all kinds of bad things. But it screams out to be filled.

We Start Back Home When We Remember that the Father Is Good

We discover the insanity of life away from the Father. The story all turns on the words "When he came to his senses" (v. 17). He could have come to them before this extremity of humiliation. He had been living in a trance. He told himself "this is living" while all the time he really knew "this is dying." How does this happen? The father enlightens us or it would never happen. He suddenly remembers that the day laborers of his father have more and better resources from the Father than he now has. The least in his father's family has more life than he.

We start home when we deliberately move from lethargy and despair. He decides, "I will set out. . . ." The emphasis is on the immediacy, "I will go at once." Life away from the Father turns us into semiparalyzed sleepwalkers. We should act at once or we will never act at all. There is a moment to stand, or never stand at all.

We start home when we make no claim except the Father's grace. Without excuse or extenuation he acknowledged it all. He gives up every claim of his own against the Father or life itself. He simply wants to get back to the Father's house, even as the lowest laborer. Anything would be an improvement. We do not come back to the Father by making claims against Him or explaining away our own insanity. We simply arise and cry out, "Make me . . . ." (v. 19). The rest is up to His grace.

Coming Home
(Luke 15:20-24)

How does God react if you come to Him or come back to Him? Tension fills the moment we return to someone from whom we have been alienated. Will he rebuke me, insult me, give me the cold shoulder, act indifferently or welcome me? How the Father receives us back is the heart of this parable. The Lord Jesus longed for us to believe that God is really like the father in this story. The very moment you make a real, actual, decisive move toward the Father, He has already received you back. Because it is a story, the parable presents in stages what actually happens in an instant.

The Lord Jesus presents God as even better than the best human father. This story answers two abiding questions about God.

How Does God Receive Us When We Come Back?

The Father actually watches for us to return. God's attitude toward us when we are away is not one of passivity. He does not respond with contempt or indifference. The emphatic word is that the Father "saw" (v. 20) the son at a distance. Both love and fear sharpen the eyesight. The father had been looking. This is the truth of the other two parables in this chapter. This father seeks like a shepherd (v. 4) or like a woman who lost a coin from her wedding jewelry (v. 7). Whether it is one sheep out of a hundred, one coin out of ten, or one son out of two, the father seeks. The most basic thing to be said about the Father is that He looks and longs for you to come back.

The Father feels deeply when we return. This father was moved with compassion, pity, and his heart went out to meet his son. The word itself refers to the moving of the viscera, the internal organs. The father felt for the son so deeply that it moved his very physical frame. This is the same thing said of Jesus in the face of human grief and loss (7:13). The father felt this before a word was even said by the son. God does not wait for our speeches before He loves us. While we were still sinners He acted in love toward us (Rom. 5:8). Before you were ever born, knowing that you would rebel, God nevertheless sent His Son for you. His compassion runs before you. For an aged Oriental man to run was incredible—it was considered beneath his dignity. This presents the depth of the Father's compassion.

The father receives tenderly when we return. The father kissed him tenderly or covered his face with kisses. Even more than in our world this was a sign of forgiveness and restoration to relationship. After Absalom had rebelled against David his father received him back this way (2 Sam. 14:33). God wants to demonstrate outwardly and obviously His tender reception when we return to Him.

The father does all of this before the son says a word. This means that there is nothing in God that should cause us to hesitate in coming back. There is no grounds for reluctance regardless of what you have done or how long you have been gone.

How Does God Treat Us After We Come Back?

God reacts with eagerness when we come back. The word "quickly" should not be ignored. The father does not even let the son repeat his memorized and rehearsed speech. God does not investigate or humiliate when we return. He interrupts the carefully crafted speech of the son with showers of honor and festivity. What God does for us He does quickly.

God reacts with generosity when we return. None of the things done for the son was in the order of a necessity. He could have come back on probation. He could have been received with reserve and coldness. He could have been welcomed with a sedate, private ceremony. But the Father gives more than enough. Salvation is more than mere pardon and an embarrassed reception back into the family. It is justification, sanctification, adoption, responsibility in the church, resurrection, and glorification. God does more than the necessary when He saves.

God reacts with dignity when we return. The son received a long, stately robe worn by nobles on state occasions. God honors us with the best when we return. We have "put on Christ" (Gal. 3:27, KJV). In spite of how we may actually be, God has covered our garments from the swine pen with dignity (Zech. 3:3-5). God shares with us His authority when we return. The signet ring indicated a person of authority and standing in a king's house. God does not merely tolerate us as a slave; He gives us the dignity of authority in His house and family. Shoes were the mark of a son, not a slave. Further, shoes could be worn in the house only by the master of the house. They symbolize possession and freedom. Far from holding us in contempt, God floods us with the tokens of adoption into His family, dignity in His household, and responsibility in His kingdom.

God reacts with celebration when we return. In all the universe, what moves heaven with hilarity? When we come back to God, heaven celebrates. There was only one fatted calf and it was reserved for the most special occasion. Nothing moves heaven like one away from the Father who comes back. What greater contrast could there be than that between the naked son longing for the carob pods of the swine and the honored son feasting with the father in the family home?

If you are away from God, this is what He desires to do for you. There is nothing in Him but a welcome when you return. Why not accept the invitation to start the celebration this very moment?

Misunderstanding Home
(Luke 15:25-32)

This is the story of two sons, both of them away from their father. One son runs away from the father to a far country. The other son stays home, but is still away from the father. We can be "in the church" but away from the Father. How do you know if you are in the church but away from the Father? What is your attitude toward the Father's feast? When someone comes back to the Father's house, He wants to celebrate. The Heavenly Father's heart longs to celebrate over finding what was lost. (vv. 7,10,32). The Father wants his family to be at a place of continuous celebration over finding what is lost.

When we feel superior to those who are lost we reveal our misunderstanding of God and His church. Spiritual superiority may not be as heinous a sin as gross sensuality, but it is more perilous. The grossly carnal know they are away from the Father. The spiritually self-righteous may be further away and not even know it. You understand spiritual home when your heart celebrates with the Father over finding the lost.

Coming Home Calls for Celebration

Says the father, "But we had to celebrate and be glad . . ." (v. 32). This story is about the necessity of celebration when someone apart from the Father comes back home. Jesus wants every Pharisee of each age to know that the Father must celebrate. It is a sacred necessity and a binding duty. You do not understand the Father if you do not feel the desire to celebrate when the lost is found. This story tells of a lavish *reaction of celebration*. The father hired a symphony and choreographed dancing for a once-in-a-lifetime event. Our Heavenly Father does the equivalent spiritually when we come home.

You misunderstand home when there is a *reaction of rejection* to the father's celebration. A dark cloud hovers over the story. Why is the son in the field? Why was he not informed his brother had come home? Did not the servants sense that he was also alienated from the father? The first words out of his mouth are contemptuous toward his father: "What's going on here?" (v. 27, author) If he had been right with his father, he should have instinctively felt that his father was right.

Even if we are at home in the church, we are apart from the Father when we do not share His celebration over those who come back to Him.

Misunderstanding Home Reveals Alienation

The elder brother is always an "inside outsider." He is close to his father, at home, but at the same time reveals that he is as far from his father as the prodigal.

Anger and *alienation* reveal apartness from the Father. The elder brother's spirit falls into a rage and becomes furious when it sees how good the father really is. It expresses itself in language of alienation. The elder brother never one time uses the word "father" or "brother" when describing his family. Even though he is formally at home, he feels no real kinship with those in the family.

Slavishness and *superiority* reveal alienation from the Father. "All these years I've been slaving for you. . . ." He has no joy in the service of his father. It is bondage, servitude. Home is a sweatshop, not a family. When that is our attitude about the church we reveal ourselves. Superiority expresses itself, "I have never disobeyed your orders." (v. 28). Other than the fact that this is not the truth, it shows the superiority complex that misses the Father altogether.

Ingratitude and *isolation* reveal alienation from the Father. He accuses his father of never giving him the minimum, when in fact his father had given him everything. He reveals the distance of his heart from the father in the isolating statement that he wants to celebrate with his friends rather than the father. He was just as far apart from his father at home as the prodigal was in the distant country.

Contempt and *comparison* show distance from the Father. "This son of yours" (v. 30) is a word of withering contempt. He compares his own self-conscious goodness with the whoremongering of his brother.

These attitudes are diagnostic of distance from the divine. If they are present in our lives, we should ask the Father to truly let us come home.

Understanding Home Invites Restoration

Everyone can be happy in the Father's home. The Father desires it to be that way.

The Father's *persistence* calls us to restoration. Just as the father went out to meet the prodigal, he also went out to meet the elder brother. His attitude toward both sons is one of initiative. God goes out after the carnal sinner and the self-righteous Pharisee.

The Father's *presence* calls us to restoration. "You are always with me." He reminds those who did not wander away morally that He has always been near. There is never a moment when we cannot immediately come into the feast and celebrate with Him.

The Father's *provision* calls us to restoration. "Everything I have is yours" (v. 31). There is nothing about life in the Father's house that He does not desire to share with us. Salvation, peace, the Spirit, the family of His church, and life that lasts forever He constantly hands to us. We should never be inside outsiders in the Father's house.

All of us need to come back to the Father. Those who left home and those who never seemed to leave home all need to be pursued, loved, and brought home. Which kind of prodigal are you?

One Who Thanks
(Luke 17:11-19)

Often this story is treated as "the nine who did not thank." But the emphasis rests upon the Samaritan—the unlikely thanker. The man least likely to bring thanksgiving became indeed the singularly most thankful.

God deserves gratitude. The thankful heart is evidence of the healthy soul. There is an anatomy of gratitude in this passage relevant for this Thanksgiving season.

One Who Thanks
Does Not Confuse Thanksgiving

Evidently the thankless nine felt they had fulfilled their obligation of gratitude sufficiently. Perhaps they confused other related attitudes with gratitude itself.

We may confuse *reverence* with thanksgiving. "They stood at a distance" (v. 12). Lepers were required to stand apart from the clean. Certainly in the instance of their relation to Jesus this represents not only the common custom, but even additional reverence for the Great Master also. A sense of awe is appropriate, even indispensable for worship. But reverence is not thanksgiving.

We may confuse *recognition* with thanksgiving. "Jesus, Master, have pity on us" (v. 13). They recognized the person and the position of Jesus. It was to some extent a confession of their faith, inadequate as it was. But the more recognition and confession of Jesus' person is not to be confused with gratitude.

We may confuse *response* with gratitude. "As they went, they were cleansed" (v. 14). Obedience is to be prized. Response to the command of God evidences good faith. But even obedience may be a grim habit without the grace of gratitude.

One Who Thanks
Does Not Refuse Thanksgiving

The one who thanked demonstrates the way to express gratitude acceptable to God.

His gratitude began with *perception*. "He saw he was healed." Acceptable gratitude must begin with the discipline of perceiving God's blessings. Even when we ask for God's blessings, we sometimes do not perceive that every good thing in life comes from His hand.

His gratitude grew with *proclamation*. "Praising God in a loud voice" (v. 15). Gratitude must move from the inward recognition to the outward representation. It belongs to the very nature of the thankful heart to say so. So the psalmist says, "Let the redeemed of the Lord say so" (Ps. 107:2, KJV).

His attitude bore the fruit of *prostration*. "He threw himself at Jesus' feet and thanked him" (v. 16). This suggests that genuine worship must be accompanied by thanksgiving. Only the thankful man was prostrate at the feet of Jesus.

One Who Thanks
Does Not Abuse Thanksgiving

Those expected to do so did not give thanks. The other nine, at least some of them, were of the house of Israel, the covenant people. Everything about their heritage should have led them to thank God.

The Samaritan outcast expressed gratitude. Jesus suggests that sometimes the only ones to thank God are the unlikely ones. How will it be this Thanksgiving? Will you belong to the company of the one or to the company of the nine?

The First Followers
(John 1:35-51)

Never more did Jesus reveal Himself as the One who knows us through and through as He did in His encounter with the first followers. In a remote part of the planet the most significant meetings of men in history took place near the river Jordan. The meeting of Jesus Christ with John, James, Andrew, and Peter has had more impact than any other such meeting in history, with the possible exception of Paul. The first followers of Jesus varied radically in temperament and needs, but the same message about the Messiah galvanized them into world-changing discipleship.

The Lord Jesus Meets Us as Individuals

For the thoughtful He answers life's big question: "What do you want?" (v. 38) James and John, who had come from the area of Bethsaida Julius north of the Sea of Galilee, were asking the big, ultimate questions of life. Their background in a Greek-influenced city had given them sensitivity to such questions. They were already agog with expectancy that God was about to do something in their lives. To them Jesus simply said, "Come and see" (v. 39). Perhaps you are already asking the big questions about life, death, and eternity. Jesus' word to them is also His word to you, "Come, and . . . see" (v. 39).

For the promising He offers new character: "You are Simon. . . . You will be called Cephas" (v. 42). Jesus gazed at Peter and through Peter as if looking at a far horizon. Simon Peter was all potential, but very little reality. His original name suggests the capricious character of a dove, flighty and unpredictable. The "dove" will become a rock, but not for a long time and only after a painful process.

Thank God that He looks at us and sees potential, not just what we are. The gaze of God looks beyond today and sees us for what we will be tomorrow.

For the reluctant He takes the firm initiative: "Finding Philip, he said to him, 'Follow me'" (v. 43). James and John sought Jesus. Andrew brought Peter. Jesus Himself stayed behind to find Philip. In some ways Philip is the dull disciple. Wherever he appears in the record, he does not understand what Jesus is doing. Nevertheless, Jesus stayed behind to find Philip. If you are reluctant to seek Him, His loving initiative will seek you.

For the cynical He reveals supernatural insight: "I saw you while you were still under the fig tree" (v. 48). Nathaniel had a tendency toward cynicism and an inclination toward the dark side of things. Unlike John, Nathaniel had to be convinced in the face of the evidence. For such distrustful belief, Jesus operated in the realm of the clearly supernatural. He revealed to the doubting man what Nathaniel had been doing and thinking in such a way that the latter knew Jesus was more than a mere man.

Christ has a way to get at every kind of needy person. He knows how to approach you if you do not run. Let Him work with you in the individual way He desires.

The Lord Jesus Meets Us All with the Same Message

The personal center of the message never varies. Christian testimony relates to Christ alone as central: "Look at the Lamb of God," cried John the Baptist. He did not point to a system or a tradition. He declared a Person. When Nathaniel hesitated in doubt, Philip called him toward a Person (v. 46). There is nothing ultimately attractive about doctrines, churches, denominations, preachers, or any other related concerns. The only attraction we have is the Person of Jesus Christ. Even His enemies admit His attractive powers. We must repeat Christ alone (vv. 29,36,39,46).

The personal priority of the message never varies: "the first thing Andrew did was find his brother" (v. 41). An encounter with Jesus is never in isolation. Inbred into the very experience is the thrust to tell. Andrew knew no theology or sophisticated system to tell Peter. He simply pointed Peter to the Person of Jesus Christ as his first priority.

The personal proximity of the message never varies: "Philip, like Andrew and Peter, was from the town of Bethsaida" (v. 44). Start with those closest when you tell. These men had grown up together, matured together, worked together, followed the path of John the Baptist together, and then they met the Christ together. Nothing is more natural and possible than for those who have done everything else together to come to Christ together. Go home and tell.

Come and See
(John 1:35-51)

Genesis 1 begins with the week that created the world. John 1 begins with a week that recreated a world. That week reveals the Master's methods with men in gathering the first followers. That week reveals the striking variety of men Jesus calls. That week also reveals the unchanging content of Christian testimony.

Although the Master's methods and men vary, the content of Christian testimony never varies.

The Master's Method with Men Varies

For the *thoughtful* He answers life's big question: "What do you want?" (v. 38)

For the *compromised* He offers new character: "You are Simon . . . . You will be called Cephas" (v. 42).

For the *reluctant* He takes firm initiative: "Finding Philip, He said to him, 'Follow me'" (1:43).

For the *cynical* He reveals supernatural insight: "I saw you while you were still under the fig tree" (v. 48).

Summary: Men come for the same faith in Christ through many different methods.

The Marks of the Master's Men Vary

The Master's men vary in potential and personality.

The Master's men vary in understanding their Master.

The Meaning of the Message Never Varies

The personal *center* of the message never varies.

Christian testimony relates to Christ alone (vv. 36,46).

The personal *priority* of the message never varies: "The first thing Andrew did was find his brother" (v. 41).

The personal *proximity* of the message never varies: "Philip, like Andrew and Peter, was from the town of Bethsaida" (v. 44).

Start with those closest.

A Taste of New Wine
(John 2:1-11)

Jesus' first miracle took place at a wedding in a tiny, remote village of His homeland. This miracle is a "sign" that points beyond itself to greater truth. It reveals to us the glory of Jesus. Jesus transforms mere religion into an exhilarating taste of new life.

The First Sign Reveals the
Personal Concern of Jesus

Jesus stands with us in our joy. It is telling that He should be a desired guest at a wedding. People desired His presence on all occasions of life, whether grief (John 11) or joy.

We can approach Jesus at every level of need. The lack of wine at a biblical wedding was a social disaster that would haunt the family for a lifetime. Although some would see it as trivial, He saw it as tremendous. Our personal needs are not trivial to Him.

The First Sign Reveals the
Spiritual Priority of Jesus

Christ relates to us a spiritual Savior before anything else. His curious reply to Mary, His mother (v. 4a), changes their relationship from son-mother to Savior-sinner. If this is the case with Mary, it is certainly the case with everyone else.

Christ deals with us according to His own timing. He said and sometimes says, "My time has not yet come" (v. 4b). As He moved toward His own cross, He walked with an acute sense of timing. As He directs our lives, He does no less today.

We can trust Christ when He is aware of our needs. Mary simply left the situation in His hands (v. 5). She had a sense that He would do the right thing, whatever.

The First Sign Reveals the
Transforming Power of Jesus

Jesus transforms empty religious forms into living faith. The six stone waterpots represent the emptiness of Jewish religion in Jesus' time. "Six" suggests something short of completeness. Everything Judaism could do was "filled up to the brim." Jesus radically and abundantly changed the situation. Out of the meaningless forms He brought a taste of new life.

Jesus does save the best for last. That is as true now as it was then. You can turn to Him with the assurance that He is the One who makes all things new.

The First Cleansing of the Temple
(John 2:13-22)

Jesus came proclaiming the rule of God, and this proclamation of necessity confronted and alienated the religious establishment of His day. Religion, particularly the Christian faith, may be institutional in either a good or a bad sense. Christianity is institutional in a good sense when its institutions are prophetically alive and instantly alert to God's presence. Christianity is institutional in the bad sense when it simply absorbs its culture, becomes an entrenched establishment, and perpetuates itself.

The first thing Jesus did the first time He came to Jerusalem pointedly confronted establishment religion. His cleansing of the temple dramatically demonstrates God's reaction to cultural, merely institutional, establishment religion. Christ comes again to His temple, the church, to cleanse and to challenge. What are some marks of establishment religion?

Religion Can Forget Its Own Purpose

Both John and the Synoptics connect Jesus' act of cleansing the temple with His first visit to Jerusalem. It was protest at first sight. Jesus passed by many *good* things that could have been done in Jerusalem to do the *best* thing, set His Father's house in order. The Old Testament ends with the promise that the Messiah will come suddenly to His temple (Mal. 3:1). Jesus is identified with that prophetic tradition.

Jesus found the outer court of the temple occupied by the "Bazaars of Annas," a fraudulent con game, a tourist trap for the rural pilgrims. Most grievous was the fact that these "money-changers" had set up shop in the one place set aside for Gentile worship, the outer court. Those responsible for the temple had forgotten its very purpose—a place where needy worshipers meet God. Jesus' response is one of the most aggressive of His entire public ministry. With His own moral authority He literally drove those out who misused His Father's house. There is literally nothing else like this in His life and work. It demonstrates the intensity of His desire that His people remain true to the purpose of His church. These are words to us when we make central that which should be peripheral, and peripheral that which should be central.

Christ Can Restore Purpose to Religion

For a golden hour, the temple in Jerusalem became what God intended it to be. With money scattered on the floor, tables overturned, and animals bleating in the confusion, the Son of God becomes the center of His temple. The face, a moment ago hard with indignation, is now radiant with compassion, as the temple becomes a place of healing for the blind and the lame. The little children gather about Him to say, "Hosanna to the Son of David!" They look in wonderment at the Godlike face of the Christ, and then on the healed sufferers. At least for a moment, God's temple was what the Father had intended; a place of instruction and healing for all men.

Religion Can Miss the Presence of the Christ

The reaction of the religious establishment was unbelief (v. 20). They found no fault in clinking coins and the bleating of nasty animals in the house of God, but they could not see the Son of God when He came. The physical temple had blinded these to the spiritual temple. We must always beware of missing the Christ.

Spiritual Harvesting

(John 4:31-38)

Everyone touched by life on a farm knows the urgency of harvesttime and the joy that follows. Jesus lived in that kind of world. His most basic parable spoke of Jesus as a Sower of seed which yielded a varied harvest (Matt. 13:3-9). When Jesus spoke with the woman at the well in Samaria, she became a spiritual harvest. He took advantage of her spiritual conversion to teach His disciples some truth about spiritual harvesting. Jesus sends you into the spiritual harvest with a sense of urgency that intensifies life.

Spiritual Harvesting Sustains Life

Spiritual harvesting brings a different understanding of life. Some live life at the physical level alone. The question of the disciples betrays life on the physical level alone: "Rabbi, eat something" (v. 31). They had a genuine concern for the hunger and physical fatigue of their Master. Jesus did have to eat, but He had moved beyond life on the merely physical level: "I have food to eat that you know nothing about" (v. 32). This statement baffled His followers.

Spiritual harvesting brings a different sustaining of life. Jesus' life was sustained by a more than physical source. He would later say, "Do not work for food that spoils, but for food that endures to eternal life" (6:27). That which sustains life more than physical food is doing the will of God. Specifically, His work of witness and winning the Samaritan woman to faith in Himself had sustained Him inwardly with a nourishment far more energizing than food itself.

Going with Christ after the lost gives to life an inward energy that nothing else can match. To share His vision of the world, to feel His compassion for the lost, and to see others come to Christ sustains life with energy and purpose that nothing else can replace.

Spiritual Harvesting Intensifies Life

In the usual physical harvest there is a long wait between sowing and reaping. During Jesus' life there were about four months between the time grain was sown in January and harvested in May. It was almost a proverb to say, "There are four months till harvest." At the very time of this story the seed had already sprouted and the young shoots of grain promised a harvest to come in the Samaritan grain fields. But they still had to wait for the physical harvest.

In the unusual spiritual harvest you can reap now. Jesus calls for a deliberate and careful gaze at humanity around you. If you will "lift up your eyes" there is a harvest already around you. Even as Jesus spoke these words the Samaritans were streaming out of the village to meet Him. Over the the next two days there was a mighty spiritual harvest of new life (v. 41). You do not have to wait for spiritual harvest—it is ready now.

Most believers spend life getting ready to witness, training to witness, or waiting for the right situation to witness. What Jesus said then He would say now. The harvest is ready. Not everyone everywhere is ready but someone somewhere is ready just now.

Spiritual Harvesting Enlarges Life

The usual physical harvest is often unfair. One person sows the seed as an act of great labor. Another person reaps the grain as an act of great joy. In Jesus' world plowing and planting were hot and tedious work. A rich landlord would come to reap the harvest long after poor servants had prepared and sowed the crop.

The usual physical harvest is more than fair. Often the sower and reaper move together. Jesus had just sown the word into the heart of the Samaritan woman. Not only did she come to Christ immediately, but also many others. But the spiritual harvest is an even greater gift. We often reap in the spiritual harvest where we have not sown. Others have gone before us to prepare the lives of those we win. Those others include the Old Testament saints, Christ, the apostles, and all the Christians in this place before us.

To be part of spiritual harvesting enlarges life. The spiritual harvest makes you part of something larger and longer than you are. Would you like to be part of something that is 2,000 years in the making? Get into the harvest. Bring someone to Christ. The harvest will enlarge the narrow confines of your life.

Share Jesus Now!

(John 4:31-39)

Share Jesus Now Is a Sustaining Necessity for Travis Avenue

"Jesus, tired as he was from the journey, sat down by the well" (v. 6). The disciples left Him thus, utterly *weary, fatigued* with the journey. He sat on the curb of the well, exhausted with the trip. Ministry *does tire.*

But when they returned there as a difference, transformation, almost a transfiguration. Absent was the fatigue, gone was the weariness. Jesus' face was animated, His eyes were kindled, there was fresh vigor and new energy. Obviously something had brought about a metamorphosis of His whole person.

The disciples' *request*—eat something. They urged, begged, and pleaded with Jesus to eat something. They did this repeatedly, all together, and each one of them.

The Master's *reaction*—a contrast between what sustained Him and what sustained them. "*I myself* have bread which *you yourself* did not know" (v. 32, author's italics).

The disciples' *response*. They did not respond to Him. They knew that their mystical Master often spoke in metaphors they did not understand. They knew He often spoke on two levels, so they did not dare to interrupt Him. *When you are not involved in Jesus' agenda it is difficult to understand His meaning.*

The Master's *reply* and *reason*—to do His will and finish the work. His resource, refreshment, renewal, recharging came from doing the will of God. The will of God was to win to Himself those like the Samaritan woman.

Jesus was *tired* in the midst of ministry. But He found *fresh* food, *surprising sustenance, resurging resources* in winning a woman to Himself.

Jesus has never once promised to keep us from *fatigue, exhaustion,* or *burnout* when we are *running along with our own agenda and not His.* We are trying to feed the body of Christ with that which cannot sustain it. Everything short of sharing Jesus now will turn to *ashes* in our mouth and be like *grit* between our teeth.

But our Lord Jesus says, "Make my agenda your agenda and you will be transformed."

Share Jesus Now Demands a Present Urgency

Our Lord turned the disciples from the *inwardness* of hidden food to the *outwardness* of white fields. He began with a prohibition. A *prohibition* against *procrastination.* This may have been a precise note of *time* but was more likely the *repetition* of a proverb of procrastination.

In all of *creation* only human beings procrastinate. But procrastination becomes more serious when it is a matter of the *harvest.* The same is true of *spiritual* harvesting. Any generation can lose the harvest if we do not act *NOW.*

Our difficulty is not *evangelism* or *Christology,* it is *procrastination.* We know *how* to do it. Our problem has never been *information,* it has been *procrastination.*

Our Lord calls for an observation—*Look* a careful, deliberate gaze. The whole of Jesus' mission can be summed up in the words *look, pray,* and *go,* in that order.

Physical vision is a mystery. But there is a greater mystery than physical vision. How will we look at Texas? Better, how do we look at our neighbors?

We can look with *indifference.* We can look with *curiosity.* We can look with *pride.* We can look with *disgust.*

We can see a harvest. As Texas Baptists, *Share Jesus Now* calls us *back to what we do best*—win to Christ. That is what we do best. Back to what we used to do!

Do You Want to Be Well?

(John 5:1-9)

In the midst of routine faithfulness the extraordinary can take place. A striking aspect of the Lord Jesus' ministry was His willingness to observe common religious customs practiced by everyone else. He went to the local synagogue in Nazareth, kept the obligatory feasts, and paid the temple tax. Even though He was the fulfillment of the Hebrew race, every feast, and the temple itself, He was not above commitment to the routine faithfulness of everyone else. We should remember this when we consider ourselves "above it all." The faithful were required to go to Jerusalem three times a year for required feasts. On one such occasion Jesus went to Jerusalem alone to avoid recognition because of His controversial presence. There He confronted a hopeless man who wanted to be well.

The Lord Jesus can make you spiritually well if you seize the moment of possibility and really want to be well.

Do You Want to Be Well in Spite of Hopelessness?

Most of us live with places and times of hopelessness. The pool of Bethesda represents such a place. The pool was northeast of the temple near the Sheep Gate where shepherds herded their flocks into the city. The pool was deep enough to swim in and was surrounded by five porches covered like an arcade. Around it gathered the hopeless people—those blind, lame, and with atrophied limbs. The picture would be comic if it were not so tragic. The blind stumbled over the lame and the paralyzed jostled with the atrophied. Their despair compounded itself because of their numbers.

At that place one person is singled out who lived in hopelessness for thirty-eight years. Time compounds hopelessness. At first he had hoped to walk again, but every year added an additional deposit of the sediment of despair to his life. By this time hope hung by a thread. For thirty-eight years he had "seen it all" around the pool and knew that there was nothing for him.

All of us have lived around the pool of Bethesda. We have been spiritually blinded, emotionally lamed, morally atrophied. Some of us have been there for so many years we have stopped hoping. That there could be radical change of life, spiritual revolution, and the dawn of a new day rests beyond our wildest dreams. Yet you must want to be whole in spite of a place and time of hopelessness.

Do You Want to Be Well at the Moment of Possibility?

Not every moment is equally possible for life change. Not every day can witness a spiritual revolution. There are a few moments in life which must be seized or the tide goes out. It is almost universally agreed by biblical scholars that verse 4 is not part of the original text written by John: "for an angel went down at a certain time into the pool and stirred up the water" (NKJV). Yet it does reflect a popular, early explanation for the bubbling up of the water from the bottom of the pool. There was probably an intermittent spring that caused the water to bubble from time to time. When that happened, the blind groped, the lame hobbled, and the atrophied lurched toward the water. The first in was made whole according to popular tradition.

This preserves a truth you should not miss. Not every moment of life is equally open to spiritual change. The Spirit of God comes, moves, and goes on His way (3:8). You cannot even make a move toward God without His initiative: "No one can come to me unless the Father who sent me draws him" (6:44). The woman at the well had a moment to drink. Bartimaeus had but one moment to see, and Zaccheus faced a split second to come out of his tree. The same is true of you. There is a moment of spiritual dawn when you must awake and a moment of high tide before the water goes out. In the moment when God speaks, seize that moment.

Do You Want to Be Well as a Point of Fact?

Jesus Christ cuts through every superficiality about our spiritual wholeness or sickness. On the surface the answer to His question looks obvious: "Do you want to be made well?" The question almost appears insulting. Certainly! A man thirty-eight years paralyzed wants to be well. But just below the surface it is a profound question. We can love our woundedness, nurture our sickness. This man escaped all responsibility by his sickness. He did not have to walk, work, or be accountable. You can love the self-pity and the escape from responsibility that comes with spiritual sickness.

We can imagine procedural difficulties. This man dodged, avoided, and evaded the awesome moment of encounter with Jesus Christ (v. 7). Like Nicodemus wondering how a man could enter his mother's womb again (3:4), the paralyzed one raised trivial difficulties in the face of tremendous opportunity.

The Lord Jesus responds with power, not another proposal or procedure. He did not simply organize a committee for the lowering of paralytics into local pools! As only He in all history has done, there was a word of power: "Rise, take up your bed, and walk" (v. 8, NKJV). The man was instantly made whole and summoned to responsible living. The credibility of the Christian message rests on His ability to do this spiritually today. Do you want to be made well?

The Life-giving Bread
(John 6:25-35,53)

The feeding of the 5,000 is the only miracle of Jesus recorded by all four Gospels. Without question it made the greatest impact on His hungering world. Most of the population never knew total satisfaction from hunger. Yet Jesus never fed them only to satisfy physical hunger. He intended the physical bread to point them to higher spiritual sustenance. His generation missed that significance. We should not make the same mistake. Jesus offers Himself to you as the only satisfaction for life's spiritual hunger.

Jesus Warns Us About Missing the Bread of Life

We may miss the bread of life because of *curiosity without commitment* (v. 25). After feeding the 5,000, Jesus had miraculously crossed the sea back to Capernaum (vv. 19-21). The crowd sensed this and wanted to know *how* and *when* He had gone so far so quickly. Jesus refused to respond. He never then or now reveals Himself to curiosity without commitment. Mere curiosity about Christ never satisfies spiritual hunger.

We may miss the bread of life because of *superficiality without comprehension* (v. 26). Jesus knows us and what is in us. He answers our needs, not our desires. He speaks to our inward heart, not our superficial questions. The crowd followed Him because they wanted full bellies, not full hearts. They had totally missed the "sign"—the higher spiritual significance of His ability to multiply physical food. He intended that to lead them to the higher, heavier, holier truth that He can satisfy the higher needs of spiritual hunger. "They saw only the bread in the sign, not the sign in the bread."

We may miss the bread of life because of *materialism without spirituality*. "Do not work for food that spoils" (v. 27). All food and physical possessions lose their sustaining power. Food itself is digested and dispersed. "Everyone who drinks this water will be thirsty again" (4:13). Even the physical food of the miraculous feeding already left them hungry. Nothing you can put in yourself or on yourself will meet the deepest hunger about yourself. Rather we are to seek that bread which abides and gives life. "Whoever drinks the water I give him will never thirst" (v. 14).

Jesus Instructs Us About Having the Bread of Life

Spiritual life does not come from *human performance* (v. 28). Human religion always asks the question, "What can we habitually practice to meet God's requirements?" The crowd questioning Jesus had in mind works (sacrifices, tithes, ceremonies, etc.) that would meet God's performance standard. Nothing you can perform will fill the higher hunger of your life.

Spiritual life does *come from an abiding faith* (v. 29). God requires not multiple "works" but a single, simple "work." The only "work" which satisfies the inward hunger is a continuous belief in the person and mission of Jesus. This is the one spiritual attitude from which satisfaction comes.

Spiritual life does not come from *miracle mongering* (vv. 30-33). The crowd implied that Jesus had not done enough to convince them. Moses supplied an entire generation with physical manna for forty years. Jesus refuses to give a dramatic miracle to those without commitment. If you do not believe Him, no additional miracle will change your mind. He had just performed a mighty miracle and they refused to believe. They would not believe another miracle any more than the first.

Jesus Explains About Appropriating the Bread of Life

Cutting through all misunderstanding, Jesus makes the bold statement, "I am the bread of life" (v. 35). Coming to Him totally satisfies spiritual hunger. How do you come to Him?

Coming to Jesus is a personal appropriation of His life and death. It is "to eat the flesh of the Son of Man and drink his blood" (v. 53). Jesus means by that an appropriation of Christ that takes Him into our innermost being. He means dwelling in Christ and Christ dwelling in you. Faith throws us onto Christ while this eating and drinking throws Christ into us.

This involves a sacrificial recognition. The separation of flesh and blood meant violent death. We appropriate the One who died for us. Out of that death comes the bread of life.

Come and Drink
(John 7:37-39)

Christ is the Source of life, and those who come to Him become themselves sources of life to others. This is the truth Jesus taught at the great Feast of Tabernacles. That great feast remembered the exodus and celebrated God's gift of rain. On each of seven days, a mighty procession carried water to the temple altar and poured it out in an impressive ceremony. On the last day of this feast, Christ stood at the critical moment of this ceremony to cry out, "If a man is thirsty, let him come to me and drink" (v. 37). By doing so, Christ dramatically presents Himself as the replacement for all outward religious ceremony, the fulfillment of every promise, and the substance behind every shadow.

Only Our Recognition of Need
Hears the Invitation of Christ

Understand our recognition of need: "If any man thirst" (v. 37, KJV). Jesus used the most basic, physical needs to indicate our spiritual needs. "Blessed are those who hunger and thirst for righteousness, for they will be filled" (Matt. 5:6). Behind Jesus' language is the scarcity of water and the constancy of thirst in the biblical world. The water salesman was a common sight in the marketplace: "Come all you who are thirsty, come to the waters; and you who have no money, come, buy and eat!" (Isa. 55:1). The only fitness Christ requires is the recognition of our need.

Hear the invitation of Christ: ". . . let him come to me and drink." Christ offers Himself. He is the slaking of every thirst. Those who drank from the ceremonial waters poured out at the feast would always thirst again. He offers Himself as the fulfillment of all ritual, everything external and formal in religion. "Everyone who drinks this water will be thirsty again, but whoever drinks the water I give him will never thirst" (John 4:13). John's Gospel presents Jesus as the final fulfillment of every hope God's people have ever had; the true Lamb of God (John 1), true brazen serpent (John 2), the true birth (John 3), the true bread from heaven (John 6), the true water from the rock (John 7), the true fiery cloud (John 8), and the true Passover lamb (John 19). Whatever your heart thirsts for, He is the fulfillment.

The Invited Christ Becomes
the Resource for Life

Two profound biblical images stand behind the truth of Christ as the resources for life. One image is from the exodus, the smitten rock that gives water in wilderness. The other is the great river that flows from the temple in the age to come.

Christ provides the source of the believer's life. Christ is the smitten Rock from whom the waters flow (1 Cor. 10:4). "One of the soldiers pierced Jesus' side with a spear, bringing a sudden flow of blood and water" (John 19:34). The water flows from the innermost being of the smitten Lord. Jesus is also the new temple from which the river of life flows. Ezekiel 47 presents a mighty river flowing from under the threshold of the temple. The further it goes, the wider it grows and the deeper it flows. It flows to the Dead Sea where it gives life. Jesus is the temple! (John 2:21). The river now flows "from the throne of God and of the Lamb" (Rev. 22:1).

The believer becomes a source of life to others. He who comes to the Rock becomes a rock from whom life flows. Christ is the ultimate Source, but those who drink deep of the living water become fountains themselves. This answers the prophet: "[You shall] be . . . like a spring of water, whose waters fail not" (Isa. 58:11, KJV).

Jesus spoke all of this of the Holy Spirit, given only after His glorification (death, resurrection, and ascension). This is the great paradox that death is the beginning of life. Christ dies and gives the Spirit of life. I die to self and become the source of living waters to others.

Why Did He Write in the Sand?

(John 8:1-11)

A daily and common experience is that of judging and being judged. The Lord Jesus could not speak to life as it is without a word about condemners and those they condemn. John 8 may be the most dramatic episode in the Gospels. We are brought to face with one judged and those who judged her. She is guilty without doubt. They judge her and call on Jesus to join in their judgment. How does Jesus respond? He instructs those who are judgmental and offers a stern mercy to the guilty.

Beware the Motives of Those Who Condemn

Those who condemn *misunderstand* Jesus' message. This act of condemnation interrupted the teaching of Jesus. In a beautiful scene, God's Son was at God's house teaching God's word. That teaching included, "Stop judging by mere appearances and make a right judgment. You judge by human standards; I pass judgment on no one" (John 7:24; 8:15). At the center of Jesus' message is a word of mercy, but not tolerance for sin. If your tendency is to judge and condemn, you are not in touch with Jesus' heart.

The *method* of those who condemn is unmerciful. The religious establishment dragged a woman before Jesus and the crowd. She had been caught in the very act. This was needless. Jesus could have judged the question in her absence. This was vindictive. It would only harden her in her sullen defiance. This was unfair. Where was her lover? He should have been there, too. The method of condemners is to expose. The method of Jesus is to redeem. Are you a redeemer or a condemner?

The *message* of those who condemn often appears to be religious. They came quoting a text (v. 5). God's law did indeed call for stoning those caught in such sin (Lev. 20:10; Deut. 22:23). Condemners are often technically correct. The judgmental recognize that the letter of the law does kill. They do not recognize that the Spirit gives life.

The *motive* of those who condemn is hidden. These judges used the woman as a pawn in order to trap Jesus. They had no concern about her, the law of God, or truth. They were concerned to make Jesus look bad in order to make themselves look good. No Jewish court could pass a death penalty. No Roman court would convict the woman. If Jesus said nothing, they would take it as permission to lynch the woman. If Jesus enforced Moses' law, he would challenge the authority of Rome, which alone had the power to execute. If Jesus refused Moses' law, He would appear to question the very Law of God. Their motive was to trap.

Observe the Method of the Master

Observe Jesus' method with the judgmental. His method is one first of *hesitation.* Those who judge hesitate at nothing. He waits. Why did He write on the ground? Surely He did so out of anger, embarrassment, and a refusal to speak. He may have written the sins of the accusers. He did write in the dust. This may have implied His willingness to let the wind of forgiveness blow away what they wished to make permanent. We would do well to hesitate in situations of judgment.

Jesus' method is one of *instruction.* They asked Him to deliver a legal verdict. He lifted the entire episode up to the level of abiding spiritual principle: "If any one of you is without sin, let him be the first to throw a stone at her" (v. 7). Moses' law called for the witnesses of a crime to throw the first stone. For many reasons they were not without sin. They owed the woman a warning before her shameful act. They could have stopped the act before she committed it; they could have intervened redemptively rather than reacted judgmentally. There is strong evidence that they had entered into a plot with her husband to trap her with her lover. Further, they had the witness of their own hearts that were not free from the same strong passion. The innocence of many results from lack of opportunity, not lack of desire. Only the sinless One has the right to execute; He refused to do so.

Jesus' method leads to *conviction.* They marched out of the temple, beginning with the eldest who had the most experience with their own hearts. Jesus cuts through to reality. Are you really free of that which you condemn?

Observe Jesus' method with the guilty. Ultimately, every sinful one of us has to do with Him alone; "only Jesus was left, with the woman still standing there" (v. 9). The judgment of others is not what matters. Only His word about my sin stands.

We are without excuse. Nothing in this story justifies this woman's act. She only speaks once, and then with no excuses (v. 11). Nothing about Jesus' attitude lessens the damning seriousness of sin.

We are given another chance by His grace. Jesus did not pronounce her worthy of stoning. However, His words are not those of forgiveness. There is no evidence of repentance or faith on the woman's part. He does release her in another opportunity for grace. "God did not send his Son into the world to condemn the world" (John 3:17). We are living in the time of His mercy.

Jesus gives us a stern mercy. "Go now and leave your life of sin" (v. 11). Amend the whole of your life, Jesus' stern mercy is not soft stuff. The only One who could condemn us does not do so (Rom. 8:33-34). But what His lordship commands His power does enable.

You live under the opportunity for that stern mercy. Do not despair; He does not condemn. Do not presume; those who receive forgiveness also repent—life is never the same again.

The Gate and the Shepherd
(John 10:7-18)

The magnificent teaching in John 10 is a comment on the sorry scene in John 9. Jesus had given sight to a man blind from birth. The Pharisees then "threw him out" of the temple (v. 34). As the Good Shepherd, Jesus found him and brought him into spiritual life (v. 35). The religious establishment of Jesus' day was pseudoministers who did not really care for the people. Jesus compared them to hireling shepherds who fled in the moment of need.

Jesus contrasts Himself to the false religious leaders. He, by implication, contrasts His true ministers with false ministers. Jesus acts as the Gate to His church and as the Shepherd to His sheep.

Jesus Serves as the Gate for His church

Jesus serves exclusively as the Gate (vv. 7,9). Twice in the Greek He makes the emphatic statement, "I, and I alone, am the Gate." Jesus declared that all approach to the fold must be "through me" (v. 9). The claim of Jesus Christ is an exclusive claim. He is the Gate into the fold (the church) for both His shepherds and His sheep. Both His ministers and every believer must come in by that one exclusive gate. Notice that He is the gate "for the sheep." The sheep are more important than the fold, the living people more important than the institutional church that enfolds them. The fold exists for the sheep, and not the reverse.

Jesus serves benevolently as the Gate (v. 9). The shepherds and the sheep—the ministers and the people—who use only Jesus as the Gate will find security ("will be saved"), liberty ("will go in and out"), and support ("find pasture"). He is only and always the Gate to life and abundance. He gives life as an enduring possession and an overflow of all that makes for life (v. 10b).

Jesus serves protectively as the Gate (v. 8,10a). Contrasted to the bright picture of the Gate is the dark picture of those who refuse to use the Gate. The religious establishment of Jesus' day harmed the sheep. Rather than giving life, they were thieves and robbers. Rather than giving abundance, they destroyed even the sheep. The words stand as a solemn warning concerning bogus religious leaders in every generation.

Jesus Serves as the Good Shepherd for His Sheep

Jesus serves exclusively as the Good Shepherd (vv. 11,14). Twice He emphatically states, "I, and I alone, am the Good Shepherd." The language indicates that He is in a class by Himself as a beautiful, noble Shepherd. There are two contrasts here. None of His under-shepherd ministers are as good as He is. In contrast to all false religious leaders, He alone is the Good Shepherd.

Jesus serves sacrificially as the Good Shepherd (vv. 11,17-18). Usually, the sheep served as a blood sacrifice for the shepherd. Uniquely, Jesus acted as a blood sacrifice for the sheep. He did this in a voluntary way (v. 18). He did it in an effective way. He not only laid down His life, but took it up again. Had He only abandoned His sheep in His death, they would today have no Shepherd. Many have died for others. Only the Good Shepherd died and took up His life again for others. The words emphasize, in the strongest way, a substitutionary death for others.

Jesus serves knowledgably as the Good Shepherd (vv. 14-15). Four times in two verses Jesus uses the word "know." The word suggests affectionate knowledge that comes from experience and appreciation. He dares to say that the mutual knowledge of the shepherd and sheep reflects the knowledge of Father and Son. All of His sheep want to sing "Savior, like a shepherd lead us, Much we need thy tender care."

The Good Shepherd
(John 10:11-18)

Jesus serves as the Gate to the fold and as the Shepherd of the flock. The favorite Old Testament image of God is that of Shepherd: "Hear us, O Shepherd of Israel, you who lead Joseph like a flock; you who sit enthroned between the cherubim" (Ps. 80:1). The mighty God of the universe, enthroned above, is also the Shepherd of His flock.

The dark backdrop of John 10 are the false shepherds of John 9. The religious establishment of Jesus' day did not care for the sheep. Jesus acts as the Good Shepherd for the flock.

Jesus Serves Exclusively as Good Shepherd

Twice in the Greek He emphatically stated, "I, and I alone, am the Good Shepherd." The language emphatically indicates that He is in a class by Himself as Good Shepherd. The word "good" here carries several emphases. He is "good" in contrast to every foul, mean, or wicked shepherd. He is "good" in the sense of competent, fit, and a model shepherd. Finally, His goodness does not consist of an austerity that repels, but an attractiveness that draws the sheep to Him.

There are two contrasts intended between the Good Shepherd and others. First, none of His under-shepherd ministers/pastors are as good as He is. Every other shepherd is derivative and dependent on Him. He calls, endows, and governs His pastors. Also, He is the Good Shepherd in contrast with all false religious leaders. Ezekiel roared against the false pastors of His day. They took care of themselves, they lived off the flock, and they ignored the hurting members of the flock. God promised to replace them and shepherd His people Himself. That was fulfilled in Christ (Ezek. 34).

True undershepherds are contrasted with hirelings (vv. 12-13). There were three levels of shepherds. The proprietor owned the flock. The shepherds kept the flock and received shares of the milk, wool, and mutton. The hireling worked for wages and received nothing from the flock. Because of that, the hireling had no personal interest in the flock. Both Jesus and Paul (Acts 20:28-29) predicted that wolflike enemies would threaten God's flock. Two things make a good shepherd: Jesus places him over the sheep and he has a concern about the sheep.

Jesus Serves Sacrificially as Good Shepherd

Usually, the sheep served as a blood sacrifice for the shepherd. Uniquely, Jesus served as a blood sacrifice for the sheep. He emphasizes the voluntary nature of His sacrifice. Four times He stated that He would "lay down" His life (vv. 11,15,17-18). Neither circumstance, friend, nor foe, took His life (13:4). When Pilate claimed to have authority of life and death over Jesus, our Lord rebuked the Roman (19:10-11). It was an accident if a Palestinian shepherd died for his sheep. Not so Jesus.

Jesus emphasized the substitutionary nature of His death for the sheep. He died "for the sheep." This is the most important preposition in history! His death was instead of the death of the sheep. A blow is about to fall on the sheep, but One interposes His body and takes the blow.

Jesus emphasized the ultimate purpose in His death. He laid down His life "[in order] to take it up again." The resurrection was not a chance circumstance, but the ultimate purpose of His death. The death of a Palestinian shepherd was a disaster for his sheep. Not so the death of the Good Shepherd. He comes back to the sheep! He ascends to the Father and sends the Spirit.

Jesus Serves Knowledgably as the Good Shepherd

Four times in two verses Jesus used the word "know." The word suggests affectionate knowledge that comes from experience and appreciation. He dares to say that the mutual knowledge of shepherd and sheep reflects the knowledge of Father and Son. Looking beyond those Jewish sheep immediately in front of Him, Jesus sees and knows "other sheep" (v. 16). He knew that His death for the sheep and His knowledge of the flock would extend around the world and down the ages. That is where we come into the picture. He knows us and we can sing, "Savior, like a shepherd lead us, Much we need thy tender care."

Does Jesus Care? Divine Timing
(John 11:1-16)

"When days are weary, The long nights dreary, I know my Saviour cares." These words reflect the simple faith of the songwriter. Does Jesus really care? John 11 presents the seventh and greatest sign-miracle of Jesus, the resurrection of Lazarus. Through this miracle we understand how Jesus cares. He cares for us in a way that shows divine timing and reveals the glory of God.

Jesus Cares by Giving
Friendships in the Faith

Even Jesus needed special places and special friendships. "The one you love [Lazarus]" suggests a special friendship between Jesus and Lazarus. Verse 5 makes it very clear that Jesus shared a special love for Lazarus, Martha, and Mary. In His human dimension, He needed special friends. He also needed a special place. Bethany was the closest thing that Jesus had to a home in Judea. He retreated there every night during the last week of His life.

Jesus extends His friendship to all who trust Him. "The one you love" (v. 3) may have become a technical term for every Christian. Our relationship to Him depends on His love for us, which never changes, not on our love for Him, which often changes.

Jesus' friends can take their needs to Him with a trusting simplicity: "Lord, the one you love is sick." They did not tell Him what, how, or when to respond. If He was aware, it was enough.

Jesus Cares by Moving According to the Timing of the Father

Divine delays do not mean divine indifference. "Yet, when He heard that Lazarus was sick, He stayed where He was two more days" (v. 6). Jesus already had supernatural knowledge that Lazarus was dead (vv. 11,14). Just because He cared, He waited, that all might see the greatest manifestation of His power and glory. In three instances, Jesus refused to move immediately when those near or dear to Him insisted that He take action (John 2:3; 7:3; and this passage). In each instance, He later did what they wanted, but only at His own timing. In no instance do Jesus' delays mean indifference.

Every move Jesus makes is measured by God's clock, not man's. "Are there not twelve hours of daylight? A man who walks by day will not stumble" (v. 9). Jesus indicated by these words an acute awareness of God's timing in His life. He was moving by signals that the others could not receive. Every believer has the capacity to move by God's special timing if we wait on Him. "Blessed are all who wait for him!" (Isa. 30:18).

Jesus Cares by Seeing Our Situation Differently

Throughout this story, everything indicates the difference between divine and human perspective. Jesus does not view our situation as we view it. Jesus saw the whole situation as an opportunity for "God's glory," while others only saw a sad story. Jesus saw opportunity in Judea, while His disciples saw only danger there (v. 8). Jesus considered Lazarus asleep, while the disciples understood only that Lazarus was dead. The most striking statement was: "Lazarus is dead, and for your sake I am glad" (11:14-15). Lazarus is dead and Jesus rejoices. Jesus sees our situation differently than we do. Throughout John's Gospel, Jesus lived and observed on a level His disciples did not.

We need to trust that Jesus sees our situation better and more clearly than we do. The loyalty of Thomas in that regard is admirable. Although He did not understand how or why Jesus was moving, he intended to be loyal (v. 16).

Consider your own difficulties and challenges. In what way could Jesus see these differently than you see them? Remember, He looks for opportunities to reveal the glory of God in the maximum way through your life.

Does Jesus Care?
Divine Revealing

(John 11:17-37)

In the last message, we saw that Jesus cares, even when divine timing creates delays. But, what happens when Jesus moves into the situation? Jesus cares by divine revealing. He reveals truths about us, about the nature of eternal life, and His own caring humanity.

Jesus Cares by Receiving Us Individually

Individuals respond to the same Christ differently. Martha and Mary reveal this in their responses to the same Christ. Their character is just what one would expect from the account of the two sisters in Luke 10:38-41. Martha is the busy housewife. She is first to be told of His presence and first to go meet Him. She is puzzled by His words, but bravely accepts them and goes away without demonstration.

On the other hand, Mary is in her private chamber, weeping. When she hears of Jesus, she hastily leaves the house to fall at Jesus' feet. At the feet of Jesus, she wails unrestrainedly. Mary expressed her faith in an outburst of emotion and sentiment. Martha expressed her faith in a quiet and reserved trust. Both of them are under Jesus' care.

A mark of security in our relationship with the Lord is our willingness to accept our experience of Christ as real, as well as that of our brother or sister. We do react differently to the same Christ.

Jesus Cares by Instructing Us Clearly

Martha shared the viewpoint of her day, that resurrection from the dead belonged to the great judgment at the last day (v. 24). Jesus countered this with one of the amazing words ever to fall from His divine lips: "I am the resurrection and the life" (v. 25). To touch Him is to touch eternal life itself. Eternal life is a personal gift from Christ Himself, now. He said "I am," not "I shall be hereafter." He did not say, "I promise," or "I procure," or "I bring," but "I am." Eternal life is not something to be distributed by Christ at the end of the age. It is a present relationship with Him now.

If you know Christ as Lord, you have as much eternal life as you will ever have. It is a quality of life that is eternal, because it is the life of God Himself.

Jesus Cares by Feeling for Us Deeply

Jesus did not work His miracles passively, as if they cost Him nothing. He was so moved by the scene that He made inarticulate sounds of mental agitation and strain. He literally shuddered at the entire scene (v. 33). The Greek gods were impassive, untouched, apathetic. Jesus reveals to us the deep feeling of God for His own.

The famous words, "Jesus wept" (v. 35), do not refer to the loud wailing of Mary, but rather to a quiet shedding of tears in light of the reality of human grief. For Jesus to weep, harmonizes with what we know of His humanity elsewhere in John. He knows thirst (4:7; 19:28), fatigue (4:6), and love (20:2). But, the greatest manifestation of His human compassion is outside the tomb of Lazarus. This chapter demonstrates as no other, the humanity and Deity of Jesus Christ. He is low enough to understand us, but He is high enough to help us.

Does Jesus Care?
Divine Power
(John 11:38-46)

"We have seen that Jesus cares by acting with divine timing and by giving a divine revealing of His Person: "I am the resurrection and the life" (v. 25). But, the ultimate expression of Jesus' care is the undisputed demonstration of His power. The resurrection of Lazarus is the greatest demonstration of His power short of His own resurrection. In confronting our impossibilities, Jesus can demonstrate His power.

Jesus Cares by Confronting
Apparent Impossibilities

We know certainly our possibilities. Our first response is often, "Nothing can be done." In spite of her earlier faith, (v. 27) Martha ultimately saw only the impossibility of the situation (v. 39). We may misunderstand Christ's intention. Martha thought He wanted to see Lazarus again, to view his remains. We may magnify only the problem rather than Christ's power and presence. Martha thought only of the dissolution of a corpse rather than the presence of Christ.

Jesus feels deeply our impossibilities. "Jesus, once more deeply moved, came to the tomb" (v. 38). In the face of skepticism (v. 37), the very presence of death, and human grief, Jesus felt a holy indignation. He is "a man of sorrows . . . acquainted with grief (Isa. 53:3, KJV).

Jesus confronts directly our impossibilities. Jesus stood boldly before the burial cave, and commanded the removal of the stone (v. 39). He does only what He can do, but we must do what we can do. He could have made the stone fly away by divine power, but instead, He commanded mere men to do it. In confronting our impossibilities, Jesus expects us to do what we can do.

Jesus Cares by Revealing the Glory
and Purpose of God

In the face of every problem, Christ intends to reveal the glory of God. Christ's intention in confronting any problem is the glory of God. He states that at the very beginning: "Did I not tell you that if you believed, you would see the glory of God?" (v. 40). The word "see" is always used of seeing spiritual and heavenly realities (cf. 1:51). He wishes us first to see His glory, not the solution of our problem. He wanted Martha to focus not on the body of Lazarus, but the glory of Christ.

God's glory is the sum total of all His attributes, so displayed that He cannot be overlooked, ignored, or avoided. Part of His glory is resurrection power: "Christ was raised from the dead through the glory of the Father" (Rom. 6:4).

In the face of every problem, Christ intends to reveal His relationship to God. Christ wants to reveal His unity in communication with the Father (v. 41). His prayer is not a request, but an expression of thanksgiving that God had already heard Him. Yet, there is no earlier prayer recorded! There is an immediate, perfect, uninterrupted unity between the Son and the Father (10:30).

Christ also wants to reveal His unity in mission with the Father: "I said this for the benefit of the people standing here, that they may believe that you sent me" (v. 42). John makes it clear that the purpose of all Christ's words and deeds is to convince us that the Father sent Him (12:30; 17:8,18,21,23,25; 20:21). In the face of Lazarus's resurrection, no one could doubt that Christ was sent from God.

Christ Cares by Demonstrating
the Power of God

Jesus demonstrates the power of God by His word alone. "Jesus called in a loud voice" (v. 43). The word "called" usually refers to the shout of a large crowd. Four times it is used in John of the crowds' call for Jesus' crucifixion. When men cried out, it resulted in the death of Christ. When Christ cried out, it resulted in life! All three resurrections performed by Christ were accomplished by His word alone (Mark 5:42; Luke 7:14). Our own resurrection at the last day will be accomplished by the call of Christ's voice alone (John 5:28-29).

Jesus demonstrates the power of God for His purposes alone. Jesus cares for us. On all three occasions of resurrection, Jesus' first interest was for the person raised. His purpose in the resurrection of Lazarus was not speculation, but belief. Lazarus did not speak; there was no sensationalism. The simple doing of the deed showed the divinity and power of Christ.

Lazarus brought his graveclothes out of the grave with him. He was going back to the grave again and would need them. When Christ rose, He left His shroud behind in the tomb (20:5,7). He would never need it. When He calls for us in resurrection, we, too, shall leave our old garments behind. We will be clothed with our heavenly dwelling (2 Cor. 5:3).

Living a Servant Life
(John 13)

John Naisbitt, in the international best-seller, *Megatrends*, predicted that our nation is moving toward a "service economy." Jesus moved His people toward a service economy long before. John 1—12 presents the public teaching of Jesus. John 13 opens the private teaching of our Lord for His own. The very first item of that private instruction is the necessity of service. Jesus gives the supreme example of how a servant loves and how love serves.

Authentic Service Ignores the Usual
Arguments About Greatness

The twelve entered the room of the last supper disputing about whom among them was the greatest. They jostled for the best seats near Jesus at the Passover meal. They ignored the common practice of volunteering to wash the street filth from one another's feet.

You cannot have the spirit of a servant as long as you measure greatness by secular standards (Luke 22:24ff).

Authentic Service Avoids the Usual Excuses About Service

In light of the circumstances, Jesus had more excuses for distraction and neglect of service than anyone else. He faced the betrayal and the cross. Yet He served to the uttermost.

A real servant acts when others neglect to serve, and a real servant acts in spite of prerogatives not to serve. A real servant acts in spite of distractions in the midst of service.

Authentic Service Acts on the Immediate Need
in a Remarkable Manner

Disciples always washed the feet of their master. It was unprecedented for a master to wash the feet of his disciples. In a remarkable manner, Jesus demonstrated service to the uttermost.

Authentic service takes the initiative and addresses the real need of the moment. Authentic Christian service always has a fuller significance than the moment. Every act of service points toward Christ's ultimate act of service on the cross. This keeps Christian service from merely being "do-gooders." List the arenas and circumstances in your life for immediate initiative of practice service.

The Holy Spirit: A Promise Kept
(John 14:15-26)

A singular promise dominated Jesus' final, private teaching to the twelve. He promised to send another Divine Personality like Himself. That Divine Personality would continue His work. He promised as His gift the Holy Spirit. He has indeed kept His promise. Every believer knows that for a fact. Have you had an experience with the Holy Spirit? You can learn from Jesus who He is and what He does in your life.

The Holy Spirit Responds to an Obedient Life

Love to Christ demonstrates itself in obedience: "If you love me, you will obey what I command." For three years, the disciples ministered to the physical needs of Christ as an expression of their love to Him. He would soon be physically absent. How do you express love to a physically absent Christ? You keep His commandments. The only way we can show love to a physically absent Christ is in obedience to His commands.

Obedience demonstrates itself in keeping His commandments. Jesus calls them "*My* commandments." The *quality* of those commands reflects those characteristics of Christ (John 13:34). The *divinity* of His commands is implied by this statement. He places His imperatives on a level with the Ten Commandments.

The Holy Spirit has an affinity for an obedient life. Verbal confession or spiritual emotion alone do not know the Spirit's presence. He resides and presides where there is obedience.

The Holy Spirit Comes at Christ's Request

The Holy Spirit comes as a gift, not an entitlement: "I will ask the Father and he will give you" (v. 16). The Holy Spirit would not have come in the natural order of things. He comes as a personal request of an ascended Lord. He further comes as a divine gift, not as a human entitlement. We do not deserve the personal presence of the Spirit of Almighty God. The Spirit is His best gift.

The Holy Spirit comes as a personal Advocate. The Holy Spirit is summoned to our side to plead, argue, convince, and instruct. As such, the Holy Spirit is a *personality,* not an impersonal force. The Holy Spirit possesses *divinity.* The Holy Spirit is the vehicle for the presence of both Father and Son in your life: "We will come to him and make our home with him" (v. 23). The Spirit comes with *durability:* "To be with you forever." The Lord Christ was physically present and then absent. The Spirit is present with the believer forever.

The Holy Spirit comes as a witness to the Truth. His name is "Spirit of Truth." He is the Spirit by whom truth finds expression and is brought to us. He will tell us truth about ourselves (16:13) and about Christ (15:26).

The Holy Spirit is unrecognized by and unavailable to unbelievers (14:17). The most powerful presence in the world is unrecognized by the world.

The Holy Spirit Comes to Continue Christ's Work

The Holy Spirit continues Christ's *provision* for us: "I will not leave you as orphans" (v. 18). In the Holy Spirit, Christ Himself comes to us as both Father (13:33) and Brother (20:17). Otherwise, we would be as bereft as orphans. He is our Provider and Protector.

The Holy Spirit continues Christ's *revelation* to us. He gives us a *continuing vision* of Christ: "you will see me" (v. 19). He gives us *continuing instruction* from Christ: "the

Counselor will teach you all things." There are dark mysteries of the faith to which our eyes must become accustomed. There are bright lights of revelation to which only the Spirit can open our eyes. He gives us a *continuing recollection* about Christ: "the Counselor, . . . will remind you of everything I have said to you" (v. 26). In all of life's circumstances, He brings to mind the appropriate and timely word from the Lord.

Abiding in Christ:
The Vine and the Branches
(John 15:1-7)

God desires reality and vitality in His relationship with believers. Such real, lively Christian living requires a daily intimacy and a conscious fellowship with the risen Christ. The Christian life is by no means merely a past transaction for forgiveness. It is a daily intimacy with the Source of life. The outcome of conscious, continuous contact with Christ Jesus is called "fruit." That "fruit" represents every aspect of inward character and outward conduct which grows naturally from moment-by-moment contact with Christ. The Lord Jesus give us illustration and instruction in order to understand.

The Lord Jesus Gives Us
an Illustration of Fruitfulness

Using that which is familiar from His world, the Lord presents a vine, its branches, and the Gardener. Behind these images stands Jesus, the believer, and God the Father.

We understand *the identity of the Vine.* "I am the true vine." This is a word of *exclusivity.* Jesus Himself alone is that great Source for the Christian. It excludes all other sources, even the church itself. This is also the language of *Deity.* Only God can say such things. No apostle or Christian would dare say to other believers, "I am the vine." Only the great I AM can claim to be the source of life for millions and for me. This is a word about *intimacy.* Our union of connection with Jesus is like that of shoots on a grapevine. Earlier Jesus claimed to be the Living Water and the Bread of Life. Yet bread must be eaten and water must be drunk. To be a branch in the vine is even more intimate than that. A branch draws its life by simply abiding, connecting with the Source.

Note the word of *reality:* "I am the true vine." Jesus is the true, ideal, and real vine. The symbol of Old Testament Israel was the vine. A guilded vine was carved into the front of the temple. Yet Israel had failed to produce the fruit God expected (Jer. 2:21) in spite of every divine advantage (Isa. 5:1-7). Jesus fulfills where Israel failed. He also is the true vine in the sense that only He gives true, heavenly life.

We understand *the identity of the branches:* "you are the branches." The believer is a shoot or branch of the vine. The emphasis rests on the Vine, not on the branches. The responsibility of the believer is to remain in the vine. In the natural world the branch does not consciously decide to remain. In the spiritual world, the Christian makes a constant choice to remain in Christ.

We understand *the identity of the Gardener:* "my Father is the gardener." The identity of the vinedresser is God Himself. He is the husbandman, cultivator, and gardener. The activity of the Gardener is to remove fruitless shoots and to prune those that are fruitful.

There is a *destructive activity of removal:* "He cuts off every branch in me that bears no fruit" (v. 2). This does not refer to genuine Christians. It does refer to superficial followers such as Judas. In February and March the gardener cut away those branches that would never be fruitful. There is a *constructive activity of improvement* "every branch that does bear fruit he prunes so that it will be even more fruitful." In August, the vinedresser pinches off some shoots so that nourishment may go to other shoots. So God purges, cleanses, and prunes the life of His own (Heb. 12:6). The agency of God's cleansing is His Word. God removes by loss of that which takes spiritual life.

The Lord Jesus Gives Us
Instruction About Fruitfulness

His instruction is a command: "Remain in me." The Christian life is not static. The Lord Jesus gives us the encouragement that while we abide in Him He most certainly will abide in us. This abiding is an act of will. It is a conscious, continual contact with the great Source. It certainly includes constant contact with His word. It means to be at home in Christ.

His instruction is a *concept:* "No branch can bear fruit by itself; it must remain in the vine." Here Jesus weaves together His illustration and His instruction. A branch must draw its life from the sap in the vine. Jesus repeatedly stated that He drew His life from the Father: "I tell you the truth, the Son can do nothing by himself; he can do only what he sees his Father doing" (John 5:19). "Apart from me you can do nothing." However successful or sensational a ministry or church may be, that only is real which comes from abiding in Christ. The nature of Christian success is not first of all mere empty activisim; it is abiding in contact with Christ.

His instruction is a *concern:* "he will bear much fruit." Christ wants to see fruit. That is a quality of character (Gal. 5:22-23), a life of praise to God (Heb. 13:15), and the extension of divine life to others through our lives (John 4:36). The fruit which comes from abiding is our inward character and outward conduct.

His instruction relates to a *consequence:* "ask whatever you wish, and it will be given you" (v. 7). The life that abides in Christ finds its will coinciding with His will. When we are so saturated with His words that they shape all of life, our prayers will reflect back to Him His own will and word. Every such prayer will be answered.

The secret to fruit bearing is abiding in Christ. This is not first effort, but relationship. Are you in the Vine?

The Best Going-away Gift
(John 16:5-11)

The farewell addresses of great leaders always merit intense attention. Those concerns of a leader's last hour with his followers are of greatest importance. This is certainly true of the final words of Jesus Christ. He promised a going-away gift, the Holy Spirit. The Holy Spirit would continue the Lord Jesus' work in the world and in the church. The Holy Spirit makes Jesus' presence universal and reveals to the lost world its true condition.

The Holy Spirit Makes Jesus' Presence Universal

What could conceivably be better than having the visible companionship and audible instruction of Jesus Christ? The disciples enjoyed that for three years and were shocked with grief at Jesus' announcement of departure (v. 6). Yet it was better for them and *is* better for us that Jesus returned to the Father out of our sight.

Jesus announces the Gift with solemnity: "I tell you the truth" (v. 7). The One who is

Truth emphatically asserts the truth. He reveals and lays bare an incredible anomaly—it is best for Him to go away.

Jesus announces the Gift as an expediency: "It is expedient for you that I go away" (v. 7b). It is not a disaster, but a great benefit and a profitable advantage that the Lord Jesus left planet Earth. The words emphasize the great help for the believer that Jesus of Nazareth goes back to the Father.

This contains the mystery of how God brings good out of evil. The wicked, cynical Caiaphas also said it was "expedient" that Jesus die (John 11:50, KJV). The crucifixion of Christ and the subsequent gift of the Spirit show how God takes the worst man can do and gives back the best.

Jesus announces His departure as a necessity: "If I go not away, the Comforter will not come." For the Holy Spirit to come, Jesus must finish His atonement (Heb. 9:24-26) and return in His risen manhood to the Father. His arrival with the Father would be signaled on earth with the gift of the Spirit. If Jesus had not returned, He would always have been local rather than universal. He would have been in the Holy Land but not Fort Worth. His return and gift make Him as real to us as to the twelve. For that reason we do not even know where the tomb of Jesus is located. He is everywhere, not somewhere!

The Holy Spirit Reveals the World's True Condition

The Holy Spirit relates to both the church (vv. 12-16) and the world. This is the only place in Scripture where the Spirit is said to perform a work in the world. The Spirit "convicts" (v. 8) the unbelieving world. This word comes from the courtroom. It pictures a thorough cross-examination which gives unquestionable proof. The Spirit will expose the world's misunderstanding of the three cardinal relations of God and man: sin, righteousness, and judgment.

Only the Holy Spirit shows us the essence of sin—a refusal to believe on Christ. The world always thinks of sin as breaking law, custom, or ceremony. The crown of all sin is rejection of Christ.

Only the Holy Spirit shows us true righteousness. Jesus' departure and return to the Father sets God's seal on Christ's righteousness. That God received Him back shows that Christ's righteousness received more than human approval. Only the Spirit shows us that we receive righteousness from Christ; we do not achieve righteousness by moral effort.

Only the Holy Spirit demonstrates that Satan has already been judged. The cross was the beginning of the end of His activity (Heb. 2:14). Surely it requires the Spirit to reveal this amidst Satan's obvious power today.

The work and witness of the church in the world is impossible without the Spirit. This is all the more reason to throw ourselves on Him in absolute dependence.

Christ Prays for Our Unity*
(John 17:20-26)

The last night before His cross, Jesus began to do what He now does perpetually. He prayed for the needs of His own disciples. A few hours before His arrest, Jesus interceded for His own disciples. He may have done so in the area of the temple itself, where the high priest of the Jews were supposed to pray for the people. He prayed not only for His immediate disciples (vv. 6-19), but for disciples in all generations to come. Beyond

His death, Jesus expected a great victory and a growing church. Jesus prays that the unity of Christians would make such an impact that the world will believe in His divine mission.

Christ Prays for the Unity of the Church

What might Christ have prayed for in the final moments before His arrest? He might have prayed for His own strength, that the eleven would support Him, that they would not flee from Him, etc. Instead, His prayer was dominated by a single great thought—the unity of the disciples. He prayed that the original disciple group would be one (v. 11). What He prayed for them, He then prayed for all believers (v. 21a). This is a comprehensive prayer for the church at rest above and the church below at work.

The pattern for the unity of believers is the unity of the Father and Son. There is literally no unity on earth like that unity. It is not merely a unity of organization, purpose, feeling, or affection. It is a vital, organic unity with an exchange of life's energy itself between persons. Just as the Father is in the Son and the Son in the Father, we are to be so related to the church.

Christians are drawn to one another because they are drawn to a common center, Christ Himself. Later, John wrote a letter to Christians "that you also may have fellowship with us. And our fellowship is with the Father and with His Son Jesus Christ" (1 John 1:3).

Christ Prays for the Impact of a Unified Church

The impact of a unified church is that the world believes God the Father sent Christ the Son "that the world may believe that you have sent me" (v. 21b). Only the manifest, visible unity of believers will convince the world of the divinity of Jesus Christ. Only the spectacle of united disciples will convince the world of the truth of Jesus' message and mission. "By this all men will know that you are my disciples, if you love one another" (John 13:35).

A truly unified community of people is a supernatural fact that must have a supernatural cause. The world is so disunited that a perfectly unified church compels the world to confess that God is at work among us. On the other hand, a disunified church reverses all the work of Christ and renders our witness to Him impotent and without effect.

Christ Prays for the Glory of a Unified Church

Christ prays that the present church on earth and the future church in heaven will see His glory. "Glory" is the visible manifestation of all the divine attributes. It is what we see when we look at God.

Christ has already revealed all the glory we can comprehend on earth below: "I have given them the glory that you gave me" (v. 22). We see in the divine manhood of Jesus Christ all the glory that our eyes are capable of seeing below. "The Word became flesh and lived for a while among us. We have seen his glory, the glory of the one and only Son, who came from the Father, full of grace and truth" (John 1:14). The purpose of showing us His glory was that "they may be one" (v. 22). Even now, when we get our eyes off one another and contemplate the revealed glory of God in Christ, we are one. That glory changes us even now: "We, . . . are being transformed into His likeness with an ever-increasing glory" (2 Cor. 3:18).

Christ will fully reveal all of His glory in heaven: "Father, I want those you have given me to be with me where I am, and to see my glory" (v. 24a). There is more to come. We will be perfectly one when we perfectly see His glory. The final object of believers' contemplation forever will be the exalted Jesus Christ. The more we look at Him, the more we will see forever. The more we see, the more we will become one forever.

That glory is the outward, visible expression of love between the Father and the Son: "the glory You have given me because you loved me before the creation of the world" (v. 24b). We will spend eternity contemplating the love between Father and Son!

Why not start now? Our church will never be fully united by looking at the pastor, program, or one another. To the extent we all look away to Jesus Christ, we will be drawn to one another. *Two slightly different sermons on John 17:20-26.

The Lord Prays for Travis Avenue
(John 17:20-26)

A principal obligation of Jesus at this very time is to pray for His church. He began this praying for His church the night before His cross. After praying for Himself (vv. 1-5), Jesus prayed for the eleven with Him in the upper room (vv. 6-19). But beyond that, He saw the future and prayed for the world church for all the ages yet to come.

In this prayer, Jesus asked only one thing—that all of His followers be one. As the church grew, the greater the risk that it would be divided. In light of that, Jesus did not pray for the church's numerical strength, financial stability, or worldly visibility. He prayed for His church's unity. That unity would ensure the victory of the church's mission in the world.

Jesus Prays for the Reality of the Unity

Jesus' singular request is "that all of them may be one." His emphasis rests on the totality of believers (all) and the necessity of the unity (one). He prays that we might continually be one. In the nature of the case, unity cannot be occasional or sporadic. This unity is not the same as unanimity or loss of identity. It does not turn us into Christian clones. You can see this unity remarkably fulfilled in the first eleven followers of Jesus with their diversity of temperament. No one could confuse Peter with John.

Jesus gives us an analogy or illustration of this unity: "that all of them may be one, Father, just as you are in me and I am in you" (v. 21a). The unity we have is like that of the Trinity. God is the center of our unity, and those who share His life are naturally drawn together as one. What holds genuine Christians together? Is it merely affection, feeling, or even purpose? No. The only thing that can hold believers together is to be caught up into the life of God Himself. There is an interchange of energy and vitality within Father, Son, and Holy Spirit. The relationship of believers is like the interchange of life within the body (Rom. 12:5). Yet in this unity, we do not lose our individuality. Just as the Father and Son are One yet distinct, so are all believers.

Jesus Reveals the Intentionality in Unity

Our unity is for a purpose: "so that the world may believe that you have sent me" (v. 21b). How does the church convince the world of the central claim of the Christian faith? We can never convince the world of the truth of our message by numbers or physical resources. The world will be convinced that Jesus' message is divine when they see believers in unity. The unity of our church is the chief testimony that Jesus is indeed God's emissary. In our kind of divided world, such a united community is supernatural. The early church did in fact do that. In Jesus Christ the deepest divisions did disappear.

Jew and Gentile, slave and free, male and female were lost in the oneness of the new life (see Gal. 3:28).

The agency of this unity is joint participation in the glory of God reveals in Jesus Christ: "I have given them the glory that you gave me, that they may be one as we are one" (v. 22). The glory of the Lord Jesus Christ is the presentation of God in His life that cannot be overlooked, avoided, or stepped around (John 1:14). When all believers gaze at that glory, they are united into one. To be drawn closer to the Light draws us close together.

For this reason, the church should not blame the world for not believing the message. We cannot point at the world and shame the world for not heeding. If we had been more perfectly one, the world would have been more perfectly believing.

Jesus Asks for Our Destiny in the Unity

As He prays, our Lord makes a specific request: "Father, I want those you have given me to be with me where I am" (v. 24). He looks ahead to our presence in heaven with Him (14:3). He had a specific reason for desiring us to be there.

The reason for the request is that we might see His glory (v. 24). He wants us to behold, gaze at, and share in His perfect glory in the presence of the Father. Even now we are being changed from one shade of glory to the next as we see him indirectly through the Word (2 Cor. 3:18). Then we will see Him and be changed to be like Him (1 John 3:2).

In a very real sense all Christians are practicing now that unity which will be fully seen only when we spend eternity gazing at His glory. To be caught up into that eternal glory will truly and finally make us to be one.

Out from Closed Doors:
The Commission and the Power
(John 20:19-23)

On the first Easter, Christ appeared to individuals and groups. He appeared under all circumstances. Around 7:00 a.m., He appeared to Mary Magdalene just outside the tomb. Soon after, He appeared to a group of women near the tomb. In the late evening, He appeared to disciples on the Emmaus Road. After 4:00 p.m., He appeared to Peter alone. But for us, the most significant appearance was to the eleven disciples and other believers in the evening. It was probably in the same upper room where He had last taught them.

Christ calls us from behind closed doors with His commission and His power for the task.

The Risen One's Church May Hide Behind Closed Doors

The church may hide behind closed doors because of fear. The first disciples were cowering behind locked doors because they feared what the unbelieving world could do. They feared retaliation. The world that crucified their Lord might do the same to them. They feared misunderstanding. There was a rumor that they had stolen the body of Jesus. They feared observation. They did not want the world to see them in their confusion and weakness.

This, unfortunately, can picture the church and individuals today. Christ's church today is often hiding behind its own closed doors, demoralized and retreating. Confronted with hostile media, a largely unbelieving academic world, and a cynical materialistic society, the church cowers behind its own doors.

In striking contrast, no closed doors can stop the Risen Christ. No closed doors can stop His *presence*. He suddenly came and stood in the midst of them. Nothing that can happen to them or to Him can stop His presence in their midst. The last time they saw Him "in the midst" was on the cross between two criminals! But nothing about the arrest, trials, humiliation, or cross could keep Him from being "in the midst" of them. The last time John would see Him, He was standing in the midst of His churches (Rev. 1). The Easter promise to our church is that nothing can keep Him from our midst except our own unbelief.

No closed doors can stop His *blessing*. "Peace be [to] you" (v. 19). His words do not express a wish, but command a fact. Because of His finished work, a state of peace does exist between God and you. These were the last words they heard Him speak in the same room before His cross. The last words of His public ministry and the first words of His resurrection presence are "peace."

The Risen One's Church Must Hear His Commission

The Risen One gives forever the *model* of His commission: "As the Father has sent me, I am sending you" (v. 21). As Jesus depended on the Father, we are to depend on Jesus. As Jesus was set apart by the Father, we are set apart by Jesus (17:19). As Jesus acted in the power of the Spirit, we are to act only in the power of the Spirit (17:22). As He came to be Light, so are we. As He came to seek and save, so are we. The reason for the failure of so much "church work" is our neglect of this commission.

The *meaning* of our Lord's commission is one of prolonging and continuing His work. We are not here to begin something new. Our only commission is to continue doing the things the Risen One is always doing.

The *method* of our Lord's commission is to use all of us, every one of us. These words were spoken to the eleven and to *all others* in the room (Luke 24:33). To limit His task to the "clergy" is the dry rot that spells the doom of any church.

The Risen One's Church Must Have His Power

Christ *gives* the power. He is the active giver. His gift of power is equal to a new creation. Jesus' words purposefully recall the gift of physical life to Adam by the breath of God. The greatest thing has happened since creation! The breath of Jesus Christ gives spiritual life.

But the gift continues His presence and work. The Holy Spirit is not a substitute for the absence of Jesus, but the vehicle for His continued presence and work. The Holy Spirit never came to lead to wild manifestations, but to continue the same witness and work of Jesus Christ.

How does Jesus' gift in the upper room relate to His gift at Pentecost fifty days later? Simply this—some of His Spirit qualifies you for more of His Spirit.

We *take* the power. We are the active receivers. The word could well be translated, "take ye the Holy Spirit" (v. 22). We are not passive in the process. There must be on our part the outreached hand, the clutching fingers. The well flows always, but we must stretch out our own cup to receive the water. The wind blows always, but we must hoist our own sails to catch the wind.

This is Easter. But we have not met to examine a long-ago, faraway event. We have met because that event means a commission and a power for Travis Avenue Baptist Church. We dare not keep the Word behind closed doors.

More Than Enough to Convince
(John 20:24-31)

The minutes of the first church conference could have recorded the words, "Thomas absent." Like a wounded animal, he had hugged his own aloneness. He must have said to the other disciples, "I told you so." Thomas had expected the worst and it had happened. We call him "Doubting Thomas." That is actually wrong. He was "Disbelieving Thomas." He positively and assertively stated his disbelief in the resurrection. His nickname "Didymus" means "twin." Perhaps that suggests the civil war within the man himself: loyal to Jesus but disbelieving His resurrection.

Thomas is an apostle for our generation. We are a generation of a ? rather than a !. The faith proclaims "He is risen!" We question. Yet Jesus always appears in a way that gives proof of the resurrection. If you do not believe, it is because you will not believe.

Unbelief Resists the Evidence

The *disposition of unbelief* resists the evidence. By nature, Thomas looked at the dark and pessimistic side of things. The other two times he appears he demonstrates that disposition. He is pessimistic about the present: "Let us also go that we may die with him" (John 11:16). He is skeptical about the future. He questions Jesus' very words about the future (14:5). Thomas had a predisposition to the dark, skeptical, and negative. Unbelief will make you look at the dark side, for there is no light.

The *isolation of unbelief* resists the evidence. Thomas's obstinate refusal to believe caused him to isolate himself from the other believers. Ten of the apostles and other disciples had gathered in belief. Thomas hid in willful doubt. In his isolation he kept himself miserable for another week. As C. S. Lewis discovered, nothing is more fatal to unbelief than being around cheerful, positive believers. Such exposure is fatal to skepticism.

The *proclamation of belief* presents the evidence. When Thomas came back, the disciples continually attempted to convince him of the resurrection. If you doubt the Easter truth, you must doubt it in the face of every church spire and 2,000 years with millions of testimonies. The Christian witness is comprehensive. Each disciple who had seen the Lord came to Thomas: the women, Mary Magdalene, Peter, James, the two on the road to Emmaus. Their testimony was convincing: "We have seen the Lord." Not only the ten apostles but many others had seen Him. When you resist the evidence, it is in the face of continual, comprehensive, and convincing evidence.

Unbelief Roots in Willfulness

Unbelief *demands its own evidence*. What is good enough for others is not enough for the unbeliever. Thomas sets up his own criteria. He must both see and touch the risen Christ. Further, the touch test must include both His pierced hands and thrusting Thomas's hand like a butcher into the wound of Jesus' side! This is the only mention of the nails in the record, and Thomas demands to see their prints! Personal unbelief is arrogant. It always sets up more and more demands in order to believe. "Get me rich, make me well, give me a job, and I will believe." The demands are endless.

Unbelief *declares its own willfulness:* "I will not believe it" (v. 25). Thomas refused the testimony of his closest friends. That testimony was more certain because it came from those who themselves did not expect a resurrection. Unbelief is unreasonable. Many blame Christians for being emotional. Nothing is more emotional than unbelief. Who would dare desire to thrust a hand into the side of a crucified friend?

Thomas did not believe because he did not want to believe. He said, "Unless I see, . . . I will not believe." That is willful refusal. Do you not believe? It is not due to the circumstances or disappointments with believers. You do not want to believe if you do not believe.

Unbelief Relents with an Encounter

Unbelief relents when it has *an encounter with believers.* The believers gathered at the same place a week after Easter because they expected to encounter Jesus on Sunday. Thomas was persuaded to be there. In the presence of expectant believers, he lost his unbelief. How do you get out of doubt? Get around believers.

Unbelief relents when it has *an encounter with Christ.* There is an *inevitability* about the presence of Christ. Even though doors were locked, Christ stood in the midst of them. You cannot close Him out. He comes into every situation. Ultimately, you will sense His presence in your home, business, social circle, and government. Christ comes into every situation, but not into every single self, unless you let Him.

There is an *intimacy* about encounters with Christ. Jesus knew what Thomas had said a week before. He had been there, unseen but more real than any other. He comprehends us completely. But then He condescends to us. Jesus did not find fault with Thomas. He offered Thomas the very test that Thomas wanted (v. 27). Thomas did not then take the test. Christ overwhelmed Thomas by letting Himself be overwhelmed. Jesus meets you again and again by stooping down to your arrogant demands. We tell Him, "Not now, wait until later." And He waits.

There is an *urgency* in encounters with Christ: "Stop doubting and believe" (v. 27). Belief and doubt are a continual process. Literally, Christ said, "Stop becoming faithless." We are in a continual process in one direction or the other—increasing doubt or growing belief. Act now as Christ calls.

Thomas moves in an instant from lowest unbelief to the highest confession of faith in the record: "My Lord and my God" (v. 28). Jesus did not want Thomas simply to believe physical evidence. He wanted Thomas to believe Him. Jesus is the same today. He offers you the evidence, but He wants you more than that to trust Him fully.

You Shall Be My Witnesses
(Acts 1:3-8)

No one reading the New Testament for the first time could mistake the intention of Jesus Christ for those who follow Him. He intended those who follow Him to give personal testimony to Him as a way of life. Something different has happened. Most polls indicate that 5 percent of Christians regularly witness to their faith. Jesus did not even tell us to build His church. He said, "I will build my church" (Matt. 16:18). Each of the Gospels ends with a commission to witness to Christ (Matt. 28:18-20; Mark 16:15; Luke 24:47-48; John 20:21). We can recover Jesus' original intention when we understand the centrality of witness in His purpose.

Understand the Basis of Witness

Only one fact justifies the Christian world witness—the actual, factual resurrection of Jesus Christ. Short of that no one had the right to ask Paul, you, or me to lay down our lives for a fraud. The resurrection is based on the *presentation of proof:* "by many infallible proofs" (v. 3, KJV). Why should anyone believe that Jesus Christ is alive? Only on the basis of the evidence. The risen Christ presented evidence which removed all doubt concerning His resurrection. He made at least eleven appearances both at day and night, inside and outside, in Jerusalem and Galilee, both to individuals and crowds. The disciples handled Him and ate with Him (1 John 1:1-4).

His resurrection had a *duration of presence*. For forty days He intermittently appeared to the disciples. This gave them time to reflect, analyze, and even invent new tests for the reality of His resurrection. They could have been stunned by a single appearance; they could not be fooled for forty days.

Appropriate the Power for Witness

While the disciples were closely crowded in a room sharing a meal with the risen Christ, He commanded them not to depart from Jerusalem, but to wait for the promise of the Father, the Holy Spirit. They were to begin their witness in the very place the facts could be validated. They had to wait for Pentecost. We no longer have to wait. The power came then and is available now.

The power for witness is *promised*. The *prophet* promised it. Joel 2:28-29 promised the coming of God's Spirit in universal power upon all people regardless of age, sex, or social standing. This would be a worldwide revolution in God's dealing with His people. The *forerunner* promised it. John the Baptist compared his physical baptisms with water to the spiritual baptism with power yet to come. The *Christ* promised it (John 14:16). The power for witness came and comes as a direct result of God's promise. We have no reason to believe any promise if we do not believe this promise.

The power for witness is *purposeful*: "You shall receive power; . . . you shall be witnesses" (Acts 1:8, NKJV). A modern tragedy of the church is the connection of the Spirit with some kinds of bizarre behavior. Healings, speaking in tongues, being slain in the Spirit and countless other eccentric activities have eclipsed the sole reason the Spirit was given. The Spirit gives power to those who witness to the facts concerning Jesus Christ.

Avoid the Evasion of Witness

We often avoid witness by *speculation* about the secondary. The disciples wanted to know if Jesus was about to restore the national fortunes of Israel (v. 6). The coming of the Messiah was connected with the overthrow of Israel's political enemies, the literal establishment of a worldwide dominion in Jerusalem. The disciples had often argued about their place in this political, national scheme (Mark 10:35ff.).

Jesus always countered speculation with a call to *duty* (Luke 13:23; John 21:22). We have replaced obedience to Jesus Christ with all kinds of speculation about church functions, organization, doctrines, and last things. He moved their attention from speculation to proclamation.

Accept the Vocation of Witness

Accept the *reality* of witness. Jesus' words are not an admonition but a statement of fact: "You shall receive power; . . . and you shall be witnesses" (Acts 1:8, NKJV). He was not giving an injunction but stating a description. His people would be witnesses. Such a witness is not just an activity but what you are in your person for the Lord Jesus.

Accept the *personality* of witness: "witnesses to Me." The Christian witness is not first of all to recount a personal experience of Christ. Although personal testimony may be part of witness, the central witness is to the mighty facts of God in Jesus Christ. We are to recount again the death, burial, and resurrection of Christ and God's offer to pardon through that death, burial, and resurrection. Our witness may be a brief word of truth, a personal testimony, or a full presentation of the gospel.

Accept the *locality* of witness. You are to begin where you are. It is always easy to avoid witness by dreaming of witnessing where you are not. They began at Jerusalem. The need for your witness is closer than you think. Your Jerusalem are those immediately around you. Go home and tell it.

Misusing and Abusing the Holy Spirit
(Acts 1; 5; 8)

The Holy Spirit changes and dwells within every believer. The normal relationship of the Christian is fullness of the Spirit. Believers have sometimes, however, tried to manipulate, deceive, or even buy the Spirit. May God grant to us a genuine and open relationship to the Spirit of God.

We May Attempt to Avoid the Holy Spirit with Our Own Plans—the Election of Matthias

Much looked right about the apostles's plan to elect a successor to Judas. Yet they avoided the leadership of the Spirit. Even though the initiation, interpretation, nomination, and election looked right, God was not in it. When we miss the Spirit's leadership, there is no direction, definiteness, or dependence in what we do. Do you subject the Spirit to your plans or your plans to the Spirit?

We May Attempt to Deceive the Holy Spirit for Our Own Reputation—Ananias and Sapphira

Ananias and his wife tried manipulation of the Spirit for their own reputation. Their act was deliberate, deceitful, demonic, and discretionary.

God presented a manifestation of judgment. God takes *genuineness* and transparency seriously, especially at times of beginning new work. There is great pressure for prominence, prestige, and visibility even in the church. We must never deceive others or the Spirit that we are more than we really are.

Some May Attempt to Buy What Only the Holy Spirit Can Do—Simon Magus

Simon thought that money could buy what only the Spirit of God could do. Although he made a personal profession of faith, he misunderstood the work of the Spirit.

Nothing can substitute for what the Holy Spirit alone can do in your life.

The Wind and the Fire: God's Fullness
(Acts 1:4-5; 2:1-4)

The New Testament Book of Acts is not so much the "Acts of the Apostles" as it is the "Acts of the Holy Spirit." The earliest history of the church shows that no major leader made a decision or opened his mouth without the direct intervention of the Holy Spirit. The Holy Spirit became a personal reality in the Christian's life on an occasion as definite as Calvary. The Spirit came in personal power at Pentecost, a harvest festival of the Jews.

Some are so afraid of Pentecostalism (a modern movement) that they miss the reality of Pentecost (a sovereign act of God). Pentecost witnessed unusual, unrepeatable acts—wind and fire. But these wrappings should not keep us from the gift. Pentecost means that God comes to me in transforming power and intimacy.

The Holy Spirit Comes to Us
Because God Keeps His Promise

God keeps His *personal promise*. The Holy Spirit comes to the believer because God promised Him. Jesus remained with the disciples forty days after His resurrection. He vowed: "I am going to send you what my Father has promised" (Luke 24:49). The Father promised His Son to send the Holy Spirit (see Joel 2:28-32; Isa. 32:15; John 14—16). Jesus told them: "wait for the gift my Father promised" (Acts 1:4). Literally, we are to "abide around the promise," as if waiting in the presence of a great expectation. My personal experience of the Holy Spirit should be so intense that it absolutely convinces me that God keeps all His promises.

God keeps His *conditional promise*. "Wait for the gift." The only contingency on the promises is that of waiting expectancy. Waiting is not wasted. The only key to effective activity is that of receptive passivity—wait for the gift. Those first Christians waited in a unique sense. They waited for the historical outpouring of God's Spirit on all believers. We wait in a different sense. We wait to prepare our hearts to appropriate what is already there. But wait we should! If they needed, how much more do we? They had been in Jesus' presence for three years, yet still needed to wait for heavenly power for effective living. Time is never lost when we wait for God.

The Holy Spirit Comes to Us
Through an Unusual Activity of God

The Holy Spirit came and comes suddenly, like a thunderclap. There is a moment when He is not within, and a moment when He is. He comes in a certain *external situation*. There is a *location*. The Holy Spirit came to the upper room, the "one place" (2:1) where they were all together. We are most likely to find God where we found Him before. In this instance it was where they had met Jesus. There is a *union*. There was a totality of unity. Nothing so hinders the coming of the Spirit in power as does division among God's people. "They were all together in one place." To experience the Spirit's power we must be in the location where we meet God and in union with other believers.

The Spirit comes with *unusual manifestations*. The Spirit came with a marked audible, visual, and verbal manifestation: "a sound like the blowing of a violent wind" (2:1). There was the echoing resonance of a gale of wind. The wind of God is a symbol of divine presence (2 Sam. 5:24; 22:16; 1 Kings 19:11; Ezek. 37:9-14; John 3:8). The blowing of the wind means life—free, mysterious, imparted life. The Holy Spirit means life.

The Spirit came with a *visual* manifestation: "They saw what seemed to be tongues of fire that separated and came to rest on each of them" (2:3). One mighty central flame entered the room and from off of that flew individual fires that rested over each single one of them. They all had one experience from one source, but each individual had a personal experience. The fire of God is a symbol of divine presence (Ex. 3:2; Ezek. 1:13; Mal. 3:2-3). The fire of God indicates His basic power—burning, purifying, energizing. The Holy Spirit means power.

The Spirit came with a *verbal* manifestation: "They . . . began to speak in other tongues as the Spirit enabled them" (v. 4*a*). The Holy Spirit sustained them as they spoke in foreign languages to those present. The Holy Spirit continually gave them solemn statements to make concerning the Lord Jesus Christ. The Spirit comes to give us bold communication concerning the Lord Jesus Christ.

We need carefully to distinguish the unique from the abiding, the gift from its wrappings. The wind, fire, and tongues were wrappings of the gift. The gift lasts—the life, power, and communication of the gospel.

The Holy Spirit Comes to Fill Us with God Himself

The most significant statement is not the most dramatic: "All of them were filled with the Holy Spirit" (v. 4*b*). There was a *totality* in the experience: "all of them." The 120 there, old and young, male and female, all experienced the gift. There was a *generosity;* they were filled. This is a filling that can be repeated and enlarged. It is a fullness to which more can be added. There was a *passivity*. The Lord Jesus acted on them. They did not fill themselves. They waited expectantly and God-in-Christ filled them in the waiting. There was a *continuity*. It was a permanent endowment and a continuing process. It is a fullness of which there is always more. Ephesians 5:18 unfolds to us the command: "Be filled with the Spirit." May we come to God with a live-or-die urgency until we know His power.

God's Design for a Blessed Church
(Acts 2:42-47)

Every sincere believer wants to belong to a fellowship that God blesses. Men do not determine what God can bless. God Himself has made simple and clear the quality of church life that He will honor. Any church may enjoy God's blessings if its members respond to His priorities.

Several chapters of Acts reveal the principles that God uses to bless His people as only He can. We have always believed that the ideals of the early church reflect God's eternal standard for His people. What kind of fellowship can God bless?

A Church that Understands Clearly its Priorities

God could bless the Jerusalem church because that fellowship keenly understood its priorities. There were four priorities to which that church devoted itself. Literally, "they adhered continuously with all their strength" to these priorities. Nothing else was allowed to stand in the way.

They gave priority to *teaching the word of God*. The word for *teaching* underscored both the work of teaching and the content of the teaching. They honored the office of the pastor-teacher and they absorbed the content of his teaching. God can only bless a people with a teachable spirit. Closely related to the priority of teaching is the priority of *devotion to the fellowship*. The early church fellowship was based around the teaching of the risen Christ. A church only experiences authentic fellowship when it places emphasis on teaching the word of God.

Following the first pair of priorities there is a second. The church adhered absolutely to the *priorities of worship*. This was expressed in the breaking of bread and in both public and private prayers. The church gave itself to the ordinances and practice of worship. The result of this was that the non-Christian fellowship in Jerusalem was in awe of the Christians (v. 44). When churches cease to worry about their "public image" and give themselves to God's appointed priorities, the public takes care of itself. This church understood the distinction between *means and ends, the processes and the purposes*. We would like to know the mechanics of the church in Acts 2 (where they met, how they were organized, etc.). God blessed them because they were more interested in His priorities than their own mechanics.

A Church that Trusts Absolutely Its Members

"All the believers were together and had everything in common" (v. 44). This passage concerning early Christian "communism" has often created difficulties for believers. We are curious about the mechanics of such intimately shared communal life. We may never understand this side of heaven exactly how they shared their goods. But what we can understand is the practical significance of that sharing: *they trusted one another absolutely*.

This mutual trust drew them together not only in public worship but also in private worship. It left them with undisturbed hearts. Externally, it brought them favor with the unchurched of the city (v. 47). We see the severity with which God responds to the breach of trust introduced by Ananias and Sapphira in Acts 5. Nothing was to be allowed to breach the trust and the confidence of the people toward one another.

How many churches do not enjoy God's blessings because their members do not trust one another? God has sovereignly chosen that He will bless only those people who live in a spirit of mutual trust and confidence.

A Church that Enjoys Daily Its Growth

The only numbers that really count are the numbers that God adds. He is unimpressed by how many bodies may be in a building on Sunday unless they are there under His priorities. When our priorities are right internally, we cannot even imagine how God would bless us. The church bold enough to be dedicated to His priorities cannot keep people away. May our church seek to discover and maintain His priorities in 1990.

A Fellowship of Astonishment
(Acts 3:11-16)

The earliest church astonished the city with the demonstration of the power and message of Christ. The very words suggest an impact which left people dumbfounded with amazement, as if shocked. There was such an excitement that it was as if people were standing outside themselves. No one could ignore the church.

On the other hand, the element of astonishment is missing from church today. The ordinary, routine, and predictable mark most of what we do. Churches today are admired, congratulated, or ignored, but we seldom astonish. When you compare the church in Acts with the church today, you see the contrast. Some things in Acts cannot be duplicated today: the wind, the fire and the tongues belonged to unique beginnings. But the astonishing quality of the Christian fellowship *should* be duplicated today. God desires our church in its demonstration and declaration to be a fellowship of astonishment.

The Demonstration of an Astonishing Church

Things happened in the earliest church that caused astonishment: "Amazed and perplexed, they asked one another, 'What does this mean?'" (Acts 2:12).

A fellowship of astonishment creates *attraction*: "all the people were astonished and came running to them" (3:11). From the inner court of the temple the Jewish worshipers ran to the eastern porch and thronged Peter and John. These people did what we long for people to do—they literally ran to the preaching of God's word and His messengers. Why?

There was the evidence of a dramatically changed life in the presence of the preacher. A forty-year-old man (4:22) lame from birth had been miraculously healed (3:1-10). In the very presence of the messengers stood an undeniable demonstration of a powerful message. No amount of promotion substitutes for such evidence. This was in the same old location, the temple. Yet the same worshipers in the same old place suddenly turned into a fellowship of astonishment.

A fellowship of astonishment lives with *expectation:* "Why does this surprise you?" Peter asked the onlookers (v. 12a). A people of faith ought to expect the astonishing. Peter reminds them that they are Israelites, sons of Abraham. Their heritage was one of the astonishing. Yet they embalmed it rather than embodied it; they remembered it rather than repeated it. The church should live with the expectation of the unusual. Yet we do the very reverse. If anything unusual happens we want to know what is wrong. A New Testament church should expect to move in an atmosphere of the supernatural, the unexplainable, the exceptional. The routine, the ritual, and the predictable should be the exception.

A fellowship of astonishment makes a clear *attribution*. The Source of everything unusual is the glorified Lord Jesus. The astonishing church is always making a disclaimer. The unusual does not happen because of "our own power or godliness" (v. 12b). We always confess that the power to do the unusual does not emanate from us. Further, anything that God does is not a reward for our piety. The astonishing is an act of sheer grace. It is only the name of Jesus and faith based on that name that makes us fully whole (v. 16). The astonishing fellowship constantly points beyond itself to the Name and Person of Jesus.

The Declaration of an Astonishing Church

The preaching and testifying of an astonishing church was personal, direct, and startling. Such preaching immediately connected the listeners with the crucifixion of the Lord Jesus. It put the hammer that nailed Him to the cross in their very hands.

An astonishing church confronts the city with the *disowning* of Christ. Peter did not hesitate to confront the city with their denial of Jesus. Two times he emphasized the baseness of it. Pilate had declared Jesus innocent and desired to let Him go. Yet Jesus stood face to face with Pilate and demanded the cross. Peter forced them to take responsibility for the cross (2:23). He puts the hammer in their hands. An astonishing church is willing to tell the city "You crucified Him." This galls and offends. If the people of this congregation really told Fort Worth, "You nailed Him to the cross," there would be an astonishing reaction.

An astonishing church confronts the city with the *dishonoring* of the Christ. We must present the contrast. The city wanted Barabbas rather than Jesus (3:14). When the city could have chosen the very best, it chose instead the very worst. The astonishing church confronts the city with choosing everyone or anyone other than Jesus. The ultimate contradiction is stated in the words, "You killed the author of life" (v. 15a). How can you put to death the Source and Prince of life itself?

An astonishing church confronts the city with the *dignifying* of Christ: "God raised him from the dead" (15b). God reverses the verdict of the city. What God does more than undoes the rejection of Christ. God vindicates Christ, exalts Him, and makes Him Lord over all. An astonishing church claims without flinching that Jesus Christ is Lord over this city *now*. We say without hesitation that God has reversed the verdict of Fort Worth on Jesus Christ, just as He reversed the verdict of Jerusalem.

Unity, Generosity, and Testimony
(Acts 4:32-37)

Any appropriate assessment of a church involves more than the sheer number of people gathered at one place. The New Testament emphasizes both the quantity of people and the quality of life in the Christian community. Acts 2:41 notes that a quantity of 3,000 were added to the church. Immediately, verses 42-47 characterize the fellowship of the church qualitatively. Again, Acts 4:4 notes there were 5,000 more in the church. Verses 32-37 highlight the quality of fellowship in that large first church.

Our church is a large quantity of people. But that does not mean much unless certain qualities mark our fellowship. In a quality church a spirit of unity leads to generosity and testimony.

A Spirit of Unity Leads to Generosity

Unity characterizes a quality church. Outwardly that first church represented a great crowd of five thousand men plus their families (Acts 4:4). They represented different ages, incomes, nationalities, temperaments, and occupations. Yet this group had "one heart" (v. 32a, KJV). In the center of their personality the same thoughts, feelings, and volitions characterized them. One heart beat in 5,000 people. The church had one soul; one great principle of life pulsated throughout the body. There were no divisions, factions, or contentions. Although this ideal situation did not last long, it was nevertheless the ideal. The glue that held them together was the joyful certainty that the Lord Jesus was risen. This genuine church unity is not forced, synthesized, or organized. It is vitalized by the shared conviction that Jesus is risen indeed.

Generosity characterizes a quality church. There was a unity at the point of generosity. It is stated literally and emphatically that "not even one" among so many considered that his or her personal possessions were peculiarly his or her own. There was a unity in which each felt he held his possessions as a trust for the whole church. If there was a need, there was not a question on anyone's part—the need was met immediately. In the early church everyone felt that way; in the contemporary church does anyone feel that way?

Generosity in the church ought to have several characteristics. Sensitivity characterizes generosity: "There were no needy persons among them" (v. 34). This did not last forever. They did not build a utopia. Later the Jerusalem church was very poor. But at its ideal best the church met every need. Spontaneity characterizes generosity. As need arose, people with resources liquidated the resources and brought the resources. Humility characterizes generosity. Affluent landowners brought their resources and laid them at the feet of unlettered fishermen. It was literally one of the most unusual days since creation.

A Spirit of Generosity Leads to Testimony

The unity which leads to generosity gives vitality to testimony. An overwhelming power characterized their testimony in those earliest days of unity. Our testimony is an obligation. Verse 33 tells us that our testimony is not a favor we give but a debt we owe. Literally the text says, "the apostles habitually paid back the debt of testimony." Our testimony concerns the resurrection. They had been arrested for proclaiming that Jesus rose from the dead (vv. 1-3). The resurrection is the crowning proof of Jesus' Deity, efficacy, and present sovereignty. Keep in mind that the power of their testimony to the resurrection rooted in their unity and generosity.

Our testimony of generosity is an attraction: "much grace was with them all" (v. 33). The unity and generosity of the Christians led to the admiration and attraction of those outside the fellowship. That loving and giving church enjoyed "the favor of all the people" (2:47). There would be a magnetism about my church that demonstrates such unity and generosity. Generosity is part of testimony. What kind of testimony will Travis give?

Three Visions
(Acts 9:1-6; 16:6-10; 18:9-11)

God intends for the believer to experience His presence in three ways. These three ways may be illustrated from three visions in Paul's life. Very few believers actually have the visions that Paul literally saw. But every believer can experience the intense, inward spiritual reality of those three visions. We must have the vision that changes us—conversion. We should have the vision that calls us—vocation. We may have the vision that comforts us—consolation.

You Must Have the Vision That Changes You

The basic Christian decision is conversion, turning, redirection. That vision came to Saul of Tarsus in the summer of A.D. 33. Very few have a "Damascus road" experience of such dramatic intensity. But the reasons for and reality of Saul's changing vision are the same for all Christians.

There are *abiding reasons* for the vision that changes life. It begins with the recognition of alienation from God. Pharisaism did not work for Paul. Even though his life was outwardly perfect, he was inwardly a civil war (Phil. 3:6; Rom. 7:23). Change begins when we recognize our distance from God.

Change continues when we hear the witness of Christians. Saul could not escape the dying agony of Stephen's face while illuminated with the light of heaven (Acts 7:54-60). Saul could not explain away the boldness and peace of Peter and other believers. Change comes when we are forced to a time of reflection. Saul's persecuting trip to Damascus forced him to stop his frenzy long enough to have to think. Many more would meet Christ if they would stop their frantic pace long enough to think.

There is *enduring reality* to the nature of the vision that changes life. For many it is sudden. Although Saul had been prepared, the vision itself came in an instant. For all it is illuminating. Saul saw a light brighter than the noonday sun. Christ brings light to life. For all it is personal. Saul saw the form of Jesus (1 Cor. 9:1) and heard himself personally addressed. For all it is individual. Others saw the light and heard the thunder, but only Saul experienced the reality. For all it is forgiving. Christ did not upbraid him for the past, but gave him a call for the future.

You Should Have a Vision that Calls You

Implicit in the vision that changes you is a vision that calls you. *Every* believer is called to a Christian vocation. This is *not* an ordained ministry, but it is the exercise of your gift in the body of Christ.

God uses several methods to call you to your task. He uses *closed doors* and *dead ends* (Acts 18:6-10). Paul tried to go west, north, and even to minister at Troas. But the providence and presence of God prohibited him. God uses *personal pleas* to call you to your task. In one vision, a man with a Macedonian cloak and hat gave a personal plea to Paul. You should listen to pleas from the pastor and the church. God speaks through them.

Mark the response to the vision that calls. The response ought to be immediate. Paul and his companion left at once (10:10). Procrastination is the enemy of obedience. The results of Paul's response were far greater than Paul anticipated. In that one decision Christianity moved west. Your own Christian life was wrapped up in Paul's response to the vision that calls. We can never imagine or measure the impact of our "yes" to God's call.

You May Have a Vision that Comforts You

Those whom God changes and calls He comforts. The response to God's call usually places you in a difficult situation. It landed Paul in the worst and vilest city of the Roman world, Corinth. Then Paul began to faint from opposition and physical threat (18:1-8). For a third time the Lord spoke to Paul in a vision. This vision brought comfort to the one God had called and changed.

The vision prohibits *fear*. This is the characteristic word that accompanies the presence of Christ (Luke 1:13; 2:10; 5:10; 8:50; 12:7). The vision is a personal presence of Christ. The words are emphatic. "I [myself] am with you" (Acts 18:10a). The vision is a promise both of protection and success. We are not promised freedom from opposition but we are promised ultimate protection. We are further promised the success of God's cause for He has "many people in this city" (v. 10b).

A Metropolitan Method for Evangelism
(Acts 19:8-10)

What interests the average person on the streets of our city? Finance, commerce, politics, travel, athletics, religion. Exactly the same things interested the person on the streets of Ephesus. Paul had an evangelistic strategy that *worked* then and *works* now.

Witness with a bold clarity where people respond, then change strategies decisively when response stops.

I. Evangelize First Where Response Appears Most Likely (v. 8)

Paul witnessed first where response was likely, the Jewish synagogue. This was his custom and their request. We must find where people in our city are most responsive and go there first.

We must go with an *habitual boldness* for a sufficient time: "Paul spoke boldly for these three months."

We must make the message *clear*, not distort it or give "religious" entertainment: "arguing persuasively."

Application: Identify the people you know most likely to respond to witness.

II. Change Evangelistic Strategy
Decisively and Creatively (v. 9)

Change to another strategy when the present one stops working.

When people grow hard

When public opposition develops

Change strategy *decisively:* "Paul left them. He took the disciples with him."

Change strategy *creatively:* "[Paul] had discussions daily in the lecture hall of Tyrannus."

Application: Find a new way to share the gospel in your circle.

III. Expect to Confront the Entire Region
with the Gospel (v. 10)

In two years, everyone dwelling in Roman Asia heard the word of the Lord. The gospel penetrated racially, geographically, economically, and vocationally.

We can find a strategy so that everyone at every level in our city hears the word of the Lord.

Application: Penetrate the different strata in **your** world with the gospel.

The Gospel:
An Obligation Without Shame
(Romans 1:14-17)

To many of us, the word *gospel* has a cozy, familiar ring. We believe the gospel, preach it, and sing it. Yet, many of us have "overheard" the gospel. That is, we have heard the very term "gospel" so many times that it has become a vague term without definite content. The gospel ought to be a precise thing that informs us and motivates our lives. The gospel places us under an obligation when we understand the power of God it reveals.

The Gospel Places Us Under an Obligation

Even before the definition of the gospel, we encounter the obligation of the gospel. Before Paul tells us what the gospel is, he tells us of the duty, debt, and obligation of those who know the gospel. To know the gospel is to have, by that fact, an inescapable duty. That duty is personal, informational, and vocational. The duty is personal because Jesus Christ lays the duty on us. The duty is informational because the gospel represents the information which *must* be shared by its very nature. (If I know a building is on fire, I have informational responsibility to share the knowledge.) That duty is vocational for those called to the ministry.

That duty is not only inescapable, but also *inclusive*. I do not have the right to qualify the people with whom I share the gospel. "Greeks and non-Greeks," means those who belong to the prevalent culture and those who do not. We have an equal debt to share the gospel with those who have intelligence and education, and those who do not. We are not to exclude anyone in our proclamation of the gospel.

The Obligation Requires that We Overcome the Shame

By the very nature of the gospel, Christians will constantly be tempted to shame concerning the gospel. Paul recognized this as a sober inevitability. Jesus Himself warned of shame concerning the gospel in awesome language (Mark 8:38). Paul had to admonish Timothy not to be ashamed of the gospel (2 Tim. 1:7-8). Peter's well-known denial underscores the intense possibility of shame.

Why are Christians ashamed of the gospel? First, the hostility of the world toward God as He really is intimidates the Christian. The world hates the real God of biblical revelation. Second, the gospel appears unimpressive, weak, foolish, and irrelevant to the world. It is preposterous to the world that one man nailed to a stick of wood, bleeding to death, saves for eternity. Because of this, Christian are personally, socially, vocationally, and intellectually ashamed of the gospel. There really is a stigma to believing the gospel in our world.

Paul refused to be ashamed of the gospel in the hardest place to tell it, Rome. We should not be ashamed in our city either.

We Overcome the Shame When We Understand the Power

The simple telling of the gospel itself possesses the omnipotent power of God. Paul himself admitted freely that the whole method and message of the gospel was foolishness (1 Cor. 1:21). To go around telling people that a man who bled to death outside the wall of ancient Jerusalem can revolutionize their life is apparently foolish. Yet in telling that story, the inherent omnipotence of an almighty God finds release. The preaching of the cross *is* power (v. 18). The Word proclaimed *is* living and active (Heb. 4:12). The very telling to the story removes sin and death, and positively makes life whole. The gospel creates the very belief or faith that make our appropriation possible. Belief is the crater that remains after the gospel has exploded on us. Tell it, and let it do the rest. The gospel is the power of God.

Right with God Alone
(Romans 1:17)

How can a mere human know with certainty that at the last he will be right with God? In that certain judgment that begins the life beyond, who can stand in the presence of a holy God? That is the central question of our faith. Martin Luther, John Wesley, and many lesser lights have discovered the amazing truth of our text. The gospel proclaimed reveals a right status which is God's gift, altogether by faith. Your assurance and happiness in Christian life depends on understanding this truth.

Right Status with God Comes as a Divine Donation

Righteousness is an *attribute* of God. In everything that He does, God is just, virtuous, and conforms to a perfect norm of moral and ethical behavior. This is foundational to all we believe. But there is no hope for you and me in that. For habitual sinners to stand in the presence of a perfectly righteous God yields no encouragement.

Righteousness is an *activity* of God. God's righteousness is not still or static, it "goes forth." It is active, energizing, and influencing all things. It diffuses itself as an active force in the world. It impels God to make men and women like Himself. In that regard, God's righteousness is like radioactivity—it transfers its energy to everything that comes in contact with it.

Righteousness is an *announcement* of God. This is the heart of the matter. God announces or declares that you are righteous when in fact you are not so at all. He does not do this for "good people." He is "the God who justifies the wicked" (Rom. 4:5). He is the author, the imparter, and the imputer of a right status that meets all His demands. What He requires of you, He freely gives to you.

This means that God *remits* all of your punishment for sin. He acquits you. He says, "Not guilty!" How? On Calvary, Christ secured a new trial for those already condemned as guilty. Christ had no sin *in* Him but He took our sin *on* Him. We have sin *in* us, but because of Christ we have no sin *on* us in God's sight. But God not only remits our punishment, He *restores* us to favor. A criminal may be discharged, but he is not a citizen; he cannot vote, etc. In Christ, God restores us to full favor. He does this instantly, completely, and irrevocably.

Right Status with God Comes Through a Divine Revelation

Your first reaction to this is probably, "It's too good to be true." The adversary then whispers, "Therefore it is not true." It is true, but only those who receive the revelation know it.

Right status by faith is *exclusively* a revelation of God. Men could never have known it, conceived it, or invented it. In the twenty-six times the New Testament uses the verb "revealed," it refers every time to that which only God could disclose, what man could never discover. The glorious fact that God freely announces you to be right with Him as a gift could never be invented.

Right status by faith is *continuously* a revelation of God. Every time the gospel is preached, God reveals this great truth to someone listening. It is happening to some here this morning. Martin Luther said that he "beat the Wittenbergers over the head with a Bible" until God revealed this truth to them. But only God can disclose it. Mere man can never discover it.

Right Status with God Requires a Human Appropriation

There are two ways of having a right status with God: human achievement or divine gift. Most seek to *achieve* a right status with God by human effort. "They did not know the righteousness that comes from God and sought to establish their own" (Rom. 10:3). Paul himself worked half a lifetime to achieve rightness with God. He frankly stated that if he could not do it by human effort, neither could anyone else (Phil. 3).

The Christian *receives* a right status with God through faith. A right status with God is "by faith from first to last." This expression means that faith is the grounds and goal of the whole process. It emphasizes the growing quality of saving faith. What is that faith? It is the "YES" of the soul to the central proposition of Christianity—Jesus of Nazareth is the Messiah and Son of God.

Warning! Faith does not merit salvation. Faith is not a work that earns salvation. Faith is the hand of a beggar reaching out for a gift. Faith is the hand of drowning man reaching out for a life preserver. Faith is itself a gift of God.

Paul wants us to understand that God has always worked this way. He quotes Habakkuk 2:4, "the righteous by faith shall be preserved alive." When the Babylonians were about to invade tiny Judah, the prophet reminded individuals that those who trusted Jehovah would be preserved alive through the ordeal. Faith alone secured the favor of God. The God of the Old Testament is the same God of the New. When we stand in His presence, our only cry will be, "Faith alone, Christ alone."

"My faith has found a resting place, Not in device nor creed; I trust the Ever-living One, His wounds for me shall plead."

The Dark Side of the Gospel
(Romans 1:18-20)

When God's holy love collides with our unbelief the collision is wrath. Calvin stated of God that "in a marvellous and divine way he loved us. . . ." More recently, Brunner claimed, "The wrath of God is the love of God in the form in which the man who has turned away from God experiences it." God's holy love requires wrath. The Bible clearly expresses the reality and the validity of God's wrath.

We Should Face the Reality of God's Wrath

Biblical Christians cannot avoid the reality of divine wrath. The reality of wrath came upon those who "killed the Lord Jesus" (1 Thess. 2:15). God's wrath remains on those who reject Christ (John 3:36). Salvation is rescue from wrath (Rom. 5:9). What is the *nature* of God's wrath? Wrath is a personal reaction of God, not an impersonal consequence of sin. God's wrath is not vindictive, violent, and malicious anger. It is even above human righteous indignation. God's wrath is the dark side of His rejected love. Wrath is God's personal reaction against sin.

The *immediacy* of God's wrath is both now and in the future. It is now being revealed but will also be revealed at the end (Matt. 3:7). The *quality* of God's wrath is not so much dramatic and supernatural as it is quiet and continual. Wrath appears in God letting us have our own way in sin (Rom. 1:24,26,28). The *inescapability* of God's wrath is expressed through Scripture (Rev. 6:16-17).

God's wrath is not indiscriminate anger. He projects His wrath at definite objects: impiety and immorality. God directs His wrath at man's irreverent neglect of Himself. Only after that is His wrath directed at immorality or misconduct.

But is God fair in His wrath?

We Should Feel the Validity of God's Wrath

Is God fair in expressing wrath toward all impiety and immorality? Does each person have sufficient evidence of God's requirements to avoid wrath? What of those who have no Bible or Christian witness, which is much of the world?

There is a sufficient revelation of God to all people at all times to warn of His wrath and hint at His love. This is the general revelation of God in nature and conscience.

Availability marks this general revelation of God. It is "among us," in our very midst. Everywhere we look God reveals Himself. *Intentionality* distinguishes this general revelation. God intends us to see His footprints in His world. *Visibility* characterizes this general revelation. In creation, God's invisible qualities "have been clearly seen." The world around us and the conscience within us shout the existence and nature of God.

Rationality, religious experience, cosmic design, and conscience all present God's existence and nature. Only willful suppression keeps us from seeing Him in all things.

What does nature show us about God? Nature shows us God's eternal power. We should see an eternal One behind everything. But nature also shows us the divinity of God, that is, the total of all His attributes and perfections. Every person on earth could know these things about God without ever seeing a Bible or hearing a sermon. Thus under God's wrath "men are without excuse."

But we have *more* than nature. On Calvary, we see God turning His wrath on Himself! At the cross, love and wrath collide in the person of Jesus Christ. He absorbed and displayed God's wrath. How can we escape if we neglect so great salvation?

Divine Footprints
(Romans 1:19-22)

Is there evidence for God's existence and nature outside the special disclosure God made in Christ and Scripture? How can God hold every human being accountable, even those who do not have His special revelation in Jesus Christ? Both the Old and New Testaments insist that God has revealed Himself in the natural world. That self-disclosure in creation is enough to make us accountable to Him. People suppress the obvious truth about God available everywhere in the natural world.

Creation Demonstrates the Availability of God's Footprints

Everything people can know about God, apart from special biblical revelation, may be discovered in creation itself. That which is knowable about God to mere man can be seen in the natural world. There is a *universality* about this natural revelation of God. It is literally "in our midst." In the world outside us and the conscience within us, we should detect divine footprints. For eyes that can see, "every bush is aglow with God." There is an *intentionality* about God's witness in nature. It is not accidental that people see God's attributes in creation. God deliberately intended it to be so: "God has made it plain to them." There is a *durability* about this disclosure of God in nature. It has been available "since the creation of the world." At all times and places in the midst of all people, there has continually been available the evidence of God's footprints in the natural world.

In the face of this is our *irresponsibility*. We "suppress the truth" (v. 18). The evidence of God's presence and power is obvious in the created world. It takes a deliberate act of suppression to avoid confronting that evidence. It burns in the eyes and roars in the ears of all people at all times.

Creation Demonstrates the Visibility of God's Footprints

The visible creation clearly demonstrates the invisible qualities of God. That the created world demonstrates the character of its Creator, is as old as the Psalms, Job, and Isaiah. "The heavens declare the glory of God; the skies proclaim the work of his hands. Day after day they pour forth speech; night after night they display knowledge. There is no speech or language where their voice is not heard. Their voice goes out into all the earth, their words to the ends of the world" (Ps. 19:1-4). A clear understanding of God's perfection may be obtained from His observable handiwork. Nature declares the eternity and the divinity of God.

The created world declares the *eternity* of God. The world around us and the conscience within us should speak of an eternal One whose power is also eternal. The created world declares the *divinity* of God. God's divinity is the sum total of all His attributes, all His invisible perfections. Creation thus implies the wisdom, righteousness, justice, and holiness (otherness) of God. Only willful suppression keeps us from seeing these qualities in His creation. Those who refuse to see God in creation are "without excuse" (v. 20).

We Have a Responsibility in Light of Divine Footprints

God's footprints should draw from us a certain *reaction*. We should give to God both glory and gratitude (v. 21). The woeful story of the race is our refusal to do so. In light of overwhelming evidence, we refuse to give Him that which is due Him. Instead, intellectually we become empty, and emotionally we are eclipsed. The reality is that while mankind claims to be wise in independence from God, we are demonstrating our foolishness. While many live in spiritual idiocy, they claim to be geniuses.

This has become an open *revolt* in which men worship things that are created rather than the Creator (v. 23). This is not only seen in ancient idolatry, but in the contemporary idolatry of self. As a famous movie star/theologian recently said, "You are God!"

Because of this willful suppression of the truth, God expresses Himself by a divine *release* of an ungrateful race: "Therefore God gave them over" (v. 24, also see vv. 26,28). God lets a revolting world take its own course. This is a reluctant release. He calls from the heavens, He speaks from the conscience, and He reveals His Word in Christ. But He also gives a reluctant release to those who persistently say, "No!"

But we have more than nature. We see the perfect self-disclosure of God in Jesus Christ. He is God's special revelation. Whereas all people are responsible because of God's disclosure in nature, we who know of Him have a double responsibility. The One who made the light walked among us as the Light of the world. May we respond in glory and gratitude.

Free but Not Cheap
(Romans 3:24-26)

Every religion and ideology has a visual symbol. Buddhism has the lotus flower. Judaism uses the Star of David. Islam puts forth the crescent. The communists use the hammer and sickle, indicating the unity of factory and field in their revolution. We all know the sinister significance of the swastika. But among these, there stands out one above all—the cross. A humiliating instrument of terrible suffering and death, it is the symbol of Christianity. We all confess that centrality of the cross. But what happened on the cross? God both liberated us and satisfied His own justice on that cross.

God Provides for Us a Free Liberation

God gives us a right status with Himself in the cross. This is the greatest truth in Romans. This is justification. But how can God do anything that wonderful?

The *manner* of justification is altogether free. Paul underscores this with two terms. We are pronounced righteous "freely." It is a gift, gratis. To make that even clearer, it is "by his grace." The whole motivation and explanation is God's grace. Nothing in us predisposes God to pronounce us right with Himself. There is no merit involved of any kind.

The *means* of God's justification is the payment of a ransom to liberate us. Redemption signifies a ransom payment of price. This implies that we are prisoners, slaves to the power of darkness. Jesus stated, "The Son of man came, . . . to give his life a ransom for many" (Mark 10:45, KJV). Jesus understood His own death as the payment of a ransom price. Repeatedly the New Testament insists on this truth. "You are not your own; you were bought at a price" (1 Cor. 6:20); "Christ Jesus, who gave himself as a ransom for all men" (1 Tim. 2:5-6). This truth underscores our bondage and the provision of God's grace to release us from that bondage.

This ransom "came by Jesus Christ." His person and work is the embodiment of the ransom. It is not some impersonal thing done for you apart from Jesus Christ. To trust Him alone for salvation is to have the ransom, the liberation.

God Provides for Himself a Final Propitiation

We needed something from the cross—liberation. God needed something from the cross—propitiation. The cross not only did something for us, it also did something for God. God needed propitiation. God needed something to avert, absorb, or deflect His wrath against sin. Remember that the wrath of God is not an emotion like human anger. It is a settled disposition of His holy character against sin. The cross absorbed the wrath of God.

In the cross, God acted *personally*. The cross was God's initiative. That is, God appeased His own wrath in the Person of His own dear Son. God did not start to love us because Christ died; Christ died because God already loved us. Christ did not win over an angry God on the cross. What God demanded, He personally provided. This keeps the cross away from any pagan idea that a mere man bribed God to change His mind.

In the cross, God acted *publicly*. "God presented him [Jesus]" (Rom. 3:25). The emphasis rests on the public display made in the cross (Gal. 3:1). The cross stands for all time to demonstrate that the wrath of God against sin has been absorbed by His own Son.

Jesus Christ is the *Person* of propitiation. "He is the atoning sacrifice for our sins. . . . He [God] loved us and sent his Son as an atoning sacrifice for our sins" (1 John 2:2; 4:10). God directed against Himself in His Son the full weight of righteous wrath.

Jesus Christ is the *place* of propitiation. The word "propitiation" actually points to a specific place often mentioned in the Old Testament, the "mercy seat." The mercy seat was the lid of the ark of the covenant (Ex. 25:22; Lev. 16:13). It was the place where God manifested Himself in glory. It was the place where the high priest sprinkled the blood of an innocent sacrifice. Jesus Christ is the final and ultimate mercy seat. He is the place and the Person where God deals forever with human sin.

God Provides for Everyone a Divine Vindication

God had a problem, so to speak. God could not offer a cheap forgiveness. God could never forgive sin in a way that implied that moral evil did not matter. God must take sin seriously. To forgive sin without the cross would call into question the righteous character of God. It would say that sin did not matter after all. God presented the cross "to be just and the one who justifies those who have faith in Jesus" (Rom. 3:26).

The cross *vindicates* God's righteousness. The suffering of Jesus on the cross shows God's abhorrence of sin. Does God take sin seriously? Look at the cross. No one less than His own dear Son suffered the cruelty of crucifixion to show that God takes sin seriously.

The cross *demonstrates* God's mercy. The cross solved your problems as well as God's. On the basis of that cross, God pronounces you "Not guilty." The cross is the final solution. God vindicated His holiness and demonstrated His mercy in the same cross. Hallelujah, what a Savior!

Overcoming Your Impossibility
(Romans 4:18-25)

Faith in God's promises confronts the impossibilities of life. Such faith acts in the realm of the future and the unseen (Heb. 11:1-2). Faith acts as if the future is present and as if the unseen is visible. Faith can always overcome impossibilities. Faith in God's power and promise may change the impossibility itself. Or faith may change us while the impossibility remains. But the assurance is that you can overcome in your impossible situation by faith in the promises of God.

Overcome Your Impossibility
by the Promise of God

Faith faces hopelessness for what it is. Abraham believed the promise of God "Against all hope, . . . in hope" (v. 18). The promise of God to the aged patriarch was beyond hope. It was no longer a human possibility. There was a twenty-five year lapse between God's first promise to Abraham and the renewal of that promise. Human hope had reached and passed its utmost limit. Abraham also hoped against hope. That is, he hoped in defiance of all human calculations. Ninety-nine-year-old men and ninety-year-old women do not have children. In both the longevity and patent impossibility of the situation there was absolute hopelessness. Abraham faced the contradiction between his and Sarah's bodies and the spoken promise of God.

Faith considers the promise of God more than hopelessness. In the face of an absurd contradiction Abraham hung everything on the promise of God. God had said, "I will make you a great nation" (Gen. 12:2). Twenty-five years later God had promised descendants as numerous as the stars (15:5-6). God promised the future as if it were already the present: "I have made you a father of many nations" (17:5). In the face of all facts Abraham depended on the promise of God alone. He refused to focus on the hopelessness but rather fastened his attention and suspended his life for a hundred years on God's promise.

The same decision belongs to us all. Will we look at visible present circumstances or the yet unseen, future fulfillment of God's promise? Whatever your impossibility—physical, financial, emotional, rational, vocational, academic—you act in faith when you focus on the promise more than the problem.

Overcome Your Impossibility
in the Face of Circumstances

Faith does not deny circumstances. Abraham fully and completely considered the deadness of his own body as to siring a child. Abraham even laughed and fell facedown on the ground when he heard that a hundred-year-old man would produce offspring

(17:17). Faith is not a sort of illusion or fiction whereby normally sane people refuse to face facts. Faith faces human impossibilities for precisely what they are.

Faith acts in the face of circumstances. Faith acts *without weakening:* "Without weakening in his faith" (Rom. 4:19). We weaken when we take God's promises less seriously than circumstances. Abraham gave more weight to the promise than to the circumstances. Faith acts *without wavering:* "he did not waver through unbelief" (v. 20). To waver suggests to dispute, to be divided in one's mind. Unbelief is not merely passive absence of faith, but a positive refusal to give credence to what God has said.

Faith acts by *growing:* "strengthened in his faith, . . . being fully persuaded" (vv. 20-21). Faith grows in the ability to rest on the promise of God alone when everything else is arrayed against it. God Himself gives that strength to faith. Faith is not only faith in the promises, but also faith in the God who has promised. His is a humble acknowledgment of His faithfulness and omnipotence. Faith acts by *glorifying:* "he . . . gave glory to God" (v. 20). No greater glory can be given to God than to accept His promises through faith. Giving glory to God is more than a verbal exercise. It is staking all of life on His faithfulness to His promise.

Your faith grows and thrives by exercise. Pick an area of life that is impossible and begin now to "faith it." You will be surprised at the growth you will see.

Faith Overcomes the Ultimate Impossibility

The ultimate impossibility is that of acceptability to God when I in fact am not of and by myself acceptable to God. How can I stand before God at the end and endure His judgment? That is faith's ultimate challenge. Our ultimate act of faith is in God's mighty act in raising Jesus Christ from the dead.

When I look at myself I see nothing in me to withstand the judgment of God. The guilt of the past, the powerlessness of the present, and the despair of the future are what human life looks like to every honest observer. Guilt, impotence, and despair mark human experience. In the face of that evidence, I choose to believe in the bare, naked, unaided promise of God. If I will trust fully His act in Christ He pronounces me not guilty, invades my life with His Spirit to help my impotence, and gives me hope instead of despair.

In the face of the ultimate impossibility will you stake everything on the Lord Jesus Christ?

A New Identity in Christ
(Romans 6:6-11)

Would you like to experience consistent triumph over temptation and sin? Would you like to end each day knowing that you had more spiritual victories than defeats? You can do so. In fact, it is your birthright as a Christian. In Christ you have a new identity. The "old you" died with Christ on the cross. The "new you" walked out of the tomb with the risen Christ. When you believe this and act on it, you can experience consistent and increasing victory over sin.

Our Old Self Dies on the Cross with Christ

An old spiritual says, "Were you there when they crucified my Lord?" The answer is an emphatic, "Yes!" You were not only there, in the most real sense you were on the cross with Him.

This is a *primary truth* of Christian living: "We know that our old self was crucified with him" (v. 6a). What Paul calls our "old self" means our old ego, our former self outside Jesus Christ. The whole reality of our life without Christ hung on the cross with Him. The totality of our whole fallen self was crucified with Him on the cross. The emphasis rests on the once-for-all decisiveness of that crucifixion. Our old self was co-crucified with Christ. This is not simply a pretty idea or a piece of fiction. It is not playing psychological mind games. This is the way God sees you at this moment.

This is a *positional truth* of Christian living: "that the body of sin might be rendered powerless" (v. 6b). When you act on the fact that your former self died with Christ, you enjoy a new position before God. Your body as a staging ground for sin is rendered inert and inoperative. The human body is not itself evil. It is, however, the instrument that sin employs to express itself. Sin cannot lie without the human tongues, steal without human hands, etc. When you truly believe that your old, former self died with Christ, your body is reduced to inaction as a staging ground for sin. This is not a matter for conjecture or even rational explanation. It is a simple reality. If you believe that your old self died with Christ, your body is paralyzed at the point of sin. Sin is deprived of its strength, force, influence, and power.

This is a *practical truth* of Christian living: "that we should no longer be slaves to sin—because anyone who has died has been freed from sin" (vv. 6c-7). Death cancels all obligations, breaks all ties, settles all old scores. If a slave is dead, his master has no more claim over him. We were once slaves to sin, but our death with Christ releases us from a hard taskmaster. We can deliberately tell the Adversary, "The person you held in bondage is now dead."

Our New Self Rises from the Tomb with Christ

It is not enough to die with Christ. We also emerged from the tomb with Him in resurrection life. This is a matter of profound *personal belief:* "If we died with Christ, we believe that we will also live with him" (v. 8). This does not refer to the resurrection of the body at the end. This points to the resurrection life of Christ that we share right now. It is an article of faith to be accepted as reality, believed in as a certainty: "we too may live a new life. . . . alive to God in Christ Jesus" (vv. 4b,11). It is a willingness to act on the fact that I now live in a whole new dimension of life. It is as if a fish lost its gills and could breathe air, or a person sprouted wings and flew like an eagle! What cannot happen in nature has happened in grace.

This is a *permanent blessing:* "For we know that since Christ was raised from the dead, he cannot die again; death no longer has mastery over him" (v. 9). Nothing can suppress, interrupt, or end our life in Christ. His life is now continuous and endless. Unlike Lazarus, He was raised never to die again. This means that no circumstance can ever cut you off from His resurrection power. If anyone else becomes your whole life, that person may die. The life that Christ now lives He lives to God (v. 10). His life forever reigns in joy and power before God. You can make a permanent move from life's basement to life's balcony.

We Must Count on This as the Truth

Your death with Christ and resurrection with Christ must be reckoned as truth, or you will not experience the power (v. 11). You must agree with God to see yourself as you are revealed to yourself by the gospel. This is not fiction. It is a fact to be appropriated in faith. You may say, "My old self is alive and kicking. If it is a corpse, it is the most lively *corpse I have ever seen."* Such excuses refuse to accept the verdict of God on your old self.

Start today to act on the fact. You have taken off the old self. You have put on the new self (Col. 3:9-10). Put off the old self. Put on the new self (Eph. 4:21-22). Welcome to the new you.

Subjects, Soldiers, and Slaves
(Romans 6:12-23)

There are two great experiences for the Christian on earth. In justification God pronounces you right with Him by faith. In sanctification God makes you right with Him as a fact. The Christian experiences victory over the power of sin. Paul describes that victory under three strong images. As a former subject in the kingdom of sin, the Christian now serves another Master. As subjects we revolt, as soldiers we change sides, and as slaves we change masters.

We Should Revolt as Subjects of Sin

Recognize the personalized reality of sin. In Romans, Paul speaks of sin as a great personality, a personal force of awesome proportions. He does not hesitate to call sin a monarch with subjects and a master with slaves. "Do not let sin reign" (v. 12a) indicates the power and intention of sin. The contemporary world ridicules the very notion of sin. The Christian takes its reality with seriousness.

Realize the realm in which sin operates: "Do not let sin reign in your mortal body." Our body in this sense is the whole of us, every capacity: physically, intellectually, emotionally, and volitionally. That body is mortal, corruptible, subject to decay. There is a word of warning and a word of encouragement about our "mortal body" (v. 12b). The warning: Do not let that which perishes rule your life. The encouragement: we will not always have a mortal body capable of sin. We will one day have a glorified body incapable of sin.

Reaffirm the revolt. For the Christian, sin is a dethroned monarch, a sovereign without a realm, a king without a crown. Sin is like a deposed ruler who constantly wants to reclaim his realm. We must constantly and actively resist and continually revolt against the reestablishment of his throne. We are no longer his subjects.

Reenlist as Soldiers of the Savior

The Christian is one who has changed sides in the battle. Negatively, *refuse* to give yourself as a weapon to the enemy: "do not offer the parts of your body to sin, as instruments of wickedness" (v. 13). This speaks of a presentation. We all offer ourselves either to unrighteousness or righteousness. This points to the things presented, parts of your body." The word means your limbs, organs, or any natural capacity. It is used specifically of the eye and the ear (1 Cor. 12:16-18). It speaks of the purpose for which we present ourselves, "instruments." The word literally means "weapons." We flatly refuse to give any part of ourself as a weapon on the side of unrighteousness. The Christian refuses habitually to hand over any part of his life as a weapon to the enemy.

Positively, we *reenlist* daily in the forces of righteousness. We make a presentation of our whole personality as a weapon on the side of righteousness. The verb emphasizes the once-for-all nature of our decision. As a practical matter, we should present ourselves every day with fresh commitment. You can literally pray, "Lord, today I present my hands, eyes, ears, and all I have as weapons to be used by You for righteousness." Never surrender your weapons back to the enemy.

Respond as a Servant

We are to *acknowledge the presence of a Master:* "Don't you know that when you offer yourselves to someone to obey him as slaves, you are slaves to the one you obey?" (v. 16) The question of being free is out of the question. Everyone is mastered by a master. Whatever is the power to which you yield yourself, that power is your master. There are ultimately two alternatives in the matter of a master. You are a slave to sin or you are a slave to obedience. Paul admits that the word "slave" could be misinterpreted (v. 19). He does not know a better word, however, to indicate total belongingness, obligation, commitment, and accountability.

Admit the power of a master. We are slaves to that which we obey, not what we profess. Jesus said, "Whosoever committeth sin is the servant of sin" (John 8:34). "No servant can serve two masters: for either he will hate the one and love the other; or else he will hold to the one and despise the other" (Luke 16:13, KJV). The slave is the exclusive property of one, and he will serve that one and no other.

Accept the payment of a master. The payoff for serving sin is death. This means inward deadness now and ultimately "everlasting destruction from the presence of the Lord, and the glory of his power" (2 Thess. 1:9, KJV). The ultimate payoff for serving obedience is final righteousness. That means that you not only will be declared righteous but will actually be made righteous in the presence of God. Sin is a master that abuses you now and bilks you later. Sin pays off in death. Righteousness is a master that blesses you now and more than blesses you later. Who masters you?

The War Within
(Romans 7:15-25)

We want to do more, but we do less. We want to reach higher, but we fall lower. We want to be better, but we turn out worse. That is often the conflict within the believer. The great apostle shares that conflict. This is an autobiographical passage in which he opens his own heart for all to see. Paul experienced the inner conflict of a Christian. "For the sinful nature desires what is contrary to the Spirit, and the Spirit what is contrary to the sinful nature. They are in conflict with each other so that you do not do what you want" (Gal. 5:17). The Christian life just begins the war within. But the war is winnable through Jesus Christ.

The War Within Exceeds Human Understanding

The psalmist asked, "Who can understand his errors?" (Ps. 19:12) For the believer there is an irrationality about the continuing war within. The fact and intensity of the battle exceeds our understanding.

The *complaint* is "I do not understand what I do" (Rom. 7:15a). Paul does not mean that he does not know what he is doing. He knows all too well what he is doing. He does not always acknowledge, approve, or condone what he does. It is as if he said, "The works I do are incomprehensible to me."

The *conflict* is "what I want to do I do not do, but what I hate I do" (v. 15b). In reality he keeps on working at or busying himself with the very things that he wishes not to do.

Paul does not mean by this that he is always defeated. He does mean that a perpetual difficulty dogs his steps in that his performance falls short of his understanding.

The *concession* is "I agree that the law is good" (v. 16). A silver lining behind the cloud is Paul's inward agreement that God's law is of the highest quality of goodness. The very presence of the conflict indicates Paul's respect for the law of God.

The *condition* is "it is no longer I myself who do it, but it is sin living in me" (v. 17). This is not an excuse but an acknowledgment of a fact. Sin usurps him, takes possession of him, and sometimes dominates him. Here Paul distinguishes between what his own essential person desires and what the intruder within actually does.

The War Within Exceeds Human Will

Even though we may understand that will of God, the capacity to do it exceeds our human wills. We can diagnose our condition, discuss our condition, deliberate about our condition, and even desire a different condition. Yet at the point of *desire* Paul says, "I have the desire to do what is good, but I cannot carry it out" (v. 18b). This does not mean that the Christian is totally ineffective. It does mean that what the believer practices actually and fully corresponds to his will. Our best actions are always stained and spoiled by egotism.

The *dilemma* of the Christian is threefold. There is an essential *shortfall*, "I know that nothing good lives in me, that is, in my sinful nature" (18a). All of the endowments of human nature, everything that is in a man, perpetually falls short of God's expectation. This shortfall produces a *takeover*, "It is sin living within me that does it" (v. 20). A usurper, intruder, or an uninvited guest remains within. The residual principle of sin takes over and dominates the mind and the will of the believer. This takeover leads to a war because of the presence of the Holy Spirit. There are two principles at war within the believer. There is a warfare between the members of his body and the law of God in his mind.

This is so intense that Paul cries out, "What a wretched man I am!" (v. 24).

The War Within Can Be Won By Christ Alone

What is the solution to this conflict? The war within can be won by Christ alone. As Luther's mighty hymn states it, "Did we in our own strength confide, Our striving would be losing; Were not the right Man on our side, The Man of God's own choosing." Our only hope in the conflict is "through Jesus Christ our Lord!" The Christian life is not difficult; it is indeed impossible. Only the supernatural resources that come from a moment-by-moment identification with Christ enable us to win the war within. Every day and in every way we must "offer [ourselves]" (6:13). We must appropriate the fact that "we are more than conquerors through him that loved us" (8:37). Your outlook determines your outcome. You win the victory by presenting yourself to the Victor.

The Victory in Christ's Ascension
(Romans 8)

Christians look *backward* at the cross and empty tomb. They look *forward* toward the second advent of Christ. But they must also look *upward* toward our ascended Lord. "Set your heart on things above, where Christ is seated at the right hand of God" (Col. 3:1). The ascending Christ looked *downward* at His disciples, *roundward* at the hostile spiritual forces, and *upward* toward the throne of God. These are the three dimensions of His victory.

The Ascending Christ Takes the Downward Look

As our Lord ascended in victory toward the Father's throne, He looked down at the disciples. He gave them two promises. He gave them the promise of the Spirit, the Paraclete. Concerning the *past,* the Spirit would remind them of everything He had said to them (John 14:26). Concerning the *future,* the Spirit would be teacher, leader, and reporter of God's will (16:13).

He gave them the promise of His presence. In the assembly of the church, He would be with them (Matt. 18:19). In the work of the ministry, He would always be with them (28:19-20). As the ascending Christ looked downward on the Christians He left on earth, He gave those two promises.

The Ascending Christ Takes the Roundward Look

As Christ ascended through the heavens, He moved through ranks, layers, and divisions of hostile spiritual powers (Col. 1:16,20b; Phil. 2:10; Rom. 8:38-39). As He passed through them, He conquered them.

He disarmed them. He took away their power to sting and torment men. He disgraced them. He put the malevolent, spiritual powers to open shame. He displayed them. Upon His arrival in heaven, He held a triumphal parade to demonstrate His victory. We need not fear the demonic powers. They cannot keep true believers in their grasp. They are defeated foes.

The Ascending Christ Takes the Upward Look

As our Lord arrived at the portals of heaven, four great realities awaited Him at His triumphant homecoming: He received His coronation as King, and His ordination as Priest.

He began His intervention as Advocate and His preparation as Forerunner.

His victory is total in every dimension, beneath, around, and above. "We are more than conquerors through him" (Rom. 8:37).

My Freedom Through His Victory
(Romans 8:1-4)

Jesus Christ won all the battles that I have lost. Because of that, Romans 8 promises a comprehensive personal victory in Christ. The vehicle for this victory is the indwelling Holy Spirit. In the face of sin's guilt, I can experience no condemnation. In the face of sin's power, I can experience personal liberation. This great chapter gives assurance of ultimate security in union with Christ. You can be free from the guilt and power of sin through Jesus Christ.

In Christ You Experience No Condemnation

This is presented as a *fact:* "There is now no condemnation for those who are in Christ Jesus" (v. 1). That means that there is no pending death sentence and no upcoming execution of that sentence. The emphasis rests on the strong word *no.* In no way whatever will the believer ever face condemnation. We are not waiting for final bad news. We already know there will be final good news. This only resumes what Paul has already stated in Romans 5:16,18.

Jesus Himself gives the beautiful assurance that whoever hears and believes Him will not be condemned (John 5:24). The only One who has the right to condemn us is the very One who defends us (Rom. 8:34). When we are "in Christ Jesus" like a branch in a vine or a limb in a body, there is no condemnation.

There is greatest stress on the *finality* of this fact. "There is *now* no condemnation." The *now* is all that time since the mighty deed of Christ. The word embraces all sin past, present, and future. The Christian is taken outside the realm of any conceivable condemnation. As a practical matter, the Christian should never feel condemnation. The Christian may feel conviction which is a fatherly correction resulting in repentance and renewal. But the Christian should refuse ever to feel condemnation.

In Christ You Experience Personal Liberation

One basis for the lack of condemnation is the increasing sense of liberation from the power of sin. The believer has moved from one governing principle to another, from one dominant influence to another, from one activating factor to another.

The believer is *liberated from an old principle:* "the law of sin and death" (v. 2a). Like spiritual gravity, the law of sin and death pulls every human down. The Ten Commandments describe sin but cannot deliver from sin. In fact, knowing the commandments of God actually aggravates and inflames the reality of sin. This leads to a vicious cycle of repeated failure. We sin, which deadens us, which leads us to more sin, etc., etc. It becomes a tyrannical rule of sin and death. Absolutely no one can liberate himself.

Christ *liberates us with a new principle:* "Through Christ Jesus the law of the Spirit of life set me free from the law of sin and death" (v. 2b). When the Holy Spirit enters a life, there is a new regulating, activating, energizing power. He is a "Spirit of life" because He animates the soul with a new life energy. This new life energy does not destroy the law of sin and death, but it does enable me to overcome the down drag of that law. Like the launching rocket that enables a payload to overcome the pull of gravity, Christ lifts you above the old law of sin and death. This does not mean a life of perfection, but you are no longer unresisting and ineffective in the fight.

In Christ You See God's Ultimate Intention

We ought to recognize the *inability of God's law:* "What the law was powerless to do . . . ; (v. 3). It is impossible for the law of God to change human behavior. The law defines sin, describes punishment, but cannot change behavior. The law is like a mirror revealing that we need to wash our faces, but we cannot cleanse our faces with the mirror. You can memorize the Ten Commandments and Sermon on the Mount, but you will not change your behavior by merely knowing the law.

We should understand *the ability of our Lord:* "God [sent] his own son in the likeness of sinful man" (v. 3). God sent His Son to assume our very liability, human flesh. Christ started with the same unpromising, unsuitable material we have. He faced all the same needs, weaknesses, and temptations. Yet in the arena where we lost, He won. On the battlefield where we were defeated, He is Victor. He entered the match with our handicap and scored perfectly. Finally, one Man conquered on the field where all others lost. He turns to you with a sweet and gracious smile as if to say, "My victory is already yours."

You participate in this when you walk "according to the Spirit." When the indwelling

Spirit of God is the regulating principle, the dominant rule in your life, His victory is yours.

Safe If Saved

(Romans 8:31-39)

How can you reduce the most profound biblical book to a single sentence? Paul did so in Romans 8:31, "If God is for us, who can be against us?" All that God says in the deep, doctrinal discussions of Romans may be reduced to that sentence. Baptist believers have stated it in a simple way, "once saved, always saved." Whoever once truly believes that Jesus was raised from the dead, and confesses that Jesus is Lord, will go to heaven when he dies.

God Is for Us

This is a presupposition, not a question. God is on our side. He is for us and not against us. He desires life in abundance. It is the resounding faith of the psalmist: "This I know [that] God is for me" (Ps. 56:9, NKJV). "In God I have put my trust; I will not be afraid. What can man do to me?" (v. 11, NKJV).

This is an affirmation. No one can ultimately prevail against me. This implies that the Christian has many enemies. This is true. In one sense, a Christian has more enemies than anyone else. Both seen and unseen opponents constantly oppose the believer. None of them will prevail.

This is a deduction. God has done the greatest conceivable thing for us—given His only Son to cruel death. Will He not do the lesser thing for us, protect us safely if saved? God has already done the inconceivably great and costly thing for us. We may be fully confident He will do what is by comparison less—protect us till we stand before Him.

No One Can Prevail Against Us

There can be no finally successful accusation against the Christian. Paul pictures a judgment scene in a courtroom: "Who will bring any charge against those whom God has chosen?" (Rom. 8:33). Many attempt to do so, including Satan himself (Rev. 12:10). The implication is that no one can successfully bring such a charge against the believer.

The Judge is already on our side. The only person who can condemn is the Judge, and He is the One who most wants to pardon and free us. The only finally effective accuser is God Himself. He is pledged to the very opposite. And from His court, there can be no appeal!

The Counsel for the Defense has done everything. He has already died for guilty defendants, taken their maximum punishment into Himself. He has risen from the dead so that He will always be available in the future. What is more, He has been exalted to the right hand of the Judge, where forever, without ceasing, He personally intercedes for every individual who trusts Him to do so. Best of all, the Counsel for the Defense is the Judge's only beloved Son!

Nothing Can Separate Us

Past experience already demonstrates this. Paul gives an autobiographical catalog of that which he had already experienced, and which had not separated him from Christ's love for him (v. 35). This was not only his experience, but that of God's people in the Old Testament (v. 36).

But what of the future? Can anything arise that will threaten our relationship? Paul considers four dimensions of reality that cannot separate us from Christ.

No state of existence can separate us from Christ. He begins with death, the greatest and ultimate enemy. "The blank horror of dying is ameliorated by the love of Christ." To die is only more of Christ (see Phil. 1:23).

No invisible, supernatural power can separate us from Christ. "Angels nor demons" (v. 38) represents all of the mysteries in the unseen, spiritual universe.

No span of time can separate us from Christ. Neither this world nor the world to come holds anything to defeat us.

No span of space can separate us from Christ. No vastness or space that exists between us below and Him in the heaven of heavens above can come between us.

Lest he omit anything, Paul added "anything else in all creation" (v. 39). There may be created powers beyond our imagination or perception. Neither can they come between Christ's love and the believer.

Take comfort from these words. You are safe if saved.

A Determination About the Cross
(1 Corinthians 2:1-5)

What is the one thing that makes Christ's church unique in this city? Is it buildings, budgets, programs, activities, or striking personalities? No. The city has all of those without the church. The one unique treasure of the church is the Person and work of the Lord Jesus, most especially His cross.

When Paul came to Corinth, he was one small man traveling on foot, living with another poor man. No heralds sounded Paul's coming, no sympathy appeared for his message, and no human resources were at his disposal. Yet his visit was the most significant in the history of the city. Paul's secret? He really did limit all he said to the Person and work of Jesus Christ.

We Make a Determination of Limitation

Limitation gives power. "I resolved to know nothing while I was with you except Jesus Christ and him crucified" (v. 2). This is a significant *determination*. We must be people of some steadfast refusals as well as affirmations. This means a renunciation. "I did not come with eloquence or superior wisdom" (v. 1). Paul did not rely upon his ability to speak or to reason in order to impress the Corinthians. Nothing about his bearing indicated that he was a rhetorician or a philosopher, the two things the Corinthians most admired. Paul was a learned man who knew the Greek poets, Greek statuary, and was able to reason like Aristotle. And yet there was a renunciation of all human cleverness as he presented Jesus Christ. He relied upon the bare presentation of the Person and work of Jesus Christ alone.

That limitation has to do with the *personal* nature of our message; it is a message about a person. At the center of our testimony is Jesus Christ—not the church, the denomination, or any theological system. But we emphasize a *particular* aspect of Jesus Christ, His cross. We point to the one thing about Him which is the most scandalous and has the greatest stigma—His blood, sacrifice, and criminal's death. From the world's point of view this is a foolish message brought by a foolish messenger. Yet God has chosen to attach His saving power to that message.

This determination of limitation must be *pervasive*. Paul was limited to Jesus Christ in all his quiet, private conversations and in all of his public preaching.

A Declaration of Personal Limitation

Should Christian messengers always present themselves as people of mastery, control, and self-possession? Paul emphasized the exact opposite about himself.

We can preach the Christ of the cross when *physically weak* (v. 3). When Paul came to Corinth he was in poor physical condition (2 Cor. 10:1,10; 12:7; 13:3). He did not come with strength, self-confidence or self-reliance. He had an extreme consciousness of his own weakness and insufficiency for the task. Yet in his very weakness the light of the message shone more brightly. We do not have to "have it all together" to preach the Person and work of Christ on the cross.

We can preach the Christ of the cross when *psychologically fearful*. Paul came to Corinth full of anxiety. He had a "phobia," not for his own safety but because of his responsibility for the gospel message. He knew that he was not up to the task. God honored that humility on Paul's part. When we admit that we personally cannot change the city, God can.

We can preach the Christ of the cross when *visibly shaken*. Paul's inward weakness and fear manifested itself in a literal outward shaking of his person. Yet the power of God poured through the shaken men. Just because of that people saw it for what it was—the very power of God.

A Declaration of Personal Motivation

There is a *motivation we refuse*. In all of our private and public work for the Lord Jesus we refuse mere human persuasion. Paul did not come with subtle arguments, clever manipulations, or overpowering logic to manipulate people into Christianity. When we rely on psychological tricks of the trade we have only human power at our disposal.

But when we rely on the gospel message alone, there is an *intervention we realize:* "a demonstration of the Spirit's power" (v. 4). When Paul—weak, fearful, shaking as he was—preached something beyond Paul happened. The Spirit put on a rigorous demonstration of the truth about Christ crucified. People were shaken to the center of their secret selves (1 Cor. 14:24-25). When Paul preached a divine power intervened in spite of Paul's weakness.

All of this is because of the *foundation we require:* "so that your faith might not rest on men's wisdom but on God's power" (v. 5). When we place at the center of our witness anything other than the Person and work of the Lord Jesus, we put faith's foundation on that which will not last. If we persuade people by cleverness, someone more clever can lead them away. If we dazzle people by reason, someone more logical can sway them away from Christ. But when we anchor people to the cross of Christ, faith's foundation lasts. The messenger can leave, but the results of the message remain.

May we commit ourselves in this city to the solemn determination that we be committed to Christ and Him crucified as our message.

Living in the Other Dimension
(1 Corinthians 2:9-15)

Not all of us who live in the same place live in the same space. Some people in Fort Worth live in one place, others live in two places. Those who live in two places at once have an extra dimension in life—the knowledge of God through His personal Spirit. Evidence supports the obvious. Around us are those blind to God and those who see Him, those deaf to Him and those who hear Him, those who are numb to Him and those who feel Him. What makes this drastic difference? The difference is the presence of God's personal Spirit.

God in Himself Is Unknowable to Mere Humans

God's *preparation* for us really exists: "What God has prepared for those who love him" (v. 9). By His initial act in eternity and continuous activity in time God prepares life in the spiritual dimension. He prepares a richness and scope of life that defies description. God has elaborately prepared a spiritual dimension of life.

Our unaided *recognition* of God's preparation is impossible. No sensory capacity we possess can recognize God's activity for us: "No eye has seen, nor ear has heard." No rational capacity we have can think of God's preparation for us: "No mind has conceived." The knowledge of the spiritual is beyond the natural capacity of humans.

God in Himself Is Knowable By His Spirit

We know God only because He reveals and unveils Himself to us. This is humbling. It slays our pride. The scientist wants to find evidence. The philosopher wants to think it through. God is closed to both approaches.

The *nature* of God's Spirit is *personal* and *probing*. God's Spirit is personal. The very word Spirit means "personal self" in biblical language. To have God's Spirit is to know God's personal self. Verse 11 offers a simple comparison. Paul moves from the human level we can understand to the divine level we cannot understand. On a human level, no one really knows what is going on inside another person except that person's own human spirit. The inner feelings, thoughts, and motives of any person are really known only to that person. Even a human has secret depths which no human can penetrate. How much more God! Only the Spirit of God knows God. Only the Spirit of God can communicate God to us.

God's Spirit is *probing*: "The Spirit searches all things" (v. 10). The activity of the Spirit is that of probing, penetrating, and piercing everything in creation. The Spirit acts as a divine sonar, penetrating and returning with knowledge of everything. This includes the deepest things of God's nature. The Spirit reflects those deep things into the heart of the person who knows God.

The *origin* of God's Spirit belongs to God Himself, not this world. Negatively, "We have not received the spirit of the world." There is a spirit of the world. It is a temperment, an outlook that gives this world its distinctive character apart from God. "The spirit of the world" is the sum total of the way life works in this world without God. We get that spirit automatically at birth and later by contact with this world. The Christian is not dominated by that spirit.

Positively, we have received the "Spirit who is from God" (v. 12). The source of our knowledge is from God Himself. The Christian lives with a confident assurance of this personal spiritual knowledge. It is more "real" than the world itself.

The *communication* about God's Spirit comes through words. Having God's Spirit does not mean simply "warm fuzzy feelings." The Spirit communicates to us through the words of Scripture. Negatively, the Spirit speaks "not in words taught us by human wisdom" (v. 13). Scripture contains the words taught the apostles by the Spirit. These words do not belong to the language of human science or philosophy. They are different. Positively, they are "words taught by the Spirit." The inspiration of the Bible goes beyond mere ideas. The very words of Scripture were taught to the authors by the Spirit of God. The Bible is verbally inspired. This does not degrade its authors into robots. Within each writer's personality, the words used were given by the Spirit.

All of this means that we are dependent and humble in order to know God. The knowledge of God comes through His Word and Spirit, not our investigation.

Our Knowledge Depends on His Provision

The *natural person* cannot know the things of God. The natural person means the person with merely animal life, the person not inhabited by the invited Spirit of God. That person misses God in two senses. First, the person has no capacity for reception (v. 14). The spiritual organ is not present to receive the Spirit of God. The pencil in your pocket cannot receive this message, in the same sense. Second, even if that person could receive the Word of God, he could not understand it. Hence he thinks it is all foolish, insipid, and stupid. Everything about Christian discipleship and stewardship appears ridiculous.

The *spiritual person* not only understands the things of God, but places all things in their proper perspective. Because the spiritual person knows the things of God, he/she is able to scrutinize, examine, and appraise the value of everything else in life. Knowing God is the key to all understanding of things as they really are. Work, play, home, family life, and death are seen in their true relationship only when you see God.

On the other hand, the spiritual person cannot be evaluated by the natural person (v. 15). You are a puzzle and an enigma to the unbeliever. You ought to be. A mark of the genuine Christian life is that of mystery to the outsider. A born-again person should be a mystery. There is literally nothing like it in this world.

Are you a mystery that cannot be explained in human terms?

Only Servants: Man's Division and God's Multiplication

(1 Corinthians 3:1-10)

How do you measure spiritual maturity? Spiritual maturity cannot be identified with age on the calendar. Neither can it be identified with the number of years you have professed Christ. Spiritual maturity reveals itself in certain reactions and evaluations. How we react in situations and how we evaluate persons can be a key to our spiritual maturity.

In the church at Corinth people were demonstrating reactions that lacked maturity and evaluations that showed a lack of growth. All of us may measure ourselves by the Word. Our reactions to situations and our evaluations of people demonstrate our level of spiritual maturity.

Spiritual Maturity Reveals Itself in Certain Reactions

We live on a higher or lower level according to the life of the Spirit. How can you tell on which level you live? Paul had founded the church at Corinth. Later he wrote them with tenderness but firmness. They still lived on the level of the world, not the spirit. How did he know this? What are the marks?

Our spiritual *age* reveals maturity: "mere infants in Christ" (v. 1). There is nothing wrong with being an infant at the very beginning of life. A newborn cannot help being an infant. But when the infantile stage continues, there is something wrong. Actually, our spiritual age is revealed by our spiritual appetite.

Our spiritual *appetite* reveals our spiritual age: "I gave you milk, not solid food, for you were not yet ready for it. Indeed, you are still not ready." At the beginning the apostle gave the the basic fundamentals of the message about Christ (2:2). There were certain rudiments that belonged to the elementary instruction of Christians (Heb. 6:1-3). These are spiritual "milk." But growing believers develop an appetite for spiritual meat (2:6-13).

Our spiritual *actions* reveal our spiritual maturity. Among the believers in the family of God at Corinth were jealousy and quarreling. The jealousy consisted of envy and rivalry, which were destructive of personal relations and individual happiness. The quarreling was a contentious temper of dissension and disputing. Paul called this the mark of the pagan world (Rom. 1:29). Paul considered such an attitude the outward evidence of spiritual immaturity.

Spiritual Maturity Reveals Itself in Our Evaluations

Spiritual immaturity reveals itself in factionalism over leadership. When God's people become partisans, some following one servant and others following another, they reveal a level of immaturity. At Corinth there were four parties in the church, each claiming a leader—Paul, Apollos, Peter, and Christ (1:12). Paul considers such reactions as evidence of life on the merely human level, not the spiritual.

Spiritual maturity reveals itself in a proper evaluation of leaders in their person and their performance. Spiritual maturity evaluates leaders as to their *person*.

The *identity* of a Christian leader is that of a servant: "only servants." The word refers to a humble household servant marked by activity in service. Paul and Apollos are not the heads of rival factions, but only servants.

The *instrumentality* of a leader is that of a channel of God's work: "Through whom you came to believe." Leaders are instruments or channels. To exalt one leader over another is simply to mistake the channel for the Source, God.

The *individuality* of a leader is given by God Himself: "As the Lord has assigned to each his task" (v. 5). The success, visibility, notoriety, and position of any leader belong only to the mercy of God. Everything we have is a gift.

Spiritual maturity not only evaluates leaders as to their person, but also as to their *performance*. Some leaders have a work of *inauguration*. They begin the work of God in a place. Other leaders have the work of *continuation*. They take what has been started and nurture it. But throughout the process it is God who gives to all the work its *energization*: "God made it grow" (v. 6). The work of those who inaugurate and those who continue is nothing without the continuous blessing of God over it all. A farmer may plant and cultivate, but he has to look to heaven for the blessings of rain and growth. Even so, all Christian leaders are desperately dependent on God for the increase.

Spiritual Maturity Reveals Itself in Our Own Confessions

Spiritual maturity reveals itself in what we confess about *ourselves:* "So neither he who plants nor he who waters is anything." Paul had a proper evaluation of himself minus the blessings of God. Minus God we are nothing.

Spiritual maturity reveals itself in what we confess about *God:* "Only God, who makes things grow" (v. 7). While we are relatively nothing, God and God alone is everything. Paul readily confessed the uniqueness and centrality of God, not himself.

Spiritual maturity reveals itself in what we confess about our *coworkers:* "The man who plants and the man who waters have one purpose" (v. 8). Christian workers are not rival leaders of competitive organizations. Paul readily confessed that he and the eloquent young Alexandrian, Apollos, were members of the same team. At the end, God will make an individual assessment of the "labor" of each of His servants. Only God is capable of doing that. In this present age, we are all coworkers.

Spiritual maturity reveals itself in what we confess about the work. Three times in verse 9 Paul underscores that the work itself is "God's . . . God's . . . God's." The church itself is God's act of cultivating and God's act of building. All nurture, building, and growth come from God, or not at all.

We can evaluate our level of spiritual maturity on the basis of these indications. May God grant that we grow up in Christ.

Freed to Be a Slave
(1 Corinthians 9:19-23)

The gospel is filled with paradoxes. To live you must die. To be filled you must be empty. To be exalted you must be humble. To be the chief one must be a servant. Paul touched on one such apparent contradiction in 1 Corinthians 9:19. The Christian is free from all people but a voluntary slave to all people. The motive for this voluntary servitude is to win more for Christ. The Christian willingly surrenders personal freedom to attract non-Christians to Christ and the gospel. The Christian accommodates himself/herself to the race, customs, and peculiarities of other people to advance the gospel. The Christian chooses to be enslaved to the needs of others to bring them to Christ.

The Authentic Christian Experiences Liberation

You can know the *reality* of freedom. Paul asked, "Am I not free?" (v. 1). It is an axiom of Christianity that Jesus Christ emancipates, frees. The scope of that freedom is, "all things," "all persons." The Christian is extricated from all entangling ties. The believer is free from all ultimate dependence on other people. The Christian is free from guilt of the past, the tyranny of sin's power in the present, and fear of judgment in the future. The Christian is free from the written law code of God (Eph. 2:15). The Christian is free from every human being in a direct relationship with God. Paul experienced and you should experience the gospel as an exhilarating freedom.

You should know the *reversal* of that freedom. "I make myself a slave to everyone" (v. 19). You cannot surrender what you never really had. The Christian is actually free but deliberately becomes a slave to others. The Christian, while free, nevertheless serves others in love (Gal. 5:13), bears with the failings of the weak (Rom. 15:1), and even washes the feet of the disciples (John 13:12). While free from all things and all people, the Christian submits himself to others.

You should know the *reason* for this reversal. The Christian does not serve others out of a weak self-image or a guilt trip. The believer serves others with a very precise goal— to win more people to Christ than otherwise would be possible. We do not practice service for service's sake. We submit in order to win people to Christ.

The Liberated Christian Practices Accommodation

In order to win many to Christ, you may accommodate yourself to the tradition, religion, and even the superstition of others. Paul gives tangible evidence of his willingness to surrender rights, to adjust behavior, and to bend his life-style to reach others with the gospel.

You may accommodate yourself to tradition. "To the Jews became like a Jew" (v. 20). Paul had been freed from the narrow, cramping, confining trivia of Jewish religious tradition. He was so free he felt as if he had lost a dead body tied to his very back (Rom. 7). Judaism was no longer real to him, but he would have dumped certain Jewish traditions to win a Jew to Christ. Thus, Paul was willing to circumcise Timothy (Acts 13:3), shave his head as a Jewish vow (18:18), or join four Jews in a temple ceremony by paying for their sacrifice (Acts 21:17-26). Although he was free, Paul subjected himself to personally repugnant religious customs to reach others for Christ.

You may accommodate yourself to *religion*. When Paul desired to win those who kept the strict code of Moses, he observed the details of the law. He did this even though he was dead to the law (Rom. 7:4), knew the law was abolished (Eph. 2:15), and cancelled by being nailed to the cross (Col. 2:14). On the other hand, when Paul was with pagans who had no written law from God, he lived as if there were no written law. He quoted pagan poets, took as his text a pagan inscription, and appealed to nature and common sense. He even changed his own name from the Hebrew Saul to the Greek Paul in order to connect with the pagan world (Acts 13).

You may accommodate yourself to *superstition*. "To the weak I became weak" (1 Cor. 9:22). To those who abstain from certain foods, beverages, and days out of superstitious scruples, Paul adapted his personal behavior. Even though he was free to eat, drink, or do anything moral on any day he bent to the needs of the timid and half-enlightened. He had the right to give up his rights.

The Genuine Believer Shapes Life
for the Gospel's Sake

Paul enlarges his frame of reference. He not only does some things but all things for the sake of the gospel. He decided where he goes, with whom he spends his time, when he does things, and how he does them—only as this is measured by impact on the gospel.

This willingness is not unrelated to personal salvation. Paul spends everything on the gospel in order that he "share in its blessings" (v. 23). It is necessary to live for the gospel in order to be a partaker of the gospel. If you refuse to accommodate yourself to anything or anyone for the gospel, you give evidence that you have no share in the gospel. Where does your life bend for the sake of the gospel? It must bend indeed if you partake of the personal blessings of the gospel.

Temptation: A Way Out
(1 Corinthians 10:11-13)

Do warnings about temptation really matter? Do you give heed to warnings? Do you listen to multiple, cumulative warnings? Paul gives some warnings and encouragements in the matter of temptation. Many people give no attention at all to warnings about temptation. If it feels good, they do it. They also suffer the consequences of such choices. On the other hand, you can choose to listen to the warnings about temptation and encouragements to find a way out. Our faithful God provides a suitable way out in every temptation.

Remember the Results of Failure to Resist Temptation

Divine biblical revelation as well as mere human history leave no doubt about the results of failure in temptation. You pay a price when you fail to resist. There are *real results* when you fail to resist temptation: "these things happened to them as examples" (v. 11). We are not without exemplary evidence that failure in the face of temptation can be fatal. Verses 6-10 list four temptations failed by Israel: idolatry, sexual immorality, testing God, and grumbling (which God takes more seriously than Baptists). These Old Testament accounts show how God will act in similar cases.

This evidence is *repeated*. If what happened were a mere fluke, we could ignore the consequences. Yet multiple, successive examples make it too clear to avoid. Failure in temptation costs. A whole train of events in Israel's history and world history demonstrate the cost of yielding.

This evidence is *recorded*. "These things . . . were written down as warnings for us" (v. 11). The record of Israel's failure was of little help to Israel; they had already failed. The biblical stories are intended for us as warnings. They are admonitions that we change our behavior before facing the same end. Indeed, we are those upon whom "the fulfillment of the ages are come." You have more examples, warnings, and clarity in the matter of temptation than any generation before you. The whole of secular and sacred history stands as a warning. Listen to it!

Understand the Results of Overconfidence

For those who are arrogant and presumptuous, there is the *possibility of overconfidence*. "That's the last thing I would ever do. I've done that before but I'll never do it again." Such statements predict a fall: "Pride goes before destruction, a haughty spirit before a fall" (Prov. 16:18). You may think that you stand fast or have security in the face of one or all temptations. You may think that this is the case because of earlier spiritual privilege or progress. Yet Israel had incredible spiritual experiences before yielding (1 Cor. 10:1-5). No kind of earlier spiritual experience exempts you from temptation.

There is the *peril of overconfidence:* "Be careful that you don't fall!" (v. 12). You may stumble so as to fall beyond recovery of testimony. You may have a moral fall that can involve personal ruin. This does not mean to "fall out of salvation." It does mean to fall in the face of temptation in such a way that you lose influence, integrity, peace of mind, and sometimes much more.

Recall the Remedy in the Time of Temptation

Such warnings could lead us to despair. If so many have fallen, how can we stand? These are words of encouragement. *Remember the limitation* on temptation: "no temptation has seized you except what is common to man" (v. 13). No temptation has come that is above human strength to withstand. There are no "superhuman" temptations. If you sin, you choose to do so. Every temptation you face has come to other humans and been resisted by other humans. No Christian can ever truly say, "It was more than I could handle. The devil made me do it."

Recall the character of God. Our mainstay in the face of temptation is the character of God. "God is faithful." God is worthy of all our reliance in times of temptation. Such times are inevitable, but God does not allow us to face temptations beyond His provision to deliver us. God always intervenes so that tempting power does not exceed our ability to resist.

Recall the provision of God. "He will provide a way out so that you can stand up under it." Temptation and possibilities of escape go in pairs. When temptation comes there is an exit, a way to get clear from the struggle. For any given temptation there is a given way out. You may or may not use it, but the way out is always present. You will not be cornered or stuck in a cul de sac. At the front end of temptation there is a way out. At the back end of sin there may not be. Find the way out at the beginning. Sometimes the way out is to run out. At other times it is prayer, reliance on Christ, and the presence of others. When temptation comes, find the way out—God always gives it.

His Resurrection and Ours

(1 Corinthians 15:35-44)

Easter has three dimensions in time. In the past Easter demonstrated a risen Lord. In the present Easter makes possible a relationship with the risen Lord. But in the future Easter touches each of us at the point of our ultimate and greatest need—the resurrection of our body at the last day. The resurrection of Christ means that you will be given a resurrected body like His glorious body.

Very early, cynical questions were asked about bodily resurrection. Some asked, "How are the dead raised? With what kind of body will they come?" (v. 35). Paul answers both of those questions. The omnipotent power of God is able to give you a body suitable for life in an eternal world.

The Power of God Will Provide a Resurrection Body

To doubt that God can bring life out of death is foolish. The evidence is there to see that life comes out of death. It is part of your own observation of all life.

Look at God's power in plant life (vv. 37-38). Every time you sow a seed you demonstrate that life comes out of decomposition. There is a disorganization of the seed followed by a reorganization of new life. Jesus recognized this principle in both the spiritual and natural worlds: "I tell you the truth, unless a kernel of wheat falls to the ground and dies, it remains only a single seed. But if it dies, it produces many seeds" (John 12:24). You are aware that the bare, naked seed you put into the ground is not the living plant that comes out of the ground (1 Cor. 15:37). The same is true of the lifeless body of a believer. What we deposit into the ground bears no relationship to what God will bring out of the ground. Would God do more for acorns and pansies than He would for His own redeemed children? Resurrection will be a creative gift of God's own power (v. 38).

Look at God's power in animal life (v. 39). The power of God has provided a body suitable to every level of physical life on earth. Paul lists the four great divisions of animal creation. God has demonstrated His power to provide a body for life on the earth, in the water, and in the air. He has given a body appropriate to every level of creation and every environment. The God who has done this in the visible known world also has the power to do so in the invisible unknown world of eternal life. There may be more difference between our present body and our resurrection body than between a man and a fish.

Look at God's power on the astronomical level (vv. 40-41). Paul turns from the inanimate body of a seed and the animate body of living things to the "heavenly bodies." Out of the same basic materials of creation God has crafted the infinite variety of stars, galaxies, and planets. The same hydrogen and carbon in your body is part of the enormous energy and size of the astronomical universe. Whereas earthly bodies have color and shape, heavenly bodies radiate light and heat. The same God who can organize the same atoms into either living people or a burning star has the power to provide a body suitable for resurrected life.

The Resurrection Body Will Be Appropriate for Eternal Life

It will be an *incorruptible* body (v. 42). The resurrection body will not be capable of decay. The most obvious truth about our present body is its subjection to deterioration, decomposition, and dissolution. The resurrection body not only will not decay, there will be nothing in it capable of decay. It will be beyond the power of deterioration. Most of our time and energy on earth relates to the decay of the body. We feed, house, clothe, medicate, and exercise our bodies to keep them from decay. That will not be necessary in the life to come.

It will be a *sinless* body (v. 43). Our present bodies are dishonored because of sin. Sin is an intruder that invades, occupies, and uses our physical bodies. All of life is a battle with indwelling sin. The resurrection body will not be capable of sin in any form. Never again by word, deed, act, or attitude will the risen Christian sin against God. The eternal heavenly day will not end with a night that calls for sad confession of failure. There will be endless celebration of endless obedience.

It will be an *unlimited* body (v. 43). The body will soar as high as the spirit can lead. On earth we are thwarted by our bodies. The thinker's mind tires with thought, the runner's legs ache with the race, the musician can imagine music that no one can play and the artist can conceive paintings that no one can paint. Our creative spirits are bounded and circumscribed by our physical weakness. This will not be so in the resurrection body. The engineer will never conceive a project, the architect will never dream of a building, the manager will never imagine an organization, and the preacher will never aspire to a sermon that is beyond realization. Every talent and ability of your life will find full and unhindered expression.

It will be a body for the eternal world: "it is sown a natural body, it is raised *a spiritual body*" (v. 44). What is placed in the grave was adequate for life in this kind of world. What comes out of the grave will be more than adequate for life in an eternal order. Our natural body was formed to be the organ of life in the natural world. Our spiritual body will be formed as an organ of life in the higher spiritual world.

Resurrection life begins now as you acknowledge Jesus Christ as Lord of life. He gives you that eternal life now which will inhabit an eternal, spiritual body then. The time to start is now.

Concerning the Collection
(1 Corinthians 16:1-6)

A discussion of the collection is an essential part of the Christian faith. The apostle has just concluded his great affirmation of the resurrection. Alongside with that, he places this discussion of the believer's giving. The historical situation is well documented. The Jewish saints in Jerusalem were enduring a time of deprivation due to persecution or famine. Paul's Gentile converts were to collect a relief offering for them. The Corinthians had asked Paul, "How do we do it?"

Paul does not appeal to the Corinthians on the basis of emotion, or play with their consciences by describing the terrible plight of the starving. The Christian life is not built on impulse, but on disciplined principle. In the area of giving, God brings order, and He removes us from the bondage to mere impulse. How do you give? By impulse or by principle?

The Principle of Planned Regularity

The apostle begins with the emphasis, "On the first day of every week" (v. 2a). That is our Sunday. The Christians celebrated the day after the Jewish sabbath as a commemoration of Jesus' resurrection. Among other things to be consecrated on *that* day are to be our gifts. As a part of the worship of the risen Christ that hallows the first day of the week, we are as a principle to give.

That is, this text calls for the formation of a *holy habit*. Some seem to be afraid of religious habits. We have habits in *every* other area of life. Personal hygiene, work, and the payment of bills are all matters or principle and habit in the life of the normal human being. We live by habit. God wants us to live by some *holy habits*. He desires us to plan, with commitment, purpose, and determination, that we will give to Him regularly. Certainly God deserves the same discipline we reserve for the utility company and the mortgage company. You should not wait for a certain spirit, impulse, or some special need to move you to give. God wishes you to give on a principle of planned regularity.

The Principle of Personal Responsibility

The apostle continues, "let each one of you put aside and save" (v. 2b, NASB). There are to be no exceptions when it is time for the collection. Had we surveyed the Corinthian church, we would have tended to exclude many of its members from the collection. This letter itself implies that the Corinthians were, by no means, people of financial ability: "not many wise according to the flesh, not many mighty, not many noble" (1 Cor. 1:26, NASB). Yet, Paul appealed to each member of this depressed community, without exception, to give to the collection. Indeed, it would have been a real disservice to the Corinthians not to have been so encouraged. God has gone on record that if the windows of heaven are to open on our lives, we must so give (Mal. 3:10ff.).

It is interesting to review the personal responsibility of the members of Travis Avenue Baptist Church. In 1985, 8.1 percent of our members (family units), gave 49.7 percent of our budget receipts. From another perspective, 21.5 percent of our members gave 75.6 percent of our budget receipts. 69.5 percent of our members gave 5.4 percent of our budget receipts. This would indicate that there are many among us who need to discover the principle of personal responsibility. Among the households in our resident membership, 37.9 percent of our members gave nothing to the cause of Christ through our church in 1985. Obviously, there needs to be a total reassessment on the part of some, with reference to giving. We are to give on the principle of personal responsibility. It is easy to hand responsibility for many things in the church to others. But, Scripture is emphatic that the collection is the responsibility of every member.

The Principle of Proportionate Return

Each member is to give "as God hath prospered him" (v. 2c, KJV). That means that every believer is to give proportionately. This bases what you give on God's activity toward you in your life. Throughout Scripture, men are called to give, never less, but sometimes more than, the tithe. Proportionate giving shows God's wisdom and fairness. All cannot give the same amount. But, all may give the same proportion. This also demonstrates God's flexibility. It lets God determine how much we will give. When you follow God's principles in giving, there is always sufficiency for what you need and for what God needs to do, and He can and will bless His giving people to do it. Why not give by principle this year?

Strong Treasures — Weak Containers

(2 Corinthians 4:7)

Have you ever said, "I am simply too weak for God to use me"? Actually, the problem may be that you are not weak enough. God does not triumph in lives conscious of their strength. God conquers in lives that are all too conscious of their weaknesses. Our weakness is the only stage on which God can display His strength.

The Weakness of Humanity Contains
the Strength of the Gospel

In the biblical world, there was a custom of burying expensive treasures in fragile, inexpensive, earthen vessels (Matt. 13:44). The weakness of the container stood in contradiction to the value of the contents.

There is the great reality of the Christian life. Every believer has a treasure. That treasure is "the light of the knowledge of the glory of God in the face of Christ" (2 Cor. 4:6). But that treasure is contained in the weakest of vessels, our frail humanity. By "clay jar," Paul refers not only to our perishing bodies, but also to our entire personalities. The Old Testament often compares powerlessness and littleness in God's eyes to a clay jar (Job 10:9; Isa. 30:14). The word points to our emotional distress and even our moral weaknesses. We are, at best, like clay jars. The message of Christianity is magnificent, but the messengers are not.

There is a reason for putting this great treasure in a fragile container: "to show that this all-surpassing power is from God and not from us" (2 Cor. 4:7b). When God prevails in us despite our weakness, it magnifies His power alone to us and to those who watch us. His power is more than sufficient to triumph over opposition. Those who watch us actually perceive that the power and ability do not belong to us, but to God. That is why we must never present ourselves as more than earthen vessels: weak, fragile people who need the treasure we carry to save us.

The Power of God Prevails
in the Midst of Difficulties

It is our very difficulties that cause God's power to shine greatly. Paul makes four statements characterizing his own difficulties that revealed God's power (vv. 8-9). In each of these, the first part of the statement reveals a human weakness, and the last part reveals the more than compensating divine strength. The thoughts come from soldiers in combat or from gladiators in a life-or-death struggle in the arena.

We can prevail in outward pressures: "We are hard-pressed on every side, but not crushed. . . . persecuted, yet not abandoned." Life put the squeeze on Paul in all things. Enemies hounded him constantly. Yet he was never hopelessly cornered or abandoned by God. The power of God shines forth even to unbelievers when we constantly overcome seemingly impossible pressures.

We can prevail against inward pressures: "perplexed, but not in despair." We may be at our wit's end, but not out of our wits! Just like you, Paul could not understand all that God permitted in his life. Yet even in his mental agitation and confusion, God's power wrought a great victory. This distracted man was able to write Romans and Ephesians! The person who is always naturally calm, cool, and collected may show great humanistic strength, but does not reveal the power of God. God's power reveals itself when our minds are about to snap, but His presence sustains us.

These pressures reach a climax: "struck down, but not destroyed." Like a warrior thrown to the ground by his enemy, we sometimes feel it is all over. Yet in the strength of God, we rise again to face the fight. This enduring grace comes only from God.

The Death to Self Releases the Life of Christ

Behind the Christian's conquest, in spite of weakness, rests a great principle. The conquering Christian reproduces the death of Christ: "We always carry around in our body the death of Jesus. . . . we who are alive are always being given over to death for Jesus' sake" (4:10a-11a). Like a Daniel, always being thrown into the lions' den, Paul was constantly on the edge of death for the sake of Christ. The daily danger and distress were sapping his very life. We may not face physical death daily for Christ, but we must face ego death daily. We must reproduce in ourselves His death to self.

When this happens, the conquering Christian experiences the resurrection life of Christ: "so that the life of Jesus may be revealed in our body." In Paul's frail, weary, battered person, he bears the dying of Jesus that the life of Jesus may be exhibited to the outside world. This is the secret source for successful Christian living. It is the life energy that comes from the living and reigning Jesus.

This is the universal principle. If you seek to save your life, you will lose it. If you lose it for His sake, you will know His life in you (Mark 10:39).

Trouble and Glory: Seen and Unseen
(2 Corinthians 4:16-18)

People of faith live by seeing invisible things. You can measure the authenticity and depth of your spiritual life by this statement: do visible or invisible things dominate your life? Faith, love, prayer, and fellowship with the risen Christ are all invisible things. Yet these invisible resources presently give you inward renewal, and ultimately will give you future glory.

Invisible Resources Give Us Inward Renewal

Two undeniable facts mark every life. Something is happening to us outwardly and something inwardly. "Outwardly we are wasting away." Not only our physical bodies but our emotions, minds, and appetites decay. This process is ceaseless and inevitable. To deny it does not change it. This decay is not only because of sin, but also because of pressure, hard work, anxiety, and a thousand other things. Paul saw it in himself; you should see it in yourself.

Something also happens to us inwardly. Outside of Christ an inward decay reflects the outward decay. But in Christ "inwardly we are being renewed day by day" (v. 16). For the Christian the true self, the inward self, is being made as good as new. "Those who hope in the Lord will renew their strength. They will soar on wings like eagles; they will run and not grow weary, they will walk and not be faint" (Isa. 40:31). This renewal is ceaseless and progressive for the growing believer. What a strange contrast: ceaseless decay of the outward life but ceaseless renewal of the inner life.

Our generation has reversed this completely. We are obsessed with the appearance, health, and grooming of the outward person while ignoring the health of the inner. For that reason there are remarkably fit people who are inwardly empty. We spend time on that which cannot last, while ignoring that which only can last.

Inward Resources Transform Present Troubles

This ceaseless, progressive, inward renewal gives us a different perspective on life's pressures and troubles. Trouble and pressure are just as real for the Christian as anyone. Paul experienced a catalogue of troubles that would demolish most of us (2 Cor. 11:23-29). His troubles, in and of themselves, were staggeringly heavy and continuous.

Yet invisible inward resources give us a different perspective on trouble and pressure. They are "light and momentary" (2 Cor. 4:17a). Our present troubles are but brief in contrast to eternity to come. Our present pressures are light compared to the "weight of glory" (v. 17b, KJV) about to come. "I consider that our present sufferings are not worth comparing with the glory that will be revealed in us" (Rom. 8:18). We think of troubles as heavy and lasting. We think of "glory" as something light and fleeting. No! For the believer, trouble is for a moment and light; splendor is forever and heavy!

Present pressure is working out future glory. Like the weightlifter, experiencing present pain for future gain, the present pressure is building spiritual muscle. Intense heat and incredible pressure produce a diamond cut of worthless carbon.

Inward Resources Demand Our Primary Attention

Inward resources dominate the attention of believers. Faith is being certain of what we do not see (Heb. 11:1). To live by faith is to live out of the unseen. Negatively "we fix our eyes *not* on what is seen" (2 Cor. 4:18). Our primary attention is not fixed on the visible world. Our gaze is not riveted on things that are seen. Everything that is seen is temporary. All of it belongs to a world that is already disappearing.

Positively, "we fix our eyes . . . on what is unseen." The Christian intensely focuses on what he cannot see *now*. That does not mean he will not see it later. "No eye has seen, no ear has heard, no mind has conceived what God has prepared for those who love him—but God has revealed it to us by his Spirit" (1 Cor. 2:9-10). What is seen now will disappear later. What is unseen now will appear later. Presently, eternal things are unseen. In the future, they will be the only things to be seen. The believer focuses primary attention on the unseen because only that lasts. Faith, love, prayer, and fellowship with Christ at the right hand of God are presently invisible. They are ultimately things that will be visible.

What dominates your life, time, resources, and attention? You can answer that question. The Christian increasingly lives for the unseen.

How God Expects Us to Give
(2 Corinthians 8:1-9,12-14)

Paul's conception of giving is a lofty one. To Him, *giving is grace*. Giving is a ministry of the Holy Spirit inwrought in personal experience and outworked in practical expression. Wherever he planted churches, the apostle made it his business to instruct the people of God in the doctrines of Christian stewardship. Particularly the churches in Macedonia—Thessalonica, Berea, and Philippi—were renowned for their charity and liberality.

In the passage before us, the apostle used the Macedonian example of generosity to challenge the Corinthian church—and us. Apparently, the Corinthian assembly abounded in the gifts of "Faith, and utterance, and knowledge, and in all diligence," (v. 7) but it lacked in the grace of giving. So, Paul confronts them with an example of giving to beget in them a sense of responsibility in Christian stewardship.

God Expects Us to Give Sacrificially

"Moreover, brethren, we make known to you the grace of God bestowed on the churches of Macedonia: that in a great trial of affliction the abundance of their joy and their deep poverty abounded in the riches of their liberality" (vv. 1-2, NKJV). Paul takes great care to show that it was not in the circumstances of prosperity that the saints in Macedonia gave their liberal offering. Some severe tests of affliction had come upon these local churches, and they had been reduced to what is described as "deep poverty" or, more literally, "down to the bottom poverty." But in all their affliction and poverty, there was joy and liberality. This is true sacrifice, and they had learned it from their matchless Savior, "who for the joy that was set before him endured the cross, despising the shame" (Heb. 12:2, KJV).

Paul makes it explicitly clear that he did not expect equal gifts, but he did expect equal sacrifice: "[It] is acceptable according to what a man has, not according to what he does not have. . . . that there may be equality" (2 Cor. 8:12-13). The genius of God's plan for giving is its fairness. Men who give radically different amounts may be totally equal in sacrifice.

God Expects Us to Give Spontaneously

"For to their power I bear record, yea, and beyond their power they were willing of themselves; Praying us with much entreaty that we would receive the gift, and take upon us the fellowship of the ministering to the saints" (vv. 3-4, KJV). The Scriptures make it plain that the grace of giving is not so much the result of *outward compulsion* as the consequence of *inward expulsion!* In a very real sense, it is "the expulsive power of a new affection." Thus, Paul admits that he had no authority to demand an offering from the Corinthian saints, but he could certainly afford them the opportunity to "prove the sincerity of [their] love" (v. 8, KJV). The pastor, the staff, and the leadership of this great church have no desire to demand an offering—indeed, we cannot, and would not if we could. We do have the solemn and joyful obligation of extending an *opportunity* for spontaneous expression.

The secret of the Macedonian giving was simply: they "gave of their own free will." This is an accurate rendering of the phrase, "they were willing of themselves." What is more, they took the initiative in beseeching Paul "with much entreaty" that he would receive the gifts. The initiative had belonged to the people, not the pastor.

God Expects Us to Give Spiritually

"And this they did, not as we hoped, but first gave their own selves to the Lord, and unto us by the will of God" (v. 5, KJV). In other words, their giving was the outward expression of their utter dedication to God. There most definitely is a kind of giving that is unspiritual, and that has ulterior motives. One form of it is a drawing attention to one's self (Matt. 6:3-4). Another form of wrong giving is with a spirit of ill will and reluctance. This runs contrary to the apostolic injunction that "God loveth a cheerful giver" (2 Cor. 9:7, KJV). The worst form of giving is that of attempting to buy off one's indebtedness to God. How different was the spirit of these. Their giving was accompanied by an act of complete self-surrender. Their giving was the measure of their love for Christ, Savior and Lord. Giving is not the only indicator of your love for God, but it will *always be one* of the indicators. These days afford us the opportunity so to demonstrate our love for Him.

The Battle We Fight
(2 Corinthians 10:3-5)

The believer battles. The Christian lives in confrontation. The faithful fight. No one could miss this in even a superficial reading of God's Word. We are to fight externally that outside us opposed to the gospel and to fight internally that within us opposed to the lordship of Christ. We are energetically reminded to "put on the armor of light" (Rom. 13:12) and "to put on the full armor of God" (Eph. 6:11). Paul commands us to "fight the good fight" (1 Tim. 1:18; 6:12). It requires endurance: "Endure hardship . . . like a good soldier of Jesus Christ" (2 Tim. 2:3). Paul heartily addresses other Christians as "fellow soldiers" (Phil. 2:25; Philem. 2).

In the Christian life as warfare we need to understand where we fight, how we fight, and the enormous potential for victory.

Christians Battle in a Real Campaign

Christians battle in the world: "We live in the world" (v. 3). We must never forget the arena in which we battle. We still live in the flesh. We have all of the infirmities, weaknesses, exposures to temptation, and limitations that go with being a human among humans. The gospel itself is a treasure, but we carry that around in fragile clay pots of humanity (2 Cor. 4:7). Jesus prayed, "My prayer is not that you take them out of the world, but that you protect them from the evil one" (John 17:15). Jesus left us in the world. We must live the Christian life in an environment that is ceaselessly hostile toward it.

Christians do not battle like the world: "We do not wage war as the world does." It is in no mere human strength that we battle the Christian war. For the conflict to tame ourselves within and to take the world without we are not dependent on anything that human nature can afford us. The church does not conquer on the basis of any kind of human strength—intellectual, physical, economic, institutional, or cultural. We do not win because we are sharper thinkers, strong fighters, richer spenders, or greater builders. We will not even make a dent in the world unless our weapons come from a supernatural source.

Christians Fight with Different Weapons

This calls for *a definite refusal:* "The weapons we fight with are not the weapons of the world." This would pit us in a battle where mere human strength encountered other human strength. God intends us to battle in a campaign where divine power confronts human strength.

This makes *an affirmation.* Our weapons have "divine power." They are powerful in God's eyes, whatever the world thinks. They are powerful through God's enablement. They are powerful for God's cause. When we fight with God's weapons we find it self-evident that there is far more than human strength behind such weapons.

What are these weapons? The unbelieving world does not consider them to be weapons at all. They are *comprehensive* weapons, both offensive and defensive "in the right hand and the left hand." They include purity, understanding, patience, kindness, sincere love, truthful speech (2 Cor. 6:6-7). The weapons include truth, righteousness, preparation, faith, assurance of salvation, and the possession of the Spirit (Eph. 6:14-17). These are first *inward* weapons, "faith and a good conscience" (1 Tim. 1:19). These are intimately *personal* weapons: "offer the parts of your body as [weapons] of righteousness" (Rom. 6:13). We are to hand over the very limbs and organs of our body to the battle. Sometimes there is more. There may be supernatural manifestations of power such as Paul sometimes used (Acts 13:8-12).

The world does not recognize our weapons as weapons at all. Yet Christ conquered on His cross through these weapons. Only victories won with these weapons are His victories.

Christians Fight with Effective Weapons

God's weapons can *conquer the unconquerable*: "to demolish strongholds." The object of Roman siege warfare was to destroy fortresses that resisted. Christian weapons can tear down every wall. Christians do not avoid strongholds or cover them up—we confront them. These strongholds may be external: enemies of the gospel outside of us. They may be internal: compulsions, obsessions, fixations, involuntary thought processes, lack of self-restraint, etc.

God's weapons can *explain the unexplainable*: "we demolish arguments" (v. 4). With Christian weapons we can demolish theories, bring down deceptive fallacies, and destroy empty speculations. The simple proclamation of the gospel in power (1 Cor. 2:4) can overcome every objection to the truth of God.

God's weapons can *assail the unassailable*: "we demolish . . . every pretension that sets itself up against the knowledge of God" (vv. 4b-5a). We witness in the face of obstacles, barriers, and walls that can be reared up by human authority against the knowledge of God. With divine weapons we can flatten such opposition.

God's weapons can *capture the untakable*: "we take captive every thought to make it obedient to Christ" (v. 5b). The believer can fight within himself and within our culture to take captive all thought for Christ. Every scheme, design, and purpose can be brought to Christ and surrendered to Him.

The intent of God is total victory for Christ. One day everything that resists and opposes will fall before Him. He will be Christ the Victor!

Strength in Weakness
(2 Corinthians 12:7-10)

Many of us spend much of the time denying what most of us know about all of us— we are people with weaknesses. Yet our point of weakness can become God's vantage ground for our greatest strength. Sometimes we wish that we were strong enough for God to use us. Actually, God's strength is most evident in the midst of our weakness.

We Should Accept the Reality of Our Weaknesses

Most Christians carry with them some definite weaknesses. They are in good company for Paul certainly did. He called his weakness a "thorn in the flesh." The word may refer to a large instrument like a stake or a narrow sharply pointed sliver like a thorn. Paul carried with him something that hurt. Some understand the thorn to be something outside Paul such as opposition or persecution. Most understand the thorn to be something inside Paul. The thorn may have been physical, emotional, or spiritual. The thorn is deliberately not named so we can relate it to our own experience.

The source of the thorn was God Himself. The passive expression "there was given me" actually refers to God's permissive will. But the thorn itself was "a messenger of Satan." Job 2 reveals that God and Satan may relate to the same human pain with different motives. Satan intended the thorn to hurt Paul. God intended the thorn to bless Paul.

The purpose of the thorn is twice repeated: "To keep me from becoming conceited because of the surpassingly great revelations" (v. 7). Paul had enjoyed an incredible vision of Paradise. Because of the extraordinary number of kinds of revelations he was in danger of spiritual conceit. There are three basic kinds of pride: pride of face, race, and grace. The ugliest pride is spiritual pride. God saved Paul from spiritual pride by giving him a thorn.

What is your weakness? Whatever it is, God intends to keep you humbly dependent on Him through it. Our thorns temper our pride.

We Should Understand the Necessity of Our Weaknesses

Our attitude toward weakness is not God's attitude. We ask God to remove our weakness. Paul persistently asked God to remove this thorn. Just as Jesus prayed three times in the garden, Paul prayed on three occasions that Jesus would remove his thorn. Paul personally requested this of the Lord Jesus. In every other instance Paul prayed to God the Father. In this instance he requested the Lord Jesus to deal with the weakness. The words suggest that he wanted the weakness removed permanently.

God's attitude toward our weakness is different from our attitude. God may inform us of the permanency of our weakness. "He said to me" (v. 9) suggests a permanent and final word from God that kept resounding in Paul's ears for years. God told Paul that he would have to live with his thorn. But God at the same time may tell us of His sufficiency in weakness. Paul was given something better than he asked for. He asked for relief. God gave Paul more grace.

The dynamic efficiency of God's power is best seen in weakness: "my power is made perfect in weakness" (v. 9). God's strength reaches completeness in our weakness. Where human strength abounds God's strength is not evidently seen. Where human strength disappears God's strength shines more brightly. From Abraham through the disciples the Bible abounds with evidence that God uses weakness rather than strength.

We Should Boast in the Sublimity of Our Weaknesses

At the mature level of Christian living we do not boast about our achievements but about our weaknesses. Paul did not present as his credentials of Christian leadership how many churches he started or converts he baptized. He never built a building or led a financial campaign. He boasted about his own disabilities.

Why? A sublime thing happened to Paul in the midst of weakness. The power of God "spread its tent" over him. The weaknesses of Paul were covered and hidden under that power of God. God's power cannot cover one who boasts of his own strength. But a sublime thing happens when we boast of our weakness and His grace. The power of God builds a tabernacle over us and around us. We can live within the walls of that tabernacle. Our life can reflect the very brightness of God's glory.

If anyone doubts this, let that person look at the Lord Jesus. When He was at His weakest on the cross He was at His strongest in redemption. So also with us.

Absolutely Free!
(Galatians 5:13-18)

The worldwide cry of this year is "Freedom!" Walls have fallen, structures of political slavery are crumbling, and instead of tyranny, liberty triumphs. No subject today compels more interest than political and economic revolution. Individual freedom calls for spiritual revolution.

Individuals can never be free under constraint of ceremonies, rites, and rituals required to please God. Individuals can be free when by faith they trust Jesus Christ alone for salvation. The Galatian Christians began with trust in Christ alone, but they were being seduced back into spiritual slavery of ritual and ceremony to please God.

You can be absolutely free by faith in Christ alone when you walk by the Spirit.

Christ Calls Us to Freedom

The *call* of the Christ is to spiritual liberty, not bondage. Every single believer without exception has the inalienable right of spiritual freedom in Christ. Regardless of what others impose by way of ceremony or ritual, you are absolutely free in Christ. God's "call" to salvation is a call to personal freedom.

The "Jew-makers" were a group of first-century Christians who hounded Paul's steps. They insisted that new Gentile Christians submit themselves to ritual circumcision. Unless a man were willing to undergo such painful surgery as a ritual, the "Jew-makers" refused him the grace of God. In the face of this, Paul cried "Free by faith in Christ alone."

The *content* of Christian freedom is both a deliverance and positive gift. What is Christian freedom? The Christian is free from the tyranny within—the guilt and power of sin (Rom. 6:18) and an accusing conscience (Heb. 10:22). The Christian is free from the wrath of God above him (Rom. 5:1) and the tyranny of Satan (2 Tim. 2:26). The Christian is also free from the curse of striving to achieve his own righteousness (Gal. 5:16).

Freedom raises a *concern*. Freedom always produces a crisis. Freedom affords both danger and opportunity. The danger: "Do not use your freedom to indulge in the sinful nature" (v. 13a). A prisoner set free may live productively or return to crime. Even so, the Christian's freedom must not become a springboard or pretext to indulge the flesh. The removal of wrath and law must not lead us to irresponsibility. The end of legalism must not be the beginning of license.

The *cure* for this concern is a life of mutual, reciprocal servanthood in love: "rather, serve one another in love" (v. 13b). The danger of our new freedom in Christ evaporates under the sunlight of mutual affection, tenderness, and genuine sympathy. In fact, the entire law of God can be condensed and fulfilled in one short sentence: "Love your neighbor as yourself" (v. 14). When this principle dominates life, Christian liberty does not become license and libertinism.

Christ Calls Us to Freedom Within Conflict

Christian freedom does not mean the absence of conflict. We are in a lifelong, close-ordered conflict with the appetites that reside in our flesh. Christian freedom does give us a way to win most of the time.

The *method* of Christian victory is positive: "Live by the Spirit" (v. 16). The legalistic method screams a negative "Thou shalt not" and is then powerless to help us. The law lames us and then damns us for limping! Christ says, "Thou shalt" and gives us His

Spirit to enable us. The Spirit is ours. We are to walk habitually in the Spirit. "Walk" (KJV) implies continuation, action, and progress in yielding to the Spirit.

Only the living can expel the dead. When we walk by the Spirit, we will not fulfill the strong desires in our flesh. It takes the tender leaves of the springtime to rid the oak tree of last autumn's withered foliage. When we walk by the Spirit we can utterly crush the flesh every time it raises its head.

The *manner* of Christian victory is a lifelong battle. If there is no battle, there is no life. The Christian's life is a constant conflict between two natures within. Flesh and Spirit are not distant enemies but in face-to-face conflict in every believer's life.

The good news is this: the Christian wins most of the time: "You do not do what you want" (v. 17). This is not a word of despair but of hope. Self and its desires can be conquered when you live by the Spirit. The winners in the Christian conflict are those who yield consciously to the Spirit, subjecting every impulse to the Spirit's mastery. Then it is no longer I that lives but Christ living in me (see Gal. 2:20). This does not eradicate your identity. You are never more you than when you are His.

The Eyes of the Heart
(Ephesians 1:15-19)

How do we know what we know? Some things we know by the perception and observation of our five senses. Other things we know by our rational, mental capacity without any observation. Still other things we know only by experiencing them. Philosophers call these three ways of knowing empiricism, rationalism, and existentialism. In today's text, Paul introduces us to a different way of knowing—seeing with *the eyes of the heart*. This is a way of knowing accessible only to the Spirit-indwelt and the Spirit-filled believer. The illumined "eyes of the heart" see things the world outside cannot even imagine, much less know. What are these things?

Only the Eyes of the Heart Perceive Christian Knowledge

Paul prays that the Father of glory will give the Christian three distinctive elements of Christian knowledge. The source of this knowledge is none other than the all-glorious Father. The glory of God in the Old Testament corresponds to the luminous splendor of His presence. This light-like presence of God illuminates the heart of men with three gracious gifts of Christian knowledge.

The *spirit of wisdom* results from that operation wherein God's Spirit creates a new human spirit or capacity of perception. Available to the believer is a deep discernment of the basic nature of things as they are. Knowledge without wisdom is a menace. Wisdom coordinates knowledge and sees into the very heart of things. *Revelation* refers to that unexpected unveiling of divine truth that takes place in the gospel. Man would have never dreamed that God was like the Father of Jesus Christ, unless God removed the veil and illumined the heart. *Knowledge* refers to full, deep, and real knowledge as distinguished from awareness or superficial acquaintance. It is the knowledge of participation and experience rather than mere observation. These gifts of wisdom, revelation, and knowledge are perceived only with the eyes of the heart.

Only the Eyes of the Heart Detect Christian Experience

The object of Christian hope is visible only to the eyes of the heart. *Hope*, as it is used here, does not refer to the subjective emotion or feeling of hope. Rather, it refers to the object and goal of Christian living. It is "the hope deposited in heaven" (Col. 1:5). Christian hope is never merely within us; it lies before us. While our inward hope may flag into despair, the great Object of our hope never varies. He is always before us. Only the eyes of the heart can fasten on this hope, like an instrument of navigation fastens to the polar star.

The church, as God's inheritance, is visible only to the eyes of the heart. The unregenerate, lost world sees the church only as another organization, building, an institution. The eyes of the heart see the church as God's inheritance, His estate, His heritage. Only the inward vision of the Christian can perceive what it means. For God to see His plan of the ages worked out in the redemption of sinners who reflect His own glory will be His inheritance. The darkened intellect cannot even imagine that, much less see it.

Only the Eyes of the Heart Comprehend God's Power

Paul exhausts his native Greek tongue to describe the power demonstrated in the gospel. In one verse, he uses virtually every Greek word for power. He successively uses words for inherent power, power expressing itself in overcoming resistance, and the actual demonstration of power. For the Christian, this massive accumulation is available in "exceeding greatness" (v. 19, KJV). But only the eyes of the heart can see this power. To the lost and blinded humanity outside Christ, the Christian life individually, and the church collectively, bespeak only of weakness and ineffectiveness. Only in the experience of the Holy Spirit through which the eyes of the heart are opened does the power of Christ become visible. Can you see it? Open the eyes of your heart! "Except a man be born again he cannot *see* . . ." (John 3:3, KJV).

The Dilemma of Us All
(Ephesians 2:1-6)

The entire gospel rests in these words, "But God. . . ." Those two words are a *continuation* of the lurid history of man in sin. But they are also a *contrast* of shattering, eternal significance. Against the background of man's cadaverous spiritual state and moribund moral immobility, there stands the One "rich in mercy, . . . great love" (v. 4, KJV). Mercy is His attitude and love is His motive cause. His mercy is that of "unsearchable riches" (3:8). That is, the mercy of God rests beyond all human comparison. What moment of your life did you receive the greatest gift of human mercy? The mercy of God extends so far beyond that as to be absolutely imcomparable, yea, to make the greatest human mercy unmerciful by comparison. How can these things be?

The Reality of the Dilemma

The revealed word of God about the human condition is *death*. That is the word because there can be no stronger term. It is categorical, final, the last word, and admits no negotiation. Man is not dying, mortal, almost dead, or desperately ill. Man is dead to God and to things spiritual by nature. Such death is no less real, concrete, or actual than physical death. In fact, the presence of physical death is only symptomatic of the reality of a far greater death at the very center of being. The tragic irony is that we only recognize we were spiritually dead once we have been made spiritually alive in Christ. The dilemma of lost man is to be dead and to think himself alive—the ultimate contradiction.

The instruments that take spiritual life are "trespasses and sins" (v. 1, KJV). Sin is the instrument that affects, the manifestation that reveals, and the consequence that remains of spiritual death. Sin is the weapon that murders, the clue that reveals, and the plot that unwinds in the saga of spiritual death.

The Reason for the Dilemma

We are not coerced to accept the biblical definition of man's dilemma. The fact of spiritual death is everywhere available for observation. Exhibit "A" for spiritual death is *conformity to the spirit of the age*. Every epoch and era of human life is characterized by certain transitory trifles. They form the mentality, the viewpoint, and the outlook of the world without God. This spirit of the age is revealed in most contemporary literature, art, and popular culture, not even to mention degenerate television and movies. The back side of this mentality is to be bored with the things of God, especially with the exposition of His Word.

Unfortunately, we are not left alone to make our choices about such conformity. There is yet darker color. Behind conformity to this age, there is a personal tyrannical and malignant power. Men have not stumbled inadvertently into spiritual death. We have not been wedded to a perishing age by accident. The New Testament faith confesses a lord-paramount of evil with an army of demonic organization. Spiritually dead man finds the very notion of Satan and the demonic hilarious, the vestige of "medieval mentality." The location of satanic influence is as pervasive as the very air. The history of the prince of evil is to be energetically at work. The result of his nefarious tactics is to leave the human race "children of disobedience" (Eph. 5:6, KJV). That is, our innate quality is obstinate opposition to the divine will.

The evidence of the prince of the air is the perpetual craving for what is unlawful, and the poisoning of life at its very wellsprings of mentality.

The Reversal of the Dilemma

Christian knowledge of God is based on verbs, not nouns. We proclaim that God has mightily acted. We do not proclaim an abstract philosophy of a remote detached deity! Paul enumerates the greatest succession of action words in the New Testament: "quickened . . . together, raised . . . together, made us to sit together" (vv. 5-6, KJV). When He first stirred to life the damp darkness of that sepulcher, we actually vivified with Him. When He walked out into the cool scented air of that garden, we walked with Him. When He sat down at the right hand of God, we sat with Him. Actually. Really. Factually. Historically. Paul is by no means speaking poetically. This is not literary overstatement. Nor is he speaking of our future with Christ. These things are done! We have no life except that life quickened, raised, seated with Him.

Do you object that such mystical things belong to the borderlands of the Christian life? Are they the territory of a few supersaints, varsity heroes of the faith? Absolutely not. Paul places them *before* his greatest statement of salvation (vv. 8-9). Union with Christ in His burial, resurrection, and enthronement is the essence of the believer's life. God has already done it, and I am part of it. We must interpret the difficulties of this life from the standpoint of faith, not the reverse. The man who wrote of enthronement with Christ is also the man who wrote of incessant shipwrecks, whippings, and death threats. These are not the words of a privileged recluse.

The great practical significance is that the Christian life begins from a place of rest, sitting together with Him. Christianity is first a great *already done,* and then later it is a great *do.* Our faith speaks of what *is,* and only after that what we *ought* to do.

The Privileges of the Christian
(Ephesians 2:19-22)

This grand chapter of biblical revelation concludes with a summary of the believer's privileges based on the foregoing themes. One saint observed that a realization of the believer's privileges would solve every problem in the Christian life. We all live far beneath our status and dignity. Out of varying degrees of ignorance we behave like hirelings rather than sons. Paul uses three figures of speech to state the believer's prerequisites: the state, the family, and the temple. He must use all three, for no one figure adequately conveys the effect of the grace of God in our lives.

The Believer Has Been Made a Citizen in God's Kingdom

Paul first states this negatively. We are no more strangers and foreigners. Taking the backward glance for another moment, the apostle reminds us of what we used to be. The words include all who by territorial distance or by absence of civic privileges are not citizens. The word "foreigner" refers to that man who dwells in a state but does not have the rights of citizenship. It could refer to those who lived outside the city walls, but not in the city. In the Old Testament it spoke of one like Ruth, halfway between an alien and a native. These words remind us that with reference to God's kingdom *everyone* began as an outsider. To receive a share in the civic privileges of the city of God is a grace gift to everyone. There are, in reality, no pioneers or latecomers in God's kingdom. We are all here by grace, not by tenure or performance.

One may always tell an alien from a citizen by three certainties. An alien will often not conform to the laws of the state. He thus demonstrates his foreign character. Further, an alien must always live on a passport, not on a birth certificate. In times of national crisis, the loyalties of aliens will be to their homeland, not to the nation where they are sojourners. So it is in God's kingdom. True citizens will live by kingdom laws. They can produce a birth certificate. In times of trial, their loyalty is to the church, not its enemies.

The Believer Has Been Born a Member of God's Family

The image of a kingdom will not suffice to explain Christian privilege. The difference between the state and the family is the difference between the general and the particular, the external and the internal, the remote and the intimate, the impersonal and the personal. Our relationship to God demands the metaphor of a family, not just a government. In this family, God is our Father and Christ is our Elder Brother.

How may you know for certain that you are a member of God's household? We are at ease among those of our own household. Do you feel out of your element when you are with God's people? We have a real and living interest in our own families. Do you delight with interest in the church? We know the family secrets of our own family, and we try to hide the bad things and to emphasize the good things. Those who are part of God's family wish it always to be seen in the very finest light. "Blood is thicker than water" is also true in God's family. Those covered by the blood of Christ may disagree, but there is a family loyalty that transcends family differences. In hours of trial, the family will be together.

The Believer Has Become a Stone in God's Living Temple

The apostle must soar still higher to express the truth about the believer's privileges. The believer is a living stone in a growing building. There is first the privilege of the *foundation*. The believer is intimately related to the same foundation laid by the New

Testament apostles and prophets, Jesus Christ. There is the privilege of the *corner-stone*, also Jesus Christ. The cornerstone binds the stones together and becomes a fixed standard for the bearings of the structure throughout. There is the privilege of the *living temple*. The image Paul suggests is that of a number of smaller buildings being joined together to form one entire structure. "Unlike dead matter this monumental structure possesses a capacity for growth and interaction. The station of each individual has been preordained with regard to the contour of the aggregate fabric. Every believer has his own niche to fill."

The Geometry of Love
(Ephesians 3:14-19)

Would you desire the very best prayer to pray for yourself or for our church fellow-ship? Your lips could find no richer words than these. This prayer is perhaps the most fervent, comprehensive, and sublime prayer in the Bible.

God can give you inner strength to comprehend His love and to experience the full-ness of God.

Strength to Love Begins with
New Power in the Inner Person

The *power* necessary to love begins through prayer. More than anything else, we need an infusion of the power, might, strength, and force of God. Paul combines words which emphasize the dynamic energy of God's power along with its inherent strength.

The *place* in which we need that power is the "inner person." This phrase indicates our whole, conscious, personal being—the secret spring of action in every person. We must experience that renewal daily (2 Cor. 4:16), because we are in a war between our inner being and the members of our body (Rom. 7:22).

The *proportion* by which God gives strength is nothing less than His "riches in glory." God does not give in proportion to our capacity or need, but His own perfection. We should not ask timidly as if we would strain the resources of God.

The *person* of Christ is thus truly at home in our heart. Paul does not refer to His initial, converting presence, but His permanent reigning presence, that He might be truly *at home* and not just a guest.

Strength to Love Grows with
a New Comprehension of Christ's Love for Us

There is *a necessary preparation* before we understand Christ's love for us. We must be "rooted and grounded" in our love for Him. We should be rooted like a tree in the soil of Christian love and founded like a building on the firm ground of love. Only love understands love. If you do not love Christ, you cannot understand His love for you.

There is a *joint participation* of all Christians as we understand Christ's love for us "with all the saints." One who fails to fellowship with God's people cannot grasp Christ's love.

There is an *eternal exploration* of Christ's love for us. We will spend forever seeking to know the unknowable and to measure the immeasurable. Paul speaks of the divine geometry of love: the extent of its breadth, the eternal duration of its length, the divinity of its height, and the humanity of its depth.

Strength to Love Finally Fills the Believer
with the Fullness of God

For eternity we are to be "filled to the brim" with the totality of God's riches that can be given to the believer. We are "partakers of the divine nature" (2 Pet. 1:4, KJV). Forever we are to receive until the limit of our capacity has been reached. Nevertheless, the distance between us and God will still be infinite.

Walking in Oneness

Ephesians 4:1-3

Jesus' final prayer begged God that believers be one, so that the world would believe His message (John 17:21). The effectiveness of Christian witness relates directly to the oneness of Christian unity. Paul's first item in the worthy Christian walk calls for unity among believers. Our congregation can make an impact on the city only to the extent we walk together in the bond of peace.

To walk in oneness requires disciplined attitudes and ceaseless activities to maintain unity.

I. To Walk in Oneness Requires Disciplined Attitudes (4:2)

Unity requires *self-effacement*—How I react in self-estimation

"Be completely humble."

Understand ourselves to be small because we are small.

Unity requires *self-containment*—How I act under provocation

Gentle—a Christlike spirit of meekness

Patient—a postponing of action or retaliation

II. To Walk in Oneness Requires Ceaseless Activities (4:2-3)

Unity requires a *restraining activity*—"bearing with one another"

The activity—"bearing with"

The actuality—"one another"

Unity requires a *maintaining activity*—"make every effort to keep the unity."

God creates the great reality—"unity."

Christians continue the great activity—"keep the unity."

This activity requires diligence to keep unity.

This activity requires vigilance to keep unity.

Applications:

1. Do your remarks, observations, and reactions enhance or undercut the unity of the fellowship?

2. Do something definite to contribute to unity in the fellowship. Write a letter, make a call, or settle a difference.

3. Make a solemn decision that if it does not unify or edify, you will not say it or do it.

The Legacy of Leadership
(Ephesians 4:11-13)

The ascended Christ leaves a legacy to His church. His benevolent bequest of leadership is for the benefit of His people. The church has not been left orphaned to make its own way in a Christless world. The divine donation of charismatic persons equips the church to meet the challenge of each generation. This God-granted gift is personal, perpetual, and purposive. The gift consists of persons, continues throughout church history, and climaxes in a purposeful conformity of the church to its Head in a new humanity. Such a grand scope of intention is instructive to the laity and inspirational to the ministry. What is its practical significance?

The Legacy of Leaders Regards
Christ's Presentation to the Church

The immediate context emphasizes the presentation by a conquering king of gratuitous gifts for his faithful people. The legacy of leaders is a *personal donation* of Christ Himself. The principal emphasis in the passage is the gracious gift-character of Christ's provision of leadership in the church. In His sovereignty "God appoints" church leaders (see 1 Cor. 12:8), but in His generosity Christ "gives" them. Christ gives the ministry to the church, not vice versa. All of the congregations and their related agencies of all the centuries cannot produce one pastor. We are an impoverished people dependent on God's donation of leadership. With reference to leadership, the church is on the divine dole.

The legacy of leaders is also a *donation of persons*. Whereas other New Testament lists emphasize impersonal services, the Ephesian emphasis falls on the services of persons. Christ endows men and then gives the men thus endowed to the church. This donation is *comprehensive:* every minister belongs to every member. Rather than members belonging to their pastors, pastors belong to their members. This renders a good deal of our bragging not only baseless but inappropriate. This donation is *communicative.* Notice the four categories of gifted persons in Ephesians 4:11. The primary thrust of each is that of proclamation or communication of the gospel. That has priority in the healthy church. The donation is *contingent* on the needs of the church. The gift of charismatic persons and services are certainly not rigid or fixed in the New Testament. Some charisms may pass away; new ones may be born. Some are provisional (apostles and prophets). Others are permanent (evangelists and teaching-pastors). Some are itinerant and others indigenous. Some are external to the church and some internal. There is a holy freedom in God's creative gifts of church leadership. We must experience it, not try to constrain or control it.

The Legacy of Leaders Reveals
Christ's Purpose for the Church

There are three purposes revealed in the gift of charismatic leaders to the church. The first purpose is a *general characterization*, the perfecting of the saints. The emphasis is upon repairing, restoring, furnishing, equipping, complete outfitting, coadjustment, and coordination. All believers thus characterized are to put on an *active demonstration*, the work of the ministry. The New Testament ideal abolishes the distinction between clergy and laity. The word used for "ministry" means a service rendered to benefit others. It knows no boundary of sacred or secular. We are men for all services in all seasons. To this there is added a *related edification*. When pastors actualize their equipping ministry, when members realize their service ministry, the body is built up. Paul mixes metaphors of "body" and "building" to emphasize both the form and the vitality of the church.

The Legacy of Leaders Reflects
Christ's Promise to the Church

There remains an ultimate promise and goal in all of this. That goal is the *experienced unity* of the church. That unity is grounded in a common personal trust and experiential knowledge of the Son of God. That goal is the *perfect humanity* of the race. The church is at work producing nothing less than God's original intention for human beings. Do you want to know what God wanted when He made Adam? Look at the mature believer in the church, for that goal finally is *ultimate maturity* which is the conformity of each member to the standard of Christ. God's final intention will not stop short of producing a new humanity of which Christ is Head and we all are the body. How that should hallow every activity of this church with the very atmosphere of the celestial.

The Marks of Christian Maturity
(Ephesians 4:14-16)

Having described the gifts of leadership showered upon the church by the risen Christ, Paul continues to delineate the impact of these gifts upon the life of the body. He gives us some clearly understandable signs of spiritual maturity and its absence. Paul took it for granted that every believer was interested in spiritual maturity. Are you?

The Attitudes of Spiritual Immaturity

Under divine inspiration, the apostle describes three attitudes that timelessly betray the presence of spiritual immaturity. Sometimes these very attitudes appear to those who self-consciously preen themselves as being spiritual. There is *childish juvenility*, "Then we will no longer be infants" (v. 14). The word refers to minors or the untaught; it could even carry the meaning of infantile or stupid. Paul intends believers to move toward an ideal whose great features are adulthood and stability in personal, family, and church life. Some attain this early. Others never attain it.

There is a *constant instability*. Their spiritual lives never show any grounded or rooted quality. Moving from preacher to preacher, conference to conference, one popular movement to another—one never knows where they will be next. Paul used both a nautical and a meteorological metaphor to describe their instability. On the one hand they are like wave-tossed ships. The apostle well knew the instability of the sea; some believers impressed him as equally unstable. On the other hand they are like the changing trade winds. They blow now this and now that wind of doctrine, every kind and degree of it. Easy prey of religious propagandists, they never recognize stability when they see it.

Finally, they demonstrate a *credulous gullibility*. They are ready to swallow anything as long as it bears the name Christian. Their gullibility is taken in by *dexterous deception,* "deceitful scheming." The word really refers to dice-playing, and it is related to our word *cube*. Just as some men may "load the dice," infantile believers are duped by the dexterity of deceivers. Immature believers are further the objects of *deliberate deception*. Those who would deceive them are clever, shrewd, and crafty at all the arts of leading astray. Such is also *designed deception,* "cunning and craftiness" (v. 14). The word means to pursue a plan, to use methods, and to deal with deceptive strategy. Paul describes a word of agile and able spiritual deceivers.

The Atmosphere of Spiritual Maturity

Before Paul describes the actual attributes of spiritual maturity, he suggests the atmosphere in which it flourishes. There is a guilelessness described, "speaking the truth in love." The very opposite of the deceptive roguery above, believers confess the truth in a loving way. There is a *growth delineated*, "grow up into him." In a loving maturity, we are to grow until we are wholly incorporated in Him, as the center and circumference of our lives. There is a *goal defined* as the direction of this growth, "the Head, that is, Christ" (v. 15). Just as a baby's body grows until it catches up proportionately with its head, so we are to grow out of the infantile until we reach the maturity of our great Head, even Christ.

The Attributes of Spiritual Maturity

In the most complicated verse of the epistle, Paul discussed the qualities of spiritual maturity. Such maturity is defined totally in relationship to the corporate Christian body. There is no room for "Lone Rangers" in the arena of maturity. Mature believers are willing parties to the *ongoing process of harmony* in the body, "joined and held together" (v. 16). They display a willingness to live in harmony and inner adaptation with other believers. Mature believers are part of a *living process of vitality*, "by every supporting ligament" (v. 16). They know that they cannot live simply by contact with other limbs in the body, any more than the hand can live because it is connected to the arm. Each as part of the corporate whole is nevertheless vitally related to the Head Himself. From Him they find a liberal supply, according to the efficiency of each individual member to appropriate. Thus New Testament spiritual maturity is defined *first* in terms of the quality of one's relationship to the corporate body. It can never be merely individual or isolated.

The Imitation of God
(Ephesians 5:1)

We learn much of what we know by imitating. Music students imitate their teachers. Young athletes imitate older, more skilled professionals. Children imitate their parents. Yet we are called to the highest imitation of all—the imitation of God. We cannot imitate some of God's attributes. He does not intend for us to be all-powerful, everywhere present, or all-knowing. He does intend for us to imitate His kindness, compassion, and forgiveness.

You can begin now to be an imitator of God.

You Can Imitate Divine Compassion

You can imitate *divine sympathy:* "be [evermore] kind . . . to one another" (4:32). The imitation of God does not begin with some difficult theological definition. To imitate God is to begin with the warmest and most appealing human quality—kindness. The word for *kindness* is used seven times in the New Testament, more often referring to God than anyone else: "love your enemies. . . . and you will be sons of the Most High, because he is kind to the ungrateful and the wicked" (Luke 6:35). The emphasis falls on our becoming evermore and more that way. This begins in the life of thought and moves outward to the life of word and deed.

You can imitate *divine sensitivity.* The word *tenderhearted* reflects a sweet sensitivity that renders us incapable of hurting one another. We should not bruise one another with words in the body of Christ. Compassion in our life should not be cosmetic but deeply ingrained.

We should live with a *dependent solidarity* in forgiveness, "forgiving each other." The implication is that in forgiving one another in the body of Christ we forgive and heal ourselves. Forgiveness circulates like the life blood of the Christian community. The very pith and marrow of our message is one of forgiveness. How inconsistent to carry a message of forgiveness and yet not forgive others in the body of Christ.

You Can Grow in the Imitation

When Paul writes of imitating God, he does not propose some radical new departure. To imitate God is to restore the very purpose of creation (Gen. 1:26). We were created to reflect both the image and the likeness of God. The imitation of God begins the recovery of that which was lost in Eden.

This imitation must be one of real *intention.* The apostle does not merely invite us to meditation. To contemplate God is necessary for imitation, but we must go beyond that. Imitation of God is not merely admiration of God. Imitation is not even the higher activity of adoration of God by prayer and by praise. The imitation of God actually reproduces the character of God in our lives.

The imitation of God calls for a *graduation* of effort. We are to move from imitating the visible to the invisible. There is a progression of thought in the letters of Paul. He urged the Corinthians to imitate him. To raw recruits from paganism Paul gave a simple, visible example of Christianity—Paul himself. Paul challenged the Thessalonians with a higher imitation: "You became imitators of us and of the Lord." Little by little they could take their eyes away from Paul and look away to the higher and the unseen. But these are only preparatory for the imitation of God Himself. This will extend beyond this life into eternity.

He adds to this a simple *motivation:* "as [little] children" (5:1). It belongs to the child heart to imitate. It belongs to the freedom and spontaneity of childhood freely and spontaneously to imitate. Like children, we are to play follow the leader with the Great Leader of all God's family.

You Can Contradict the Imitation

Suddenly like a chill wind surprising us on a warm day, Paul writes of the contradiction of the imitation. He lists specific practices in life which Satan writes like graffiti over the image of God. There are aspects of the physical, mental, and verbal life that must not even be named among those who would imitate God. Paul is explicit in listing behavior that defaces the image of God from our life.

But the image of God can never be spoken of in merely negative terms. We are to practice thanksgiving. From our lips should come no pollution but a clear stream of glad thankfulness that bathes our lives in light and life. Thanksgiving—gratitude—helps make us invulnerable in the inner life. It is both a symptom of and a means toward the development of the imitation of God.

The Church that Is and Is to Be
(Ephesians 5:23-27)

The life of every church is sustained by the great Head of the church, the risen Lord Jesus Christ. In the past Christ so loved the church that He handed Himself over for the church, even to the cross. His purpose was to set apart a living organism—the church—that would be different from any other gathering in the world. Nothing will keep Him from doing just this thing. Although the church in this age will never be perfect, He will at the last great Day present to Himself a perfect church.

Paul moves easily from a discussion of the married life on earth into the most sublime truths about Christ and His church. All things were so sacred to him that he could move from the hearth and home to heaven and back again with ease.

Christ Sustains the Church that Is

Christ is the Head of the church. This is exclusively His function. No one other person is the Head. Not a pope or pastor, not a deacon or layperson. No collection of people is the head of the church. We sometimes call a Baptist church a democracy. This does not mean that the church determines itself. The church is a Christocracy or it dies. As the Head of the church Christ is both its Leader and its Life. He is the Head in terms of being Governor. But He is also Head in terms of the very life of the church. A decapitated life dies. Christ is not only Head of the universal church, He is the only Head of Travis Avenue Baptist Church.

The headship of Christ is always true, but at some times in the life of the church it is even more critically true. In days of transition this truth is even more critical than ever.

Christ loved the church. Jesus Christ loved the church before its existence (1:3-7). He loves the church in spite of its deficiencies, imperfections, or inadequacies. Christ loves the church that really is, not an imaginary perfect church. He loved the churches at Corinth, Galatia, Colossae, and Thessalonica, even though those churches had serious spiritual and ethical problems.

If our church is worthy of Christ's love, it is worthy of your love. Self-deluded people look for a church without a fault so they can love that church. The church as it is reflects the church that Christ loves. Your church needs your love now.

Christ's love acts for the church. He "gave himself up for her" (v. 25). Christ proved His love for Travis Avenue by the great giving over of Himself to the cross. His love is a verb; it acts. Your church does not need your emotion, sentiment or deep feeling in the days to come. It needs your presence, your gifts and your labor.

Christ's love for the church is purposeful. Christ loves the church for the purpose of separating the church and making it actually different from every other gathering. The way the church organizes, leads, reacts, and spends is on a different basis from other institutions. Christ has set the church apart to be different from homes, schools, banks, theaters, and everything else.

Christ has made the church different by cleansing the church through His Word: "cleansing her by the washing with water through the word" (v. 26). The church is the great lavatory of life, the laver of living. The church is the bathing place of the Word. In connection with the utterance of the gospel the church is made clean. For that reason the Word needs to be central in the church. For that reason you need to be present under the Word in the church.

The church is a gathering of people called out to be different, and kept that way only by bathing in the Word of God.

Christ Presents the Church that Is to Be

The church that is in this age is a church imperfect. That will not always be so. The great goal of the cross is a final presentation of the church in pristine perfection.

Christ will present the church at the end of the age. In the background of this passage is the thought of a bridegroom presenting his bride at his side. At the end of the age, Christ Himself will present the church to Himself. He will present the church for Himself as a perfect church. Christ will do that regardless of all obstacles; He cannot be stopped in that purpose.

Christ will present the church gloriously. In that great Day the church will be presented as it actually is, a thing of glory. There will be no labels or denominations, no controversies or division. He will present His church to Himself "arrayed in glory."

At that time the church will be "without stain." In this age the church is besmirched with stain, spot, blemish. As the church builds and battles in the world, stains splash upon the church. These stains come from without and from within. At that time the church will be "without . . . wrinkle" (v. 27). A wrinkle is the sign of age, decay, and death. Denominations and local churches may die in this age. In that age the church will be sustained ever new, always youthful, never showing a sign of decay or age.

It would be shocking at a wedding to see the bride enter with a badly stained wedding gown, her face deeply carved by ineffaceable wrinkles. To the outward observer the church appears that way. But another Day is coming. In that Day all we have aspired to be we shall be. He himself will present to Himself a glorious church.

This and this alone is the hope and goal of Travis Avenue. Some day all the pastors and people of the generations of this church shall stand in His presence. Then all we have hoped to be we shall in an instant be, not because of us but because of Him.

The Christian Conflict
(Ephesians 6:10-13)

At last the apostle writes "Finally." That does not, however, suggest he has finished. The expression means "what you have still to do in addition to what has been said." One vital, decisive area of Christian life has yet received no treatment in the letter. Paul has written of the Christian's resources without and within. He has also reminded us of the weakness that resides within. But he has to this point said nothing of the foe that assails from *without*. The finale of this letter is the most vivid warning in the New Testament concerning Satan and his assaults. If there were no personal power of evil that actively attacks Christians, this passage would be patently ridiculous. Scripture, history, and personal experience combine to underscore the existence of such an enemy. What are the battle lines?

The Strength Demanded

For this conflict there is demanded a strength *personal in its appropriation,* "be continuously clothed with power." Paul writes out of the most intensely personal experience of divine inner resources. Otherwise he would be like a blind man describing great art or a deaf man discoursing on symphonies. Paul had known that strength *initially* at conversion (Acts 9:22). He enjoyed it *perpetually* in Christian living (Phil. 4:13). He confessed it *finally* in his last correspondence (1 Tim. 1:12). At the end it was a strength that did not dissipate with mental and physical capacities; it endured.

Such strength must be *supernatural in its origination,* "in the Lord." Paul leaves no question that our conflict engages no merely human foe. We must have supernatural strength for a supernatural battle. You are already defeated if you understand Christian living as a contest between two principles, good and evil, or between conscience and evil passions. We fight as living persons against living demonic personalities. As such we need an appropriation of heavenly strength that is active, conscious, and incessant.

The Enemy Confronted

Our enemy stands *close in his proximity:* "we wrestle" (Eph. 6:12, KJV). The biblical expression was normally used for hand-to-hand conflict, individual encounter at the closest quarters. Make no mistake about the perverse and pernicious proximity of actively evil personalities with supernatural origin. Our spiritual battles are face-to-face and hand-to-hand with nearby opponents. Our enemy is *supernatural in his personality:* "not against flesh and blood." Our fight is not with man in his corporal, intellectual, and spiritual weakness. We badly misunderstand the nature of the Christian conflict within and without when we think of our opponents in human terms. Paul spares no efforts to picture the supramundane personality of our foes. Our enemy is *organized in his hierarchy.* C. S. Lewis preferred to call the satanic organization a "lowerarchy"! "Rulers of the world darkness" represent the princes and those of first rank in the demonic contingents. "Powers" stands for those potentates of lesser authority, but of no less danger. "World-rulers" (v. 12, ASV) describes those demonic personalities that hold sway over the present world order characterized by hostility to God and His church. Evil is active, not passive. It is personal, not a principle. And it is organized, not at random. This opponent is *superterrestrial* in his territory, "in the heavenlies." The word describes that area that is above the earth but below the heavens. Elsewhere Satan is described as "the prince of the power of the air" (Eph. 2:2, KJV). His presence and reign is as pervasive as the very air itself.

More than anything else, our antagonist is *strategic in his methodology.* His "wiles" (v. 11, KJV) represent his planned, analytical, and crafty strategems for each of us. He knows ultimately the crack in the armor of each of us. Our Achilles heel is his familiar territory. He works purposefully on us, not ignorantly.

The Conflict Anticipated

The conflict *demands comprehensive defense.* We are to put on the panoply (the whole armor) of God. This describes the extent, the source, and the nature of our defenses. Our physical bodies are not equally vulnerable at every point, but our spiritual life is. We may receive a mortal wound anywhere. We must be able to *discern an inten-*

sive attack, "the evil day" (v. 13*a*, KJV). Not all days and not every moment is equally open to satanic attack. We must be on our guard for those malicious moments of extraordinary attack. These may come because of illness, fatigue, depression, or a spectrum of reasons. Finally, we must *demonstrate our conclusive stance,* "having done all, to stand" (v. 13*b*, KJV). The Christian goal is to hold our position neither dislodged nor felled. There is much to be said for the man who merely stands his ground. There can be no Christian advance until there is first a firm Christian stance.

Overcoming Temptation:
Spiritual Warfare
(Ephesians 6:10-13)

The Christian life is a real, arduous, difficult, and dangerous conflict. The phrase "let go and let God" can be totally misleading. It can suggest a passive, quiet, inert Christianity which passes through life with comfort and ease. New Testament Christianity—the real thing—is very different. Our brief years on earth present a constant battle in preparation for an eternity at rest with the Lord.

Only a sufficient source of strength and only an adequate supply of protection can make us victors in the fight. We are indeed in a superhuman battle against a supernatural foe. The only way to stand our ground, no less prevail, is to fight with weapons given by God. Victors in temptation overcome only with the weapons God provides because they know the strength of the enemy.

The Battle Requires Adequate
Preparation for the Christian

Understand the *source* of the preparation: "be strong in the Lord and in his mighty power" (v. 10). Literally, we are to "be strengthened in the Lord." The source of our energy for spiritual warfare must and does rest outside of us. These words do mean "pull yourself together." Our preparation for spiritual warfare is an appropriation of dynamic energy from beyond ourselves. In this battle we can quickly come to the end of our hoarded resources. We must enter the battle in the vigorous operative strength that is inherent in God Himself. We move into the battle as if surrounded with a spherical shield or protective bubble of divine strength.

This strength must be constant in its appropriation. There is no once-for-all donation of such resources. Daily and repeatedly we enter into that strength from beyond ourselves.

Remember the *scope* of this preparation: "put on the full armor of God" (v. 11). There is an element of urgency in this as if it were a military command: "Put it on at once." There is not time for apathy or delay in light of the enemy's activities. The emphasis rests on the comprehensive nature of the armor required to stand in such a battle: "full armor." The word suggests the Roman legionnaire with his full complement of defensive and offensive weapons. The suggestion is obvious: to be unprotected at any point can be dangerous. Paul presents the armor in Ephesians 6:14-18.

But this is not armor which you invent. It is the armor whose source is God Himself. We may attempt to design all kinds of tricks to get us through the day. Only God gives the armor that survives spiritual warfare.

Grasp the *significance* of this preparation: "so that you can take your stand against the devil's schemes" (v. 11). We are not dealing with the impersonal conflict between an internal principle of evil and good within ourselves. We are dealing with an external and powerful adversary who has access to us and superhuman intelligence in dealing with us. He uses various forms of craftiness, strategy, and expert methods. In the face of this, God desires us to take our stand. For each of us there is a critical position on the battle-field. God desires that we take it and hold it. That position may be standing for Christ in our home, neighborhood, school, church, or job. Only God can enable you to take that stand and hold that ground.

The Battle Requires Appropriate Identification of the Enemy

Do not misunderstand *the nature of the battle:* "our struggle is not against flesh and blood" (v. 12). We must have the armor God provides because we are not engaging in hand-to-hand conflict with a mere human foe. We are not wrestling with the physical, intellectual, and spiritual limitations of mere humans. The consequences of losing to our spiritual enemy are far worse than being pinned to a mat in a wrestling arena.

Do understand *the enemy.* Paul parades the entire army of hostile spiritual forces before us. There are ranks and assignments in that army of darkness. The words em-phasize the tyrannical strength and hardness of the spiritual sovereigns in that dark world. Their seat of power is not located on the earth. Although they do not belong to the heaven of God's throne, they are nevertheless more than earthly in their origin and power.

Also understand the *time of the conflict.* Not every day is equally a day of battle. There is the "day of evil" (v. 13). Fortunately, God's strength is always equally available every day. As an equal blessing our spiritual enemy does not attack equally every day. He does depart for a season, only to return. But there are days of evil, awful days of attack in the conflict. For those days we must be prepared in advance. In those awful days of attack your goal is that "after you have done everything, to stand." There are bright days of advance in which it is all we can do to stand our ground. On those days a man or woman has been a spiritual hero simply to stand neither dislodged nor floored, but to hold onto the ground already gained. There can be no advance until there is a stance.

Inventory Time

(Philippians 3:4-8)

Most of us pause at some time to take stock of what really matters in life. In lesser ways we do it all along. At life's dramatic intersections we do it in great depth. Most people in prison take stock. When Paul was in prison for Christ he had much time to assess his circumstances. Paul made an enormous trade-off to serve Christ. He turned his back on family heritage, a comfortable place in the religious establishment, and certain personal security. It landed him in jail while waiting for a verdict on his life. Paul concluded that the trade-off was worth it all.

We should all take this ultimate inventory. The personal knowledge of Jesus Christ diminishes all other personal assets.

Most of Us Have Some Real Personal Assets

We have some assets that we inherit. By God's grace most of us inherit some good things in life. Our background, family, associates, and surroundings are often good gifts to us. We may have an excellent heritage. Paul did. He was "circumcised on the eighth day." That is, he was born in the strictest conformity with the highest norms of his race.

We may have a proud parenthood. Paul was "of the people of Israel." He was not a proselyte or convert, but of direct Israeliteish descent, a Jew with unmixed blood. We would say that Paul was a "blue blood," a person with exalted family heritage.

We may have an excellent brotherhood. Paul was "of the tribe of Benjamin." Benjamin was considered the elite tribe of Israel. Paul came from an exemplary family rooted in the favorite region of his Jewish people. The people and the places of Paul's life were all the very best.

We may live in the right neighborhood. Paul was a "Hebrew of the Hebrews." Although he lived in a Greek city, Tarsus, Paul's family were strict Jews. They lived a kosher life. They retained the Hebrew language in spite of inconvenience and oddity. All of these were very real assets in Paul's life.

For many of us our family, friends, region, schooling, and surroundings are very real assets. That is good. Yet compared to knowing Christ, they diminish.

We have some assets we achieve. Paul had improved what life had given him. By his own discipline he achieved rare status in the Jewish world.

We may achieve elitism. Paul was "in regard to the law, a Pharisee" (v. 5). By his own rigorous discipline he belonged to the elite religious achievers of his time. We may achieve a level of enthusiasm that marks our lives as particularly vital. As for Paul's zeal, he was "persecuting the church." Paul lived with a burning vitality that belonged to his own intensity. That is indeed an asset. We may live with a rigorism, "as for legalistic righteousness, faultless" (v. 6). No one could find a flaw in Paul's outward observance of God's requirements.

For some of us personal achievement and rigorous discipline are a way of life. That is good. Yet compared to knowing Christ, that too diminishes.

In Comparison to Christ, All Other Assets Diminish

Life's assets of inheritance and achievement are real. Yet we must compare those assets with something of greater reality and value—the knowledge of the Son of God.

We must make a reevaluation of life's assets. "Whatever was to my profit I now consider loss for the sake of Christ" (v. 7). There is a rationality in this reevaluation. This was no instant replay. Paul deliberately, carefully came to this conclusion. The finest and best things in his life were like losses compared to knowing Jesus Christ. When the sun rises, all other stars disappear. When a great man enters the room, lesser men fade. When Christ comes into life, assets can look like liabilities.

The cause of the reevaluation is "the surpassing greatness of knowing Christ Jesus my Lord." The words refers to the personal, daily knowledge of the risen Christ. No credential, pedigree, achievement, or promotion can stand in the same place with simply knowing Jesus Christ.

The cost of this evaluation may be enormous: "For whose sake I have lost all things" (v. 8). Legally, familially, educationally, religiously, economically, and in every way Paul had lost everything most would live for. Yet he had come to count these things as rubbish compared to Christ.

When you take inventory, what value do you put on the knowledge of Christ? When a ship is about to sink, the passengers begin to throw cargo overboard. If you had to throw away the things of value in order of importance, would only Christ be left at the end? All Paul had was Christ and Christ had all of Paul. Considering history, did Paul really lose anything that counts? Will you?

Holy Amnesia
(Philippians 3:12-14)

The growing Christian races toward spiritual maturity. The race demands a single concentrated commitment. The growing believer forgets past defeats and triumphs. He reaches forward to grasp a prize that is ever before him. The upward call of God puts in a flow that disregards everything hindering him from the goal—the full experience of Christ.

Growing Believers Confess Holy Discontent

Paul's situation was Roman imprisonment toward the end of his ministry. He deliberately, carefully formed a confession. That confession was a denial. He had not captured full knowledge of Christ or reached abiding spiritual maturity. He was on a journey, not at the destination. The implication is that some Philippians claimed to have reached ripe Christian perfection. "Not for me," said Paul. Christ had captured him on the Damascus road. He wishes to capture Christian maturity.

Are you satisfied with your level of Christian growth?

Growing Believers Achieve a Single Commitment

Paul states a priority: "One thing!" He had one aspiration toward which he moved with total concentration. Limitation gives power. That priority works itself out in *a process.*

Forgetting the past: Live with a holy amnesia. Paul equally forgot the guilt that could paralyze him and the attainments that could slacken him.

Straining toward the goal: This is like a runner with body bent over, hand stretched out, head fixed forward. Orient life toward a future fuller encounter with Christ.

Identify the past things that distract you from future growth. Confess them and move on.

Growing Believers Race Toward a Certain Climax

Our *fixation* is the "Goal-Marker." We rivet our attention to the post at the end of the race. What is it? Anyone or anything that comes up on the course. Our *motivation* is the heavenward call of God.

In the games, specially honored athletes were not crowned below in the stadium but were called above to the emperor and crowned there. The call is upwards always. The race, the cross, then the crown.

These Truths We Proclaim
(1 Timothy 3:15-16)

The church is the "pillar and foundation of the truth." In this world by our proclamation we display the truth as if elevated on a pillar, and we support the truth as if a foundation. There are certain items of timeless truth that the church both displays and supports. The truth does not rest on the church. The church rests on that truth. But the continued presentation of the truth in the world depends on the faithfulness of the church as a "pillar and foundation" of that truth. Each local congregation has that obligation as well as the entire church.

Paul gave to Timothy a simple hymn or spiritual song which expressed that truth in six statements. The hymn contains the confessedly great and wondrous revelation of Jesus Christ. That revelation begins in heaven, descends to earth, and returns in glory to heaven. Our congregation through its proclamation must hold up and support these truths in this generation.

We Hold Up the Incarnation of God in Christ

We hold up His *manifestation* in the flesh: "He appeared in a body." In Christ the invisible God appeared in our very form. He appeared "in fashion as man" (Phil. 2:8, KJV). "The word became flesh and dwelt among us" (John 1:14). He took part in our own flesh and blood (Heb. 2:14). This implies His preexistence. The fact that He "was manifested" clearly states that Jesus Christ existed before His birth in Bethlehem. It also states His virgin birth. Along with the Gospels Paul understood the virginal conception and birth of Christ (Rom. 1:3; Gal. 4:4). But the statement includes still more. The entire life of Christ was a manifestation of the invisible God. Every attribute of Jehovah in the Old Testament appears visible in the ministry of Jesus.

We hold up His *vindication* by the Spirit: "He was indicated by the Spirit." The end of His earthly manifestation was a shameful public death on a stick of wood. He died a criminal's death that was a ghastly aggregate of horrors. The power of God intervened to vindicate the claims of Jesus Christ. He claimed to be the Son of God in His Person and to be sinless in His performance. In a preliminary way God vindicated Him by His baptism and transfiguration. But in the final approval God vindicated Him by the resurrection (Rom. 1:4).

In this place our congregation must hold these truths up as if on a tall pillar and support them as if a strong foundation.

We Hold Up the Proclamation of God in Christ

The apostle emphasizes the widest possible proclamation of Christ in the next two statements. Jesus Christ revealed God to the two greatest extremes of rational creation. He revealed God to those closest to God, the angels. He also revealed God to those furthest from God, the Gentile nations.

He is the object of *angelic observation.* "He . . . was seen by angels." We should remember that before the coming of Jesus Christ, God Himself was invisible to angels. These superhuman intelligences took the deepest interest in everything about Jesus' career. They carefully marked His birth, temptation, resurrection, and ascension. But more than that, the coming of the Christ taught the angels things they could never have known about God in any other way. The angels learned truths about the multifaceted wisdom of God they would have known no other way (Eph. 3:10). With breathless interest the angels looked at how Christ fulfilled Old Testament prophecy (1 Pet. 1:12).

He is the subject of *universal proclamation:* "He . . . was preached among the nations." While the angels of heaven longed to observe Him, His followers on earth proclaimed Him to the entire world. He was made known by direct vision to the angels and by preaching to the nations. This bespeaks the dignity of the church's preaching task. We are proclaiming what intrigues heaven itself.

Our congregation has the responsibility to proclaim in this generation and city the Truth. We are to hold it up like a mighty pillar and buttress it like a great foundation.

We Hold Up the Consummation for Christ

We hold up *His reception in the earth:* "He . . . was believed on in the world." Jesus Christ has not been believed by the entire world, but He is believed on by many in the world. From north, south, east, and west a worldwide church has accepted the truths of the Lord Jesus. It should never cease to amaze us that the Galilean's message now circles the planet, that what began with a dozen followers now claims millions who call Him Lord.

We hold up *His glorification in heaven:* "He . . . was taken up in glory." The glorious and glorified Jesus has been gloriously lifted up to heaven itself. At the end of His earthly manifestation He was elevated to another world. He had a glorious reception on His return. He now sits in a glorious position at the right hand of the Father. He now has a glorious occupation as our Intercessor and Advocate. He is still the unseen support of those who believe in Him here in the world below.

Thus this confession begins and ends in the heavenly world. He was there before His manifestation and He is there now. Travis Avenue Baptist Church in this city may do many good things. But the essential things are to hold up and protect these six truths about our glorious Lord Jesus Christ. These are the only truths that save, forgive, and give eternal life. These are the only truths for living with confidence now and forever.

Advance Foundation Work
(1 Timothy 6:17-19)

You can build a foundation for life that will last into the age to come. That foundation depends on what you do with your wealth. The words of this text are addressed to the "rich." In contrast to the biblical world, that includes most of us. By any global standard of comparison, most people hearing this message are affluent. Paul urges the young pastor Timothy to give an authoritative and repeated warning to affluent people. That warning applies to most of us. That warning needs to be repeated because the negative temptations and the positive opportunities of the affluent are always with us.

By the use of your wealth in the present age you are building a foundation for the age to come. What you give does not earn your salvation but it does affect your standing in the age to come. You are building a foundation forever as you use your wealth in the present.

Your Feelings About Wealth Build a Foundation

There is a careful negative and positive description of how we should feel about our wealth. Negatively, *we should reject a certain attitude toward people* and toward *wealth.* Toward people, we should "not . . . be arrogant." Toward those who have less, those who have more should not be haughty, arrogant, or superior. It is common for those who have more to demand and even expect that those who have less look up to them, pay them deference. This overestimate of self is exactly the opposite of the Christian attitude which "in humility considers others better than themselves" (Phil. 2:3). The one who is affluent in this age ought to confess his spiritual poverty and take his position alongside all his brothers (Jas. 1:10).

We should also reject an *attitude toward wealth:* "Command those who are rich not . . . to put their hope in wealth." We are never to put our hope or anchor our confidence in the uncertainty of riches. The main characteristic of wealth is its uncertainty. "Cast but a glance at riches and they are gone, for they will surely sprout wings and fly off to the sky like an eagle" (Prov. 23:5).

Positively, all should "put their hope in God." The one certain security of our life should be God. When you think about your ultimate security, what first comes to your mind? Bank accounts, stocks, real estate, pensions, or the equity in your home should not be the first things to come to your mind. When you think of security you should first think of God. Our confidence in God is not divorced from His provision for us. He is by nature a giving God. He provides for us quantitatively and qualitatively. The purpose in His provision is that we enjoy the good things of life. God intends us to enjoy the pleasures of physical life. They are to be a joy. But they are not to take God's place as objects of ultimate hope and security.

Your Functions with Wealth Build a Foundation

Your *activity* with wealth builds a foundation forever. "Command them to do good, to be rich in good deeds." As a habit of life, the affluent are to continue to do good, beneficial things for others. The world speaks cynically about "do-gooders" because the world has no intention of doing good as a habit of life. Jesus went about doing good. Christians are lifelong do-gooders. We are to "abound in every good work" (2 Cor. 9:8). We are "not to become weary in doing good" (Gal. 6:9). We are not to minimize doing good, but "to be rich in good deeds." The more affluent you are in money, the more lavish you are to be in good deeds. We should be a people on the lookout for when, where, to whom, and how we can do good.

Behind this activity of doing good there must be an *attitude*. We are to be "generous." Paul uses a rare word which means to be bountiful, ready to impart, open-handed like God. Doing good cannot be a shallow activity without a deeper attitude or it will not last. You develop an attitude of generosity by imitating God and practicing generous acts.

Your *accessibility* to need builds a foundation. "Willing to share" (v. 18) means literally "keep on fellowshiping." We are not to hold aloof or be inaccessible. We must be affable and ready to welcome others who have need. The Christian person is to be open to fellowship with all brothers and sisters in Christ, especially those with real need.

Your Foundation Stands Sure for the Future

You can't take it with you, but you can send it ahead! It is a *fact* that you lay up treasure for yourself in the life beyond (v. 19). Everyone is storing up something. Some are storing up wrath in the life beyond by their stubborn and unrepentant hearts (Rom. 2:5). Others are storing up a treasure by their use of wealth in this life. What you give away in this age meets you in the age to come (Rev. 14:13). You can send some it ahead and the rest of it follows you.

The *firmness* of this foundation enables you to stand upon it while you "take hold of the life that is truly life." To reach out and grasp the life that is life indeed you must stand on a foundation of generous giving. What the world calls "life" is a mere phantom that ends immediately with death. What the Christian calls life always exists and does not end with death. The grasping person who does not give has every reason to question whether he has experienced the life that is life indeed. What you do with your wealth provides the foundation for the future. Build carefully.

The Lord Jesus:
A Friend in Temptation
(Hebrews 2:17-18; 4:15-16)

It helps to have a close friend with a similar experience to our own. If you name a handicap, a medical condition, or a life-disturbing problem, you will probably find a support group to help the victims of that problem to cope. Most of us seek identity in life's crises with someone who understands because they had the same experience.

The Letter to the Hebrews repeatedly stresses Jesus' identification and sympathy with us in our temptations. He cannot identify with us in our sins; sin is foreign to Him. He never had personal experience in sin. But He had the most extensive and intensive experience of temptation of anyone ever. Out of that He not only sympathizes with us but makes successful provision for us in tempting times. It will be of practical help in tempting times to understand His ability to encourage.

We Should Understand His Identification with Us in Temptation

He identifies with us in the *situation* of human life: "he had to be made like his brothers in every way" (2:17). For Christ to do His work it was a *necessity* that He identify with us in every way. He could not have been the sacrifice for sin or an encouragement against temptation without such identity.

His identification was with the *totality* of the human condition. He identifies with us "in every way." He knows every situation in life that beclouds us, weighs us down, and wears us away. This includes all of the toils, perils, and conflicts of life. He took on flesh and blood and worked as a carpenter. He was rejected by His own people and faced with the misunderstanding of His own family. In all of this He shares the necessities of our own situation.

He identifies with us in the *temptation* of human life. The emphasis rests on the *duration* of temptation: "he himself suffered when he was tempted" (18). All of His life He faced the temptations that we all face. But beyond that, He faced the temptations that related directly to His role as Savior. He was tempted directly by Satan, by circumstances, by the hardness of the Jews, and by the slowness of His own disciples.

Yet there was a great *exception* in His temptation: "yet was without sin" (4:15). This means more than the fact He did not sin. It further means that there was nothing in Him that sin could touch. His sinless nature found nothing that responded to temptation. Some of our worst temptation comes from previous sin. Yet because of us He felt the full force of every temptation.

We Should Accept His Compassion for Us in Temptation

His compassion comes from His *identity*. He is a "merciful and faithful high priest" (2:17). The word for "priest" actually suggests someone who is a bridge builder. He is God's great bridge builder, never more so than in times of temptation. As God's great bridge builder, He is merciful. That is, He has compassion for us in our wretched situations. In some instances the Jewish priests were cruel, insolent, and greedy. Our great high priest identifies with the needs of each sinful person. He is also faithful. We can trust Him to do what He has promised to do. He is loyal both to God and to us.

His compassion comes from His *sympathy*: "we do not have a high priest who is unable to sympathize with our weaknesses" (4:15). We should never think that because Christ is at the right hand of God in glory that He is unable to sympathize with us in temptation. He has an habitual sympathy. This is more than compassion that regards our sufferings from without. This is the feeling of one who enters into suffering and makes it His own. It is not really feeling *for* us, but feeling *with* us. He truly feels our weaknesses. He was acquainted with weariness, disappointment, desertion, and pain. His sympathy is not that of a remote observer but a feeling participant. Do not make your own temptations an exception. He understands them.

We Should Appropriate His Provision for Us in Temptation

We should appropriate His *ability:* "he is able to help those who are being tempted" (2:18). While there will be continual temptation there will also be continual help. We could be in the presence of someone suffering agonizing temptation and not even know it. Even if we did know it, we could not always help. He is able to give actual, immediate help.

His ability to help relates to our *access* to Him: "Let us then approach the throne of grace with confidence" (4:16). In the moment of temptation we have an invitation to draw near to God's throne. The *quality* of this approach is one of confidence. We can come to Him with an open face, with freedom, frankness, and without concealment. We can give utterance to every thought, feeling, and wish.

The *destiny* of this approach is the throne of grace. It is not a throne of judgment, probation, or law. There are no degrees of acceptability before God. It is all grace or not of grace at all. When we tremble with temptation, remember that our help comes from a throne that is all grace.

The *immediacy* of this approach is "grace to help us in our time of need." Help is of no avail if not on time. It will do little good to have strength for tomorrow for the temptation of today. God's help is timely. Ask now and find help now.

God's Living, Powerful Word

(Hebrews 4:12-13)

It is a wonderful statement that the Word of God can refer both to the living Word, the Lord Jesus Christ, and to the written Word, the Bible. Our text does not make it clear to which it refers. This is of God. God has so joined His living Word to His written Word that they cannot be divided in our thinking. The only Christ we know is the Christ who comes to us on the pages of Scripture. The Word lives because it is His Word. That Word alone gives life.

God's Word Lives

God's Word lives because *it is the Word of the living God.* God has chosen to pour His very life into His Word. He identifies Himself repeatedly as the "living God." He vivifies His word with His very life. Jesus asserted, "The words I have spoken to you are spirit and they are life" (John 6:63). Our own words die. The words of mere people notoriously date themselves. God attaches His very life to the written Word.

God's Word lives because *it gives life.* Peter reveals, "You have been born again, not of perishable seed, but of imperishable, through the living and enduring word of God" (1 Pet. 1:23). When you first encounter the Word of God you are dead spiritually. It brings you to life and sustains that spiritual life within you. God's Word has an indescribable vitality which breathes, speaks, pleads, and conquers. It wrestles, smites, comforts, smiles, weeps, sings, and whispers. It lives!

God's Word lives because *it has inherent energy.* When Jesus was arrested, a word from Him forced His adversaries to the ground (John 18:6). Christ will win His final victory over all opposition with His energetic word (Rev. 19:15). The Word of God has an energy that is never without results. It is always full of activity for salvation or for judgment. All spiritual life depends on continued contact with that Word. If you are listless, lifeless, and lethargic spiritually, it relates in some way to separation from the living, written Word. Contact with it gives life.

God's Word Cuts

God's Word cuts *superlatively*: "Sharper than any double-edged sword" (v. 12). God's Word cuts keener, better, and sharper than the sharpest weapon. A double-edged sword cuts both ways as it moves. "Take . . . the sword of the Spirit which is the word of God" (Eph. 6:17). The Word suggests the short, daggerlike sword of the Roman soldier. As God's Word cuts, it also heals. There is no healing without the cutting that first kills. We must let the Word cut the desires, obsessions, and fixations of our life in order to be healed by the same Word.

God's Word cuts *thoroughly*: "it penetrates even to dividing soul and spirit, joints and marrow" (Heb. 4:12). The Word of God alone penetrates to show us everything that inheres in our spiritual and earthly, bodily life. The Word makes the most decisive separations and divisions in life. It separates spirit from soul. Spirit is that part of our life which comes from God. Our soul is the seat of all thoughts, emotions, feelings, desires, volitions, and actions. In lost persons the soul has been separated from the life of the Spirit. God's Word identifies this. The Word of God penetrates our very physical life in the same way. It confronts us with the most radical kind of separations, bones from marrow. Taken together, this Word means that God's Word lays bare the entire person before God with absolute thoroughness. It completely reveals what is spiritual and what is fleshly about us all.

God's Word Exposes

God's Word exposes *personally*: "It judges the thoughts and attitudes of the heart" (v. 12). God's Word sifts, scrutinizes, and exposes the impulses and secret thoughts that belong to the emotional life as well as the designs and purposes that belong to our rational, thinking life. In so doing, God's Word goes to our very hearts. The Book of Hebrews warns us about the heart, the location of who we really are. We must not harden the heart (3:8), for it tends always to stray (v. 10), and God must write His law within our heart (8:10). We must draw near to God with a sincere heart (10:22), and we can do that only with a heart strengthened by His grace (13:9).

God's Word exposes *universally*: "Nothing in all creation is hidden from God's sight." Not only does God search us personally with His Word, but no created thing will escape His search. What He says of mere people He also says of angels, archangels, demons, and all else that exists. Nothing in all creation is invisible to Him. His Word penetrates all.

God's Word exposes *powerfully*: "Everything is uncovered and laid bare before the eyes of him to whom we must give account" (v. 13). In the sight of God everything is stripped of all artificial covering (naked) and laid out prostrate before Him. The word itself refers to a wrestler who throws back his adversary and holds back his head so as to expose it thoroughly to sight. Creation which would bow its head and withdraw from God will be powerfully revealed in the presence of God.

What a potent thing is the Word of God. To know the life it gives we must saturate ourselves in that very Word. We must let it cut, penetrate, expose, and then give the only healing that is healing indeed.

Hold Fast

(Hebrews 10:19-25)

Without perseverance nothing else ultimately lasts. Real Christian faith perseveres. Faith does not quit God or the visible church. Triumphant fortitude and steadfast endurance are the marks of the faith that lasts. The New Testament Letter to the Hebrews addressed Jewish Christians who were about to leave the church to return to the temple, leave the gospel to return to the law, leave Jesus to return to Moses. The author admonishes them repeatedly to hold fast. Although God holds us, we must hold fast.

Holding Fast Begins by Drawing Near to God

The Christian lives with the privilege of drawing near to God. In the ancient world such a privilege belonged to the priest alone. In Jesus Christ every believer is a priest with access to God immediately. Perseverance continues to press on toward God without ceasing for any reason. The text gives us four reasons why we can draw near to God.

We can draw near to God because of who we are. There are two qualities that characterize those drawing near to God. We draw near "with a sincere heart." The heart is the seat of personal character. There can be no divided allegiance, double-mindedness, or reservations for the one who presses into God's presence. We must also draw near "in full assurance of faith" (v. 22). We must banish any disbelief as to our acceptance with God through Jesus Christ. Full assurance means no reliance upon myself, my merit, or my performance, but all reliance on Christ.

We can draw near to God because of what God has done. We have received access to God as a gift. Drawing on the images of the Old Testament, the text gives us two things God has done for us that enable us to draw near. Inwardly, our hearts have been sprinkled. In the Old Testament the Hebrew people and priests were sprinkled with the blood of a sacrificial animal (Ex. 24:8; 29:21). We have been sprinkled with the blood of Jesus Christ. This has liberated us from a bad conscience. Outwardly, our very bodies have been washed with pure water. Body and soul God has made us fit to stand in His presence. God's provision should stir us mightily to press into His presence and hold fast our right of access.

Holding Fast Continues by Holding onto Our Hope

Because we are held, we are to hold on. "Let us hold unswervingly to the hope we profess" (v. 23). Hope is faith looking forward. Now the life of faith is difficult. The objects of our faith are in the future and are invisible. The risen Christ, the throne of God, the resurrection of our bodies all belong to throne of God, the resurrection of our bodies all belong to an unseen and future time. Faith holds onto the hope of all this.

Yet we hold because we are faithfully held. "God . . . is faithful" (1 Cor. 1:9). Our hope does not rest in our own fickleness and faithlessness. To break His promise is the contradiction of God's very nature. Because He holds us, we hold onto the hope. The fidelity of God challenges our own fidelity. If He is that faithful, so must I be!

Holding Fast Bears the Fruit of Mutual Encouragement

We encourage each other individually. "Let us consider how we may spur one another on" (v. 24). We are consistently and continually to prod one another in a ministry of loving confrontation. Literally, we are to "lay our minds down on one another." We are to observe and mark how to encourage each other. The quality of our encouragement is expressed by a tremendously energetic word which suggests irritation, incitement, and stirring up to rivalry. The goal of our encouragement is to be "good works." I am to incite in you the desire to deeds which are attractive and winsome to those who see your life.

We are to encourage one another in the church. "Let us not give up meeting together" (v. 25). Why do you come to church? The proper reason for church attendance has little to do with "what I get out of it." Your presence in the gathering of God's people has to do first with the encouragement of others. Some were abandoning the fellowship. The effect of this was discouragement on those who remained. Every filled seat in God's house is a testimony of encouragement to the pastor and people. Every empty seat is a symbol of discouragement.

The Christian lives all of life under the aspect of the Coming Day. That Day is our face-to-face encounter with the living God. The Word connects your presence at God's house directly with that encounter. You are to persevere in your presence with God's people. Heaven keeps church records, too.

Sure of the Future and Certain of the Invisible
(Hebrews 11:1-7)

We have an inclination to name eras of time. The 1980s were called the "me generation" because of an obsession with individual fulfillment. The 1990s may be called the "we generation" because of the emphasis on family. We speak of ages—industrial, atomic, space ages.

What if the periods of your life were given a title? Have you ever entered the "faith age"? Faith shapes life in three dimensions—future, past, and present.

Only Faith Can Make the Future Certain

This passage is not really an exhaustive definition of faith. Rather it gives the chief characteristics of faith. The emphasis is upon *any kind* of faith, whether Christian or otherwise. First, there is emphasized *the arena in which faith operates*. There exists a definite sphere with which faith has to do—the future ("things hoped for") and the invisible ("things not seen" 11:1, KJV). To speak of the life of faith is to ask how you relate to those two spiritual frontiers. Old Testament men and women had nothing to rest upon except the promises of God, without any visible evidence that they would ever be fulfilled. Yet they regulated the whole course of their lives on the basis of those promises. That is faith. They could do that because of *the certainty which faith achieves*. Faith gives solid ground and acts as the title-deed to things hoped for in the future. Things which in the present have no existence as yet become real and substantial by the exercise of faith. Faith makes the future present! All of this is contingent upon *the attitude which faith demands* (v. 6). Even the initial approach to God must believe in His existence and His interest in us. Such a belief enables one to seek Him with a persistent diligence.

Only Faith Can Explain the Past

Faith does not deal exclusively with the future; it likewise enables us to have any comprehension of the past. Only faith explains history. Faith about the certainty of the future rests squarely on our faith that understands the past. Faith thus helps us to understand the two most significant things about the past.

First, we understand by faith only that the world was created by the Word of God. That the cosmic universe of time and space came into existence because of a specific utterance of God is a confession of faith. That faith rests squarely upon the Genesis account of creation. But it is faith that gives validity to that revealed Word and to our highest thinking about creation. The belief that the world exists as an expression of divine will is fundamental to a life of faith. Second, the world does not contain its own explanation. As Weymouth translates, "What is seen does not owe its existence to that which is visible" (v. 3). Material causation is not enough. The visible universe was not made out of what we see. That is not the confession of science; it is the triumph of faith.

Only Faith Can Enable Us to Please God in the Present

So far we have dealt with abstract definitions. We need to see an embodiment of what faith is. The entirety of this chapter relates the incarnation of faith in the life of specific people with definite problems.

Only faith enables us to please God in our *giving*. Abel's stewardship was more excellent than Cain's because of Abel's faith. This may mean that his gift was quantitatively more or qualitatively better. God specifically testified that Abel's gift was right because he gave it in faith. Further, faith enabled Abel to give with abiding significance. We must give in faith if our giving makes any durable difference.

Only faith enables us to please God in our *living*. All we know about Enoch can be said in a sentence—he walked with God and was not. His fellowship with God in a corrupt age was an expression of faith. Faith makes fellowship acceptable. On the other hand, Enoch's kind of fellowship with God is an evidence of faith.

Only faith enables us to please God in our *serving*. Noah's faith differed from that of Abel and Enoch in that it was directed to a special revelation. Noah was told to prepare for that which was unprecedented in the history of the world. Noah's faith consisted in taking God at His word and making the required preparations. Faith enabled Noah to pay careful heed to the word of God. Such faith vindicated Noah who through his faith "put the whole world in the wrong" (v. 7, NEB). Only faith enables us to serve in the present when the vindication of our service is in the future.

Choosing By Faith
(Hebrews 11:24-28)

Nothing is more important than being able to make the right choices in life. In the life of Moses we see faith crowned as the greatest aid in making the right decisions. Moses' life begins another epoch of faith. The faith of the patriarchs represented that epoch in which faith enabled patient maintenance of the unseen hope. But Moses inaugurates that epoch in which faith makes decisive choices, acts on those choices, and changes all history. Moses appears in this chapter because of the great, right choice he made. In sharing with us the choice, the writer also shares with us the secret of making a right choice, and then of carrying through on the right choice.

Faith's Choice Begins with Renunciation

The choices of faith always involved a renunciation. At a critical time when he was forty years old Moses "refused to be called the son of Pharaoh's daughter." The original language dictates this choice was so absolute that Moses would not even allow himself to be so called in private conversation. His renunciation was complete. Ancient sources give Moses incredible stature in Egyptian society. One makes him the inventor of the alphabet. Another indicates that Egypt owed her civilization to him. Philo insists that Moses might have rationalized his choice away by thinking he could do more for the Hebrews by staying in Pharaoh's court and using his influence there. Had he done that, we would never have heard of Moses.

To decide by faith means you must make renunciations throughout life. It is to live on the basis of "things hoped for" and "things not seen." At the forks of the road, is your faith enabling you to make such hard choices?

Faith's Choice Continues with Identification

Whatever specific choice you must make by faith, one thing is certain—that choice will always identify you with the people of God. If your choice by faith—whether vocationally, economically, domestically, or educationally—does not identify you closely with God's visible people, you did not choose by faith. This is the touchstone of any choice faith makes.

Faith enables us to suffer with the people of God. Faith enabled Moses even to see the people of God in the despised Hebrew slaves. To the Egyptian court it was ludicrous to suppose that a slave people would be God's people. Once Moses by faith had seen them to be God's people, he *had* to identify with them or be guilty of disowning his heritage. His choice of values was clear—he could "enjoy sin for a season" in Egypt or take the consequences of identifying with God's people. Faith always identifies with God's people. Do you?

Faith enables us to bear the stigma of God's people. The choice of identity with God's people always bears a stigma when it is truly made. In some ways Moses bore "the reproach of Christ." Moses chose by anticipation to share in the sufferings of Christ. This may mean that the exodus was typical of or prefigured the greater redemption of Christ. Perhaps it means that Moses bore the same reproach at the hand of the Egyptians that Christ bore at the hands of the Jews. It certainly means that Moses endured the stigma the world always reserves for those who sacrifice a life of comfort and advancement for a life of the apparent uncertainties of faith. How can one do this? Moses did this by keeping his attention fixed on the reward in the invisible world. Remember, faith can only operate when it is certain that God is a Rewarder of those that seek Him (v. 6).

Faith enables us to live with patient courage. Moses' first attempt at bringing about an exodus failed miserably (Ex. 2). He had to flee to Midian for forty years in the "backside of the desert" (3:1, KJV). Faith gave Moses the patience to abandon his attempt to do God's work in Moses' way. At first Moses was the right man with the right mission doing it the wrong way. Faith enabled Moses to accept a life in inaction in the wilderness while waiting for God's hour to strike. Perhaps this is the hardest choice that faith must make—to wait on God when we would do otherwise.

Faith's Choice Gives a Demonstration

The celebration of Passover in Egypt (v. 28) was a great demonstration of Moses' faith. Here Moses burned his bridges behind him. To shut people inside their houses with blood on the doorposts and to wait quietly for the mighty intervention of God was the total risk of faith. If God acted, all was won. If God did not act, all was lost. The faith that renounces and the faith that identifies is also the faith that will risk everything on the intervention of God at the crucial moment.

In the Arena of Faith
(Hebrews 12:1-3)

More than any other figure of intensity the New Testament compares the Christian life to the races and games of the arena. We ought to run purposefully to get the prize

(1 Cor. 9:24). We should take care that we do not run the race in vain (Gal. 2:2; Phil. 2:16). At the end we should be able to say that we had fought a good fight and finished the race (2 Tim. 4:7). The author of Hebrews reminds us that we run our race in a spiritual stadium surrounded by former runners who now witness to the reality and triumph of faith.

Run Your Race

Run the race in light of the encouragement. The encouragement is twofold. Former participants in the same race pack the stadium. They are the heroes of Hebrews 11. They are witnesses in the sense that they speak to us of God's faithfulness in the race. They have run and won. Our race is being run in a stadium full of victorious athletes. But they are not only former participants, they are present spectators. We are in some sense to be cheered onward by the fact of their observation. Indeed, their numbers have increased greatly since the author wrote of those heroes in Hebrews 11.

We ought to take courage by the thought of both biblical and historical Christians who witness to us through their lives and with the thought of their present observation of our race.

Run the race without the impediment. We are to act with decisiveness in laying aside anything at all that hinders us in the race: "let us throw off everything that hinders" (12:1). Originally this word referred to the bulk of the body. The runner abstains in order to be sleek and swift. It also referred to an arrogant bearing which exudes all undue confidence. But mostly it refers to any burdensome load. We are to free ourselves from anything, however innocent, which hinders us in the race. It could be any relationship, possession, or habit which slows us in the least. The strong word "throw [it] off" speaks of stripping oneself of a garment that entangles the feet and hinders the effort. There is an immediacy, urgency, and radical call to be done with impediments.

If this is true of things in and of themselves innocent, how much more certainly true is it of known sin. Such sin "easily entangles." The author is realistic about us and our sin. We are susceptible and sin is easily contracted. The word suggests the fatal easiness with which sin stands around us and then encloses us. There are those sins toward which we are inclined because of temperament, weakness, and environment. We are encircled by the opportunity to sin and we are encircled by witnesses to encourage us. To which will you give heed?

Fix Your Eyes

This is the supreme motive and the highest encouragement. Above the cloud of all human witness is our King. Far more than any other contestant has He faced the battle we now face. He endured suffering beyond all others and received glorious joy beyond the battle.

Fix your attention on Jesus. The human name "Jesus" emphasizes our Lord in His humanity. We are especially to pay attention to what He suffered in His human nature. This means that we must continually look away from distractions. The very word suggests looking away from some things in order to look toward one thing. We are to see in the Lord Jesus the great Example and the great Giver of faith. He is the great example of faith in the life of His own divine humanity. He lived by the unseen and the future. He both began and ended His life as the great Example of faith.

But He is also the great Giver of our faith. He is the Originator of our faith and will be the Completer of our faith. This is true of the faith of every person of faith in the biblical record. Moses wrote of Christ (John 5:46). Abraham saw Christ's day (8:56). Wherever you find the first stirrings or the final victory of faith you find the Person of the Lord Jesus. He is the Example and the Giver of faith.

He enables us to look beyond present discouragement to the future encouragement of a life of faith. Our Lord Jesus was enabled to endure the shame of dying the death of a criminal considered by His executioners accursed of God (Gal. 3:13) because of the joy that followed the conflict. He was willing to trade the pain to reap the joy.

This is a basic decision which the life of faith makes initially and continually. We must say with the apostle Paul, "I consider that our present sufferings are not worth comparing with the glory that will be revealed in us" (Rom. 8:18).

Cornerstone
(1 Peter 2:4-8)

Your name usually gives you an interest in others who have the same name. Evidently when Jesus gave Peter the name "Rock," Peter came to be interested in every rock in the Bible! In this magnificent passage Peter examines all that God says about stones. He finds that Christ is the Cornerstone, you are a living stone, but for some He is a stumbling stone.

Jesus Is the Cornerstone

Today a cornerstone is merely decorative. In biblical times such a stone was structurally significant. It bound the building together. The Old Testament prophet foresaw God's coming Cornerstone (Isa. 28:16). Jesus openly identified Himself as that Stone (Matt. 21:42). In what way is Jesus the Cornerstone of the church?

He is a living stone. These words are a violent contradiction, direct opposites in our experience. Yet they express a truth that can be expressed in no other way. In Christ there is the fixedness of a stone yet the vitality of life itself. Anytime God touches a stone that stone takes on new life.

He is a chosen stone. Twice the text emphasizes that Christ is the man of God's own choice. After testing Him, mere men rejected him. But God has already chosen Him and that choice stands. He chose Him in eternity and in time. He chose Him at Bethlehem, Jordan, transfiguration, and resurrection. What man emphatically rejected, God eternally chose.

He is an honored stone. A Jewish legend tells of the rock chosen for the cornerstone of the temple having been lost and neglected. Finally it was rediscovered and elevated to its place of significance. God has given to the Cornerstone His place of preeminence and man shall not take it away.

Christians Are the Living Stones

Christians are like their Lord. As He is alive, so are they. Peter must have remembered that occasion when he received his name (Matt. 16:18). Christ promised to build His church upon the Great Confession. Men such as Peter would become the living stones built upon that great Rock. Here Peter imagines those stones mysteriously attracted to that great Cornerstone. One by one they come from all ages and places to take their place upon the Rock. Their contact with the living foundation makes them living stones. As such they form a new temple with a living sacrifice.

Christians are a spiritual temple. Jesus predicted that He would raise up a new temple (John 2:19). The new temple is not local or material like that of Solomon, but universal and spiritual. God now literally dwells in the community of His people. We are collectively the house of God. It is a spiritual house because the Holy Spirit brought it into existence and pervades its life.

Christians are a holy priesthood. Suddenly the one image dissolves into a new image. Christians are not only stones in the wall, they are also priests serving within those walls. In the old order and among pagans, priests were a separate caste—set apart like the sons of Aaron. In contrast, all those in the living temple are priests with direct access to the God whom they serve.

Christians bring spiritual sacrifices. This completes the picture. Every temple with priests must have sacrifices. In the old order there were material, animal, and vegetable sacrifices. In the new temple of living stones where every person is a priest, the sacrifices are different. They are the sacrifices of praise and worship (Heb. 13). Indeed, before a man brings any other sacrifice he brings himself as a living sacrifice (Rom. 12:1-2). Do not miss the clear fact that Peter is speaking of what Christians are collectively. None of this is done alone. I am part of the temple because my life is cemented to yours in the church. I am part of a body of priests who come together to God. There are no free-lance Christians according to this word. We are alive in Christ *together*.

For Some Christ Is a Stumbling Stone

He is either your Cornerstone or your Stumbling Stone. Some men look at God's Cornerstone as an object that blocks their path. They have no desire to build on Him. They want to be rid of Him. They are like men rushing upon a great fixed stone. They cannot dislodge the stone. They only break themselves over the stone.

How do people stumble over Christ? We stumble over Christ because we actively and deliberately refuse to obey the truth about Him. This means more than passive disbelief. The test suggests those who examine Him and then reject Him. There is no neutrality. Sometimes to refuse to make a decision is to make a decision.

Why do people stumble over Christ? God has sovereignly ordained that those who disbelieve Christ will stumble. It is no mere accident that lives crash when Christ is rejected. An invisible hand is operative in the process. Ultimately, we do not reject Christ. God rejects those who fail to believe in His Son. He will have the last word.

Are you building on the Cornerstone or falling over the stumbling stone?

Fellowship and Forgiveness in the Light
(1 John 1:5-7)

John describes Christians as those who are in fellowship with God and with one another. To be a Christian is not just to look back to a past experience but to participate in a present fellowship. Only those whose conduct is "walking in the light" can have fellowship with God and with other believers. The belief that "God is light" has a profound implication for our walk with Him and with one another. First John 1:5 tells us what God *is* and verses 6-10 tell us what we are bound to *be* in the light of that fact. Those who walk in the light know the fellowship of forgiveness.

Light Reveals the Nature of God

"God is light" represents one of the three great statements John makes about the nature of God. Elsewhere he tells us that "God is spirit" (John 4:24) and "God is love" (1 John 4:8). Whereas others tell us what God *does*, John tells us what God *is*.

Consider the *source* of this statement: "we have heard from him" (1 John 1:5). Some believe the Lord Jesus made this statement but that it was not recorded in the Gospels. Still others understand this to be a summary of all Jesus said about God. The purport of everything Jesus said and did reveals God as light.

Consider the *significance* of this statement. Positively, it is a word about the Person, purity, and purpose of God. The *Person* of God is light. Light is the divine essence, the physical accompaniment of the presence of God. God dwells in light that is unapproachable (1 Tim. 6:16).

Light also refers to the *purity* of God. Christians have put on an "armor of light" (Rom. 13:11-12). Believers are all "sons of light and sons of day. We are not of night, nor of darkness" (1 Thess. 5:5, NASB). You cannot separate the Person of God from the purity of God. The early Gnostics taught that one could know the Person of God without knowing the purity of God. John says this is never true.

Light refers to the *purpose* of God. Light pervades everything unless it is shut out. God reveals Himself. He does not conceal Himself. In that medium of self-revelation is where God and man meet. In the physical world we are revealed to one another only in the physical light. In the spiritual world we meet with Him and one another only in His light.

Negatively, in God there is no darkness. This does not mean that we can know everything there is to know about God. It does mean that there is nothing that hides, no secret reserve in God. We can know all of Him that we desire to know.

Light Reveals the Nature of Fellowship with God

Negatively, there is a false *claim*. Those who claim to have intimate experience with God and yet who habitually walk in darkness are deceived. The Gnostics taught that one could know God spiritually yet do anything one desired with the body physically. Fellowship with God and a life in the darkness are mutually exclusive.

There is a *contradiction*. The person who claims to share life with God and yet walks in the darkness morally does not do the truth. Truth is not only to be believed; the Christian *does* the truth. Talk is cheap; only walk really counts.

Positively, there is a *conduct* that reveals true Christian character. That conduct is to "walk in the light." The psalmist could say, "The Lord is my light and my salvation" (27:1). This light comes from the written Word of God: "Thy word is a lamp unto my feet and a light unto my path. . . . The entrance of thy words giveth light" (119:105,130).

The *consequence* of walking in the light is twofold. In relationship to God and other believers, "we have fellowship with one another" (v. 7). This means a daily, intimate sharing of all life. In relationship to sin, we experience continual cleansing through the blood of Jesus Christ. One experiences the initial cleansing of salvation only once. One experiences the daily cleansing of Christ's blood repeatedly (John 13).

This is a word of warning and encouragement. It is a warning to those who habitually live a dark life they must conceal and hide. Such do not belong to God or the light. Those who walk in light, however, can know daily renewal of their fellowship with God. Where do you walk?

We Shall Be Like Him
(1 John 2:28 to 3:3)

Authentic Christians live in anticipation of a face-to-face encounter with Jesus Christ in the presence of God. The last chapter of the Bible promises "They will see his face"

(Rev. 22:4). In the present, faith deals with the invisible. In the future, faith will become sight and we will see the object of our faith. Jesus prayed, "Father, I want those who you have given me to be with me where I am, and to see my glory" (John 17:24). Genuine believers live with the compelling hope that we will see Jesus Christ.

The fact that we shall be like Him in the future energizes Christian living in the present.

A Persistent Desire Marks Those Who Shall Be Like Him

Those who shall be like Him desire a perpetual relationship: "dear children, continue in him." John's definition for the Christian life is abiding in Christ, being at home in Christ, constant union with Christ. Christianity is not an initiation at the beginning, but a relationship throughout life. We must not misrepresent Christianity as a mere transaction that changes eternal destination. There is a large difference between meeting someone casually and moving into the same house! Jesus saves by moving in.

There is an *ultimate reason* for continuing in Christ: "so that when he appears, we may be confident." *Confidence* is a favorite word for John. He desires that we be confident in prayer (1 John 3:21; 5:14) and confident in the presence of God. Such confidence pictures the freedom of a child relating to a father rather than a slave to a master. This confidence indicates an undismayed frankness and freedom of speech in the presence of a judge. When you abide in Christ, you can finally stand before God's throne with that confidence.

This confidence means we will be "unashamed before him at his coming" (2:28). The opposite of confidence is to shrink away from Him with an averted faith. When you live in union with Jesus Christ, you can anticipate meeting Him face to face and looking into His eyes with bold confidence.

There is an *immediate evidence* of readiness for that meeting. Meeting Jesus Christ face to face belongs to the invisible world of the future. There is a visible test in the present which reveals my fitness for the future. That test is based on the character of God as it is revealed in the conduct of my life.

God's character is righteous, meaning everything that is right in conduct and inner character. We all have an immediate, intuitive awareness of that truth. The proof that I know Him and am ready to meet Him is in my conduct as it reveals that character: "Everyone who does what is right has been born of him" (v. 29). I do not have to guess. There is a definite family likeness in God's family—righteousness as a practice.

A Present Dignity Encourages Those Who Shall Be Like Him

Believers recognize that present dignity. It is an exclamation and an astonishment: "How great is the love the Father has lavished on us" (3:1). We should never lose the wonder of the unearthly love that God has given us which is foreign to human experience. That God took hostile rebels and made them obedient children defies comparison.

Yet the world does not recognize us as children of God. We look very much like everyone else around us. There are no halos, angel's wings, or beams of light shining from us. The world around us has no conception of who we are; the world cannot have (1 Cor. 2:14). Far from discouraging us, this is a prime motivation; it is evidence that we really belong to God.

The deeper reason the world does not recognize us is that the world did not recognize Jesus Christ as the Son of God when He came (3:1). The world did not recognize the Son of God, and it does not today recognize the sons of God. Christians are not "in." We are definitely "out." This is a proof that we belong to Him.

A Promised Destiny Motivates Those Who Shall Be Like Him

We live between the "now" and the "not yet." We now have the dignity of being the children of God. We do not yet have the destiny of being the children of God.

Our destiny is *concealed:* "what we will be has not yet been known." Our future state of existence cannot be imagined. We do not have the faculties to understand it. We can no more understand the world to come than our house cat could appreciate Mozart. We see through a glass darkly (1 Cor. 13:12). Our best conception of the life to come is like looking into a bad mirror.

Our destiny is *compared:* "we know that when he appears, we shall be like him, for we shall see him as he is" (1 John 3:2). We may rest in this. When we gaze at Him, we shall instantly be made like Him. Even now the contemplation of our Lord Jesus changes us (2 Cor. 3:18). In the future His power will enable Him to bring all things under His control and He "will transform our lowly bodies so that they will be like his glorious body" (Phil. 3:21). This will happen as a result of the impact of seeing Him as He is.

Our destiny is *compelling:* "Everyone who has this hope in him purifies himself, just as he is pure" (1 John 3:4). This compulsion is comprehensive and inclusive, "Everyone." There will be no exceptions in this preparation. Without holiness no one will see the Lord. Do not entertain false hopes in that regard. Those who prepare for the encounter practice a habitual and strenuous self-purification. The word indicates purity maintained with effort in the midst of defilements. While "the blood of Jesus Christ . . . cleanseth us from all sin" (1:7, KJV), we also actively and watchfully purify ourselves inwardly and outwardly. Just as we prepare carefully for other meetings, we must prepare ultimately for this meeting.

The Vision of the Exalted Christ
(Revelation 1:9-20)

The Gospel stories shape our image of Jesus. We think of Him as the humble traveling teacher and healer. We see Him at His trial, on His cross, in His humiliation. Yet the final picture of Christ in the New Testament is anything but that of an humble victim. As an old man, the apostle John was exiled to the island called Patmos, a tiny six-by-ten-mile rock off the coast of Asia Minor. He was there "because of the word of God and the testimony of Jesus." John was the last surviving apostle. The churches were under persecution by the Emperor Domitian. The Christian churches seemed so fragile and vulnerable.

In that context a vision of Christ as He really is broke in upon John. He sees the cosmic Christ, the exalted King, the everlasting Lord Jesus uplifted to incomparable dignity. We all need a vision of Christ exalted over the church and the world.

The Function of the Exalted Christ in His Church

What is the Lord Jesus Christ doing today as His principal concern? He walks among His churches caring for and judging them.

The function of the church is the illumination of the world. The seven churches of Asia Minor are called "seven golden lampstands." The seven-branched candelabra had burned in the Jewish temple as a symbol of God's light. That famous candelabra was now gone. Now the church must illumine the world with the light of God. The church only shines by deriving its light from Christ. The church is not self-consumptive like a candle. It is fed by the oil of the Holy Spirit. A lampstand requires constant renewal of oil in order to shine (Zech. 4).

The church lights the world in its diversity and its purity. The seven churches of Asia Minor were diverse in their character and contribution (Chs. 2—3). None of the churches was perfect, and several were severely flawed. Yet each of them is still a center of light. God's ideal for the church is that of a "golden lampstand." The purer the gold, the brighter the light. The call is for purity in the churches.

The function of the risen Christ is the care of the churches. The last vision of the risen Christ in the Bible presents Him in the midst of His churches. The location of Christ today is among His churches, walking among the assemblies of His people. He walks among us as the "Son of man." That is His favorite title, a title of humble identity with our weakness and need. Yet He walks among His churches in dignity (His long robe) and ceaseless activity (the robe girded around His waist).

The Identification of the Exalted Christ in His Church

As John examines the cosmic Christ, the exalted risen Lord, He sees Him in His sevenfold character. The number seven throughout this book indicates the perfection of God Himself.

His eternal duration: "His head and hair were white like wool." We need the assurance of the One who was, and is, and always will be. John's world disintegrated before his eyes. Our world changes with such velocity that we cannot conceive what is happening. Above it all, the eternal Christ reigns.

His penetrating vision: "his eyes were like blazing fire" (v. 14). In a world that conceals so much, the gaze of the risen Christ penetrates all things. When we think that nobody knows or understands, we should remember that His sight pierces every detail.

His active judgment: "his feet were like bronze glowing." That metal was associated with the activities of judgment. Few things are more evident than the lack of justice in this age. The risen Christ assures that all will be set right.

His resounding authority: "his voice was like the sound of rushing waters" (v. 15). As John listened to the waves crash against the rocky island coast, it reminded him of the resonant authority of Jesus' voice. He is our eternal contemporary. Every other voice is silenced or becomes irrelevant. His is always fresh with authority.

His grasp of concern: "in his right hand he held seven stars" (v. 16a). These stars seem to be the pastors of the seven local churches (v. 20). This suggests that the ministry of the church rests in His hand. The call, equipment, and preservation of the ministry belongs to Him—not to the church or to the world.

His weapon of conquest: "out of his mouth came a sharp, double-edged sword" (v. 16b). The short Roman dagger had a tonque-shaped appearance. All of Jesus' victories are won by His word alone (Heb. 4:12). He does not fight Rome with the kind of power Rome knows. His victory is that of His word alone.

His brilliance of appearance: "His face was like the sun shining in all its brilliance" (v. 16c). The composite impact of this vision was like looking at the sun filtered through thin clouds. He is the Light that gives the church all their light.

This vision is not to be explained so much as to be an encounter with Christ as He is.

The Reaction to the Exalted Christ

There is a reaction of reverence: "I fell at his feet as though dead." The characteristic response to a vision of the divine is one of total submission out of reverent awe.

There is a reassurance of care. The risen Christ does not desire to overawe us into terror. It is just the opposite. His first words are "Do not be afraid." We should have no fear because of His eternity, "I am the First and the Last" (v. 17). He has been and always will be with us. We should have no fear because of His victory, "I [became] dead." He has entered into the worst that can happen and emerged victor. More than anything else He wants us to understand that. We should have no fear because of His mastery, "I hold the keys of death and Hades" (v. 18). Whatever life holds now and in the beyond, He grasps the key that opens the door. We shall forever and ever honor and exalt the One Who so loved us and gave Himself for us.

Worship that Is Worthy
(Revelation 4:8-11)

There are four popular motives for attending worship services. Some simply think that it is the decent thing to do. Others are fans of popular preachers. Still others think attendance is good for their personal reputation. There is a fourth group for whom worship is a glorified aspirin tablet to guarantee peace of mind.

There is really one reason why the living God wants His people assembled in worship: to ascribe to Him the worth and value that are His. A. W. Tozer called worship "the missing jewel in the evangelical church." We preach, evangelize, educate, organize, but do we really worship? In Revelation 4 and 5, John witnessed the continuous, perfect worship in heaven itself. What better model could we find? *Worship ascribes to God His worth and surrenders to Him in light of that worth.*

Worship Commences When We
Acknowledge the Authority of The Lord

We acknowledge His *sovereignty,* "Him who sits on the throne" (v. 9). When John observed the perfect worship of heaven, one thing dominated—a throne. Nine times in this passage he writes of the throne. Worship begins with the confession, "I am coming to a throne." The colors of that throne suggest the righteousness, sacrifice, and covenant of the One on the throne. Everything arranges itself around that throne: all created life, the church, and the angelic world. When you worship you acknowledge that all authority, power, dominion, control, supremacy and command belong to Him.

We acknowledge His *eternity.* We "worship Him who lives forever and ever" (v. 10b). We acknowledge His authority over time and space. He is the One whose very name means "I AM THE GREAT I AM." We worship the One for whom a thousand years are as a day. We are time-bound slaves to our watches and calendars. In worship we confess that there was a time when we were not, but there was never a time when He was not. We confess that there is a time when I shall not be as I am, but there is never a time when He shall not be as He is.

We acknowledge His *activity.* We acknowledge His activity in *creation* and in *re-demption.* When we acknowledge His creation of "all things" we affirm that the entire universe came from His hands. But the highest praise, the greatest worship, the loudest hallelujah is reserved for His activity in redemption. The God who created billions of stars hung on the cross for me.

Worship Continues When We Yield
to the Authority of the Lord

This yielding demands a *submission.* All of the redeemed prostrate themselves before the throne of God. This means to lay oneself flat in humility or adoration. Repeatedly in the Revelation those around the throne do this very thing (5:8,14; 11:16; and 19:4). Our only appropriate reaction to the sovereign, eternal God is to fall down before Him in submission.

This yielding demands an *abdication*: "they lay their crowns before the throne" (v. 10). Redeemed humanity takes its own crown off its head, its own sign of achievement and accomplishment, and lays it down at the feet of Him on the throne of God. This language sounds strange to us now. But those who first read Revelation understood its significance. It meant that those taking off the crown renounced the right to rule their own lives and gave it to another.

Worship Consummates When We Ascribe Worthiness to God

The highest act of worship is when we tell God that He alone is worthy of the three things that men most seek: glory, honor, and power. When we worship, we ascribe or attach to God glory, honor, and power. Simply put, we tell Him in front of the world that He alone is worthy of it all.

We tell Him that He is worthy to receive *glory*. The word means heaviness, weight, or substance. We take God weightily. We reflect back to God the light and splendor of His visible presence. Glory is the over and aboveness of God: more than light, more than beauty, goodness, mercy, and splendor. The longer we praise Him, the more we praise Him. The doxologies increase in length and splendor (1:6; 4:11; 5:13; 7:12).

Worship is both private and public. Private worship is the artesian well. Public worship is the river that flows from it. There is no more sense in private worship without public worship than there is in a single individual saluting a flag all by himself, at the post office, alone, when no one is there.

Worship is private and public. Response is public. Should your response be public at this time?

Persons and Places Index

Subject Index

Scripture Index